Exploring Language through Second Language Acquisition Research

Routledge Introductions to Applied Linguistics is a series of introductory level textbooks covering the core topics in Applied Linguistics, primarily designed for those beginning postgraduate studies, or taking an introductory MA course as well as advanced undergraduates. Titles in the series are also ideal for language professionals returning to academic study.

The books take an innovative 'practice to theory' approach, with a 'back-to-front' structure. This leads the reader from real-world problems and issues, through a discussion of intervention and how to engage with these concerns, before finally relating these practical issues to theoretical foundations. Additional features include a glossary of key terms, and discussion questions.

Following the back-to-front approach of the series, the book takes problematic issues in language pedagogy as its starting point. These are then examined in terms of second language acquisition. Each chapter begins with a look at the pedagogical proposals found in teacher guides and then asks 'Do these proposals accord with what we know about how languages are acquired?' Pedagogical topics covered include teaching methods, syllabus design, explicit instruction, comprehension versus production-based instruction, task-based instruction, authentic materials, the role of the learners' first language in the classroom, error correction and catering for individual differences.

Including a glossary of key terms and questions for discussion at the end of each chapter, and assuming no prior knowledge of second language acquisition, this is the ideal text for all students studying language teaching methods, language teacher education, English teaching methodology and second language acquisition modules in advanced undergraduate and postgraduate/graduate TESOL and Applied Linguistics courses.

Rod Ellis is Distinguished Professor in the Department of Applied Language Studies and Linguistics, University of Auckland. He is also a professor in the EdD in TESOL programme at Anaheim University, USA and a visiting professor at Shanghai International Studies University (SISU) as part of China's Chang Jiang Scholars Programme. He is currently editor of the journal *Language Teaching Research*.

Natsuko Shintani is an Assistant Professor at the National Institute of Education, Nanyang Technological University, Singapore. She obtained her PhD from the University of Auckland in 2011. She has worked as a language teacher in Japan and New Zealand, including in her own private language school for children. Her research interests are the role of interaction in second language acquisition, corrective feedback and meta-analysis as a research tool.

Routledge Introductions to Applied Linguistics

Series editors:

Ronald Carter, *Professor of Modern English Language, University of Nottingham, UK*

Guy Cook, *Chair of Language in Education, King's College London, UK*

Routledge Introductions to Applied Linguistics is a series of introductory level textbooks covering the core topics in Applied Linguistics, primarily designed for those entering postgraduate studies and language professionals returning to academic study. The books take an innovative 'practice to theory' approach, with a 'back-to-front' structure. This leads the reader from real-world problems and issues, through a discussion of intervention and how to engage with these concerns, before finally relating these practical issues to theoretical foundations. Additional features include tasks with commentaries, a glossary of key terms and an annotated further reading section.

Exploring English Language Teaching: Language in Action
Graham Hall

Exploring Classroom Discourse: Language in Action
Steve Walsh

Exploring Corpus Linguistics: Language in Action
Winnie Cheng

Exploring World Englishes: Language in a Global Context
Philip Seargeant

Exploring Health Communication: Language in Action
Kevin Harvey and Nelya Koteyko

Exploring Professional Communication: Language in Action
Stephanie Schnurr

Exploring Language Pedagogy through Second Language Acquisition Research
Rod Ellis and Natsuko Shintani

Exploring Vocabulary
Dee Gardner

Exploring Language Pedagogy through Second Language Acquisition Research

Rod Ellis and
Natsuko Shintani

Routledge
Taylor & Francis Group

LONDON AND NEW YORK

First published 2014
by Routledge
2 Park Square, Milton Park, Abingdon, Oxon OX14 4RN

Simultaneously published in the USA and Canada
by Routledge
711 Third Avenue, New York, NY 10017

Routledge is an imprint of the Taylor & Francis Group, an informa business

British Library Cataloguing in Publication Data
A catalogue record for this book is available from the British Library

Library of Congress Cataloging in Publication Data
A catalog record for this title has been requested

ISBN: 978-0-415-51970-0 (hbk)
ISBN: 978-0-415-51973-1 (pbk)
ISBN: 978-0-203-79658-0 (ebk)

Typeset in Sabon
by Saxon Graphics Ltd, Derby
Printed and bound in Great Britain by
CPI Group (UK) Ltd, Croydon, CR0 4YY

Contents

Learner differences   283

11 Catering for learner differences through instruction   285

PART V
Conclusion   319

12 Teaching for learning   321

    Glossary   334
    References   347
    Index   383

Figures

List of tables

Series editors' introduction

The Introductions to Applied Linguistics series

This series provides clear, authoritative, up-to-date overviews of the major areas of applied linguistics. The books are designed particularly for students embarking on masters-level or teacher-education courses, as well as students in the closing stages of undergraduate study. The practical focus will make the books particularly useful and relevant to those returning to academic study after a period of professional practice, and also to those about to leave the academic world for the challenges of language-related work. For students who have not previously studied applied linguistics, including those who are unfamiliar with current academic study in English-speaking universities, the books can act as one-step introductions. For those with more academic experience, they can also provide a way of surveying, updating and organising existing knowledge.

The view of applied linguistics in this series follows a famous definition of the field by Christopher Brumfit as

> The theoretical and empirical investigation of real-world problems in which language is a central issue.
>
> (Brumfit 1995: 27)

In keeping with this broad problem-oriented view, the series will cover a range of topics of relevance to a variety of language-related professions. While language teaching and learning rightly remain prominent and will be the central preoccupation of many readers, our conception of the discipline is by no means limited to these areas. Our view is that while each reader of the series will have their own needs, specialities and interests, there is also much to be gained from a broader view of the discipline as a whole. We believe there is much in common between all enquiries into language-related problems in the real world, and much to be gained from a comparison of the insights from one area of applied linguistics with another. Our hope therefore is that readers and course designers will not choose only those volumes relating to their own particular interests, but also use this series to construct a wider knowledge and understanding of the field, and the many cross-overs and resonances between its various areas. Thus the topics to be covered are wide in range, embracing an exciting mixture of established and new areas of applied linguistic enquiry.

The perspective on applied linguistics in this series

In line with this problem-oriented definition of the field, and to address the concerns of readers who are interested in how academic study can inform their own professional practice, each book follows a structure in marked contrast to the usual movement *from* theory *to* practice. In this series, this usual progression is presented back to front. The argument moves *from* Problems, *through* Intervention, and *only* finally to Theory. Thus each topic begins with a survey of everyday professional problems in the area under consideration, ones which the reader is likely to have encountered. From there it proceeds to a discussion of intervention and engagement with these problems. Only in a final section (either of the chapter or the book as a whole) does the author reflect upon the implications of this engagement for a general understanding of language, drawing out the theoretical implications. We believe this to be a truly *applied* linguistics perspective, in line with the definition given above, and one in which engagement with real-world problems is the distinctive feature, and in which professional practice can both inform and draw upon academic understanding.

Support to the Reader

Each chapter concludes with a list of questions to help readers review the contents and reflect on some of the key issues. The book also provides a glossary of key terms.

The series complements and reflects the Routledge Handbook of Applied Linguistics edited by James Simpson, which conceives and categorises the scope of applied linguistics in a broadly similar way.

Ronald Carter
Guy Cook

Reference

Brumfit, C. J. (1995) Teacher Professionalism and Research. In G. Cook and B. Seidlhofer (eds) *Principle and Practice in Applied Linguistics*. Oxford: Oxford University Press, pp. 27–42.

Part I

Introduction

There are many 'introductions' to second language acquisition (SLA) theory and research (e.g. Ellis, 2008; Ortega, 2009; Gass and Selinker, 2001). These books aim to survey the research and theory that has investigated and explained how learners acquire an additional language. The field of SLA is dynamic and growing and doubtlessly there is a continuing need for an updated survey. However, that is not the purpose of this book. Our aim is to draw on SLA theory and research to examine pedagogical issues and problems. Our starting point is not SLA but language pedagogy. We want to explore to what extent various pedagogical practices are supported by what is currently known about how learners acquire another language. Thus we are not seeking to 'apply' SLA to language pedagogy but rather to 'use' it as a resource to investigate the kinds of claims that characterize pedagogical accounts of how to teach a language.

Language teaching is an inherently practical affair while SLA constitutes a research discipline. As Hirst (1966) pointed out:

> To try to understand the nature and pattern of some *practical discourse* in terms of the nature and patterns of some purely *theoretical discourse* can only result in its being radically misconceived.
>
> (p. 40)

In terms of language teaching, 'practical discourse' refers to the moment-by-moment decisions that teachers make in the process of conducting a lesson and that manifest themselves in teaching-as-interaction. In making these decisions, teachers typically draw on their 'practical knowledge' of what works in a specific instructional context – knowledge shaped more by experience than study. 'Theoretical discourse' embodies the 'technical knowledge' that is available in expository accounts of teaching and learning. It consists of statements about what and how to teach and the theoretical rationale for these. Language teachers may also draw on this technical knowledge both in planning a lesson and in implementing it in the classroom, although teachers' primary concern with practical action does not readily allow for the application of technical knowledge. 'Technical knowledge', however, is important. It serves as a resource that teachers can use when planning a lesson and also, less easily, when coping with the exigencies of real-time teaching. It also provides a body of information that teachers can draw on to reflect on their teaching and to experiment with new possibilities.

This book explores 'technical knowledge' about teaching and learning. This type of knowledge itself, however, is not monolithic. The kind of technical knowledge found in teacher guides is fundamentally different from the kind of technical knowledge found in published research about language teaching and learning. We refer to the former as 'pedagogic discourse' and the latter as 'research-based discourse'. The differences are evident in their epistemological bases. Pedagogic discourse draws on authors' prior knowledge of such discourse and on their own practical experience of teaching a language. As Underhill (in Scrivener, 2005) wrote in his general introduction to the MacMillan Books for Teachers 'we take a "Learning as you go approach" in sharing our experience with you' (p. 9). Pedagogic discourse is intended for teachers and thus is written in a form that is accessible to this audience. Its aim is to be 'practical' – to offer suggestions for what might work in the classroom. Research-based discourse, in contrast, draws on well-established formats for conducting and reporting confirmatory and descriptive research in order to demonstrate validity or trustworthiness. It is intended for fellow researchers and although it may propose a number of 'practical' applications, it is primarily directed at theory-testing or theory-building. Frequently, it is couched in language that is not accessible to outsiders. However, in Hirst's terms both pedagogic discourse and research-based discourse constitute 'theoretical discourse'.

This book is an exploration of the relationship between the pedagogic discourse found in teacher guides (e.g. Harmer, 1998; Hedge, 2000; Ur, 1996; Scrivener, 2005) and in the research-based discourse found in published SLA research. It seeks to examine the proposals for teaching found in the guides in the light of the findings of SLA research. It delves into the theoretical assumptions that underlie the practical proposals found in the guides and then attempts to evaluate these through reference to SLA research.

In adopting this approach, we were aware of a number of problems. First, the distinction between pedagogic discourse and research-based discourse is not always clear-cut. Some (but certainly not all) authors of the teacher guides are familiar with SLA theory and research findings and drew on these in shaping the advice they offered teachers. We struggled at times with deciding what constituted 'pedagogic discourse' and 'research-based discourse'. For example, some of the writings of one author of this book (Rod Ellis) are both 'pedagogic' and 'research-based'. Clearly there are hybrid discourses. Many SLA researchers also position themselves as teacher educators. We resolved this problem by electing to focus on a well-defined set of teacher guides and practical articles about language teaching whose intended audience was clearly teachers, on the one hand, and books and articles plainly intended to provide information about SLA and primarily directed at researchers or would-be researchers, on the other.

Another problem is that the teacher guides do not always agree about specific proposals although, on the whole, we did find a high level of commonality in the positions they adopted. There is, for example, general agreement that teachers should avoid excessive metalanguage when teaching grammar and that they should use a variety of corrective feedback strategies when correcting learner errors. In part, the recommendations for teaching found in guides appear to reflect received opinion about what constitutes effective teaching. SLA researchers also do not present a uniform picture. In particular, there are clear differences in how interactionist–cognitive theories and Sociocultural Theory view second language (L2) acquisition. We have attempted to address these differences by pointing them out and by offering alternative evaluations of the pedagogic proposals we discuss.

In short, this book aims at what Widdowson (1990a) termed a 'conceptual evaluation' of a set of established pedagogic practices as reflected in the pedagogic literature through reference to what is currently known about how learners learn an L2. The aim is not to demonstrate that established pedagogic practices lack validity but rather to submit them to scrutiny. We have attempted to make use of one type of theoretical discourse (research-based discourse about SLA) to examine the claims found in a different type of theoretical discourse (pedagogic discourse). Our hope is that in this way it will be possible to achieve a symbiosis to the mutual benefit of each.

We are aware that the tentative conclusions that we arrive at as a result of our evaluation will not always be accepted by either teacher educators or SLA researchers. Many of the issues we address are controversial. The conclusions we offer reflect *our* interpretations of both the nature of the pedagogic proposals and the SLA research. Other interpretations and, therefore, other conclusions are doubtlessly possible. But by offering our own views we hope to stimulate debate between those engaged in these two types of theoretical discourse.

In line with our stated purpose, the majority of the chapters in this book take as their starting point a specific pedagogic construct or proposal, which is then considered from the perspective of SLA research. However, we feel that it will help readers not familiar with work in SLA if they are given a brief introduction to SLA. This is the purpose of the chapter in this opening section of the book – to set the scene for the subsequent chapters by providing the reader with a general background in SLA. To this end the chapter offers a brief historical survey of SLA, tracing the development of SLA over the five or so decades since its inception. Then, drawing on a general survey of work in SLA, it presents a number of general principles about instructed second language learning. These principles will serve as a point of reference for the evaluation of the specific pedagogical issues addressed in the chapters that follow.

1 Instructed second language acquisition

As a field of study, SLA is relatively new. While there had been interest in L2 learning for a long time, the empirical study of how an L2 is actually learned began relatively recently, dating from the 1960s when some of the first studies were undertaken. We begin by tracing the development of SLA from the early years to today, move on to consider key areas of research in SLA and conclude with a number of general principles of instructed SLA.

Behaviourist vs mentalist accounts of L2 learning

Interest in investigating L2 learning empirically originated in the challenges to behaviourist theory. This viewed L2 learning as the same as any other kind of learning, including L1 acquisition. It treated language learning as a mechanical process of habit formation, which involved 'conditioning' (i.e. the association of an environmental stimulus with a particular response produced automatically through repetition and with the help of reinforcement). This view of learning was challenged by Chomsky (1959) in his review of Skinner's *Verbal Behaviour*. Chomsky argued that L1 acquisition was distinct from other kinds of learning and could not be explained in terms of habit-formation. He staked out a strong case for viewing it as a mental rather than a behavioural phenomenon. Learning happened *inside* the learner's head and was driven by an innate capacity for language (what Chomsky then called the 'language acquisition device'). Verbal behaviour was simply a manifestation of what had been learned not the source of learning. This led a number of applied linguists to ask whether L2 learning was a matter of behaviourally induced habits or a mental phenomenon governed primarily by internal mechanisms.

Behaviourist accounts of learning viewed old habits as an impediment to the formation of new habits. Applied to L2 learning this meant that the learner's L1 was a source of interference, resulting in errors. According to mentalist accounts of L2 learning, however, learners draw on their innate language learning capacity, to construct a distinct system, which came to be called 'interlanguage' (Selinker, 1972). Learning was seen not as the accumulation of correct habits but as an organic process of gradual approximation to the target language. It followed from such a position, that errors were not just due to the influence of the L1 but also the product of the learner's 'creative construction' of the L2. The competing claims of behaviourist and mentalist accounts of learning led to research that investigated: (1) the nature of the errors that learners produced and (2) whether L2 learning was a matter of accumulated habits, or a process that involved stage-like progression in the acquisition of specific grammatical features.

Early research in SLA provided clear evidence that many of the errors that learners produced were intralingual rather than interlingual. That is, to a large extent they were universal (i.e. all learners irrespective of their L1 background make the same errors). Such errors were the product of omissions (e.g. 'She sleeping'), additions (e.g. 'We didn't went there'), misinformations (e.g. 'The dog ated the chicken') and misorderings (e.g. 'What daddy is doing?') – see Dulay et al. (1982). These errors, it was claimed, were 'developmental' in the sense that they arose as a result of the learner attempting to confirm or disconfirm hypotheses about the target language on the basis of limited experience (Richards, 1971). Furthermore, many of the errors L2 learners were seen to make were the same as those found in L1 acquisition, suggesting that they would disappear in due course. In other words, errors were no longer viewed as evidence of non-learning but as part and parcel of the natural process of learning a language.

Early SLA research also involved case studies of naturalistic L2 learners (i.e. learners who were learning through exposure to the L2 rather than through formal instruction) – see, for example, the longitudinal studies reported in Hatch (1978a). These descriptive studies provided evidence about two important characteristics of L2 acquisition. They showed that learners mastered grammatical morphemes such as English plural-s, past tense-ed, and third person-s in a fixed order suggesting that they had their own built-in-syllabus, which they followed irrespective of differences in their L1 or the linguistic environment in which they were learning. Also, and arguably more importantly, they did not master such features one by one but rather gradually, often taking months to fully acquire a specific feature. The acquisition of structures such as English negatives and interrogatives was characterized by a series of transitional stages as learners approximated step by step to the target structure. For example, an early stage in the acquisition of negatives typically involved using 'no' before a verb (e.g. 'No coming today'), followed later by the use of 'not' after an unmarked auxiliary verb (e.g. 'He do not come') and finally the use of 'not' after auxiliary verbs correctly marked for tense and number (e.g. 'He did not come yesterday').

The case studies of naturalistic learners also provided evidence of three other general aspects of L2 acquisition. Some learners – adults as well as children – elect for a 'silent period' during which they function only as listeners. After time when they have acquired some L2 resources through listening, they begin to speak. Their early speech often consists of formulaic chunks – either complete routines such as 'I don't know' or patterns which have one or more empty slots (e.g. 'Can I have a – ?'). Subsequently, researchers have suggested that L2 acquisition proceeds when learners are able to break down these fixed chunks into their parts and in so doing discover their grammatical properties.

In other words, they bootstrap their way to grammar. As this takes place learners start to produce their own 'creative' utterances, but these typically involve both structural simplification (i.e. they omit grammatical words and inflections) and also semantic simplification (i.e. they omit content words when these can be inferred from the context). For example, they produce sentences such as 'Mariana no coming' when meaning 'Mariana isn't coming today'.

Interlanguage theory

These findings could not be explained by a behaviourist view of learning. L2 learning was clearly not a matter of externally driven habit-formation but rather a learner-driven, organic process of gradual development. This led to the claim that learners possessed an *interlanguage* (Selinker, 1972) – that is, they constructed an internal system of rules that was independent of both the learner's L1 and the target language and which evolved gradually over time. Subsequent research was directed at uncovering the characteristics of this interlanguage. These are summarized in Table 1.1. It should be noted, however, that some of the claims made by early interlanguage theory have subsequently been challenged. For example, not all SLA researchers now agree that fossilization occurs. Some current theories of L2 acquisition emphasize that learning never ceases completely as small changes are ongoing in any person's language system (Larsen-Freeman and Cameron, 2006).

Input and interaction

The recognition that L2 learning is best explained in terms of interlanguage theory led researchers to ponder what role the linguistic environment played. Self-evidently, learning can only take place when learners are exposed to input. In the 1980s, researchers began to ask questions such as 'What kind of input are learners exposed to?' and 'How can interaction facilitate the process of interlanguage development?' These are questions that have continued to inform SLA right up to today.

Early research on input focused on *foreigner talk*. This was the special register that native speakers adopt when talking to non-native speakers. Research showed that under some circumstances native speakers resort to ungrammatical foreigner talk – for example, they delete copula *be*, omit auxiliaries and articles, use the base form of the verb and special constructions such as 'no + verb'. Interestingly, many of these features of foreigner talk are the same as those observed in learners' interlanguage. However, not all foreigner talk is ungrammatical. Simplifying input to make it comprehensible to learners need not entail ungrammatical modifications. Teachers rarely use ungrammatical foreigner talk.

The input addressed to L2 learners, even when it was grammatical, was found to be characterized by a number of 'modifications'. That is, when native speakers addressed learners, in comparison to when they addressed other

Table 1.1 Interlanguage theory

Key premises	Description
Learners construct a system of abstract linguistic rules, which underlie comprehension and production	The rules constitute 'an interlanguage'. They account for the errors that learners make and they are systematic (i.e. learners behave in accordance with the rules they have constructed). An interlanguage is a 'system in its own right'.
Learner grammars are permeable	An interlanguage grammar is unstable. It is amenable to penetration by new linguistic forms and rules and thus evolves over time. The new rules may be derived internally, as when a learner overgeneralizes an existing rule, or externally through exposure to the target language input.
Learner grammars are transitional	Learners constantly revise their interlanguage grammars, which therefore manifest an 'interlanguage continuum'. This is reflected in identifiable stages in the acquisition of specific grammatical features.
Learner grammars are variable	At any one stage of development, the language produced by learners will display systematic variability (e.g. they will sometimes say 'She no coming' and sometimes 'She is not coming'). This is because the learner has access to both an 'old' rule and a 'new' (more target-like) rule. Variability is systematic in the sense that identifiable factors such as who the learner is speaking to or the time available to plan an utterance influence which feature the learner accesses.
Interlanguage development reflects the operation of cognitive learning strategies	A number of key strategies have been identified – simplification, overgeneralization and L1 transfer (no longer viewed as causing 'interference' but as one of many resources learners draw on).
In using their interlanguage, learners may draw on communication strategies	Faced with having to communicate ideas with limited linguistic resources, learners draw on such strategies as paraphrasing, word-coinage, code-switching and appeals-for assistance.
Interlanguage systems may fossilize	Fossilization occurs when learners' interlanguage stops developing short of the target language rule. This accounts for why most L2 learners fail to achieve full target language competence. However, this premise is controversial as some SLA researchers argue that development never ceases completely.

native speakers, they typically spoke more slowly, paused more, used simpler high-frequency vocabulary, used full forms rather than contractions (e.g. 'She is coming' rather than 'She's coming'), moved topics to the front of a sentence (e.g. 'John, I like him') and avoided complex subordinate constructions. Researchers such as Hatch (1983) suggested that such modifications might help learners by making it easier for them to process the input and making grammatical features more salient. Another key finding was that these modifications were dynamic. Teachers, for example, were shown to vary in the extent to which they modified their input depending on the proficiency of learners: the more proficient the learners, the fewer the modifications.

Other researchers began to examine the interactions that learners participated in. Long (1981), for example, reported that the native speakers he investigated were more likely to make interactional modifications than input modifications when speaking to L2 learners. Interactional modifications involved both the management of discourse and the repair of communication problems. Examples of the former are the various strategies native speakers use to make a topic salient – for example, by starting an interaction with a question and by treating topics simply and briefly. In the case of the latter, researchers focused on the *negotiation of meaning*. They identified sequences of talk consisting of a 'trigger' (i.e. an utterance that caused a breakdown in communication), an 'indicator' where a speaker signals he/she has not understood and a 'response' where an attempt is made to resolve the problem. Such negotiation, it was suggested, helps learners' comprehension and provides them with input for learning, as this example illustrates:

> NS: we got a plant
> NNS: plant
> NS: yeah, um it's kind of like a fern, has a lot of big leaves; it's in a pot
> (Pica, 1992)

This research on input and interaction led to two hypotheses that spawned further research and that also had a marked influence on language pedagogy. Krashen's (1985) Input Hypothesis claimed that L2 acquisition takes place when a learner is able to understand grammatical forms that are a little more advanced than the current state of the learner's interlanguage. Krashen argued that L2 acquisition was input-driven; that is, output (speaking or writing) played no role in acquisition. He claimed that all that was needed to ensure successful learning was *comprehensible input* and a low *affective filter* (i.e. learners were motivated to attend to the input and were not prevented from doing so by anxiety). Long's (1983b) Interaction Hypothesis also emphasized the importance of comprehensible input but argued that this is best achieved through interaction, especially when problems arose and meaning was negotiated. Later, Long (1996) revised the hypothesis to allow for other ways in which negotiation could assist acquisition – through the feedback that learners received when their errors led to communication problems and through the modified output they produced when learners self-corrected (as illustrated in the example above). Long was responding to Krashen's Input Hypothesis by arguing that output had a role to play in acquisition.

The role of output

The claim that input alone was responsible for acquisition contradicted the pedagogic assumption – explicit in many mainstream methods – that learners need plenty of production practice. It was challenged by Swain (1985), who noted that learners in immersion programmes (i.e. programmes where the L2 was taught by using it as the medium of instruction for teaching the content of other school subjects) failed to achieve high levels of grammatical accuracy even though they were exposed to plenty of comprehensible input. Swain argued that *comprehensible output*, where learners were pushed to produce in the L2, was also needed. Later, Swain (1995) identified a number of ways in which output could assist acquisition: (1) it served as a consciousness-raising function by helping learners to notice gaps in their interlanguages, (2) it provided a means for testing hypotheses about the L2 and (3) it helped to develop metalinguistic understanding of L2 rules when learners talked about their own output. Swain subsequently referred to this last function as 'languaging'. She and her co-researchers conducted a number of studies that showed that talk about language did indeed contribute to acquisition. It should be noted, however, that the kind of output that Swain was talking about was not the same as that which arises in grammar exercises but rather in the performance of various kinds of communicative tasks.

The role of consciousness

Krashen's Input Hypothesis was based on the assumption that L2 acquisition was a subconscious process; that is, learners automatically and naturally acquired new L2 features as a result of comprehending the input they were exposed to. Long's early Interaction Hypothesis also viewed L2 acquisition as not requiring any conscious attention to grammatical forms in the input. However, the later version of the Interaction Hypothesis and Swain's Output Hypothesis both claimed that L2 acquisition is, in part at least, a conscious process. They drew on work by Schmidt (1990, 2001), who presented a strong case for a role for consciousness in L2 acquisition.

Schmidt first pointed out that the term 'consciousness' needs to be carefully defined. He distinguished consciousness as 'intentionality' and as 'attention'. Learning can take place both intentionally when learners make a deliberate attempt to learn something or incidentally when they are focused on meaning rather than form and pick up something through exposure to input. This is an important distinction as one way of distinguishing different approaches to language teaching is in terms of whether they cater to intentional or incidental learning. Schmidt argued that irrespective of whether learning is intentional or incidental it involves consciousness at the level of attention. That is, in order to learn, learners need to notice specific forms in the input and also learning is facilitated when they notice the gap between an interlanguage form and the equivalent target language form in the input. Schmidt's claims about the importance of conscious attention have since become known as the *Noticing Hypothesis*. It has led to studies that have investigated whether: (1) learners do notice linguistic forms in the input and (2) whether this results in learning. These studies have shown that learners tend to notice some features (e.g. lexis and word order) but are less likely to notice others (e.g. morphological features such as third person-*s*). This finding has been used to explain why many learners fail to acquire some grammatical features. For example, they do not notice features such as third person-*s* because they are semantically redundant (i.e. they do not convey any additional meaning in a sentence) and thus they do not acquire them.

The Noticing Hypothesis has also informed research that has investigated the conditions that are likely to promote noticing. Long (1996), for example, proposed that the negotiation of meaning directed learners attention to those linguistic forms that they used incorrectly. That is, it induced both noticing and noticing-the-gap. Other researchers experimented with various ways of highlighting problematic features in the input that learners were exposed to (e.g. by embolding them in a reading passage) in order to increase the likelihood of learners paying attention to them. VanPatten (1996) argued that learners will rely on default input processing strategies, unless their attention is specifically directed at the target language forms needed to comprehend a sentence correctly. For example, the First Noun Principle states that learners will automatically assume that the first noun in a sentence is the agent, which works in a sentence such as:

Mary bit the dog.

but not in a sentence such as:

The dog was bitten by Mary.

VanPatten proposed that to overcome such default strategies, a special type of instruction, which he called Processing Instruction, was needed. This directs learners' conscious attention to the grammatical markers that signal that the default strategy is inoperable. In the case of passive sentences, these are the use of 'be', the past participle, and 'by'.

However, the role played by consciousness remains controversial. Krashen has continued to insist that L2 acquisition is essentially a subconscious process. Also, some studies have suggested that this might indeed be the case – at least to some extent. Learners do seem to be able pick up some features of which they have no conscious awareness. Schmidt (2001) later modified his original claim (i.e. no noticing, no learning) by suggesting that learning is more likely to occur when learners attend consciously to linguistic forms (i.e. more noticing, more learning).

Explicit and implicit L2 knowledge

Schmidt (1993) also suggested a third way in which consciousness figures in L2 learning – in terms of the conscious understanding of linguistic forms and rules that learners develop. This is different from noticing as it entails an explicit representation of L2 features and rules (i.e. explicit L2 knowledge). Running throughout the history of SLA has been a concern for the role that explicit L2 knowledge plays in learning. In the 1990s, however, this particular issue began to receive detailed attention.

Just about all theories of L2 acquisition acknowledge the distinction between implicit and explicit knowledge. By and large these theories have addressed how learners develop implicit L2 knowledge as this is the type of knowledge that is considered primary, in the sense that it is required to become a fluent, competent user of an L2. But SLA researchers have also, increasingly, been concerned with how explicit knowledge can assist the development of implicit knowledge. This is, of course, a key issue for language pedagogy as teachers need to know what value there is in teaching explicit knowledge of the L2.

Table 1.2 provides definitions of these two types of knowledge in terms of their key characteristics (see R. Ellis, 2005). There is disagreement about how best to conceptualize implicit knowledge. Some theorists view it as 'symbolic' in nature (i.e. as consisting of 'rules'). Other theorists view it as simply a network of 'connections' and 'procedures', some of which become so firmly ingrained that they give the appearance of 'rules'. Controversy also exists regarding the role of age in the development of implicit knowledge. Some researchers argue that once learners are past a critical age (often given as the beginning of puberty) they lose the ability to acquire implicit knowledge and thus must rely on explicit knowledge. Other researchers, however, maintain that the ability to acquire implicit knowledge declines gradually with age but does not entirely disappear. We will put these issues aside for now and, instead, focus on the issue crucial to language pedagogy – the relationship between explicit and implicit knowledge.

Three very different positions have been advanced to explain the relationship between explicit and implicit knowledge:

1 The non-interface position (e.g. Krashen, 1981; Paradis, 1994)
   This draws on theory and research that shows that implicit and explicit L2 knowledge involve different acquisition mechanisms, are stored in different parts of the brain (Paradis 2009), and are accessed in performance by means of different processes, automatic vs controlled. It claims that explicit knowledge cannot transform directly into implicit knowledge as it is neurolinguistically distinct.
2 The strong interface position (e.g. DeKeyser, 1998)
   This claims that explicit knowledge can transform into implicit knowledge through practice. That is, learners can first learn a rule as a declarative fact and, then, by dint of practising the use of this rule in controlled and communicative activities, construct an implicit representation, although this need not entail (initially, at least) the loss of the original explicit representation.
3 The weak interface position (e.g. R. Ellis, 1994; N. Ellis, 2005)
   The weak interface position exists in three versions, all of which acknowledge the possibility of explicit knowledge assisting the development of implicit but posit some limitation on when or how this can take place. One version posits that explicit knowledge can transform into implicit knowledge through practice, but only if the learner is developmentally ready to acquire the linguistic form. The second version sees explicit knowledge as contributing indirectly to the acquisition of implicit knowledge by assisting 'noticing' and 'noticing-the-gap'. The third version proposes that learners can use their explicit knowledge to produce output that then serves as 'auto-input' to their implicit learning mechanisms.

Table 1.2 Key characteristics of implicit and explicit knowledge

Characteristics	Implicit knowledge	Explicit knowledge
Awareness	Learner has no conscious awareness of linguistic norms but does intuitively know what is correct.	Learner is consciously aware of linguistic norms.
Type of knowledge	Implicit knowledge is 'procedural'; that is, available for automatic processing.	Explicit knowledge is 'declarative'; it consists of 'facts' about language that are only available through controlled processing.
Systematicity	Implicit knowledge is variable but systematic.	Explicit knowledge is often anomalous and inconsistent as learners may have only a partial understanding of a linguistic feature.
Use of L2 knowledge	Implicit knowledge is only evident when learners use it in communication.	Explicit knowledge is used to monitor L2 production; it is used when learners lack the requisite implicit knowledge.
Self-report	Implicit knowledge consists of internalized constructions and procedures that cannot be directly reported.	Explicit knowledge can be reported. Reporting requires access to metalanguage.
Learnability	There may be age limits on learners' ability to acquire implicit knowledge (i.e. a 'critical period').	Explicit knowledge is learnable at any age.

These different positions afford very different views about the role that language pedagogy should play in L2 acquisition, which we will consider in Chapter 4. Briefly, advocates of the non-interface position argue that nothing – or very little – is to be gained by instruction directed at explicit knowledge, while advocates of the strong interface position consider that it is helpful (and in the case of older learners maybe even necessary) to first develop learners' explicit knowledge and then help them to proceduralize this through practice. Advocates of the weak interface position propose that instruction should be predominantly directed at developing implicit knowledge through communicative activities but that explicit instruction can assist its development indirectly by making learners aware of their linguistic problems. The interface positions and the associated pedagogic proposals continue to be debated today.

Social perspectives on L2 acquisition

The research that we have considered to date was based on a psycholinguistic view of L2 acquisition. That is, it was primarily concerned with explaining the cognitive processes involved. In recent years, however, a debate has arisen centred around the general approach to theory-building in SLA with some researchers viewing SLA as essentially a cognitive enterprise and others seeing it as a social phenomenon. As Firth and Wagner (2007) put it:

It appears that SLA has, over the last decade in particular, undergone a bifurcation between a cognitive SLA (which is being termed mainstream in a number of publications)...and a sociocultural/sociointeractional SLA.

(p. 804)

What view of L2 acquisition does sociocultural/sociointeractional SLA offer?

In fact, a social perspective was not entirely missing from early SLA research. Schumann's (1978) Acculturation Theory was closely linked to interlanguage theory. It proposed that the speed in which and the extent to which learners' interlanguage developed depended on the degree to which they acculturated to the target language community, which in turn depended on the social distance between the learners' social group and the target language community. Social distance was determined by such factors as the social status of the two groups (i.e. whether or not they were 'equal', whether both groups welcomed assimilation and the extent to which the two groups shared the same social facilities). The theory claimed that where there was minimal social distance, learners advanced quickly and were less likely to fossilize and that where the social distance was great, learning was slower and learners were more likely to develop a pidginized (i.e. highly simplified) variety of the target language. Schumann's theory, however, received limited support from studies that investigated the relationship between social distance and success in L2 learning. Also, it was essentially a deterministic theory, failing to acknowledge that learners are not just subject to social conditions but also through their own agency can create social contexts that are favourable to learning.

Other social theories of L2 learning emphasize the learner's contribution to the social context in which learning takes place. Norton (2000), for example, proposed that the learner's social identity plays an important role in creating opportunities for learning. Her Social Identity Theory is concerned with the relationship between power, identity and language learning. Norton saw social identity as multiple, contradictory and dynamic. To obtain the 'right to speak', learners need to be able to see themselves as legitimate speakers of the L2. To achieve this they may need to challenge the social identity that is often thrust upon them by target language speakers and to assert the right to communicate on an equal basis by insisting on a social identity that confers a non-subservient status. Norton illustrated her theory in research on adult female immigrants to Canada. In some cases, these women were successful in establishing a social identity that afforded them opportunities to speak and thus to learn; in other cases, they were not successful and withdrew from contact with native speakers.

Both of these theories examine the social conditions that promote contact with target language speakers and afford opportunities to learn. However, they do not specify what these opportunities are. That is, they do not consider the actual interactions that learners participate in and how these 'shape' learning. Sociointeractional theories, in contrast, seek to do just this. They view interaction not just as a source of input but as a socially negotiated event. They claim that to understand how learning takes place in interaction it is necessary to examine the social context in which interaction occurs and the social relationships of the interlocutors. Furthermore, they see learning not as something that happens as a result of interaction but as taking place within interaction itself. That is, learners create their own linguistic resources (which may or may not correspond to target language norms) in the course of achieving inter-subjectivity with other speakers (who may or may not be native speakers) and in so doing demonstrate acquisition taking place in flight.

The theory that has most clearly articulated this view of L2 learning is Sociocultural Theory (SCT). This draws on the work of Russian psychologist Lev Vygotsky, who argued that learning arises when an expert (i.e. a teacher) interacts with a novice (i.e. a learner) to enable the novice to perform a task collaboratively that the novice is incapable of performing independently. When this happens, the expert and the novice jointly construct a *zone of proximal development* (ZPD). SLA researchers such as Lantolf (2000a) have proposed that interaction is therefore essential as it mediates L2 learning. They see learning as manifesting itself first in social interaction and only subsequently becoming internalized. Initially, development takes place with the help of the 'scaffolding' provided by an interlocutor; subsequently what has been learned is internalized and thus is available for self-regulated use. SLA researchers have also proposed that ZPDs do not require the assistance of an expert; they can arise in interaction between learners. Swain (2006), for example, explored how the 'languaging' (i.e. talk about language) that arises in tasks that invite learners to collaborate in selecting linguistic forms to achieve a communicative outcome, helps to construct ZPDs that give rise to learning and to subsequent internalization of new linguistic forms.

Research based on sociointeractional theories has tended to be qualitative in nature. That is, it consists of the detailed analysis of interactional sequences involving learners, frequently employing the techniques of Conversational Analysis to describe the orderliness, structure and sequential patterns of the interactions. In this respect it differs from mainstream SLA, which has preferred quantitative methods to describe different aspects of interaction or experimental methods, to examine cause-and-effect relationships between aspects of interaction/input and learning. Swain's research, however, although firmly sociocultural in orientation, combines qualitative and quantitative approaches as it aims to investigate not just learning-in-flight but also the extent to which internalization has occurred.

Instruction and L2 acquisition

Much of the early SLA research was motivated by the wish to improve language pedagogy. Researchers believed that if they were able to provide accurate descriptions of learner-language and how it changed over time and if they could then develop theories to explain what they found, they would be in a position to make sound proposals about how to teach an L2. In other words, they believed that for instruction to 'work', it had to be compatible with how learners learn. They also recognized, however, that there was a need to investigate the effects of instruction on learning empirically. Such research had a two-fold purpose: it provided a means of testing the claims of specific theoretical positions and it might contribute to better, research-based pedagogy.

Instruction can be non-interventionist or interventionist. Non-interventionist instruction aims to create the conditions for acquisition to acquire naturally. This can be achieved either by providing the learner with plenty of comprehensible input or by means of task-based teaching, where learners perform a variety of input-based and production-based tasks, all of which have a primary focus on meaning rather than form (Ellis, 2003b). Non-interventionist instruction, therefore, is *meaning-focused instruction* (MFI). Interventionist instruction involves the direct teaching of specific linguistic forms – typically by means of explicit instruction combined with some form of input-based or production-based practice. Interventionist instruction is typically referred to as *form-focused instruction* (FFI).

Meaning-focused instruction (MFI)

MFI is premised on the assumption that the development of true competence in an L2 (i.e. implicit knowledge) is best catered for through the incidental learning that takes place when learners are engaged in processing input and output in communicative contexts. Such contexts can be created in a variety of ways – through exposure to comprehensible input as in the Natural Method (Krashen and Terrell, 1983) or extensive reading programmes, through content-based language teaching, or in immersion programmes. It is the last of these that has been subject to closest scrutiny.

Immersion programmes were first introduced in Canada but have since sprung up in all parts of the world (see Johnson and Swain, 1997). There are different types of programmes (e.g. early vs late immersion; immersion programmes for majority language or minority language students) but they all have in common an attempt to develop L2 proficiency by teaching a range of normal school subjects through the medium of the L2. The Canadian programmes were reviewed by Swain and Lapkin (1982) and by Genesee (1984). These reviews showed that learners in these programmes developed a normal standard of L1 proficiency (despite being educated in the L2) and demonstrated the same or better level of academic development. They tended to have less rigid ethnolinguistic stereotypes than students in regular school programmes. They also manifested a high level of L2 proficiency, developing a native-like control of discourse. However, immersion learners did not typically develop high levels of grammatical proficiency and did not always demonstrate an ability to use the L2 in sociolinguistically appropriate ways. In sum, immersion programmes lead to considerable communicative skills and confidence in using the L2, but not to high levels of linguistic competence.

This led researchers to suggest that although incidental learning does occur in MFI, there are limitations. They noted that when learners are primarily engaged in communicating, they fail to pay attention to grammatical features that are not important for realizing their meanings and, like classroom learners in general, have limited opportunities for production in the L2. As a result, they fail to require non-salient or redundant features. In some respects, then, immersion learners manifest the same characteristics as many untutored learners – their speech remains, to a degree, 'pidginized'.

SLA researchers have continued to maintain the importance of MFI for developing communicative ability. Currently, this is reflected in proposals for task-based language teaching (TBLT) (Ellis, 2003b; Samuda and Bygate, 2008). This is an approach to teaching that emphasizes holistic vs discrete learning, learner-driven rather than teacher-centred education and communication-based vs form-focused instruction (Van den Branden et al., 2009). However, TBLT does not entirely exclude attention to form. Rather, it proposes that attention to form should be embedded in the communicative interactions that tasks give rise to. This has come to be referred to as 'focus on form', defined by Long (1991) as follows:

> Focus on form overtly draws students' attention to linguistic elements as they arise incidentally in lessons whose overriding focus is on meaning or communication.
>
> (pp. 45–46)

Researchers have investigated how focus on form takes place in MFI (e.g. Ellis et al., 2001) and also whether it has an effect on L2 learning (e.g. Loewen, 2005). There are strong theoretical reasons for claiming that focus on form is not just facilitative of learning but may even be necessary. The research shows that it arises frequently in teacher-led MFI but less commonly in MFI activities performed by learners in small groups. There is growing evidence that it does result in learning.

Form-focused instruction (FFI)

There is a rich history of research investigating FFI in SLA. FFI research in the 1960s was 'method' oriented; that is, it investigated the relative effectiveness of different methods, in particular those that aimed at teaching grammar explicitly (e.g. grammar-translation and the cognitive-code method) or implicitly through controlled practice exercises (e.g. the audiolingual method). These studies were largely inconclusive: they failed to find any clear difference in the learning outcomes of the different methods. In the 1970s, researchers adopted a different approach to investigating FFI. They sought to compare groups of instructed learners who were presumed to have received FFI with groups of untutored learners. Long (1983a) reviewed a number of such studies and concluded that the instructed learners achieved higher levels of proficiency. Pica (1983) adopted a slightly different approach. Basing her study on the finding that there was a natural order of acquisition for English grammatical morphemes, she investigated three different groups of learners (an instructed group, an untutored group and a mixed group), to see whether there were any differences in the accuracy with which they produced the same set of morphemes. She reported no overall difference in the accuracy orders of these groups but she did note that the groups differed in the accuracy with which they produced specific morphemes (e.g. the instructed group produced plural-*s* more accurately than the untutored group). Other studies in the 1970s and 1980s also found that the order of acquisition was not affected by instruction. Thus, while the research indicated that FFI resulted in higher levels of achievement, it also suggested that it did not affect the overall process of L2 development.

The results of these early FFI studies led researchers to propose that FFI was beneficial but needed to be made compatible with the learning process. One way in which this might be achieved was by ensuring that the target of the instruction was 'teachable'. That is, it had to be directed at a target feature that learners were developmentally ready to learn. Pienemann (1989) reviewed a number of studies that showed that FFI was effective if it took account of the learners' developmental stage but was not effective if it did not. However, it is difficult to see how this can be applied to everyday language teaching as teachers have no ready way of determining which target features their students are ready to learn.

Subsequent FFI research has shifted tack. Rather than asking 'Does FFI have an effect on L2 learning?' it asked 'What effect do different types of FFI have on L2 learning?' The various types of FFI that were investigated were based on theories of L2 learning. For example, VanPatten (1996) argued that the goal of FFI should be to assist learners to abandon default processing strategies and that to achieve this it was necessary to direct learners' attention to key grammatical markers in the input, rather than to try to elicit the correct target features in production. He and his co-researchers (and other researchers) conducted a series of studies comparing the effects of structured input (i.e. input specially designed to induce processing of a grammatical structure) and traditional production activities. While these studies produced results that were not entirely uniform, they did point to the general effectiveness of input-based instruction, which was shown to result in learning no matter whether this was measured by comprehension or production tests. Other studies, however, indicated that production-based instruction can also be very effective, especially if this focused not just on linguistic form but also on form-function mapping (i.e. the meanings realized by different target forms). Harley (1989) and Day and Shapson (1991) investigated the effects of instruction consisting predominantly of functional, production activities and reported results, indicating that this kind of instruction resulted in increased accuracy in the use of the target features in free production. Recent studies by Swain and her co-researchers (e.g. Swain and Lapkin, 1998) have also produced results that show that production can assist learning.

Yet another set of FFI studies set out to investigate competing theoretical claims regarding the role of corrective feedback in L2 learning and the type of feedback most likely to promote learning. Corrective feedback was found to help learning. Different studies have shown that both feedback that provides learners with the correct target language form and feedback that prompts learners to self-correct their own errors can be effective.

FFI has also been conceptualized more generally in terms of whether it is implicit or explicit in nature. This distinction cuts across the various other types of FFI. That is, input-based instruction, production-based instruction and corrective feedback can all be distinguished in terms of whether they involve implicit or explicit instructional activities. While the implicit/explicit distinction can be defined in different ways, the essential difference lies in whether the instruction involves rule explanation/guided discovery of the rule (in the case of explicit instruction) or whether it leaves it to learners to work out what the target is (in the case of implicit instruction). Norris and Ortega (2000) reported an analysis of FFI studies of implicit and explicit instruction. They found that explicit FFI was more effective than implicit FFI.

The goal of much of this research has been to establish which type of FFI is universally more effective. However, there are reasons to believe that in fact this may not possible. The effectiveness of different types of FFI has been shown to depend on: (1) the linguistic feature that is the target of the instruction and (2) the instructional context. For example, a number of studies indicate that whereas explicit instruction is more effective than implicit instruction in the case of simple grammatical structures, the opposite can be true for complex structures. However, as De Graaff and Housen (2009) pointed out 'no generally agreed definition or metric of structural complexity exists' (p. 739). Also, Spada and Tomita's (2010) meta-analysis of studies that had investigated the effects of FFI on simple and complex structures failed to support the claim that the type of structure interacts with the type of instruction. Thus, no clear conclusions can be drawn yet about the effect of instruction on linguistic features of different complexity. The research is clearer where the instructional context is concerned. The findings of studies of corrective feedback are indicative of the importance of taking the instructional context into account. For example, Lyster (2004) found that in a French immersion context, prompts, which pushed learners to self-correct, were more effective than recasts, which provided learners with the correct form, while Lyster and Mori (2006) found the opposite in a Japanese immersion programme in the United States, where learners were more oriented to attend to form. There is also a third factor that can influence the effect of FFI – the individual learner. This will be considered in the following section.

This plenitude of FFI studies helps to illuminate when, why and to what extent FFI is effective. However, as De Graaff and Housen (2009) noted 'it is hard to formulate generalizable conclusions, and even more difficult to formulate implications or recommendations that are relevant to, and useful for, teaching practice' (p. 742). In part, this is because FFI is a very complex phenomenon. In part, it has to do with problems with the research. Not only has the same type of instruction been operationalized in very different ways in different studies, but also the learning that results from the instruction has also been measured differently. This makes it very difficult to compare results across studies. Nevertheless, some findings are clear cut (i.e. FFI does benefit learning!) and the research has certainly led to a much better understanding of the factors that influence the success of FFI and provides an empirical basis for examining proposals for teaching grammar found in handbooks for teachers.

Individual differences (IDs) in language learning

In all the above sections, we have been concerned with the universalistic aspects of L2 acquisition. But there is also a rich history of research into individual learner differences. In fact, much of the research predates the inception of SLA as a field of study. Carroll, for example, began his work on language aptitude (i.e. the special ability believed to be important for learning an L2) in the 1950s.

Horwitz (2000) noted a marked shift in the way in which individual differences have been viewed over the years. Much of the earlier research regarded learners as either innately endowed with or lacking in language learning skills. They were seen as 'good' or 'bad', 'intelligent' or 'dull', 'motivated or unmotivated'. One of the main purposes of the early research was to identify those learners likely to be successful if selected for a foreign language course. This research focused on developing tests such as the Modern Language Aptitude Battery (Carroll and Sapon 1959) in order to predict which individual learners would be successful. From the 1970s, however, researchers became more concerned with identifying the characteristics of those learners who were 'good language learners' in order to provide guidance to other learners about how best to learn. Researchers now viewed learners as possessing different kinds of abilities and predispositions that influence learning in complex ways.

The bulk of research into individual learner differences, however, has continued to examine the relationship between different learner factors (e.g. language aptitude, learning style, personality, motivation, language anxiety) and language achievement or proficiency. A typical study involved correlating measures of an ID factor with measures of language learning. Such studies enabled researchers to identify which ID variables were most influential in language learning. It became clear that two factors – language aptitude and motivation – were strongly related to learning outcomes. These two factors function independently. That is, learners who are strong in language aptitude do not necessarily possess a strong motivation to learn and vice versa. The most successful learners are those who are strong in both language aptitude and motivation. Much of the research was also directed at defining and measuring constructs such as 'language aptitude' and 'motivation'. These are highly complex factors and it is, therefore, not surprising to find different theoretical perspectives and a range of instruments for measuring them. L2 motivation research, in particular, has evolved considerably over the last forty years, from the early work of Gardner and Lambert (1972) on the roles of instrumental and integrative motivation in the Canadian context with its two official languages (English and French), to the current work on the situated and dynamic nature of motivation and the role played by how learners view an L2 in terms of their 'ideal' selves (Dörnyei, 2005). There has also been growing interest in how teachers can enhance those factors that are mutable – such as motivation – (e.g. Dörnyei and Csizér, 1998).

In general, however, research into individual differences has taken place alongside and separate from mainstream SLA research, where the primary concern has been with the processes responsible for L2 acquisition (e.g. noticing and noticing-the-gap). One reason for this is that universalist and differential approaches have distinct agendas: the former seeking to explain the mechanisms responsible for the commonalities observed in the process of language learning (e.g. the 'natural' order and sequence of L2 acquisition), the latter directed at examining how and why learners differ.

It is, however, clearly important from the perspective of language pedagogy to develop an understanding of how individual factors affect the way in which a learner responds to and performs specific instructional tasks. While such research is limited, it is now beginning to appear. Learner factors such as language aptitude and language anxiety have been shown to influence the extent to which learners benefit from instruction. For example, Erlam (2005) found that language analytic ability was not related to gains resulting from deductive-type instruction but was to gains from an inductive type. Again, though, results have not been consistent. Other studies (e.g. DeKeyser, 2000) suggest that more explicit types of instruction favour adult learners with higher levels of analytic ability. Manolopoulo-Sergi (2004) proposed that the type of motivation – whether it was extrinsic or intrinsic – would influence how learners processed input. That is, intrinsically motivated learners could be expected to process input in a more elaborated, deeper manner. Evidence in support of this claim was available in a study by Takahashi (2005), which showed that Japanese learners of English were more likely to report paying attention to the linguistic aspects of complex requests if they were intrinsically motivated.

Researchers have also had a long-standing interest in the learning strategies that individual learners employ (see, for example, Oxford, 1990, 2011). Learning strategies are the techniques that learners employ when engaged in intentional language learning. Examples are 'grouping' (i.e. classifying items to be learned into meaningful units), 'practising', 'setting goals and objectives', 'taking risks' and 'asking for clarification'. The choice of such strategies defines the approach that a learner consciously adopts to learning an L2. Researchers have used a variety of methods, including questionnaires, learner diaries and interviews to investigate the strategies that learners report using. Studies have also examined the relationships between learners' reported use of learning strategies and their achievement or proficiency in an L2 in an attempt to identify those strategies that are more effective. In addition, there have been ongoing attempts to discover the strategies used by the 'good language learner' (i.e. by learners who are acknowledged to have been very successful in learning an L2) (e.g. Gan et al., 2004). Such research is of obvious value to language pedagogy as it opens up the possibility of training students in the use of those strategies that have been shown to promote L2 learning. A number of training studies have been conducted in the last twenty years (see the review of these in Hassan et al., 2005). However, these have produced somewhat mixed results in part because there is still no clarity as to which strategies or combination of strategies are the important ones for language learning. Also, it is not clear what role such strategies play in incidental as opposed to intentional learning.

Principles of instructed language learning

This brief historical review shows how SLA has grown into a highly complex subdiscipline of applied linguistics. It has spawned a plethora of theories that address the linguistic, cognitive, social and psychological aspects of L2 learning. It has employed a variety of research methods – descriptive, ethnographic, correlational and experimental. It has produced findings documenting different aspects of learner language and the factors that influence its development. While these findings are not always easy to interpret and are often apparently contradictory, they do provide a basis for identifying a set of general principles that can inform the role that instruction plays in L2 learning. Drawing on Ellis (2003a), we conclude this chapter with a brief account of these principles, which we will refer to in subsequent chapters.

Like the principles proposed by Long (2006), the Principles of Instructed Language Learning constitute design features that are motivated by SLA theory and research findings. Long distinguished 'principles' and 'procedures', arguing that whereas the former constitute 'language teaching universals', the latter consist of a 'potentially infinite range of options for instantiating the principles at the classroom level' (p. 376). In the account of each principle that follows, we have suggested a number of 'procedures' for implementing it.

Principle 1: Instruction needs to ensure that learners develop both a rich repertoire of formulaic expressions and a rule-based competence

Proficiency in an L2 requires that learners acquire both a rich repertoire of formulaic expressions, which cater to fluency and their immediate functional needs as well as knowledge of underlying rules that enable them to use the L2 'creatively'. Traditionally, language instruction has aimed at developing rule-based competence but, arguably, formulaic expressions are more important in the early stages of language learning. A complete language curriculum needs to ensure that it caters to the development of both formulaic expressions and rule-based knowledge.

Principle 2: Instruction needs to ensure that learners focus on meaning

As we have seen, there is now ample evidence to show that meaning-focused instruction (MFI) is highly effective in enabling learners to develop fluency and confidence in using an L2. MFI is also seen as a means of developing learners' linguistic resources in the L2. Immersion programmes, content-based language teaching and task-based language teaching all constitute ways of providing learners with the input and interactional opportunities they need to develop the implicit knowledge required for effective communication. However, this principle does not preclude the need for attention to form. We have pointed out that MFI does not guarantee high levels of linguistic accuracy. Thus, to be effective, instruction must also direct attention onto form, as proposed by the following principle.

Principle 3: Instruction needs to ensure that learners also focus on form

There is now a widespread acceptance that acquisition also requires that learners attend to form. As we have already noted, some theories of L2 acquisition consider such attention is necessary for acquisition to take place. Instruction can cater to a focus on form in a number of ways:

- Through the explicit teaching of grammar.
- By means of consciousness-raising tasks that assist learners to discover grammatical rules for themselves and to develop an explicit representation of them.
- Using input-based or production-based practice activities.
- By means of 'focus on form' techniques (i.e. methodological options that induce attention to form in the context of performing a meaning-focused task).
- FFI can involve an *intensive* focus on pre-selected linguistic forms or it can offer *extensive* attention to the forms of a range of features through corrective feedback in task-based lessons.

Principle 4: Instruction needs to be predominantly directed at developing implicit knowledge of the L2 while not neglecting explicit knowledge

Given that it is implicit knowledge that underlies the ability to communicate fluently and confidently in an L2, it is this type of knowledge that should be the ultimate goal of any instructional programme. How then can it be developed? There are conflicting theories regarding this (see earlier discussion of the interface positions). Irrespective of these different theoretical positions, however, there is a clear consensus that learners need the opportunity to participate in communicative activities to develop implicit knowledge while there is also a case for teaching explicit knowledge. First, explicit knowledge is useful for monitoring and, given time, also for formulating messages. Second, according to the weak interface hypothesis, explicit knowledge can facilitate the processes of noticing and noticing-the-gap. Accordingly, instruction needs to be directed at developing *both* implicit and explicit knowledge, giving priority to the former.

Principle 5: Instruction needs to take into account the order and sequence of acquisition

One of the key findings of SLA is that learners manifest an order and sequence of acquisition that is to a large extent universal and reflects the gradual process of acquiring grammatical features. How, then, can instruction take account of this gradual process? There are a number of possibilities:

- Adopt a zero grammar approach, as proposed by Krashen. That is, employ a task-based approach that makes no attempt to predetermine the linguistic content of a lesson.
- Ensure that learners are developmentally ready to acquire a specific target feature. However, this is probably impractical as teachers have no easy way of determining where individual students have reached and it would necessitate a highly individualized approach to cater for differences in developmental levels among the students.
- Focus the instruction on explicit rather than implicit knowledge as explicit knowledge is not subject to the same developmental constraints as implicit knowledge.

It should be noted, however, that not all researchers accept that there are developmental constraints on what learners can learn and, therefore, what can be successfully taught. The strong interface position claims that explicit knowledge of a grammatical structure can be converted into implicit knowledge at any time, given the right amount and type of practice. Similarly, Sociocultural Theory rejects the view that L2 acquisition progresses along a relatively predetermined mental path. Chapters 3 and 4 provide a discussion of this issue.

Principle 6: Successful instructed language learning requires extensive L2 input

As we have already noted, much L2 learning is incidental rather than intentional and this requires access to massive amounts of input. It can be claimed with confidence that if the only input students receive is in the context of a limited number of weekly lessons based on some course book, they are unlikely to achieve high levels of L2 proficiency. How then can teachers ensure their students have access to the extensive input they need? Teachers need to:

- Maximize use of the L2 inside the classroom. Ideally, this means that the L2 needs to become the medium as well as the object of instruction, especially in a foreign language setting. However, this does not mean that the L1 has to be excluded entirely. See Chapter 8 for a detailed discussion of the role of the L1 in the L2 classroom.
- Create opportunities for students to receive input outside the classroom. This can be achieved most easily be providing extensive reading programmes

based on carefully selected graded readers, suited to the level of the students, as recommended by Krashen (1989). Learners can also seek out opportunities to experience the language outside class time and need encouragement and guidance in how to do so.

Principle 7: Successful instructed language learning also requires opportunities for output

The importance of creating opportunities for output, including what Swain (1985) has called 'pushed output' (i.e. output where the learner is stretched to express messages clearly and explicitly), constitutes one of the main reasons for incorporating tasks into a language programme. Controlled practice exercises typically result in output that is limited in terms of length and complexity. They do not afford students opportunities for the kind of sustained output that theorists argue is necessary for interlanguage development. Classroom research has shown that extended talk of a clause or longer in a classroom context is more likely to occur when students initiate interactions in the classroom and when they have to find their own words. This is best achieved by asking learners to perform tasks as these provide them with the opportunity to perform a range of language functions associated with initiating as well as responding roles in interaction.

Principle 8: The opportunity to interact in the L2 is central to developing L2 proficiency

Hatch (1978b) famously put it 'one learns how to do conversation, one learns how to interact verbally, and out of the interaction syntactic structures are developed' (p. 404). Thus, interaction is not just a means of automatizing existing linguistic resources but also of creating new resources. What then are the characteristics of interaction that are deemed important for acquisition? Johnson (1995) identified four key requirements for an acquisition-rich classroom:

- Creating contexts of language use where students have a reason to attend to language.
- Providing opportunities for learners to use the language to express their own personal meanings.
- Helping students to participate in language-related activities that are beyond their current level of proficiency.
- Offering a full range of contexts that cater for a 'full performance' in the language.

Creating the right kind of interaction for acquisition constitutes a major challenge for teachers, especially in teacher-centred classrooms. One way is to exploit the interactive opportunities afforded by small group work. When students interact amongst themselves, acquisition-rich discourse is more likely to ensue although there are also a number of dangers (e.g. excessive use of the L1 in monolingual groups and exposure to interlanguage errors).

Principle 9: Instruction needs to take account of individual differences in learners

There are a number of ways in which teachers can adapt their teaching to take account of individual learner differences. One way is by matching the instruction to suit individual learners. However, this is not practical in many teaching situations as learners vary in so many different ways. However, teachers can cater to learner variation by adopting a flexible teaching approach involving a range of different instructional activities. They can also use simple learner-training materials (e.g. Ellis and Sinclair, 1989) to make students more aware of their own approaches to learning and to develop their awareness of alternative approaches. They can try to increase the range of learning strategies at learners' disposal and to assist learners to achieve self-regulation. Strategy training – despite the problems referred to earlier – may help to make learners more flexible in their approach to learning. Finally, but perhaps most importantly, teachers need to find ways of fostering motivation in their students (see Dörnyei, 2001). They should accept that it is *their* responsibility to ensure that students are motivated and stay motivated and not just blame a lack of motivation on their students. While it is probably true that teachers can do little to influence students' extrinsic motivation, there is a lot they can do to enhance their intrinsic motivation.

Principle 10: Instruction needs to take account of the fact that there is a subjective aspect to learning a new language[1]

This principle is based on a much broader view of what is involved in learning an L2 and draws on the ideas about social identity discussed earlier. It acknowledges that language teaching involves much more than developing students' linguistic and communicative abilities. It also involves developing them as people. As Kramsch (2009) noted 'language…is not just an unmotivated formal construct but a lived embodied reality' (p. 4). Kramsch argued that learners have the opportunity to develop their subjective selves by taking on new identities and even a new personality. Learning an L2 can change how people view reality and how they see the world around them when the new language enters into their lives and transforms them. For Kramsch, teaching a new language needs to cater to the 'construction of perceptions, attitudes, beliefs, aspirations, values' (p. 7). Also, it needs to encourage learners to examine the practices and beliefs of their own world-view critically.

Kramsch suggested a number of ways in which instruction can help develop what she called 'symbolic competence' in learners. Teachers need to become 'critical educators' and learners to become politically, socially and personally aware. This requires instructional activities that encourage language play and emotional identification with the language. One way in which this can be achieved is through the introduction of literature and creative writing into the L2 curriculum.

Principle 11: In assessing learners' L2 proficiency it is important to examine free as well as controlled production

Norris and Ortega (2000) conducted a meta-analysis of FFI studies. A meta-analysis is a statistical procedure that enables researchers to compare the relative effectiveness of two types of instruction. Its advantage is that it examines a large number of studies and thus can show which type of instruction is overall the most effective. The meta-analysis demonstrated that the extent of the effectiveness of instruction is contingent on the way in which it is measured. They distinguished four types of measurement:

1 metalinguistic judgement (e.g. a grammaticality judgement test)
2 selected response (e.g. multiple choice)
3 constrained constructed response (e.g. gap-filling exercises)
4 free constructed response (e.g. a communicative task).

They found that the magnitude of effect was greatest in the case of (2) and (3) and least in (4). Yet, arguably, it is (4) that affords the best measure of learners' L2 proficiency, as it is this that corresponds most closely to the kind of language use found outside the classroom. The ability to get a multiple choice question right amounts to very little if the student is unable to use the target feature in actual communication. Free constructed responses are best elicited by means of tasks.

Conclusion

A fundamental assumption of this book is that good teaching is teaching that proceeds in accordance with how learners learn. Instruction that is not compatible with the way L2 acquisition takes place cannot be successful. Thus, the goal of 'SLA-for-language pedagogy' must be to: (1) to provide a clear and usable account of how learners acquire an L2 both outside and inside classrooms and (2) propose how instruction can take account of what is known about L2 acquisition.

This is not an easy enterprise, however, in part because SLA has grown into an epistemologically diverse area of enquiry affording varying and sometimes conflicting accounts of the same phenomena. Thus, there is no simple SLA recipe that can be applied to language pedagogy. Our approach, therefore, has been to try to draw out of the review of SLA in the first part of this chapter a set of general principles that can guide decision making in pedagogy. In the rest of the book, we will explore these principles and the SLA research that informs them in greater depth as we examine specific issues in language pedagogy.

Note

1 This principle was not included in the original list of ten principles published in Ellis (2003a). It was added because we recognize that the other principles focused on how instruction can assist the development of linguistic or communicative competence and there is a need to recognize that language instruction can – and in many cases, probably should – have wider goals.

DISCUSSION QUESTIONS

1. What are the 'competing claims of behaviourist and mentalist accounts of L2 learning'?
2. What evidence is there to support the claims that learners develop an 'interlanguage'?
3. What are the implications of Interlanguage Theory for language teaching?
4. What is meant by claiming that 'L2 acquisition is input driven'? To what extent is this claim justified?
5. What kinds of input facilitate L2 acquisition?
6. In what ways can 'output' (i.e. learner production) also contribute to L2 acquisition?
7. Schmidt distinguishes two senses of 'consciousness' – 'intentionality' and 'attention'. Explain the difference and then consider which of these is more important for acquisition.
8. What is a 'default processing strategy'? Think of examples.
9. The interface positions address the relationship between implicit and explicit knowledge in L2 learning. Briefly describe each position and then discuss which one you favour and why?
10. In what ways can social factors influence how learners acquire an L2?
11. How 'learning' is conceptualized differs in cognitive-interactionist and Sociocultural Theory. Explain the difference.
12. The chapter distinguishes two types of language instruction – meaning-focused instruction (MFI) and form-focused instruction (FFI). Give examples of instructional activities characteristic of each type. What does SLA tell us about the effectiveness of the two types?
13. In what ways can individual difference factors such as language aptitude and motivation affect L2 learning?
14. Discuss each of the Principles of Instructed Language Learning in terms of your own experience as a learner or a teacher. Do you consider some of the principles more important than others?
15. Is there an additional principle of instructed language learning you would like to propose?

Part II

Language pedagogy and SLA: an external perspective

The purpose of this book is to evaluate different aspects of language pedagogy through reference to SLA research. These aspects have been drawn from what we refer to as an 'external' and 'internal' view of language pedagogy.

When we adopt an external view, we see teaching in terms of the overall approach (e.g. traditional, weak communicative, strong communicative language teaching), curricular goals (e.g. Type A and Type B syllabus), materials for realizing these goals, classroom activities (e.g. 'exercises' or 'information gap tasks'), methodological procedures, viewed either in macro terms (e.g. accuracy vs fluency based) or in micro-terms (e.g. the provision of opportunities to plan prior to performing a task) and devices for measuring student progress. The external view of language teaching is enshrined in handbooks for language teachers (e.g. Harmer, 1983; Ur, 1996). These describe and sometimes prescribe how teachers can teach. They provide blueprints for actual lessons. The external perspective is realized in the lesson plans that teachers devise – as statements about what and how to teach. When teachers contemplate and discuss language teaching they are likely to adopt an external view.

The internal view requires us to adopt Allwright's (1984) dictum – 'interaction is the fundamental fact of language pedagogy'. That is, we need to treat teaching as an interactional event – or, more properly, as a series of interactional events. Teachers talk to students. Students sometimes talk to teachers and, in some classrooms, talk to each other. How is all this talk accomplished? What kinds of speech events do teachers and students enact when they talk to each other? In what way does classroom talk vary from one interactional event to another? What are the factors that cause this variation? Most crucially, what kinds of talk are most likely to promote language learning?

In this section of the book we will focus on evaluating a number of pedagogic constructs that belong to the external perspective. Perhaps the clearest example of such a construct is the 'method' construct. A method is defined in terms of the content teachers are supposed to teach and the methodology for teaching it. Methods exist as the descriptions found in books on language teaching (e.g. Richards and Rodgers, 1986, 2001). The method construct serves as the ideal starting point for investigating how SLA can inform an external perspective on language pedagogy. Subsequent chapters focus on a number of other pedagogic constructs – linguistic syllabuses (Chapter 3), explicit instruction (Chapter 4), comprehension-based vs production-based instruction (Chapter 5) and task-based language teaching (Chapter 6) – all of which embody theoretical notions about what and how to teach.

2 The method construct and theories of L2 learning

Introduction

Traditionally, language teaching has been conceptualized in terms of 'methods' and 'approaches'. These terms are not quite synonymous. 'Method' is used to refer to a set of clearly defined techniques and procedures for teaching a language. In contrast, the term 'approach' refers to a set of general principles that can guide the choice of specific techniques and procedures. Examples of 'methods' are Grammar Translation, the Audiolingual Method, Total Physical Response, the Silent Way and Community Language learning. Examples of 'approaches' are Communicative Language Teaching and Task-Based Language Teaching. However, the distinction between a method and an approach is, at best, a fuzzy one. Methods are generally underpinned by theories of language and language learning and the general principles that these provide. Similarly, 'approaches' entail the use of specific techniques and procedures although these are not so narrowly prescribed as in a 'method'. In this chapter, we will not make a distinction between these two terms but use 'method' as the general cover term.

Readers might like to google *language teaching methods*; they will find clear evidence of the prevalence of viewing language teaching in these terms as well as brief descriptions of the various methods/approaches that have been proposed over the years. Thus the method construct constitutes a good starting point for our exploration of language pedagogy and second language acquisition research. After all, one way of evaluating the claims of different methods is by examining to what extent they are compatible with what is known about how learners learn an L2.

Anthony (1963) provided a framework for examining different methods/ approaches. Somewhat confusingly, this framework consists of three central constructs: *approach*, *method* and *technique*. He used the term 'approach' to refer to the theory of language and learning that underlies a particular method/ approach. The second construct, 'method', refers to the 'overall plan for the orderly presentation of language material' and covers what is now called 'design' (the objectives, choice of content and how this is organized). 'Techniques' consist of the 'particular trick, stratagem, or contrivance used to accomplish an immediate objective'. Anthony saw these three constructs as interconnected levels of conceptualization – that is, 'techniques carry out a method which is consistent with an approach' (p. 63).

Richard and Rogers (1986, 2001) provided descriptions of a number of different methods based on Anthony's framework. Kumaravadivelu (2006) proposed classifying these methods into those that were: (1) language-centred, (2) learner-centred and (3) learning-centred. Language-centred methods are organized around linguistic forms (usually grammatical structures) which are systematically practised with a focus on accuracy. Learner-centred methods are directed at meeting the learner's linguistic and communicative needs. Like language-centred methods they also preselect and practise specific elements of language. Both of these types of methods cater to intentional language learning. Learning-centred methods define the content to be taught in non-linguistic terms (e.g. tasks or topics) and aim to promote the social and cognitive processes involved in learning. They cater more for incidental learning.

Table 2.1 uses Anthony's framework to provide brief descriptions of three specific methods, one from each of Kumaravadivelu's types: (1) the Audiolingual Method was popular (especially in the United States[1]) in the 1950s and 1960s and continues to exert an influence on language pedagogy up to today; (2) Communicative Language Teaching first appeared in the 1970s and has had a major impact on thinking about language teaching since;[2] (3) Task-based Teaching attracts considerable attention today, largely because of the support it has received from SLA.

Problems with the method construct

Prior to the 1990s the method construct served as the major way of conceptualizing language teaching. Since then, it has come under attack as both impractical and theoretically unsound. For many teachers and teacher educators, it is no longer seen as constituting an adequate basis for the design and implementation of a language teaching programme.

Practical issues

There are a lot of methods for teachers to choose from. In the first edition of their book *Approaches and Methods in Language Teaching*, Richards and Rodgers (1986) discussed eight methods (but also mentioned a number more). In a later version of the same book published in 2001, the number discussed in detail doubled. Thus, the most compelling issue facing teachers is to decide which method to adopt. One possibility – one that educational research (e.g. Goodlad, 1982) suggests is all too common – is that teachers opt to teach in accordance with how they were taught. There are two problems with this. First, teachers may simply elect to adopt the techniques they experienced themselves as learners with no real understanding of the underlying principles that inform them. Second, the techniques may not be appropriate for the aims of the course or the needs of the learners. A second possibility is to undertake some form of evaluation of the different methods in order to determine which one is best suited to a particular group of learners. This calls for knowledge of the criteria that can be used to conduct such an evaluation.

Table 2.1 Three levels for conceptualizing proposals for teaching an L2

Level of conceptualization	Definition	The Audiolingual Method	Communicative Language Teaching	Task-based Language Teaching
Approach	'a set of correlative assumptions dealing with the nature of language teaching and learning'.	Language learning is like any other kind of learning. It consists of developing habits that become ingrained so that learners automatically use the L2 correctly. Habits are developed mechanically by ensuring that learners respond correctly to behavioural stimuli.	The language needs of specific groups of students are defined in terms of notions and functions (e.g. 'expressing possibility' or 'apologizing'). The aim is to develop 'communicative competence' rather than 'linguistic competence'. No clear learning theory underlies this approach but recognition is given to the importance of learning through communicating.	Language learning arises incidentally when learners are engaged in the effort to communicate and when attention is directed to linguistic form in a context where learners are primarily focused on meaning. Learning involves mapping form onto meaning.
Method	'an overall plan for the orderly presentation of language material, no part of which contradicts, and all of which is based upon, the selected approach'.	The initial focus should be on oral skills and ensuring that learners avoid making errors. This is achieved by systematically teaching the patterns of the L2 one by one, focusing in particular on those patterns that differ from the L1. Teaching should consist of practice rather than the explicit description of the target patterns.	The syllabus consists of a graded list of functions and notions and their linguistic exponents. The methodology is 'accuracy'-oriented, involving the presentation and practice of selected exponents of each function/notion. Attention is also given to sociolinguistic appropriateness. Both oral and written media are addressed.	No attempt is made to specify the linguistic content to be learned. Content is specified in terms of a series of communicative tasks that learners perform. Tasks can involve any of the four language skills. A lesson can involve (1) a pre-task stage, (2) a main-task stage and (3) a post-task stage but only (2) is required.
Technique	'A technique is implementation...It is a particular trick, stratagem, or connivance used to accommodate an immediate objective... Techniques must be consistent with a method, and therefore in harmony with an approach as well.'	The L2 is taught by means of drills of various kinds (e.g. repetition, substitution, and transformation drills). The drills present learners with stimuli that carefully control the learner's responses. Dialogues are also provided for the learner to memorize and repeat.	Key techniques: (1) situational presentation of a function/notion e.g. by means of a dialogue, (2) controlled practice (e.g. substitution or sentence completion) and (3) free production using a communicative task. Teaching materials are (semi-)authentic (i.e. bear a relationship to natural language use). Importance is attached to learners working in pairs or small groups.	The L2 is learned through performing a variety of different types of tasks (e.g. information-gap and opinion-gap tasks) in either whole-class or small group interaction. Tasks can be input-based or output-based. Attention to form arises when a linguistic or communicative problem occurs and corrective feedback is provided. Opportunities to focus more directly on form occur in the pre-task and post-task stages of a lesson.

Richards and Rodgers (1986) outline the questions that need to be asked when evaluating methods. These questions, however, are directed more at the professional evaluator than the teacher faced with the task of choosing a method. For example, teachers are unlikely to be able to answer a question such as 'How does the method compare with another method (e.g. when used to attain a specified type of competency)?' Also, none of the questions address what we would see as the central question – 'To what extent are the methods compatible with what is known about how learners learn a second language?' Richard and Rogers go on to suggest the kind of data needed to conduct an empirical evaluation of methods – descriptive data, observational data, effectiveness data and comparative data. Again, though, teachers are unlikely to have the time and may not have the skills needed to collect such data, analyse it and reach a conclusion about which method to employ. In short, it is unlikely that a busy teacher will be able to undertake the kind of evaluation that Richards and Rodgers have in mind. Thus, any evaluation that teachers undertake will probably be based on their experience as learners and teachers and on their beliefs (often not explicit) about how languages are learned. There is, though a clear need here – to make available to teachers information about what method evaluation studies have shown. We will attempt to provide such information for two of the theories shown in Table 2.1 later in this chapter.

Once teachers have selected a method, they face another problem – they need to be able to implement the method successfully in their classrooms. 'Method' is essentially an 'external' construct; it comprises descriptions of a set of techniques. The teacher needs to execute the techniques and this requires making countless and immediate decisions 'online'. In other words, the method construct needs to be ultimately understood in terms of the processes that arise in the classroom – what we call the 'internal' view of teaching. Mackey (1965) made a similar distinction when he noted that 'method analysis determines how teaching is done by the book; teaching analysis shows how much is done by the teacher' (p. 139).

To illustrate the problem that can arise when implementing a technique, let us consider one teacher's attempt to conduct the kind of drilling recommended by the Audiolingual Method. The teacher, who was very experienced in teaching this method, wished to elicit a plural sentence pattern from a beginner-level learner in an ESL class. Below is an extract (taken from Ellis, 1984b) from the actual lesson. The teacher adopts a standard technique of the Audiolingual Method, namely asking questions designed to elicit the target pattern ('These are + plural N') and contrasting this with another pattern ('This is a singular N'). The first point to note is that this learner fails to produce the complete target pattern in any of her turns. The teacher responds to the difficulty the learner experiences by attempting to scaffold the correct pattern (e.g. 'These are –' in turn 6), by providing the complete pattern for the learner to imitate ('These are rulers' in turn 13) and by explicit correction ('Not "a"' in turn 16). These are all standard audiolingual techniques of 'reinforcement' but they are not successful. The episode concludes with the teacher accepting the learner's partial production of the pattern (turns 18 and 19). What we see happening here, then, is the teacher working hard to elicit the correct response but failing. This raises two questions. The first is 'Is this bad audiolingual teaching?' Arguably it is not, as the teacher was responding to the learner's obvious frustration with this drill (which is quite evident when listening to the audio recording of the lesson). The second is 'Why did this learner fail to produce the correct pattern given all the support she was given?' To answer this question it is necessary to know something about the process by which learners acquire an L2 grammar (see Chapter 1). The key point, however, is that teachers are not just implementers of a technique. They have to negotiate its implementation with their learners by reacting to the learners' responses and adjusting their own behaviour turn by turn.

Extract 1:

1. T: Now, Tasleem.
2. T: What is this? (T. holds up pen.)
3. S: This is a pen.
4. T: What are these? (T holds up two pens.)
5. S: This are a pen.
6. T: These are ____?
7. S: Are pens.
8. T: What is this? (Teacher holds up a ruler.)
9. S: This is a ruler.
10. T: What are these? (Teacher holds up two rulers.)
11. S: This is a...are...
12. S: This are a rulers.
13. T: These are rulers.
14. T: What are these?
15. S: This are a rulers.
16. T: Not 'a'.
17. T: These are _____?
18. S: Rulers.
19. T: Rulers.

Teaching by method, then, is problematic in two major ways. First, it requires teachers to decide which method to employ. This requires teachers to possess the knowledge, skills and time needed to evaluate methods, which in many instances they are unlikely to have. Of course, this problem can be circumvented if the method is chosen for the teacher – for example, by selecting a textbook that embodies the method and mandating its use in the classroom. However, this does not prevent the second problem from arising, namely that classroom exigencies may result in the teacher failing to implement the techniques as required by the method. This suggests that there may be something fundamentally wrong with the 'method' construct.

Theoretical issues

There have been a series of attacks on the method construct starting in the late 1980s (Pennycook, 1989; Kumaravadivelu, 1994; Richards, 1996; Bax 2003). These attacks were based on the postmodernist perception that teaching was and ought to be more of a bottom-up than a top-down affair informed by the needs of learners and teachers working in specific sociocultural contexts. Teacher educators argued that no single method is appropriate for all situations and that, in any case, teachers never simply implement the blueprint specified by a particular method, but rather 'construct' teaching fluidly in accordance with their understanding of what works for the particular students they are teaching on particular occasions – as the above extract illustrates.

The method construct were seen as limited in a number of key ways:

- By and large, methods only address how to teach relative beginners; they do not cater to instruction for more advanced learners. Thus they cannot serve as a basis for teaching learners of all proficiency levels.
- The method construct assumes that there is a universal way in which to teach all learners, ignoring the fact that learners are individuals, with different needs and different ways of learning. For example, learners vary in perceptual learning style (Reid, 1987), so a method such as the Audiolingual Method that insists on the primacy of teaching oral before written language will not suit learners with a preference for a visual learning style.
- It also takes no account of the sociocultural milieu in which the teaching takes place; that is, it assumes that the aims and techniques of the method are equally relevant to all classrooms, irrespective of the economic, political and social context in which the teaching is taking place. For example, a number of commentators (e.g. Bax, 2003; Littlewood, 2007) have pointed out that Communicative Language Teaching is not compatible with the beliefs and traditions that inform teaching in many Asian countries and, as a result, teachers face major obstacles in its implementation. It has been suggested that the imposition of a method, such as CLT, that originated in the West, constitutes a form of 'technocratic imperialism' (Sampson, 1984).
- It positions the teacher as being in thrall to the chosen method. That is, it deprives the teacher of autonomy by requiring him/her to teach in accordance with the prescriptions and proscriptions of the method. Thus it denies the importance of teachers' own practical experience of what constitutes effective teaching.
- As such, it deprofessionalizes teachers by discouraging innovation and reflective teaching.

These criticisms led to the claim that 'method is dead' (or ought to be) and to proposals for a 'postmethod pedagogy'. Kumaravadivelu (2001) rather grandly proposed that this could be conceptualized in terms of a 'three-dimensional system consisting of the parameters of "particularity", "practicality" and "possibility"'

(p. 538). Particularity refers to the need to ensure that language pedagogy is based on 'context-sensitive knowledge'. Practicality involves enabling teachers to develop their own theories of teaching based on their practical experience. Teaching needs to be based on a 'teacher-generated theory of practice' (p. 541). Possibility refers to the importance of awareness of the sociopolitical factors that shape learners' identities and of actively helping them transform themselves by resisting social inequality (see the account of Norton's Social Identity Theory in Chapter 1). Kumaravadivelu emphasized that in a postmethod pedagogy both teachers and learners are autonomous.

It should be clear from these proposals for a postmodern pedagogy that the emphasis has shifted from 'techniques' to 'approach' (to use Antony's terms). That is, Kumaravadivelu defines a postmodernist approach in terms of a set of abstract axioms or maxims that can guide teachers in selecting and implementing instructional activities. He does go on to suggest the 'actions' that teachers and learners can perform but there is clearly a reluctance to propose specific techniques. Indeed, the essence of a postmodern pedagogy is that the teachers are left to decide on the nuts and bolts of actual practice for themselves. As Kumaravadivelu (2001) put it, teachers 'theorize from their practice and practice what they theorize' (p. 541).

Postmodern pedagogy is not without its critics, however. Block (2001) noted that:

> While method has been discredited at an etic level (that is, in the thinking and nomenclature of scholars) it certainly retains a great deal of vitality at the grassroots, emic level (that is, it is still part of the nomenclature of lay people and teachers).
>
> (p. 72)

He might also have added that not all scholars have dispensed with the construct. Indeed, task-based language teaching grew out of the theorizing and research of SLA scholars. Nor is it really clear that the proposals for a postmethod pedagogy are really so incompatible with the method construct. Bell (2003) suggested that it might be better to view method and postmethod as dialectically related – 'method imposes practices top-down; postmethod constructs practices bottom-up' (p. 332). That is, methods have value in that they equip teachers with both the practical tools needed to teach and a sense of belief in what they are doing, while postmethod pedagogy encourages teachers to guard against over-routinization. Bell also pointed out that the method construct is, in fact, far from dead. He noted that many of the principles of a postmethod pedagogy advanced by Kumaravadivelu are in fact part and parcel of current proposals for teaching language through communication. In a post-postmodern pedagogy, therefore, there is arguably a place for the method construct. Klapper (2006), following his own survey of a number of mainstream methods,[3] saw merit in familiarizing teachers with these methods on the grounds that 'the study of different approaches focuses attention on how theory and practice is integrated and thus is fundamental to the process of reflective continuing professional development' (p. 123). Klapper's own approach – a wise one – is not to reject the method construct but rather to present each method and then to consider the problems with it.

Evaluating and investigating methods

There are many ways in which the method construct can be subjected to evaluation. Our concern in this section is limited to examining how SLA can inform our understanding of the strengths and limitations of teaching-viewed-as-method. We will consider two questions:

1 To what extent are specific methods compatible with how an L2 is learned in an instructed setting?
2 What do studies that have compared different methods show about their relative effectiveness?

To answer these questions we will focus on two specific methods that have had a considerable influence on language teaching in general – the Audiolingual Method and Communicative Language Teaching. We will examine to what extent each of these methods is compatible with the principles of instructed language learning introduced in Chapter 1 and then examine a number of comparative method studies that investigated the effectiveness of these methods in relation to other methods.

The Audiolingual Method

This method grew out of the work of structural linguists such as Fries and the experience of teaching languages to army personnel during the Second World War. Fries (1948) described the approach adopted in an article written for the first issue of *Language Learning*. This involved:

- Drawing up descriptions of the target language patterns, using native speakers as informants.
- Carrying out a contrastive analysis of the patterns in the learners' L1 and those of the target language to provide a basis for selecting and grading the patterns to be taught.
- Preparing materials to teach the target language patterns.

The method was later underpinned by behaviourist learning theory. Brooks (1960) and Lado (1964) outlined the psychological principles that they believed needed to be followed to ensure successful implementation of the method. These emphasized that learning consisted of changes in behaviour brought about by experience, that language learning was a mechanical process of habit formation, that old habits (i.e. L1 habits) would interfere with the development of new (L2) habits, that learning proceeds by analogy rather than analysis and that, therefore, there is no need to teach grammar explicitly, and that errors were to be avoided at all costs. The specific techniques were based on these principles; they involved mechanical pattern practice, the use of 'reinforcement' to address errors whenever these occurred, memorizing dialogues and the avoidance of explicit grammar teaching. They also emphasized developing oral skills first and limiting the teaching of vocabulary until the patterns had been firmly established.

Theoretical evaluation

Table 2.2 evaluates the Audiolingual Method in terms of the Principles of Instructed Language Learning. It should be clear that, in the main, the AM does not accord with these principles. In particular, the AM fails to acknowledge the learner's own contribution to learning and the importance of providing opportunities for meaning-focused language use. It is also limited by its rejection of explicit instruction. The emphasis on teacher-controlled drilling will inevitably lead to a highly restricted form of classroom interaction consisting of initiate-respond-follow-up (IRF) exchanges – as illustrated in Extract 1. As a result, learners are exposed to a very limited input and have no real opportunity for pushed output in contexts where they can express their own personal meanings. The emphasis on error avoidance also fails to acknowledge that L2 learning is a slow, organic process, with errors not only inevitable but potentially facilitative of learning as learners test out their hypotheses. In short, the insistence on viewing language in terms of structural patterns and of viewing learning in terms of behaviourist learning theory is highly limiting.

Audiolingualism came under attack in the 1960s as a result of Chomsky's (1959) critique of behaviourism and experimental and clinical evidence showing that language development was biologically as well as environmentally determined (Lenneberg, 1967). As we saw in Chapter 1, studies of L2 learners demonstrated that grammatical structures were not acquired as 'accumulated entities' – as habit-formation theory assumed – but in stages, involving transitional constructions that all learners manifested on route to the target language pattern. In other words, how L2 learners learn simply does not conform with the psychological principles on which AM was based. Nor does it with the finding that early L2 acquisition is primarily lexical in nature.

Perhaps the overriding problem with the AM rests in the fact that it fails to cater for *transfer appropriate learning* (TAP). Lightbown (2008) defines this as follows:

> The fundamental tenet of TAP is that we can better remember what we have learned if the cognitive processes that are active during learning are similar to those that are active during retrieval.

(p. 27)

The AM engages learners in highly controlled language production. It positions learners as responders to stimuli. Clearly, this is of very limited use if the goal is to prepare learners to participate in spontaneous face-to-face communication where they will need to play an initiating as well as a responding role. The TAP predicts, correctly, that learners taught by the AM will have difficulty in using the L2 for purposes of everyday communication.

It is, however, worth standing back to ask whether AM is entirely worthless. Many learners were taught with the AM and although they often failed to develop the ability to communicate easily and freely, they did learn something. Does memorization and repetition play no role in language learning? Is learning patterns through controlled production practice totally without value? Is 'reinforcement' not a useful teaching strategy for dealing with errors? Clearly memorization is important for language learning, although perhaps more so for vocabulary than for grammar. It constitutes a learning strategy that many 'good language learners' make use of. Cook (1994) staked out the case for repetition in language learning, noting that it occurs commonly in caretaker–child discourse and contributes to L1 acquisition. A number of studies (e.g. Weinert, 1987; Myles et al., 1998) have reported that classroom learners learn ready-made chunks as a result of engaging in controlled practice activities directed at teaching them specific grammatical structures. That is, teaching patterns may not result in the acquisition of the underlying structures but it may result in learners internalizing formulaic sequences that are of communicative value to them (see Principle 1 in Chapter 1). SLA research also provides evidence in support of 'reinforcement' (relabelled 'corrective feedback'), although this is seen as more likely to contribute to learning if it occurs when learners are focused on meaning rather than form (Lightbown, 2008). Thus, although audiolingualism may not pass muster as a 'method', some of the 'tricks', 'strategems' and 'contrivances' that constitute its 'techniques' can contribute to learning and, indeed, continue to figure in contemporary language teaching.

Empirical evaluation

A key tenet of the Audiolingual Method was that language learning proceeds by means of analogy rather than analysis and that, therefore, there was no need to teach explicit grammar rules. This tenet directly contradicted other methods that were popular at the time, namely Grammar Translation and the Cognitive Code Method, both of which emphasized the importance of deductive instruction involving the provision of explicit rules. The 'language teaching controversy' (Diller, 1978) led to a number of large-scale empirical studies designed to establish which approach – the inductive approach of the AM or the deductive approach of Grammar Translation and the Cognitive Code Method – was the more effective.

In the Colorado Project, Scherer and Wertheimer (1964) compared the Grammar Translation Method and the Audiolingual Method. They investigated

Table 2.2 Theoretical evaluation of the Audiolingual Method

Instructed Language Learning Principles	Audiolingual Method
1. Instruction needs to ensure that learners develop both a rich repertoire of formulaic expressions and a rule-based competence.	AM is directed at 'behaviour' not 'competence. It aims to teach 'patterns' (i.e. the underlying structure of specific utterances) but in fact may succeed only in teaching formulaic expressions.
2. Instruction needs to ensure that learners focus on meaning.	It is doubtful if mechanical drills and the rote-memorization of dialogues focus learners' attention on meaning.
3. Instruction needs to ensure that learners focus on form.	The drilling clearly does focus attention on form. This is achieved entirely through production-based practice.
4. Instruction needs to be predominantly directed at developing implicit knowledge of the L2 while not neglecting explicit knowledge.	AM seeks to develop 'habits' which can be seen as analogous to 'implicit knowledge'. However, the nature of the instructional activities makes it unlikely that implicit knowledge results as learners are primarily focused on form. AM sees no merit in teaching explicit knowledge.
5. Instruction needs to take account of the order and sequence of acquisition.	AM claims that learning is entirely environmentally determined. It assumes that learners will master the patterns in the order in which they are taught. There is no recognition that learners may go through a 'silent period' or that early L2 speech is predominantly lexical.
6. Successful instructed language learning requires extensive L2 input.	The only input learners receive – at least in the early stages – is in the form of drills and dialogues. This is not likely to create an input-rich learning environment.
7. Successful instructed language learning also requires opportunities for output.	AM is entirely output-based. That is, it assumes that learners learn through producing patterns correctly. However, the output they produce is very controlled; there is no opportunity for 'pushed output'.
8. The opportunity to interact in the L2 is central to developing L2 proficiency.	Interaction is entirely controlled by the teacher; initiate–respond–follow-up exchanges are likely to dominate. There is no opportunity for learners to express their own personal meanings or to engage in a 'full performance' in the language.
9. Instruction needs to take account of individual differences in learners.	AM treats all learners the same. However, Lado (1964) did acknowledge the importance of motivation, seen as the 'need and urge to communicate through language' (p. 34). It is unlikely, however, that pattern-drilling and memorization foster such a motivation.
10. Instruction needs to take account of the fact that there is a subjective aspect to learning a new language.	No account is taken of this – language learning is conceptualized purely in linguistic terms.
11. In assessing learners' proficiency, it is important to examine free as well as controlled production.	Lado (1964) emphasized that testing needed to focus on assessing learners' ability to produce the patterns of the target language correctly by means of selected response and constrained constructed response items. He is dismissive of tests involving metalinguistic judgements and sees limited value in tests involving free constructed responses (e.g. a written composition).

beginner-level, college-level students of L2 German over a two-year period. The Audiolingual Method proved superior at the end of the first year in all tests with the exception of a translation test. However, at the end of the second year, no overall significant difference between the two methods was found. While the Audiolingual Method group did better at speaking, the Traditional Method group did better in reading, writing and translation. In other words, each method resulted in learning products that reflected its instructional emphasis. The Colarado Project initiated a critical appraisal of the claims of the Audiolingual Method (Hayn, 1967).

The Pennsylvania Project (Smith, 1970) compared the effects of three methods – (1) 'traditional' (i.e. Grammar Translation), (2) 'functional skills' (essentially the Audiolingual Method), and (3) 'functional skills plus grammar' – on beginning and intermediate French and German classes at the high-school level. Student achievement in the four skills was evaluated at mid-year and at the end of the year using a battery of standardized tests. The results in general showed no significant differences between the three methods, except that the 'traditional' group was superior to the other two groups on two of the reading tests. After two years, the 'traditional' group again surpassed the 'functional skills' group in reading ability but did significantly worse on a test of oral mimicry. No differences were found in the students' performance on the other tests.

In the Gothenburg/Teaching/Methods/English (GUME) Project (Levin, 1972), six studies, all similar in design, were carried out comparing the Implicit Method and the Explicit Method. The Implicit Method is described as corresponding to 'an inductive-oriented audiolingual method' and the Explicit Method as corresponding to 'a deductive-oriented audiolingual method' with the grammatical explanations provided in English (i.e. the L2) in some studies and in Swedish (the L1) in others. By and large, no significant differences between the implicit and explicit school groups were found. In some groups very little learning was evident, but even in those where learning did take place, the type of instruction made no difference. In the case of an older group of high school students, a clearer advantage was found for the Explicit Method. Also, the adult learner group benefited most from the Explicit Method. In both of these groups, the explicit explanation of grammar points was provided in Swedish. Levin concluded that the main results 'tend to support the cognitive-code learning theory' (p. 193) but only at the upper secondary school and adult learner levels. However, none of the group differences were statistically significant.

These studies were all carefully designed studies (for their time) and yet they failed to provide a clear demonstration that one method was superior to another in terms of overall language proficiency. While short-term differences were sometimes evident, these disappeared over the long term. What was clear was that the claims made by advocates of the Audiolingual Method – namely that learners would achieve far higher levels of proficiency especially in oral skills – was not borne out. Indeed, if anything, the results pointed to a slight superiority for methods that included explicit instruction, at least where older learners were concerned. Perhaps, the most reasonable conclusion to draw from these studies, however, was that the choice of method did not matter. This was one reason why the 'method construct' began to fall out of favour, first with researchers (see Allwright, 1988) and later with teacher educators such as Kumaravadivelu (1994).

These projects also pointed to some inherent problems in conducting large-scale comparative method studies. We will reserve consideration of these until we have completed our examination of the other method – Communicative Language Teaching.

Communicative Language Teaching

Communicative Language Teaching emerged at a theoretical level in the 1970s (Wilkins, 1976; Brumfit and Johnson, 1979; Widdowson, 1978) and at the same time in published materials for learners (Abbs and Freebairn, 1982). A weak and strong version of the communicative approach can be distinguished (Howatt, 1984). The aim of both is to develop 'communicative competence' but they differ in how this is to be achieved.

It is the 'weak' version of CLT that is described in Table 2.1. This is predicated on a Type A syllabus (White, 1988) that itemizes features of communication to be taught and employs a traditional 'accuracy'-oriented methodology (Brumfit, 1984) to teach it. It draws on theories and descriptions of language that emphasize the functional and social side of competence (e.g. Hymes' (1971) model of communicative competence and Halliday's (1973) functional grammar). These afford a clearly defined content for specifying what is to be taught, as in the notional functional syllabuses that began to appear in Britain in the 1970s (Wilkins, 1976). The accuracy-oriented methodology used to teach this content is typically 'PPP' (present–practice–produce), a borrowing of the procedures used in the pre-communicative era. However, Brumfit (1984) proposed an alternative – produce–present–practice – which involved starting with a communicative task in order to identify learning problems that could then be addressed through presenting and practising specific linguistic features. In effect, the 'weak' version of CLT differs from traditional approaches to language teaching only in minor ways.

The 'strong' version offers a far more radical alternative to traditional approaches. In this version, no attempt is made to specify the teaching content in terms of a set of gradable linguistic items. Instead, the content consists of a set of 'tasks', which the teacher and students carry out in the classroom. The methodology is fluency oriented – directed at getting students to *use* language for communication rather than to *practise* correct usage. As Hughes (1983) pointed out, the strong version is predicated on the principle that classroom language learning will proceed more efficiently if it occurs in a similar way to 'natural' language learning. The preferred label for the strong version today is 'task-based language teaching' (see Table 2.1).

Theoretical evaluation

Given the differences between the weak and strong versions of the CLT, it is clearly necessary to evaluate them separately. The focus of the theoretical evaluation in this chapter will be on the weak version. The strong version will be examined in detail in Chapter 5. Table 2.3 presents an evaluation of weak CLT in terms of the Principles of Instructed Language Learning.

Weak CLT is far more successful in satisfying the principles than the Audiolingual Method. Interestingly, the mainstream literature on CLT makes almost no reference to research on L2 acquisition. Key publications (e.g. Widdowson, 1978; Brumfit and Johnson, 1979) are almost entirely devoid of references to SLA. CLT was driven by theoretical constructs drawn from linguistics and sociolinguistics and by the practical language teaching experience of teachers. Yet, many of the proposals emanating from them were very compatible with what is known about how learners acquire an L2. It was not until later that advocates of CLT began to draw on the findings of SLA research to provide a rationale for proposals that had originated from other sources.

The compatibility of CLT and SLA is perhaps most evident in the suggestions advanced for instructional activities and how they should be implemented – i.e. the 'methodology' of CLT. Johnson (1982), for example, proposed four principles that could guide the design of 'communicative exercises':

- The information transfer principle (i.e. transferring information from one medium to another).
- The information gap principle (i.e. the transferring of information from one person to another).
- The jigsaw principle (i.e. the assembly of information from different sources and different people).
- The task dependency principle (i.e. the completion of one task requires the successful completion of a prior task).

These principles pre-date work by SLA researchers on 'tasks' designed to promote L2 acquisition but are very similar to the 'dimensions' that Long and Crookes (1987) had in mind, when they argued the need for 'organizing tasks in terms of their potential for second language learning on the basis of psycholinguistically motivated dimensions'.

In one major respect, however, weak CLT is limited. Teaching notions and functions is likely to result in the learning of some useful formulaic sequences and thus provides a sound basis for the early stages of L2 learning. It is doubtful, however, whether it will result in the rule-based knowledge needed to use the L2 creatively in later stages. What is missing from weak CLT is any account of how grammatical competence is to be developed. For example, although it places great importance on 'interaction', there is no explanation of how this fosters grammatical competence. Indeed, CLT methodologists appear to see 'interaction' as catering to 'fluency' rather than 'accuracy'. It serves as the means for using

Table 2.3 Theoretical evaluation of weak CLT

Instructed Language Learning Principles	Weak version of communicative language teaching
1. Instruction needs to ensure that learners develop both a rich repertoire of formulaic expressions and rule-based competence.	A notional/functional approach provides a framework for systematically teaching formulaic expressions. For example, the function of 'requesting' is realized by such patterns as 'Can I have ...?' and 'Would you mind ...?' It is uncertain whether it provides a basis for teaching the generative rules of grammar that make creative language use possible.
2. Instruction needs to ensure that learners focus on meaning.	Learners' attention is focused on both semantic and pragmatic meaning of linguistic forms. However, a primary focus on meaning only occurs in the free production stage of a lesson; in other stages, the primary focus is on form.
3. Instruction needs to ensure that learners focus on form.	Focus is directed at the oral and written form of formulaic sequences – both routines (i.e. ready-made chunks) and patterns (i.e. chunks with one or more empty slots).
4. Instruction needs to be predominantly directed at developing implicit knowledge of the L2 while not neglecting explicit knowledge.	The aim is to develop the ability to use the L2 correctly, fluently and naturally. However, the fact that the activities are largely controlled or guided makes it more likely that learners will develop automatized explicit knowledge than implicit knowledge. No attempt is made to develop explicit knowledge of grammatical features.
5. Instruction needs to take account of the order and sequence of acquisition.	It can be argued that weak CLT achieves this as it makes no attempt to teach grammar. There are no obvious psycholinguistic constraints on the acquisition of formulaic sequences. The acquisition of morpho-syntactic features is left up to the learner.
6. Successful instructed language learning requires extensive L2 input.	CLT materials (e.g. Abbs et al., 1975) provide much more extensive input than audiolingual materials, in part because there is less control of vocabulary. However, input still remains somewhat limited.
7. Successful instructed language learning also requires opportunities for output.	The teaching of speaking and writing figures strongly in CLT. Tasks that create 'a condition of unexpectedness' and also satisfy the 'task dependency principle' (Johnson, 1982) are likely to push learners to use resources that are at the limits of their competence.
8. The opportunity to interact in the L2 is central to developing L2 proficiency.	Opportunity to interact is central in weak CLT. The 'practice' stage of the lesson is likely to result in highly restricted interaction but the 'produce' stage creates opportunities for a 'full performance' of the language. Group work ensures that learners play an initiating as well as a responding role.
9. Instruction needs to take account of individual differences in learners.	The literature on CLT (e.g. Brumfit and Johnson, 1979) makes no mention of adapting instruction to suit individual learners.
10. Instruction needs to take account of the fact that there is a subjective aspect to language learning.	No account is taken of this – the focus of weak CLT is the development of communicative competence.
11. In assessing learners' proficiency, it is important to examine free as well as controlled production.	Proposals for communicative tests were forthcoming (e.g. Morrow, 1979). Communicative tests assess 'performance' and are 'holistic' rather than discrete points. In terms of Norris and Ortega's (2000) four test types, a communicative test assesses 'free production'.

the language that has been previously presented and practised 'communicatively'. There is no recognition of the need for learners to attend to form while they are interacting and no suggestions for how this might be promoted methodologically.

In short, weak CLT lacks a principled basis for developing grammatical competence. Subsequently, this was remedied as notional/functional syllabuses were abandoned in favour of hybrid syllabuses that included a grammar component. Also, due in part to the growing influence of SLA on language pedagogy, proposals were forthcoming for how interaction could be made to work for the acquisition of grammar as weak CLT morphed into strong CLT (i.e. task-based teaching).

Empirical evaluation

The disappointing results of the global method studies carried out in the 1960s led to disillusionment with such studies. It is, therefore, perhaps not surprising that there have been relatively few studies that have attempted to compare CLT with other methods. The results of these studies are difficult to synthesize as CLT was not implemented in a consistent fashion – reflecting the fact that it is more of an 'approach' than a 'method'. We will focus here on a number of studies that investigated weak CLT, leaving a consideration of studies of strong CLT to Chapter 6.

One of the earliest studies compared communicative language teaching and traditional teaching. Savignon (1972) investigated three university classes of French as a foreign language. All three classes received the same number of hours of traditional form-focused instruction. However, one group had an additional 'communicative hour' where they performed tasks, another group an extra 'cultural hour' and the third group spent the extra hour in a language laboratory. There were no differences among the three groups on measures of grammatical proficiency, but the communicative group outperformed the other two groups on measures of communicative ability. This study suggests that a mixture of traditional and communicative instruction is more effective than purely traditional instruction.

The advantages of combining traditional and communicative instruction have been confirmed by other studies. Montgomery and Eisenstein (1985) compared the gains in the proficiency of two groups of learners. One group attended regular ESL classes aimed primarily at improving grammatical accuracy. The other attended the same classes but also enrolled in a special oral communication course, involving field trips that gave them opportunities to communicate in English. The proficiency of both groups improved but the learners in the oral communication programme showed greater gains in grammar and pronunciation. However, it should be noted that these learners received more instruction overall which may have accounted for their better performance.[4]

A more direct comparison of 'communicative' and 'traditional' instruction was carried out by Palmer (1979). In this study, one group of Thai university students was taught by a method involving mechanical and meaningful drills that focused on specific linguistic features. A second communicative group also followed a structural syllabus but was required to use the target structures in communicative activities. Learning was measured by means of achievement tests measuring listening, grammatical accuracy and punctuation and communicative tests that required students to elicit information from an interlocutor, in order to identify the correct picture and to react quickly and appropriately to communication problems that arose in an oral interview. There were significant positive correlations between the communicative and formal achievement measures in the results for the communicative group but none for the traditional group. However, as Krashen (1981) noted, the differences between the groups on the communicative measures were not significant.

This somewhat disappointing result was replicated in a study by Allen et al. (1990). They adopted a somewhat different approach to the other method studies. Instead of defining 'method' externally, they set out to distinguish classes in terms of whether they involved 'experiential' and 'analytic' teaching strategies (Stern, 1990). As Table 2.4 shows, these correspond broadly to communicative and traditional teaching. They used a classroom observation scheme – (Communicative Orientation of Language Teaching, or COLT) to examine classrooms that varied in terms of these teaching strategies. They administered a battery of tests to measure different aspects of communicative competence (grammatical, sociolinguistic and discourse), expecting to find that the analytic classes did better in the writing and grammar tests and the experiential classes better in the tests of sociolinguistic and discourse competence. However, this did not happen. There were few statistically significant differences between the two most experiential and the two most analytic classes. Allen et al. admitted that the results were 'somewhat disappointing'.

Overall, these method studies failed to demonstrate that communicative language teaching is superior to more traditional methods. Two of them (Savignon, 1972; Montgomery and Eisenstein, 1985) did find that providing

Table 2.4 Experiential and analytic features in language pedagogy (from Stern 1990)

Experiential features	Analytic features
1 Substantive or motivated topic or theme (topics are not arbitrary or trivial).	1 Focus on aspects of L2, including phonology, grammar functions, discourse, and sociolinguistics.
2 Students engage in purposeful activity (tasks or projects), not exercises.	2 Cognitive study of language items (rules and regularities are noted; items are made salient, and related to other items and systems.
3 Language use has characteristics of real talk (conversation) or uses any of the four skills as part of purposeful action.	3 Practice or rehearsal of language items or skill aspects.
4 Priority of meaning transfer and fluency over linguistic error avoidance and accuracy.	4 Attention to accuracy and error avoidance.
5 Diversity of social interaction.	5 Diversity of social interaction desirable.

opportunities for using language communicatively produced better results than traditional, form-focused instruction. But these opportunities were supplementary to traditional instruction, not in place of it. They showed that a combination of form-focused instruction and communicative opportunities is more effective than form-focused instruction alone. The two studies that carried out a direct comparison of form-focused and communicative instruction (Palmer, 1979; Allen et al., 1990), failed to find any significant differences even in tests that favoured the CLT groups.

There are two explanations for these disappointing results. One is that CLT is really not superior to more traditional methods. The other is that comparative method studies are fundamentally flawed. We will now turn out attention to this latter possibility and, at the same time, revisit the central question posed by this chapter, namely whether the method construct is of any value to language pedagogy.

Conclusion

We began by pointing out that the method construct has held a central position in thinking about language pedagogy. Its attractions are obvious. It constitutes a means of specifying not just what and how teachers should teach but also underlying theoretical principles. Thus, it constitutes, in some respects at least, a construct that bridges theory and practice in language teaching. It is, therefore, not surprising that the method construct has been influential in teacher training and teacher education programmes. Trainers can base their training on a specific method. Educators can encourage reflexivity by inviting teachers to undertake evaluations of a number of different methods (see, for example, Klapper, 2006). However, notwithstanding the utility of the method construct, there are some obvious problems. There is a danger of decontextualizing teaching by assuming that a single method is suitable for all situations and of deprofessionalizing teachers by positioning them as mere implementers of a method. These problems led to proposals for a postmethod pedagogy.

The perspective we have adopted in this chapter is that individual methods need to be subjected to evaluation – both theoretically in terms of what is currently known about how learners learn an L2 and empirically by conducting comparative method studies. We have illustrated this approach by conducting evaluations of two methods that have been influential in language teaching – the Audiolingual Method and weak Communicative Language Teaching. The results of our evaluations demonstrate two points:

1 At a theoretical level it is possible to distinguish the potential effectiveness of different methods by examining the extent to which they satisfy a set of general principles about instructed language learning. We have seen, for example, that weak CLT is, in general, more compatible with what is known about how learners learn an L2 than the Audiolingual Method.

2 At an empirical level, however, the comparative method studies have been unable to show that one method is clearly superior to another. There is no clear evidence, for example, that CLT is more effective than more traditional methods that emphasize formal accuracy.

The question arises, therefore, as to why a method that is theoretically sound does not emerge as empirically superior in method comparison studies.

The answer lies in the difficulties in designing and carrying out comparative method studies (see Ellis, 2012). In particular, many of these studies were methodologically weak in that they did not control for the teacher variable (i.e. the groups taught by different methods also had different teachers). Crucially, no attempt was made to establish that the instructional treatments were carried out in accordance with the external descriptions of the methods. Thus, it is not clear that the methods differed in terms of actual classroom processes. Also, in most of the studies no account was taken of the very real possibility that different learners will benefit from different kinds of instruction.

The fact that the global method studies have generally failed to demonstrate that one method is more effective than another suggests that the critiques of the method construct may be right – it is fundamentally flawed. Many researchers would concur with such a view, arguing that what is important is not external prescriptions of what and how to teach, but the study of the instructional processes that arise in the classroom and the learning that results. Allwright (1988), for example, documented how researchers abandoned method studies in favour of the detailed observation of actual classrooms.

We believe, however, that a case can still be made for conducting method comparison studies and that the method construct is still of potential value. Sheen (2006) argued that it is dangerous to advocate new methods such as task-based language teaching on purely theoretical grounds. We agree. As long as the method construct is alive – and there is no real sign of its demise – there is a need to evaluate the claims made by different methods. What is needed is not the abandonment of method studies but better designed studies. Ideally a comparative method study needs to: (1) establish through observation that the instructional processes resulting from the methods are different, (2) ensure that the testing regime is not biased in favour of one of the methods and (3) investigate the effect on individual learners, not just on groups. Perhaps, rather than 'global' studies that are longitudinal, involve large samples of learners and investigate the effects on general language proficiency, 'local' studies that are short-term, making it easier to control extraneous variables, investigate a smaller sample of learners and focus more narrowly on the acquisition of specific linguistic features, would be more profitable. We will examine a number of such studies in subsequent chapters.

Notes

1 A somewhat similar method was popular in Britain around this time – the Oral Approach. Like the Audiolingual Method, this emphasized the importance of intensive and controlled oral practice of specific grammatical structures by means of drills and dialogues. It differed from the Audiolingual Method in the importance it attached to teaching the structures situationally.

2 The version of Communicative Language Teaching outlined in Table 2.1 is the version illustrated in early textbooks that employed this approach (e.g. Abbs and Freebairn, 1982). It constitutes what Howatt (1984) called a 'weak form' of CLT. Subsequently, proposals for organizing the teaching content around 'tasks' rather than 'notions/functions' were made. These eventually led into fully fledged proposals for 'Task-based Language Teaching', which is treated separately in Table 2.1.

3 The methods that Klapper (2006) considered were: Grammar-Translation, Direct Method, Audiolingualism, Communicative Language Teaching and Task-based Instruction.

4 Further evidence in support of a combination of form-focused and more communicative learning opportunities comes from Spada (1986), who found that learners who experienced form-focused instruction inside the classroom and greater contact with English outside the classroom, performed better in tests of grammar and writing than learners who experienced the same instruction but had less contact.

DISCUSSION QUESTIONS

1. What is the difference between a 'method' and an 'approach'?
2. Kumaravadivelu distinguished three types of method in terms of whether they were: a) language-centred, b) learner-centred and c) learning-centred. Examine the methods you are familiar with and decide which type it represents.
3. If teachers were to decide to base their teaching on a particular method, what criteria would you recommend they consider when selecting the method?
4. Consider the pros and cons for basing language teaching on a specific method. What conclusion do you reach about the usefulness of 'method' in language teaching?
5. '[T]he method construct needs to be understood in terms of the processes that arise in the classroom.' Explain what is meant by this. What kinds of 'processes' need to be considered?
6. Why do you think Communicative Language Teaching (CLT) has continued to be the favoured approach to language teaching, even though the evidence from comparative method studies has not convincingly shown it to be more effective than other, more traditional methods?
7. Explain the differences between a 'theoretical evaluation' and an 'empirical evaluation' of a method?

8. What are the problems with large-scale comparative method studies? Do you think there is any value in continuing with such studies?
9. This chapter provides a theoretical evaluation of two methods – the Audiolingual Method and Communicative Language Teaching. Choose ONE other method/approach you are familiar with and carry out a theoretical evaluation of it based on the Instructed Language Learning Principles.
10. The alternative to basing teaching on a method is to adopt an eclectic approach that takes account of the specific learners and instructional context. Can you see any problems with adopting an eclectic approach?

3 Linguistic syllabuses and SLA

Introduction

A syllabus is a statement of teaching content in the order in which it is to be taught. It is 'an official, explicit, public statement intended to control the teaching activity' (Sinclair and Renouf, 1988: 140). The syllabus is a central feature of the 'design' level of a method; it links the levels of 'approach' and 'procedure' (see Chapter 2). As Richards and Rodgers (1986) pointed out, 'different approaches to language teaching manifest themselves in different design elements in language-teaching systems' (p. 20). Equally, different syllabuses are associated with different sets of teaching procedures.

Traditionally, the content of a language teaching course has been specified in terms of the grammatical patterns to be learned (e.g. Hornby, 1959). The Grammar-Translation Method, the Audiolingual Method, the Cognitive-Code Method and the Oral-Situational Method all involved a grammatical syllabus. However, in the 1970s, alternative views about how to specify the teaching content arose, leading to a debate about what kind of syllabus was best suited to developing communicative ability in a second language (L2). These proposals, however, were still based on theories of language rather than language learning. That is to say, they were still linguistic in nature, albeit viewing language in ways that differed from the 'structural' perspective that informed traditional syllabuses. It was not until the late 1980s and 1990s that an entirely different way of conceptualizing the content of a course in terms of 'tasks' was proposed. This new type of syllabus drew very directly on work in second language acquisition (SLA). However, mainstream language courses have continued to draw on linguistic syllabuses of one kind or another. Thus, there is a current need to evaluate such syllabuses. This is the goal of this chapter. We will address the key question – 'In what ways is a linguistic syllabus compatible with how learners' acquire an L2?' The starting point will be an examination of the different kinds of linguistic syllabuses. This is followed by a review of the research that has investigated how the learner's 'interlanguage' develops and the apparent problem this poses for linguistic syllabuses. In a final section we will advance a number of ways in which a linguistic syllabus can be made compatible with what is known about L2 acquisition and thus provide a valid basis for a language course.

Types of linguistic syllabuses

Linguistic syllabuses can be distinguished in terms of: (1) the level of language and (2) whether the organizational principle of the syllabus is 'form' or 'meaning'. Language is traditionally viewed as involving three levels: phonology, vocabulary and grammar. Inventories of the elements in each of these levels derived from linguistic descriptions provide a basis for designing a syllabus. Language at the levels of vocabulary and grammar involves a matching of 'form' and 'meaning'. For example, the sounds/letters that make up the word 'cat' constitute its form, while its meaning is that provided in a dictionary (e.g. 'a four-legged furry animal with sharp claws'). In the case of grammar, '-s' constitutes a morphological form that can realize a number of different meanings in English (plurality, possession and third person). Linguistic syllabuses can be organized in terms of either 'forms' or 'meanings'. When form is used as the organizing principle, the syllabus lists the forms to be taught and the meanings they realize as in a grammatical syllabus. When meaning serves as the organizing principle, the syllabus lists the meanings to be taught and the linguistic forms required to express them as in a 'notional syllabus' (Wilkins, 1976). The debates about syllabus design that we will now consider centre around whether content should be defined in terms of grammar or vocabulary and whether it should be specified in terms of forms (and their meanings) or meanings (and their forms).

Irrespective of whether the syllabus is grammatical, lexical or notional, the overall approach corresponds to what White (1988) referred to as Type A. That is, it involves the pre-selection of the language to be taught which is divided into small bits representing the learning objectives of individual lessons. Type A syllabuses are interventionist, other-directed and thus external to the learner.

A major issue that needs to be addressed in any discussion of linguistic syllabuses is which variety of the target language to select as a basis for the syllabus. This not just a question of choosing British or American English but also whether it is appropriate to select a native-speaker variety at all. It has been pointed out that learners are as likely to use the L2 with other learners as with native speakers and that a more appropriate basis might be a variety called 'English as an International Language', which acknowledges the use of English across a range of contexts throughout the world (Jenkins, 2000) or 'English as a Lingua Franca', which recognizes that 'English is being shaped at least as much by its non-native speakers as by its native speakers' (Seidlhofer, 2005: 339). Attempts have been made to provide systematic descriptions of these varieties based on corpora of learner language (e.g. the Vienna-Oxford Corpus of English). We see this as an admirable development but also as unlikely to lead to learner varieties replacing native-speaker varieties as the foundation of a linguistic syllabus. To attempt to do so confuses the 'target' with the 'end result'. Many learners, when asked, indicate that they aspire to achieve target-language norms while acknowledging that the variety they actually learn will display the kinds of linguistic features found in learner varieties. To our mind, it is entirely appropriate to base linguistic syllabuses on native-speaker varieties as long as, when implemented, it is recognized that the end result is likely to be a learner variety. Such a position also accords with the SLA research we will consider in this chapter. Interlanguage theory (see Chapter 1) assumes the end state is native-speaker norms but it also acknowledges that learners progress slowly towards this end state and, in many cases, do not reach it. However, our view is not shared by others. Hall and Cook (2012), for example, take completely the opposite view: 'native-speaker models of English and the goal of cultural integration into English-speaking countries are no longer needed, or even desirable' (p. 272).

Grammatical syllabuses

The grammatical syllabus has proved enormously robust as is evident from an inspection of current course books. Few authors of textbooks are prepared to abandon at least a grammatical strand and indeed feel the need to introduce grammar at the beginning level (i.e. in lesson one). There are many reasons why grammar has come to be seen as so central to language teaching and learning. Some are purely linguistic. Grammar, unlike vocabulary, is finite and more or less stable (i.e. there are a finite number of grammatical forms and rules for their combination and grammar changes only very slowly over time). Grammar is not just a set of items: it is a system and affords generalizations (in the form of 'rules') that can be applied to a number of instantiations. Also, grammar is, in a sense, absolute. That is, although variation in the use of grammatical rules is well attested in native-speaker usage (Labov, 1970), there is nevertheless a common core of grammatical features in a standard variety. Thus teaching grammar, unlike teaching vocabulary, seems manageable, economical and purposeful.

Perhaps, though, the stronger argument for placing grammar at the centre of a language curriculum lies in its importance for ensuring effective communication. Widdowson (1990b) pointed out that words by themselves often suffice to communicate meaning effectively but only when the context enables the missing grammar to be inferred. So, when a surgeon says 'scalpel!' in the context of an operation, his assistant will readily interpret this as 'Give me the scalpel'. There is no need for a verb, an indirect object pronoun or the definite article. Grammar is redundant. However, not all communication can rely on indexical meaning in this way. As Widdowson noted, 'grammar frees us from a dependency on context and the limitations of a purely lexical categorization of reality' (p. 86). In order words, whenever context is insufficient to enable the meaning of a word or group of words to be inferred, grammar is needed. Clearly, effective communication cannot always rely on context, so grammar is needed. Nevertheless, as we will see, the early stages of L2 acquisition are essentially lexical in nature.

There is another reason for emphasizing grammar. The goal of just about all language courses is to help learners achieve membership in an acceptable community of L2 users. Learners whose development stops at an early 'pidginized' stage of development may be capable of basic everyday communication but are not likely to be considered members of an accepted community of L2 users. To achieve this, learners need to be capable of expressing themselves accurately using a range of grammatical structures in ways that are appropriate for the social settings in which they find themselves. In other words, they need grammar to ensure that both their 'usage' conforms reasonably to the norms of educated native speakers (e.g. they say 'children' and not 'childrens') and their 'use' reflects how such native speakers deploy grammar in context (e.g. they say 'I'd be grateful if...' rather than 'I want you to...' when asking for a favour that constitutes an imposition on the hearer).

For these reasons, the grammatical syllabus has held pride of place in language courses, although in many contemporary courses, grammar exists as a strand in a multidimensional syllabus rather than serving as the complete syllabus.

One might expect to find considerable variation in the content and organization of different grammatical syllabuses. In fact, this has not occurred. Krahnke (1987), for example, noted 'except in the case of uncommonly taught languages, the grammatical structure of the language being taught is well-known'. Yalden (1983) compared the grammatical content in four ESL textbooks written for beginning and intermediate levels and found that the content was ordered 'in a remarkably similar fashion'. The situation has not changed today. There would appear to be general agreement that for English morphological features such as 'be', demonstratives ('these/those'), present and past tense forms, plural and possessive nouns are taught early while constructions such as question tags, conditional clauses and passive voice are taught late. As we will see later, this sequencing bears no resemblance to the order of acquisition evident when learners are acquiring a language in a naturalistic setting, nor what actually occurs when learning takes place in a classroom.

Grammatical syllabuses are sometimes criticized for focusing only on grammatical form, to the exclusion of the meanings that these forms realize in communication. However, while this might have been true of some traditional syllabuses, it is almost certainly not true of a contemporary grammatical syllabus. Crace and Wileman (2002) in *Language to Go*, for example, quite clearly see grammar as a resource for expressing meaning. The grammatical strand in their course includes such features as 'modal verbs for giving advice' and 'present simple and continuous for future'. Even where grammatical items are listed in purely formal terms (e.g. 'passive constructions'), the actual treatment seeks to teach form in relation to meaning. Thus, a modern grammatical syllabus does not assume that grammar is just an inventory of forms. It acknowledges the form-meaning mapping that lies at the heart of grammar. However, as we will shortly see, this does not absolve grammatical syllabuses from the problem referred to above; learners construct form-meaning networks as they learn an L2 but these networks evolve gradually and evolve transitional stages.

Lexical syllabuses

As Sinclair and Renouf (1988) pointed out, vocabulary has typically been regarded as simply the means for exemplifying other, more important aspects of language. In a traditional grammar-based course, the aim has been to restrict the vocabulary taught to enable the focus to be placed on grammar (Lado, 1964). However, in the 1980s, the development of software for analysing large corpora of native-speaker texts (oral as well as written) made it possible to identify not only the frequency with which specific words are used but also the words that they typically co-occur with. Projects such as the Cobuild Project (Sinclair, 1991) provided detailed information about how words worked together, which could serve as a basis for the development of a lexical syllabus.

One of the clearest findings of the work on learner corpora was that much of native-speaker language production is formulaic in nature. Sinclair (1991) advanced the Principle of Idiom:

> A language user has available to him or her a large number of semi-preconstructed phrases that constitute single choices, even though they might appear to be analyzable into segments. To some extent this may reflect the recurrence of similar situations in human affairs; it may illustrate a natural tendency to economy of effort; or it may be motivated in part by the exigencies of real-time conversation.
>
> (p. 110)

It followed from such a principle, that knowledge of a language did not consist of separate components for grammar and vocabulary but rather, in part at least, involved lexical chunks which become internalized as a result of exposure to frequent collocations. Sinclair claimed that the Idiom Principle could account for most of the texts he analysed. Sinclair was in fact providing empirical evidence in support of Pawley and Syder's (1983) claim that linguistic competence consists to a large extent of a 'store of familiar collocations' (p. 192). In other words, learning a language did not so much involve learning abstract patterns and then slotting words into them but rather figuring out which words go together and then storing these as memorized chunks. In other words, lexis, not grammar, was primary.

It seemed logical, then, to think about how to organize the content of a language teaching programme around lexis rather than grammar. West (1953) proposed a number of criteria for selecting the vocabulary to be taught: frequency, coverage, range, availability and learnability. However, of these it is frequency that has been most commonly used. The availability of electronic texts has made it possible to identify the frequency with which different lexical items occur in a particular corpus. There are now lists of the most frequent words at the 1000 up to the 10,000 level in several languages (e.g. Laufer and Nation, 1995) and also an academic word list (Coxhead, 2011). The case for using frequency as the main criterion for the selection and grading of items has been reinforced by research which shows that a large proportion of a text comprises those words that are most frequent in a language (see Nation, 2001: 144) and thus teaching learners these words is likely to assist successful comprehension.

Sinclair and Renouf (1988), however, argued that a lexical syllabus must consist of much more than a list of the most frequent words. They pointed out that it is necessary to consider not just the frequency of word forms but also of word meanings (e.g. 'certain' can mean 'specific' as in 'in certain circles' or 'sure' as in 'I'm not very certain about that', with the former meaning accounting for 60 per cent of occurrences in the Cobuild corpus and the latter only 18 per cent). They also point out that because the most frequent forms are function words (e.g. 'the', 'and', 'to'), it is important to also include lower-frequency words in a beginner level course.

Moreover, 'a simple list of words is not nearly explicit enough to constitute a syllabus' (Sinclair and Renouf, 1988). It is also necessary to consider the central patterns of a word's use and the combinations that a word enters into. Words do not just have lexical meaning, they also have discoursal and pragmatic meanings. For example, 'see' is frequently inserted parenthetically into a statement to indicate concern (e.g. 'You see, I was feeling lonely'). This use is actually more common than the use of 'see' to refer to vision. Sinclair and Renouf argued that the 'essential patterns of distribution and combination... will be included in a lexical syllabus'. For example, some common verbs ('give', 'make', 'take') are often used delexically in phrases such as 'give advice', 'make a discovery', and 'take note of'.

A lexical syllabus does not aim at just teaching learners words, their common uses and their typical combinations. It also aims to teach grammar. Sinclair and Renouf argued 'if the analysis of the words and phrases has been done correctly, then all the relevant grammar should appear in a proper proportion'. In effect, then, grammar is no longer seen as abstract rules but rather as entrenched combinations of words, some of which have an open slot. Thus, a lexical syllabus aims to offer learners 'reasonable exposure to the common patterns of the language' (Willis, 1990: 52) from which grammar will emerge. Grammar in this sense involves the constraints that govern which type of word can complete an open slot in a pattern, in accordance with Sinclair's (1991) second principle – the Open-Choice Principle.

The fullest account of a lexical syllabus can be found in Willis (1990). He described how he and J. Willis set about constructing the syllabus for the Cobuild English Course (Willis and Willis, 1988). First, they established the targets for the three levels of this course – 850 words for Level 1, 850 more words for Level 2, and a further 950 words by the end of Level 3. The choice of words was based largely on frequency in the Cobuild corpora but it also proved necessary to include other words from outside the high-frequency list. For each word there was a 'data sheet' consisting of a headword followed by information and examples about the meanings of the headword, its combinations with other words and the patterns in which it occurs. It should be noted that the headwords included functors such as 'would' and 'any' and, therefore, considerable grammatical information was explicitly present in the syllabus. In addition, a set of 'topics' were chosen by analysing the topics that figured in twenty of the most widely used ELT course books at that time. Tasks were designed based on these topics and these were then performed by native speakers. This resulted in a number of 'spontaneously produced texts'. These texts were ordered according to the Willis's intuitions about the difficulty of the texts and tasks. They were then computer analysed and the concordances checked against the data sheets of the target words to establish that they had been adequately 'covered'. In effect, then, the Cobuild syllabus was not a 'pure' lexical syllabus. Rather it was a combination of a lexical, topic-based and task-based syllabus. The starting point, however, was the frequency lists of the words to be taught.

A lexical approach to teaching language has also been advocated by Lewis (1993, 1997). Lewis argued that grammar is not the basis of language acquisition, lexis is. Like Willis he argued that words should not be taught in isolation but in the 'chunks' in which they commonly occur. Lewis, however, had little to say about how to design a lexical syllabus except to suggest, somewhat vaguely, that the language material should be text and discourse based. He offered no guidance as to how the texts should be selected and organized into a coherent package, relying instead on the Krashen-like view that all that was needed was 'comprehensible input'.

Notional syllabuses

Notional syllabuses work in the opposite way to grammatical syllabuses – they take as their starting point 'meanings' and then specify their linguistic exponents. The theoretical basis for notional syllabuses emerged in the 1970s in the work of Hymes (1970) and Halliday (1973), both of whom emphasized the importance of examining language as used in actual communication. The impetus for the development of meaning-based syllabuses came from the re-evaluation of foreign language education that took place under the auspices of the Council of Europe. A group of language educators (Trim, Van Ek and Wilkins) sought 'to establish a framework for adult language learning based upon the language needs of the learner and the linguistic operations required of him (*sic*) in order to function effectively as a member of a large community for the purposes, and in the situations, revealed by those needs' (Trim, 1973).

One possibility was to define the units that comprised the framework in grammatical terms but this was rejected on the grounds that a grammatical syllabus has 'low surrender value' (i.e. learners needed to learn a lot of grammar before they can begin to communicate) and that therefore it was demotivating for learners who needed to see some immediate practical return for their efforts. Thus, it was proposed that the needs of the learners and the units designed to meet these needs should be meaning based. Wilkins (1976) distinguished 'synthetic' and 'analytic' syllabuses. In a synthetic syllabus, 'different parts of language are taught separately and step-by-step so that acquisition is a gradual process of accumulation of the parts until the whole structure of the language has been built up' (p. 2). The stereotypical synthetic syllabus is a grammatical one. In an analytic syllabus, there is no attempt to regulate the learning process by presenting it bit by bit. Instead, the units in the syllabus are defined semantically and functionally, allowing for much greater variety of linguistic structure to be present from the beginning. In a synthetic syllabus, the learner's task is to reassemble (i.e. synthesize) the bits and pieces of language that have been taught. In an analytic syllabus, the learner's job is to learn and then analyse the chunks of language taught as exponents of general meaning categories. A notional syllabus is one type of analytic syllabus.

Wilkins distinguished three types of meaning for defining the behavioural units of a notional syllabus. The first type consisted of semantico-grammatical categories. General examples are 'time', 'quantity' and 'relational meaning'. Each of these was further broken down into subcategories. For example, 'relational meaning' included 'agent', 'initiator', 'object', 'beneficiary' and 'instrument'. The second type of meaning was 'modal meaning'. This included general categories such as 'certainty', 'intention' and 'obligation'. The third type of meaning involved communicative functions such as 'judgement and evaluation', 'approval and disapproval' and 'prediction'.

The linguistic exponents are then established. This is achieved by looking for the typical (i.e. recurrent) linguistic forms used to realize a given meaning category. Given that a single meaning category can be realized in many different ways, it is inevitable that there will be considerable structural diversity in a notional syllabus. For example, the communicative function of 'suggesting' can be realized linguistically by a whole range of different linguistic forms:

I suggest that...
Shall we...?
How about...?
Have you thought of...?
Suppose we...
Another possibility would be...

Whereas it is reasonably clear what guides the selection of the meaning content of a notional syllabus (i.e. content is chosen by first determining the communicative needs of a specific group of learners), it is somewhat less clear what guides the sequencing of the categories of meaning in a syllabus. For example, should 'certainty' precede 'obligation' or vice versa? One possibility – acknowledged by Wilkins – was that the syllabus should draw on the familiar criteria for grading linguistic content (e.g. frequency, range, availability and complexity of form – see Mackey, 1965). These could be used to help determine the order in which different meaning categories and the linguistic exponents for expressing them would be taught. In other words, in choosing which semantic categories to teach first it was necessary to consider not only which ones were of greatest importance to the learners, but also which ones the learners could be expected to handle at their particular stage of development. It is perhaps not surprising that courses based on a notional syllabus (e.g. Abbs and Freebairn, 1982) first introduced communicative functions such as 'greeting' and 'introducing' because the linguistic exponents of such functions were linguistically simple (e.g. 'Hello, what's your name?'). To deal with the fact that the exponents of a function such as 'suggesting' vary considerably in linguistic complexity, Wilkins proposed that notional syllabuses should be cyclical (i.e. a specific semantic category could be repeated with different linguistic exponents at different stages of a course).

Acquiring an L2

Linguistic syllabuses, whether grammatical, functional, lexical or a combination of these, are premised on the assumption that learners will learn what they are taught. However, research on how learners acquire the various linguistic systems suggests that this may not be the case. Allwright (1984), drawing on early work on how learners acquire an L2, pointed out that: (1) learners do not learn everything they are taught (which he suggested is not so surprising) and (2) they manage to learn things they are not taught (which he considered more interesting). In other words, learners may have their own 'built-in syllabus' (Corder, 1967), which may not conform to the teaching syllabus. Evidence for a built-in syllabus came from studies of the kinds of errors that learners make when learning an L2 and from studies that plotted the order and sequence of acquisition of grammatical structures. Selinker (1972) coined the term 'interlanguage' to refer to the mental grammars that learners construct and then restructure to account for the regularities that have been observed across learners (see Chapter 1). Researchers have also shown that, contrary to the assumption of a grammatical syllabus but more compatible with the assumptions of a notional or a lexical syllabus, learners have a natural propensity to acquire 'chunks' rather than 'rules', as evidenced in the formulaic nature of many of the utterances they produce in an L2, especially in the early stages.

We will now review what SLA research has shown about how learners acquire an L2. This will serve as a basis for considering whether linguistic syllabuses can serve as a basis for teaching an L2, and, if so, how.

L2 learner errors

Early work on how learners learn an L2 focused on the errors that they typically make. This was motivated largely by the Contrastive Analysis Hypothesis (the CAH), which claimed that errors were largely the result of interference from the learner's first language (L1) and that this fact needed to be taken into account in designing teaching materials:

> Those structures that are similar (between the L1 and the L2) will be easy to learn because they will be transferred and may function satisfactorily in the

foreign language. Those structures that are different will be difficult because when they are transferred they will not function satisfactorily in the foreign language and will have to be changed.

(Lado, 1957: 59)

It followed that what was needed was a contrastive analysis of the learners' L1 and the target language in order to identify which structures were the same and which were different. A linguistic syllabus would then consist of those structures that were different and thus difficult to learn for a particular group of learners. The 1960s saw a number of such contrastive analyses for the main European languages (e.g. Stockwell et al., 1965).

Researchers, however, began to question the underlying assumption of the CAH, namely that 'difference equals learning difficulty'. They collected samples of learner errors and submitted these to analysis. Dulay and Burt (1974b), for example, classified the sample of errors they collected in terms of whether they were:

- Developmental (i.e. the errors were the same as those observed in children acquiring the target language as an L1).
- Interference (i.e. the errors reflected the structure of the learners' L1).
- Unique (i.e. the errors were neither developmental nor interference errors).

Of the 513 clear errors made by Spanish-speaking learners of English, Dulay and Burt claimed that the vast majority were developmental. Overall, less than 5 per cent of the errors were attributed to interference. Dulay and Burt's analysis, however, was criticized on the grounds that their assignment of errors to the different categories was arbitrary. Other studies (e.g. George, 1972), in fact, reported a much higher level of interference errors. Also, in some cases, errors may arise as a result of both interference and natural developmental tendencies. For example, Spanish learners of English tend to use preverbal negation (e.g. 'No Mariana coming'), which suggests interference as Spanish is a pre-verbal negation language, but German learners make similar errors, at least in the early stages, even though German is a post-verbal language (e.g. 'Mariana kommt *nicht*' = 'Maria comes not').

Overall, however, the error analysis studies showed that many errors were not the result of interference but were 'developmental'. This suggested that natural learning processes are involved in L2 learning and that, to a degree, these processes are the same in L1 and L2 acquisition. The research lent support to nativist theories of L2 learning, which emphasized the importance of the learner's internal mental processing, and led to a rejection of the behaviourist theories that underscored the CAH and the Audiolingual Method. In other words, it was clear that Lado's thesis about the necessity of taking into account the learner's L1 in designing language courses was, at best, only partially correct.

A key question, however, was whether the kinds of developmental errors that Dulay and Burt and other researchers found were also evident in classroom learners. The learners who many of the error analysis studies investigated were not pure classroom learners – they were either entirely naturalistic learners or 'mixed' learners (i.e. 'second' rather than 'foreign' language learners who had exposure to English outside the classroom). It is possible that instruction based on a grammatical syllabus enables learners to avoid developmental-type errors. To investigate this possibility, Felix (1981) carried out a longitudinal study of German children learning English in a classroom setting. The children produced exactly the same kind of errors in English negation as had been reported for naturalistic learners. For example, even though they were taught how to use 'don't' and 'doesn't' with a main verb, they still opted to position the negative auxiliary before the subject of the utterance (e.g. 'Doesn't she eat apples' instead of 'She doesn't eat apples'). Felix noted a marked difference between the correctness of their L2 production in drills and the errors they made in their spontaneous speech in English. It was clear, then, that instruction did not prevent developmental errors from occurring.

The classroom studies also provided another interesting finding. Some of the 'unique' errors that were observed in instructed learners were 'induced' (i.e. arose as a result of instruction). Stenson (1974) reported examples of such induced errors in the classroom speech of Tunisian learners of English. For example, telling the students that 'any' has a negative meaning gave rise to the students using 'any' to mean 'none'. Svartvik (1973) suggested that Swedish learners of English produced errors such as 'He proposed her to stay' as a result of being drilled in the pattern Subject + verb + direct object + infinitive (e.g. 'He asked her to stay'). Lightbown (1983) found that the classroom learners she investigated overused the present progressive verb tense (V-*ing*) as a result of the intensive drilling in this structure.

These studies suggested that instructed learners, like naturalistic learners, have a natural tendency to simplify and overgeneralize and that this occurs irrespective of the instruction they receive and sometimes because of it. Simplification is evident in the common omission of grammatical functors (e.g. 'She sleeping') and in reliance on a basic word order (e.g. 'What daddy is doing?'). Overgeneralization is evident in the tendency to employ a common grammatical pattern in linguistic contexts where it is not used in the target language (e.g. 'My father made me to do it') and in what Dulay et al. (1982) called 'misinformation' (e.g. 'The dog ated the chicken'). Such errors have also been observed in the L1 acquisition of English. They constitute strong evidence that there are 'natural' processes at work in L2 acquisition, raising the question as to whether instruction based on a linguistic syllabus is capable of circumventing them. Indeed, one of the pedagogic recommendations emanating from the findings of the error analysis studies is that teachers need to be tolerant of learner errors.

Much of the research on errors was conducted in the 1970s and 1980s. It stopped once the key finding – namely, that many of the errors of even instructed learners were developmental in nature – was established. However, recently interest in error analysis has undergone a rebirth. Computer-based analyses of corpora allow for the large-scale analysis of errors. A number of projects such as the International Corpus of Learner English (Granger, 1998) and the Standard Speaking Test Corpus (Izumi et al., 2004) have produced a wealth of information about the typical errors committed by learners from different language backgrounds. These projects have largely confirmed the results of the earlier studies. Some errors are clearly traceable to the learner's L1 but many are developmental or unique.

Order of acquisition

In the 1960s, a number of seminal studies of how children acquire the grammar of their first language were carried out. These studies provided evidence to show that L1 acquisition was incremental involving a relatively clearly defined order of acquisition. Brown (1973), for example, reported a longitudinal study of three children learning English as their mother tongue. He showed that grammatical morphemes such as V-*ing*, plural-*s*, regular past-*ed*, and third person-*s* were mastered by all three children in the same fixed order. De Villiers and de Villiers (1973) found a very similar order for the same morphemes in a cross-sectional study of a large number of children. They examined the accuracy with which the children used the different morphemes at one time and then claimed that the accuracy order they found reflected the order of acquisition. These studies – and many others (see in particular, Wells, 1985) – testify to an order of acquisition for L1 learners of English. Other studies have shown that child learners of other L1s also manifest a well-defined acquisition order for morphemes (e.g. Perez-Pereira's (1989) study of the L1 acquisition of Spanish morphemes). This led to researchers asking if L2 learners also demonstrate a well-defined order and whether this is the same or different from that attested in L1 acquisition.

In the 1970s, a number of 'morpheme studies' were carried out, using the same methodology as de Villiers and de Villiers (i.e. cross-sectional samples of learner language were analysed to determine the accuracy with which the morphemes were used and then accuracy order was equated with acquisition order). Dulay and Burt (1973, 1974a) investigated Spanish and Chinese children learning L2 English. They found that the 'acquisition order' for a group of English morphemes was the same for both groups of learners. Bailey et al. (1974) carried out a similar study on adults. The acquisition order they found correlated significantly with that reported by Dulay and Burt. Larsen-Freeman (1976) found that the learners' L1 made little difference to the accuracy order. However, she did find that different elicitation tasks produced somewhat different accuracy orders. In particular, she noted that some morphemes (e.g. plural-*s* and third person-*s*) were used more accurately in writing than in speech.

Pica's (1983) morpheme study is a special interest as it compared the accuracy orders in three groups of learners – naturalistic, instructed and mixed. This study is important because it addresses whether the linguistic environment influences the order in which learners acquire grammatical features. Pica reported the same accuracy order in all three groups of learners, suggesting that instruction had no influence on how the learners mastered the grammatical morphemes. However, when Pica investigated specific morphemes, she did find evidence of some differences among the three groups. The instructed group used plural-*s* more accurately than the naturalistic group, while the naturalistic group was more accurate than the instructed group in using V-*ing*. Pica suggested that instruction might be effective in the case of simple grammatical features (such as 3rd person-*s*) but might induce overuse in the case of features that are formally simple but functionally quite complex (such as V-*ing*). Despite these differences, however, there were clear similarities in the way in which the three groups of learners mastered English grammar, providing support for Corder's (1967) claim that learners have a built-in syllabus – irrespective of whether they are learning in the real world or in a classroom.

The morpheme studies have not produced entirely consistent results, however, and they also suffered from a number of methodological problems. It was not clear whether accuracy order could be equated with acquisition order in the way that researchers such as Dulay and Burt claimed. Some grammatical morphemes were found to manifest a U-shaped pattern of development. For example, irregular English verbs forms went through stages of development where learners first learned the correct irregular form (e.g. 'ate'), but later overgeneralized the regular-*ed* form (e.g. 'eated') before finally reverting to the target language form. Clearly, it is not possible to use accuracy as a measure of acquisition of this morpheme. Ideally, morpheme studies needed to be longitudinal but few were. Two that were (Rosansky, 1976; Hakuta, 1974) did not find the same 'acquisition order' as that reported in the cross-sectional studies. Hakuta, for example, found that the learner he investigated – a five-year-old Japanese girl learning English – learned plural-*s* much later than Dulay and Burt's learners, possibly because this morpheme had no equivalent in the learner's L1. These and a number of other studies (e.g. Shin and Milroy's (1999) study of young Korean-American children's acquisition of ten grammatical morphemes) suggest that the learners' L1 influences the order of acquisition and that, for this reason, the L2 order is not exactly the same as the L1 acquisition order. Another criticism of the morpheme studies was that they only examined a small set of grammatical morphemes which, in fact, were a rag-bag of disparate features involving very different kinds of learning problems.

Nevertheless, as Larsen-Freeman and Long (1991) argued 'there are…too many studies conducted with sufficient methodological rigor and showing sufficiently consistent general findings for the commonalities to be ignored' (p. 92). In other words, by and large, there was an identifiable order of acquisition for English grammatical morphemes. The obvious question, then, was why learners followed such a natural order. Goldschneider and DeKeyser (2001) examined some twenty morpheme studies, investigating which factors could account for the order. They were able to show that the phonological salience of a morpheme, its syntactic category, and its frequency in input to learners all had an influence on when a particular morpheme was acquired. They concluded that there was a single general factor that could explain the order of acquisition – 'salience'. In other words, learners first learn those morphemes whose meanings are transparent and whose form is readily discernible in the input. An alternative explanation is that the order of acquisition reflects the frequency with which morphemes appear in the input. However, as we will see in Chapter 7, input frequency alone cannot provide an adequate explanation.

Later research on the order of acquisition has focused on the acquisition of self-enclosed grammatical subsystems, thus addressing the criticism regarding the rag-bag nature of the features investigated in the earlier morpheme studies. Bardovi-Harlig (2000), for example, reviewed a range of research that studied how L2 learners acquire the tense-aspect system of different languages. These studies adopted a different way of defining 'acquisition' – that is, in terms of 'emergence' rather than 'accuracy'. They provided clear evidence of a consistent order of acquisition. Learners initially employ some basal verb form (e.g. the simple verb form in English) and then systematically accrue the different tense-aspect morphemes. In her own longitudinal study of sixteen learners of L2 English from four different language backgrounds, Bardovi-Harlig found the following order:

PAST > PAST PROGRESSIVE > PRESENT PERFECT > PAST PERFECT

Such studies, which were methodologically much sounder than the earlier morpheme studies, again demonstrated that learners acquire L2 grammar in a largely fixed order.

Sequence of acquisition

Whereas 'order of acquisition' is defined in terms of the order in which different grammatical features are mastered or first emerge in learners' production, 'sequence of acquisition' refers to the stage-like process by which individual grammatical features are acquired. Learners pass through transitional stages in acquiring specific grammatical structures such as interrogatives, negatives and relative clauses.

We have already noted that a common error in L2 English is the use of preverbal negation. In fact this constitutes an early step in learners' acquisition of negation. Early negative utterances are typically propositionally reduced (i.e. both content words and grammatical functors are omitted) with the negator (usually 'no') positioned before or sometimes following a noun, adjective or pronoun:

No very good.
Me no.
Me no ruler.

A little later negative utterances with verbs appear, preceded by the negator:

> Mariana no coming.
> Me no stay.

'Don't' appears in commands:

> Don't sit in that one chair.

Also 'not' begins to be used in statements:

> Not that one.
> Not climbing.

However, early learner language continues to demonstrate simplification. When modal verbs begin to appear, the negator is positioned correctly between the modal and main verb but such utterances may still not be well-formed:

> The man is can't read it the book.

Gradually different auxiliary verbs appear in utterances that are increasingly well formed:

> The man is not shouting.

However, it is not until later that negatives with the auxiliary correctly marked for tense become common:

> I did not throw paper on the floor.

This whole process can take months even for successful learners who are highly motivated. The stages are not well defined, however. Rather they overlap with considerable backsliding to earlier negative forms. In other words, the acquisition of negatives is slow, gradual, dynamic and variable. However, although there is no instant mastery of the target language structure, the pattern of development is systematic and predictable.

Sequences of acquisition – such as that for negatives – have been noted for a wide range of grammatical structures, morphological as well as syntactic, and for a number of different languages. Pienemann et al. (1988), for example, identified a sequence of acquisition for German word order rules, claiming that the sequence constitutes 'probably one of the most robust empirical findings in SLA research' (p. 222). Drawing on this research, Pienemann (1998, 2005) proposed his Processability Theory, which sought to explain acquisition sequences such as that for German word order rules in terms of a set of universal and hierarchical processing procedures. As Pienemann (2005) put it 'processing devices will be acquired in their sequence of activation in the production process' (p. 13). In other words, the failure to master a low-level procedure blocks access to higher-level procedures, making it impossible for learners to acquire those grammatical features that depend on them. Table 3.1 describes the different processing procedures and indicates how they relate to the sequence of acquisition for German word order. In order for learners to acquire the full range of German word rules, they have to master the procedures involved one at a time. Thus, for example, it would be impossible for learners to acquire inversion following an adverb (as required in German) unless they had already mastered lemma access, the category procedure and the phrasal procedure. The procedures are not just applicable to German word order rules, however, but to all developmental features, including morphological, in any L2. For example, third person-*s* in English is not acquirable until the *S*-procedure is available.

Table 3.1 Processing procedures involved in the acquisition of grammar (based on Pienemann, 2005)

Procedure	Description	German word order
1. Lemma access	Learners can only access L2 words but these are invariant in form and have not been assigned a grammatical category.	Learners simply string + single words together (e.g. 'kind spiel da' = child play there). They may also learn some formulaic chunks.
2. Category procedures	Words are now assigned a grammatical category (e.g. 'adverb') but there is no exchange of grammatical information between phrases.	Adverb preposing – learners can position an adverb in sentence initial position but cannot invert the subject and verb as required when a clause begins with an adverb (e.g. 'da kinder spielen' = there children are playing).
3. Phrasal procedures	Learners are able to vary the order of words within a phrase by moving an element in the phrase to a different clause position.	Verb separation – learners can move non-finite verbal elements into clause-final position as required in German (e.g. 'alle kinder muss die pause machen' = all children must the pause make).
4. S-procedure	Learners can handle the exchange of grammatical information across phrases.	Inversion – learners can now invert subject and verb following an adverb and in interrogatives (e.g. 'da spielen kinder' = there children play).
5. Subordinate clause procedure	Learners are able to process grammatical information across clause boundaries and to distinguish word order in main and subordinate clauses.	Learners are able to position the verb at the end of the subordinate clause (e.g. 'er sagte dass er nach hause kommt' = he said that he home comes).

A key question is whether this pattern of acquisition can be changed through instruction. Pienemann (1984) reported a study that showed that instruction directed at a particular grammatical was only effective if a learner had already obtained access to the processing procedure immediately preceding that required for the target feature. One learner, who had not yet mastered phrasal procedures, was not successful in producing utterances with inversion (the target feature), while those who had mastered it demonstrated acquisition of inversion. Ellis (1989) reported a study that compared the sequence of acquisition for German word order rules of a group of adult-instructed learners with that reported for naturalistic learners. He found that both sets of learners manifested the same sequence even though the order in which the instructed group was taught the word order rules was different. Spada and Lightbown (1999) tested the claims of Processability Theory by investigating the effects of instruction on English interrogatives. They found that by and large the instruction only enabled learners to produce interrogatives belonging to the next stage to the one they had already reached prior to the instruction. However, there were a number of learners who did not progress at all and one or two learners who skipped a stage. The general conclusion that can be drawn from these and other studies is that instruction generally does not change the natural sequence of acquisition but can assist learners to move more rapidly through it.

These studies then lend support to Pienemann's (1985) Teachability Hypothesis. This 'predicts that instruction can only promote language acquisition if the interlanguage is close to the point when the structure to be taught is acquired in the natural setting (so that sufficient processing prerequisites are developed)' (p. 37). However, there is also plenty of evidence to suggest that instruction is effective in speeding up the process of acquisition. Ellis (1989), in the study mentioned above, found that the classroom learners he investigated demonstrated more rapid progress in acquiring the German word order rules than has been reported for naturalistic learners. A key question, then, is how instruction based on a grammatical syllabus helps learners move through an acquisition sequence.

The acquisition of language functions

There has been far less research that has investigated how learners acquire language functions such as requests. There are no theoretical grounds for proposing an order of acquisition for language functions. The functions that learners acquire will reflect their particular communicative needs. However, there are grounds for suggesting that there will be regularities in the way in which learners acquire the linguistic exponents of specific functions, as this depends in part on the processing constraints we considered above.

Kasper and Rose (2002: 140) drew on three longitudinal studies of L2 learners' acquisition of requests (Schmidt, 1983; Ellis, 1992; Achiba, 2003) to suggest that the development of requests involves five stages:

1 The pre-basic stage (i.e. requesting utterances are context-dependent and typically lacking in verbs – e.g. 'another paper please').
2 The formulaic stage (i.e. reliance on unanalysed formulaic sequences and imperatives – e.g. 'give me my paper'; 'can I have paper please?').
3 The unpacking stage (i.e. formulaic sequences are analysed allowing for more productive use and a general shift to conventional indirectness – e.g. 'Could you go over there please?').
4 the pragmatic expansion stage (i.e. the pragmalinguistic repertoire is extended, greater mitigation, more complex syntax – e.g. 'I'm sorry, but I'll have to go at 6pm. Would you mind coming a bit earlier?').
5 The fine-tuning stage (i.e. adjusting the force of a request in accordance with the participants, goals and context).

Two of these studies (Schmidt and Achiba) investigated naturalistic learners but Ellis's study examined the requests produced by two classroom learners over a two-year period. The general pattern of the development was the same irrespective of the setting, although the learners' in Ellis's study only reached Stage 3. There was little evidence of pragmatic expansion and no evidence at all of any ability to modify the form of requests in accordance with audience or purpose. Ellis suggested that the somewhat limited development evident in the two learners' requests, might have been because the classroom context did not create any need for sociolinguistic variation. Another possibility, however, is that the learners were not directly taught how to make requests. Other studies (e.g. Lyster, 1994) have also shown that classroom learners' pragmatic development is often very limited.

An important question concerns whether learners acquire grammar and then put this to use to convey pragmatic meanings or whether the need to perform language functions drives the acquisition of grammar. This question is of direct relevance to the choice of syllabus. If grammar is the starting point, then it would make sense to base teaching on a grammatical syllabus, but if grammar originates out of the need to perform language functions, a notional (functional) syllabus would be preferable. It is also possible, of course, that pragmatic and grammatical development take place concurrently with each feeding off the other. Studies of naturalistic learners (e.g. Schmidt, 1983; Achiba, 2003) suggest that the early stage of acquisition is essentially pragmatic rather than grammatical. That is, learners grab at the slender linguistic resources at their disposal (formulaic sequences, simple lexis and intonation) to perform those functions that are communicatively important to them. However, this may not be the case at later stages. There is considerable evidence to show that the acquisition of grammar is needed for the performance of more subtle pragmatic meanings. For example, learners cannot be expected to perform polite bi-clausal requests (e.g. 'Would you be so kind as to help me with my car?') until they have mastered subordinate clauses. As Kasper (2001) pointed out, in the later stages of development, grammatical forms may be first acquired in relation to their core semantic meanings and only take on a pragmatic function later. What is clear is that learners' awareness of what constitutes correct grammar and appropriate pragmatic use of the L2 are not closely related (Bardovi-Harlig and Dörnyei, 1998), with foreign language learners more likely to be aware of formal correctness and second language learners more aware of pragmatic appropriateness.

Formulaic sequences

Wray (2000) defines a formulaic sequence as 'a sequence, continuous or discontinuous, of words or other meaning elements, which is, or appears to be, prefabricated; that is stored and retrieved whole from memory at the time of use, rather than being subject to generation or analysis by the language grammar' (p. 465). It is useful to distinguish two basic types of formulaic sequences – 'routines' which are totally unanalysed units and learnt as wholes (e.g. 'I don't know') and 'patterns', which are partially analysed units consisting of a chunk with one or more open slots (e.g. 'Can I have a –?').

It is not always easy to decide whether a learner utterance is formulaic or rule based. For example, 'I don't understand' may constitute a memorized whole or it may have been derived from knowledge of the target language rule for negation. Myles et al. (1998) proposed a number of criteria for determining whether an utterance is formulaic:

1 At least two morphemes in length.
2 Phonologically coherent (i.e. fluently articulated, non-hesitant).
3 Unrelated to productive patterns in the learner's speech.
4 Greater complexity in comparison with the learner's other output.
5 Used repeatedly in the same form.
6 May be inappropriate (syntactically, semantically or pragmatically or otherwise idiosyncratic).
7 Situationally dependent.
8 Community-wide in use.

However, these criteria are not easy to apply. The two key criteria appear to be (3) and (4).

Despite the problems of identification, there is now widespread acceptance amongst researchers that formulaic sequences play a major role in both L2 production and L2 acquisition, especially in the early stages. Specific sequences emerge tied to the performance of specific language functions. For example, 'Can I have – ?' is used to perform a request, 'Why don't we – ?' to perform a suggestion, and 'I'm very sorry' an apology. Ellis (1984a) found that the classroom learners he investigated rapidly acquired a repertoire of formulas to enable them to perform the functions that met their classroom communication needs. Formulaic expressions, it should be noted, are common in the speech of both children and adults and in both naturalistic and classroom learners.

A key question raised by Hakuta (1976) is: 'To what extent do these routines and patterns facilitate or hinder the acquisition of TL grammar?' Krashen and Scarcella (1978) argued that formulaic speech and rule-created speech are unrelated but the prevailing view today is that learners unpack the parts that comprise a sequence and, in this way, discover the L2 grammar. In other words, formulaic sequences serve as a kind of starter pack from which grammar is generated. Some of the clearest evidence of this comes from a longitudinal case study of five Spanish-speaking children learning L2 English (Wong Fillmore, 1976). Nora, the fastest of the five learners, used two formulas:

I wanna play wi' dese.
I don't wanna do dese.

and then discovered that the constituents following 'wanna' were inter-changeable:

I don't wanna play dese.
I wanna do dese.

Wong Fillmore commented that this 'formula-based analytical process...was repeated in case after case' (p. 645). Ellis (1984a) found evidence of the classroom learners he studied systematically unpacking the constituents of what were initially routines. For example, by analysing the routines

I don't know.
I don't understand.
I don't like.

the learners learned the construction 'don't + verb'. Myles (2004) also argued that formulas constitute an important starting point. In her study, those classroom learners who failed to acquire a set of formulas showed very little development. There is also evidence (Weinert, 1987; Myles et al., 1998) that attempts to teach learners grammar may only result in learners extracting ready-made chunks from structural practice exercises rather than internalizing the underlying rule. These chunks, which often contain verbs, contrast with the verbless utterances that figure in the pre-grammatical stage of acquisition. They seem to provide learners with data which can feed into their creative speech.

Summary

The research we have examined lends support to Selinker's (1972) claim that learners possess a mental grammar that undergoes constant restructuring during the process of L2 acquisition (i.e. an 'interlanguage'). This inter-language differs markedly from the target language grammar, which constitutes just the end point of the developmental continuum. It is manifest in the following ways:

1 Learners make errors which partly reflect their L1 grammar but are largely developmental in nature.
2 Learners acquire the grammatical morphemes of an L2 in a relatively fixed and universal order reflecting the overall salience of the different grammatical features.
3 Specific grammatical structures manifest a sequence of acquisition. That is, they are acquired gradually involving overlapping stages of development resulting in considerable variability in L2 use.
4 Learners manifest a developmental profile in the acquisition of the linguistic exponents needed to perform language functions, such as requests.
5 Learners acquire formulaic sequences. These are used to perform language functions that are communicatively important to them but also provide them with data which is analysed and fed into their grammatical development.

This pattern of development is evident in both naturalistic and instructed learners. Instruction does not appear to have much effect in preventing developmental errors, changing orders of acquisition or enabling learners to bypass stages in acquisition sequences. Natural learning processes are paramount, indicating that instruction is only successful if learners are developmentally ready to acquire the target feature. Instruction can also impede learning (e.g. induce errors that otherwise might not occur) or alternatively it can result in learners learning something other than what was intended (e.g. when learners acquire formulaic sequences rather than rules from grammar practice exercises). However, instruction is beneficial: it assists learners to develop more rapidly than purely natural exposure to the L2.

Teachers may find this account of L2 acquisition somewhat puzzling and contrary to their own experience of how instructed learners learn. For example, they may feel that beginner learners can be taught how to perform target-like negatives. In a way they are correct. Learners can certainly be taught the target language rule for negatives and then apply this rule consciously to produce correct negative utterances. The account of L2 acquisition we have presented in this chapter, however, is not based on learners' consciously monitored production but on their spontaneous, communicative language use. If the goal of instruction is to enable learners to use the L2 effectively in such use – and we would argue this is the primary goal of most language courses – then it is essential to ask if and how linguistic syllabuses can contribute to the way in which learners build their knowledge of an L2 grammar.

Evaluating linguistic syllabuses: problems and solutions

The essential problem in the design of a linguistic syllabus is how to select and sequence the linguistic content in a way that accords with how learners learn an L2. This problem is somewhat different for grammatical, lexical or notional syllabuses so we will examine its nature and possible solutions for each type of syllabus separately.

The grammatical syllabus and L2 learning

There are some good reasons for rejecting a grammatical syllabus as the basis of a language course. As we have seen, the research on learner errors, grammatical morphemes and the sequence of acquisition of syntactic structures, indicates that L2 acquisition is gradual and dynamic involving internal mental processes that cannot be easily controlled externally through instruction. As Ortega (2011) concluded in her own evaluation of the significance of developmental sequences and processes for language teaching: 'Instruction cannot affect the route of L2 development in any fundamental way' (p. 98). She also noted that 'instruction can be ineffective and even counterproductive when it ignores developmental readiness' (p. 99). However, she also acknowledged that 'instruction has large positive effects on rate of development and ultimate level of achievement' (p. 100). What is needed then is to examine how instruction based on a linguistic syllabus can be made compatible with how learners learn the grammar of an L2.

One possibility might be organizing the syllabus in such a way that it matches the learner's order and sequence of acquisition. This might be possible in the case of grammatical morphemes given that these are mastered in a fixed order. There are, however, several problems with this. First, information is only available about a relatively small set of grammatical morphemes. We do not know where morphemes such as comparative-*er*/-*est* or determiners such as *some*/*any* fit into the order. Second, researchers have lumped together some morphemes (e.g. the articles *a* and *the*) that constitute very different kinds of learning problems for learners.[1] Third, and perhaps most important, morphemes may be 'mastered' in a fixed order but their development, like syntactical structures, is a gradual process sometimes involving U-shaped patterns of development. Thus, even though a morpheme such as V-*ing* has been shown to be mastered early, its acquisition is characterized by marked fluctuation involving overuse as learners struggle to distinguish the meanings that it performs from the meanings of other verb forms. Also, acquisition does not entail the mastery of grammatical forms but of form-meaning mappings that are subject to ongoing revision as new forms enter interlanguage.[2] Finally, the grammar of a language involves much more than grammatical morphemes. A grammatical syllabus needs to incorporate a broad range of grammatical features including simple and complex syntactical structures. The research on grammatical morphemes provides a very incomplete picture of the grammar that learners need to acquire. In short, it would appear that what is known about the order of acquisition of grammatical morphemes does not provide a basis for organizing a grammatical syllabus.

The impossibility of matching the contents of a grammatical syllabus to the order and sequence of acquisition becomes even clearer when we consider acquisition sequences. As we have seen, learners typically progress through transitional stages before acquiring the target language form of a structure. This is incompatible with a linear syllabus that assumes that acquisition is a process of accumulating discrete entities (Rutherford, 1988). If learners are not ready to acquire a specific feature, they will not acquire it no matter how intensively it is taught. In fact, attempting to teach it 'discourages learners from taking risks, which may delay development' (Ortega, 2011: 99). A possible solution to this problem might be to try to determine when learners are ready to acquire the target structure. But establishing this will be beyond most teachers and, in any case, the learners that make up a particular classroom will not all be at the same stage of development (i.e. some of them may be 'ready' but others will not be). Also, there is no way of taking account of 'readiness' in a syllabus that consists of a predetermined ordering of grammatical features.[3]

There is, however, a possible solution to these problems. Ellis (1993) suggested that although a grammatical syllabus was incompatible with what is known about how learners acquire grammar, it might still serve as a basis for teaching explicit knowledge of grammar. In Chapter 1 we pointed out that knowledge of a language can be implicit or explicit. Implicit knowledge is procedural and thus available for use in online communication. In contrast, explicit knowledge is declarative and available for use only in controlled processing. The research on the order and sequence of acquisition, which we considered earlier in this chapter, examined how learners develop implicit knowledge. That is to say, the gradual, non-linear nature of acquisition that we described is only evident in how learners use their L2 in communication. There is no reason to believe that explicit knowledge is subject to the same kind of developmental constraints as implicit knowledge. The factors that govern the learning difficulty of different grammatical structures as explicit knowledge are of an entirely different nature. Ellis (2006) suggested that these are the 'conceptual clarity' of different structures (i.e. the extent to which the form and meaning of a structure can be explained simply and clearly and the extent to which there is a transparent, general rule that can be articulated) and the metalanguage needed to describe a feature (i.e. whether a structure can be described adequately using only semi-technical language or whether more technical language is needed). These are precisely the criteria that have been used to grade structures in a grammatical syllabus. In other words, even though grammatical syllabuses are directed at developing learners' implicit knowledge, in fact they are organized in terms of the designer's understanding of what constitutes grammatical complexity as explicit knowledge. Ellis's (2003a) proposal is that the problems with grammatical syllabuses can be overcome if they are used as a basis for teaching explicit rather than implicit knowledge.

This raises another issue, however, namely the legitimacy of a syllabus that is geared only to teaching explicit knowledge. To address this, it is necessary to consider the role played by explicit knowledge in L2 use and acquisition. There is general agreement that explicit knowledge is of value in L2 use, especially of the planned kind. That is, when learners are not required to use the L2 spontaneously, they are able to draw on their explicit knowledge to help them formulate what they want to say or write and also to monitor their output. However, as we saw in Chapter 1, there is less agreement about the role played by explicit knowledge in L2 acquisition (i.e. the development of implicit knowledge). According to the non-interface position, explicit knowledge plays no role. However, both the strong interface position and the weak interface position see a role for it. According to the strong interface position, learning begins with explicit knowledge which is then automatized through practice. According to the weak-interface position, explicit knowledge does not transform into implicit knowledge but can facilitate some of the processes involved in developing implicit knowledge (i.e. by helping learners to 'notice' features in the input and to 'notice-the-gap' between the input and their own interlanguage). The strong interface position is compatible with a grammatical syllabus but runs up against the problems we have already identified, namely that the development of implicit knowledge is gradual and non-linear. It was for this reason that Ellis argued for a weak-interface position. He proposed that a grammatical syllabus can be usefully employed to teach explicit knowledge on the grounds that this will assist the development of implicit knowledge – but over time rather than immediately.

To sum up, grammatical syllabuses are problematic if they are intended to serve as a basis for teaching implicit knowledge. Implicit knowledge is not 'teachable'; it is only 'learnable'. However, a grammatical syllabus may have legitimacy as a basis for teaching explicit knowledge. Clearly, though, a grammatical syllabus does not constitute a sufficient platform for developing full competence in an L2. Learners need to experience the conditions that foster the development of implicit knowledge and, arguably, this cannot be achieved by an approach that assumes L2 acquisition in a linear process. In other words, a grammatical syllabus can only be used alongside a non-linguistic syllabus, that caters to the kinds of acquisition processes involved in the development of implicit knowledge. How this might be achieved will be considered in Chapter 6 when we discuss task-based language teaching.

The lexical syllabus and L2 learning

Willis (1990) argued that just as the lexicographer can arrive at a description of a language through the careful examination of a language corpus, so the learner can also derive a working knowledge of the language in the same way. In effect, then, he is claiming that a lexical syllabus, consisting of the words and the chunks in which they occur, is compatible with the way in which learners learn an L2. He is not alone in this. N. Ellis (2002) likewise argued that language learning (including grammar learning) is the 'piecemeal learning of many thousands of constructions and the frequency-based abstraction of regularities within them' (p. 144). He sees acquisition as entailing a general developmental sequence from 'formula, through low-scope pattern, to construction'. In other words, grammar learning involves the gradual extraction of the underlying patterns to be found in the collocations the learner has stored. The whole process is driven by input frequency which determines the order in which collocations are acquired and provides learners with the data needed to extract the underlying patterns. Learners, he argued, engage naturally in an 'incessant unconscious figuring' that enables them to discover the statistical regularities in the chunks they have acquired. This is a view of language learning that is clearly supported by the research that we examined on formulaic sequences and the role they play in learning. It would seem then that a lexical syllabus of the kind proposed by Willis has solid support from theories of L2 acquisition that emphasize implicit language learning.

There are, however, problems with lexical syllabuses. The content of a grammatical syllabus is derived from a well-established and finite description of grammar as a 'system': texts only figure as a methodological device for implementing the syllabus not as the source of the grammatical content. In contrast, the content of a lexical syllabus is based on 'items' that do not comprise any 'system' and are potentially infinite: texts serve as the source of the content, as words and collocation are selected on the basis of the frequency in which they occur in these texts. This raises questions about the validity of a lexical syllabus. Is frequency an adequate basis for selecting the lexical content? Can a lexical syllabus provide adequate coverage of the lexical items learners need to learn? Can it ensure the development of grammatical competence?

Frequency counts simply tell us how often specific lexical items and constructions appear in a given set of texts. That is, they provide information about 'token' frequency. But what is of greater importance for language learning is 'type' frequency (i.e. the number of different lexical items that can occur in a given construction). Productivity in the use of specific items is determined by type rather than token frequency. N. Ellis (2002) explained why this is. When learners encounter a number of different lexical items in a construction, they are more likely to form a general category and extend this category to new items. Type frequency also strengthens the mental representation of the category. This suggests that a lexical syllabus needs to be based not on the frequency of individual words but rather on constructions (i.e. assemblages of words) which are selected and graded not on their raw frequency, but on the frequency with which different words can occur in them. It may be possible to design a syllabus based on type frequency but, to date, lexical syllabuses have not attempted this nor is it clear whether they can. In this respect, therefore, they are not ideal for language learning.

Coverage is a problem no matter whether the syllabus content is based on token or type frequency. Either way there are a massive number of items and constructions that will need to be covered. The Cobuild Course consists of three levels that overall introduce 2,450 words together with some of their common collocations. This constitutes only a small number of the total number of words and collocations that learners must acquire to achieve a high level of competence in a language. It is difficult to see how a lexical syllabus can satisfactorily provide coverage of the huge amount of lexical material a learner needs to master a language, although, it might be argued, it can constitute a basis for the early stages of learning. The problem of coverage has been acknowledged by Lewis (1997) who draws on Krashen (1985) to argue that what is needed is massive exposure to 'comprehensible input' (i.e. input that has been tailored to the level of the learner). However, this is catered for most effectively not by means of a syllabus specifying the lexical items to be learned but by providing learners with a rich input. One obvious way in which this can be achieved is through an extensive reading programme consisting of graded readers (see Chapter 7). It is worth noting that the preparation of such readers has always drawn on frequency lists of individual words. What might be useful, therefore, is not a lexical syllabus, but a checklist of lexical items that can be used as a basis for ensuring that learners are exposed to lexical items in context, in accordance with what is known about their overall frequency. As Nation (2001) pointed out, it will also help to ensure that learners know the meanings of high frequency words as this will help to make input comprehensible. There is, however, no need for a lexical syllabus and no need to teach the collocations of words. By and large, learners will need to figure these out for themselves as they encounter them in context.

Proponents of lexical syllabuses do not ignore grammar. In accordance with usage-based accounts of language and language learning (e.g. N. Ellis 1996, 2002), they view grammar as the extraction of patterns from the collocations they have acquired – a matter of implicit learning. However, N. Ellis also acknowledged that explicit instruction can facilitate the extraction process. The question that arises is how best to organize this instruction – a matter of syllabus design. There is merit in raising learners' consciousness about the patterns that underlie collocational sets. One way that this might be done is by presenting learners with raw data (based perhaps on a pre-selected concordance of the collocations that manifest a specific pattern) and asking them to draw their own conclusions about the underlying regularity. Peppard (2010) provides an illustration of how this might be done for the 'V about N' pattern in such collocations as 'think about the future', 'forget about the gym' and 'talk about something'. But how are the patterns and their collocations to be identified and organized into a syllabus? Once again we run up against the problems discussed above. The collocations are endless and the patterns, while finite, too numerous to accommodate in a syllabus. A better and more practical way might be to use a traditional grammatical syllabus as a basis for explicit instruction (as proposed in the previous section) and allow learners to make use of this to fine-tune the implicit processes involved in extracting patterns.

Language learning involves both exemplar-based learning and rule-based learning (Skehan, 1998) (see Principle 1 in Chapter 1). As Skehan points out 'there is a danger...that an exemplar-based system can only learn by accumulation of wholes, and that it is likely to be excessively context bound, since such wholes cannot be adapted easily for the expression of more complex meanings' (p. 89). The key question is how to assist rule-based learning. On the basis of the arguments presented above, this cannot be efficiently achieved by means of a lexical syllabus consisting of 'items' (words and their collocations). As Thornbury (1998) argued, the lexical approach affords 'a journey without a map' (p. 7). It may be true that 'language consists of grammaticalized lexis, not lexicalized grammar' (Richards and Rodgers, 1986: vi) but it does not follow that a lexical syllabus provides the best way to organize the teaching of a language. It is not so surprising, therefore, that the Cobuild Course, based on a lexical syllabus, was not so well received by teachers (Taylor, 1991).

The notional syllabus and L2 learning

Wilkins (1976) claimed that a notional syllabus was 'analytic', in contrast to a grammatical syllabus that is 'synthetic'. However, it is not clear that a notional syllabus is analytic in the sense intended by Wilkins. Widdowson (1979) argued convincingly that a notional syllabus is in fact 'synthetic' since it too presents 'isolates' (i.e. the linguistic means for performing specific semantic and functional meanings) to be accumulated and stored. The essential difference between a notional and a grammatical syllabus lies in how these isolates are organized. In a notional syllabus, they are organized in terms of the specific notions and functions to be taught. We can ask, therefore, whether this way of organizing linguistic material is compatible with how learners acquire an L2.

We have seen that L2 learning is functionally driven – that is, learners seek out ways of performing the semantic and functional meanings that are important to them. To a considerable extent – especially in the early stages of learning when learners have very limited linguistic knowledge – they achieve this by means of formulaic sequences. That is, they internalize ready-made chunks of language that are closely linked to the performance of specific semantic and functional meanings. For example, to make a request, they learn the pattern 'Can I have – ?', to apologize they learn 'I'm sorry', and to invite somebody to do something they learn 'Would you like to – ?'.[4] These routines and patterns may be picked up incidentally through interacting in the L2. Can they also be taught explicitly through presentation and practice? Are formulaic sequences 'teachable'? Given that they do not involve the processing operations involved in the acquisition of grammar, there is no reason why they cannot be explicitly taught. Pienemann's lowest level of processing – available to learners from the beginning – is 'lemma access'. Words and formulaic sequences, then, are not subject to the same constraints that govern the acquisition of grammar. It seems reasonable to conclude, then, that a notional syllabus provides a basis for the exemplar-based learning that characterizes one aspect of L2 acquisition. Teaching learners formulas will give learners a start on the developmental path they will follow and will also help them achieve fluency in comprehending and producing the L2.

In this respect, a notional syllabus is much more promising than a lexical syllabus. Notions constitute a relatively closed class of entities; lexis constitutes an open class. Thus, the coverage problem that we saw as inherent in a lexical syllabus is solved. It is a relatively straightforward task to identify the specific notions that beginner learners of a language will need to perform. They will need to greet, to request, to invite, to accept or refuse, to apologize, to suggest and to express such notions as ability and future and past time. Nor is it difficult to identify simple formulaic expressions that will realize these notions. It is also possible to design a notional syllabus for learners with specific purposes for learning an L2, as their needs can be more easily defined in notional than in purely linguistic terms. It is less clear, however, if a notional syllabus can cater effectively to more advanced learners who require to express more complex ideas involving more complex language. As we noted above, the acquisition of a language involves a rule-based as well as an exemplar-based competence. We need to ask, therefore, whether Wilkins's claim that a notional syllabus can also cater to the development of a rule-based system is justified. We have seen that there is evidence that L2 learners do naturally unpack the grammatical detail in a formula – they 'analyse' them in the way that Wilkins suggests. However, this occurs implicitly by means of the frequency-based abstraction of the regularities within the chunks they have acquired (N. Ellis, 2002). Earlier we showed how this takes place. At issue, then, is whether a notional syllabus should seek to direct the process of analysing formulaic sequences, or just specify the formulas to be taught and rely on the capacity of the learner to carry out the business of analysing them implicitly. Wilkins avoids this problem. He acknowledged that the 'need for the learner to benefit from significant generalizations cannot be ignored' but then goes on to say that 'whether or not the aspects of language structure involved are to be bought explicitly to the learner's attention is a methodological matter and does not concern us here' (p. 14). In other words, he does not consider developing the learner's rule-based competence the responsibility of a notional syllabus.

In effect, then, a notional syllabus addresses only one of the goals of a language syllabus – how to organize the linguistic content for exemplar-based learning. It rejects the need to cater for rule-based learning. This is its strength as it avoids the problems inherent in a grammatical syllabus (see previous section). But it is also a limitation as it fails to provide a basis for the full development of competence in an L2. Recognizing this, many language courses (e.g. the *Cambridge English Course* – Swan and Walter, 1984) have adopted a hybrid syllabus consisting of a notional/functional strand and a conventional grammatical strand. Such an approach – especially if the grammatical strand is directed at learners' explicit rather than implicit knowledge – would seem to afford the most effective way of organizing the teaching content in a linguistic syllabus.

Conclusion

In this chapter we have examined to what extent linguistic syllabuses are compatible with what is known about L2 acquisition. We have considered three types of linguistic syllabuses – grammatical, lexical and notional. The position we have taken is that linguistic syllabuses can only serve as a basis for teaching a language if they are able to take account of the order and sequence of acquisition (see Principle 5 in Chapter 1). To this end, we examined research that has documented the natural route of development that learners follow. We considered the kinds of errors that learners commit, the order and sequence of acquisition, and formulaic sequences. We have advanced arguments to support the following conclusions:

1 Grammatical syllabuses cannot easily accommodate the essential nature of L2 acquisition. A grammatical syllabus assumes that acquisition consists of the serial acquisition of 'accumulated entities' (Rutherford, 1988) whereas the acquisition of implicit knowledge is a dynamic and gradual process involving constant restructuring. However, we also noted, in accordance with Principle 4 in Chapter 1 ('Instruction needs to be predominantly directed at developing implicit knowledge of the L2 while not neglecting explicit knowledge'), that a grammatical syllabus can provide a basis for raising learners' consciousness about explicit L2 knowledge. This suggests, however, a need to rethink the traditional goal of a grammatical syllabus by, for example, using it as a basis for teaching explicit knowledge. We will consider the possibility in greater depth in the next chapter.

2 The view of language that underlies a lexical syllabus accords with a usage-based account of how learners acquire an L2. It is, however, not clear how the lexical content of such a syllabus can be organized in such a way as to ensure adequate coverage of the words and chunks, given the sheer volume of lexis that learners need to achieve advanced levels of L2 competence. Nor is it clear if such a syllabus can assist learners with the implicit processes involved in extracting rules and patterns from the lexis they have acquired. This requires exposure to massive amounts of comprehensible input. However, a case can be made for the explicit teaching of the meanings of high-frequency vocabulary to help learners comprehend input. This point is also considered further in the next chapter.

3 A notional syllabus affords a systematic way of teaching learners the formulaic sequences for performing key language functions. It receives support from Principle 1 ('Instruction needs to ensure that learners develop a rich repertoire of formulaic expressions'). Because the content of such a syllabus is defined in terms of 'chunks' (which can be learned explicitly) rather than 'structures', the problem of how to match the external syllabus with the learner's internal 'syllabus' does not arise. However, such a syllabus can only cater to exemplar-based learning; it does not address rule-based learning (i.e. the process of extracting regularities from the chunks that have been taught) and thus does not address the final part of Principle 1 ('and a rule-based competence').

Robinson (2011a) states the fundamental issue for syllabus design that arises out of a consideration of how learners learn an L2 is as follows:

> Is the L2 best learned explicitly, by understanding and using a series of formal units of language, however characterized, or is it best learned incidentally from exposure to the L2 during communicative activities and tasks?
>
> (p. 294)

Linguistic syllabuses are premised on the assumption that teaching discrete elements of language (grammatical structures, lexis, or formulaic sequences) is the best way to develop the implicit knowledge that is fundamental to L2 acquisition. We have argued that this assumption does not readily accord with how learners acquire an L2. However, we have also argued that linguistic syllabuses can serve as a basis for teaching explicit L2 knowledge, which is of value for both L2 use and L2 acquisition. In the next chapter we consider the possibilities for explicit language instruction.

Notes

1   English articles are multifunctional. Acquisition involves gradually learning the different meanings performed by *a, the* and zero article.
2   The problem concerning the gradual mastery of grammatical morphemes might be addressed in a 'cyclical syllabus' of the kind proposed by Howatt (1974). In such a syllabus, grammatical features are introduced and then later retaught. However, this raises the additional problem about when exactly to reintroduce a previous taught feature in the syllabus.
3   It might be possible to take account of learner readiness if the grammatical content takes the form of a checklist (i.e. a list of putative structures to be taught when the teacher considers learners are ready) rather than a fixed syllabus. However, the problem of determining readiness remains.
4   Teaching materials based on a notional syllabus typically present and practise the formulaic sequences required for performing a specific notion or function. For example, in a unit labelled 'Degrees of certainty about the future', Abbs and Freebairn (1982) introduce the patterns 'Knowing –, he/she will + verb' and '– might + verb, but I doubt it'.

DISCUSSION QUESTIONS

1.   A syllabus is a 'statement of the teaching content'. What are the different ways in which the linguistic content of a syllabus can be specified?
2.   'Linguistic syllabuses can be organized in terms of forms of meanings'. Explain the difference.
3.   Some applied linguists have argued that it is no longer appropriate to base a linguistic syllabus on a native-speaker variety (i.e. standard British or American English) and have proposed instead basing it on 'English as a Lingua Franca'. What view do the authors of this book take on this issue? Do you agree?
4.   '[T]he grammatical syllabus has held pride of place in language courses.' Why is this?
5.   Review the arguments in favour of a lexical syllabus. If you had to choose between a grammatical or lexical syllabus, which would you choose and why?
6.   What are the arguments in support of a notional syllabus? Are there any drawbacks in specifying the linguistic content of a syllabus in notional/functional terms?

7. '[O]ne of the pedagogic recommendations emanating from the findings of the error analysis studies is that teachers need to be tolerant of learner errors.' Do you agree that teachers should be tolerant of learner errors? In what ways could they practise such tolerance?

8. Why would it be difficult to base a syllabus on what is known about the 'order of acquisition'?

9. Pienemann's (1985) Teachability Hypothesis 'predicts that instruction can only promote language acquisition if the interlanguage is close to the point when the structure to be taught is acquired in the natural setting (so that sufficient processing prerequisites are developed)' (p. 37). What are the implications of the Teachability Hypothesis for a grammatical syllabus?

10. SLA researchers have shown that the early stage of naturalistic acquisition is essentially pragmatic rather than grammatical. What is meant by this? What are the implications for syllabus design?

11. Which type of linguistic syllabus is most compatible with the finding that language learners acquire 'formulaic sequences' rather than 'rules', especially in the early stages of L2 acquisition?

12. 'The essential problem in the design of a linguistic syllabus is how to select and sequence the linguistic content in a way that accords with how learners learn an L2.' Do you agree this is the essential problem? How can this problem be overcome?

13. Why does Ellis (1993) propose that a grammatical syllabus should serve only as a basis for teaching explicit L2 knowledge (not implicit L2 knowledge)? How convincing do you find this proposal?

14. Summarize the advantages and disadvantages of a lexical syllabus from the perspective of how learners acquire an L2.

15. 'A notional syllabus addresses only one of the goals of a language syllabus – how to organize the linguistic content for exemplar-based learning. It rejects the need to cater for rule-based learning.' Make sure you understand the difference between 'exemplar-based' and 'rule-based' learning and then explain why a notional syllabus only addresses the former. How might the teaching of notions and functions be carried out so as to facilitate rule-based learning?

16. The chapter ends with Robinson's (2011a) questions:

> Is the L2 best learned explicitly, by understanding and using a series of formal units of language, however characterized, or is it best learned incidentally from exposure to the L2 during communicative activities and tasks?
>
> (p. 294)

After reading this chapter, what answer would you give to this question?

4 Explicit instruction and SLA

Introduction

In the previous chapter we considered ways of organizing the content of a language course in terms of linguistic categories. The focus was on 'design'. In this chapter we will consider one of the main ways of implementing a linguistic syllabus – through explicit language instruction. The focus is on the specific techniques for teaching grammar and vocabulary. In this way we can examine further some of the claims – and doubts – about the feasibility of intervening directly in interlanguage development which we raised in the last chapter.

Explicit language instruction caters to intentional language learning in students. That is, it makes it clear to the learner what is the instructional target and provides activities to assist them in learning it. Explicit instruction is usually discussed in relation to grammar where it refers to activities that require 'some sort of rule being thought about during the learning process' (DeKeyser, 1995). However, vocabulary teaching can also be explicit where target items are presented and then practised. Implicit instruction caters to incidental language learning. Learners are not told what the instructional target is but simply engage in activities that provide them with input containing the target feature and opportunities to use it in output as in task-based language teaching (see Chapters 6).

De Graaff and Housen (2009) elaborate on this basic distinction between explicit and implicit instruction (see Table 4.1). In one respect, however, their definition of explicit instruction does not accord with how it is discussed in the pedagogic literature. As we will see, both explicit grammar and vocabulary teaching frequently include activities involving 'free use of the target form'.

As indicated in Table 4.1, explicit instruction involves two main components – presentation and practice. Presentation can be undertaken deductively or inductively. A deductive presentation starts with an explicit explanation of the target feature and usually also includes examples of the feature in sentences or longer texts. An inductive presentation begins with examples and requires the learners to induce the grammatical rules from them.

Once again, we will begin by examining how explicit instruction is handled in the pedagogic literature before considering the theoretical issues that SLA has addressed and the relevant empirical research.

Table 4.1 Implicit and explicit forms of form-focused instruction (De Graaff and Housen, 2009: 737)

Implicit instruction	Explicit instruction
• attracts attention to language meaning	• directs attention to language form
• language serves primarily as a tool for communication	• language serves as an object of study
• delivered spontaneously and incidentally (e.g. in an otherwise communication-oriented activity)	• predetermined and planned (e.g. as the main focus and goal of a teaching activity)
• unobtrusive (minimal interruption of communication of meaning)	• obtrusive (interruption of communication of meaning)
• presents target forms in context	• presents target forms in isolation
• no rule explanation or directions to attend to forms to discover rules; no use of metalanguage	• use of rule explanation or directions to attend to forms to discover rules; use of metalinguistic terminology
• encourages free use of target form	• involves controlled practice of target form

Pedagogical accounts of explicit language instruction

The dominant approach to teaching linguistic forms explicitly is present–practice–produce (PPP). In this chapter we will focus on the 'presentation' and 'practice/production' stages of this approach.

Presentation

Deductive vs inductive presentation

In a deductive presentation of a target structure, learners are given an explanation of the target structure and, typically, examples are provided to illustrate its form, meaning and use. In an inductive presentation, however, there are only examples aimed at helping learners work out for themselves the meaning and use of the target form. This can involve 'guided discovery' (Scrivener, 2005) where the teacher 'helps the learner to tell himself' (p. 265). The idea here is to 'nudge the learners towards key points' (p. 268).

The advantages and disadvantages of both types have been examined by teacher educators (e.g. Ur, 1996; Thornbury, 1999; Scrivener, 2005; Borg, 1999). Gower and Walters (1983) suggested that a deductive presentation is appropriate when the target structure is entirely new to learners but an inductive presentation is more effective if the learners are already familiar with the target forms. Ur (1996) suggests that the decision should be made depending on the situation and states that 'if the learners can perceive and define the rule themselves quickly and easily, then there is a lot to be said for letting them do so{...}but if they find this difficult, you may waste a lot of valuable class time on sterile and frustrating guessing or on misleading suggestions' (p. 83). However, some teacher educators encourage using an inductive approach. Scrivener (2005), for example, states 'explanation given before learners really know what is being discussed often seem to make no difference' (p. 267). Interestingly, however, grammar practice books tend to employ deductive presentation rather than inductive presentation. Ellis's (2002b) analysis of seven published grammar practice books found that only two of them employed inductive rule presentation. The advantages and disadvantages of each approach are summarized in Table 4.2. Each approach is then considered in greater detail below.

Deductive presentation

Deductive presentation involves a consideration of how rules are explained, the use of metalanguage and the provision of examples to support the explanation.

Table 4.2 Deductive and inductive presentation

	Deductive presentation	*Inductive presentation*
Advantages	• It is a quicker and easier way to teach the rule to learners. • It respects the intelligence and maturity of learners, especially adult learners. • It confirms many students' expectations about classroom learning, particularly adult learners or analytical learners who want to know 'what they are studying'. • Time-saving (explaining rules is usually quicker than guessing from examples). The class time can be used for more practice.	• Discovering rules by learners is likely to lead to more 'meaningful, memorable, and serviceable' knowledge (Thornbury, 1999: 54). • It involves greater depth of processing which assists memory. • It encourages the students' active involvement in grammar learning. • It is more challenging than simply receiving explanations. • It can be done collaboratively in the classroom. • Figuring out the rule by themselves might encourage learner autonomy. • Acquirers develop the skills needed to analyse language. • A discovery-based approach enables learners to recognize that grammar is 'conventional rather than logical' (Ellis, 2002b:165).
Disadvantages	• Grammar explanation tends to be teacher-fronted and does not actively involve learners. • Grammar explanation might be cognitively demanding for young learners. • Starting with grammar explanation might demotivate learners. • It leads to the belief that learning language involves just knowing the rules.	• Time consuming – it takes up time better spent on practice. • Inferring rules might result in learners misunderstanding the rule. • It places high demands on teachers for class preparation. • It might frustrate students who are used to a deductive type of learning.

RULE EXPLANATION

One major issue that teachers and material developers encounter is how detailed the rule explanation should be. This reflects whether to base the explanation of the rule on a 'descriptive grammar' or on a 'pedagogic grammar'. To illustrate the difference we will compare how 'plurals' are handled in the *Oxford English Grammar* (Greenbaum, 1996) and in *Impact Grammar* (Ellis and Gaies, 1999), a course book for low-intermediate learners of English. The former devotes seven pages for 'plurals'. These are summarized in Table 4.3. The latter provides a succinct explanation in less than a page. Both explanations refer to the key point – namely, that only count nouns can be pluralized. Both also refer to the different plural morphemes involved. However, there are some obvious differences. The descriptive grammar deals with the irregular plurals in great detail and also distinguishes written and phonological forms of the plural morphemes. In doing so, it makes use of extensive metalanguage (e.g. 'voicing of final consonant', 'collective nouns', 'mutation plurals' and 'sibilant'). The aim is to provide a comprehensive account of pluralization in English. In contrast, the pedagogic grammar only specifies the main categories of plural nouns, provides no account of the phonological variations and uses only simple metalanguage (e.g. 'countable nouns', 'singular' and 'plural'). The aim is to provide the learner with a clear explanation that accounts for the main features of pluralization.

Teacher educators (e.g. Swan, 1994; Thornbury, 1999; Ur, 1996) are very clear about what kind of explanation should be given to learners. They argue that descriptive rules of the kind found in the *Oxford English Grammar* are overwhelming for the learner and that, therefore, it is preferable to make use of simple, clearly formulated pedagogic rules of the kind found in *Impact Grammar*. However, they also consider what constitutes a 'good' pedagogic rule, suggesting that it needs to achieve a good balance between 'truthfulness' (as in descriptive rules) and 'usefulness' for L2 learners. Ur (1996), for example, proposed that a rule explanation should cover the great majority of instances learners are likely to encounter and some obvious exceptions, but avoid too much detail. She commented 'a simple generalization, even if not entirely accurate, is more helpful to learners than a detailed grammar-book definition' (p. 83). Thornbury (1999) likewise pointed to the need for a compromise between the truthfulness and the pedagogical usefulness of a rule. Drawing on Swan (1994), he proposed a number of criteria that could inform pedagogical rules:

- Truth: rules should be true to use in the real world.
- Demarcation: the limitations of the rule should be clearly presented.
- Clarity: ambiguity or obscure terminology should be avoided.
- Simplicity: rules should be simple enough for learners to understand.
- Conceptual parsimony: rule explanation should involve familiar concepts for the learner.
- Relevance: a rule should only include the points that the learners need to know. For example, some aspects of a linguistic rule might not be relevant to the learners whose L1 shares the same rule as the L2.

Table 4.3 Explanation of pluralization in a descriptive and pedagogic grammar

	Oxford English Grammar (Greenbaum, 1996: 100–101)	Impact Grammar (Ellis and Gaies, 1999)
General explanation	Count nouns make a distinction between singular and plural. Singular denotes one, and plural more than one (p. 100).	Countable nouns such as 'forest' and 'beach' can have a singular form ('a forest') and a plural form ('forests').
Regular and irregular forms	Regular plurals: 'in writing, the regular plural ends in -s'. Variations in writing and pronunciation are also explained.	You can make most countable nouns plural by adding -s.
	Irregular plurals: 1) voicing of final consonant, 2) mutations, 3) zero plurals, 4) foreign plurals, 5) uninflected plurals, 6) binary plurals, 7) inflected plurals, 8) collective nouns and 9) plurals of compounds.	Some nouns do not have a plural with -s. (irregular) Some nouns are same in the singular and the plural. Nouns that end in -ch or -sh add -es.
	Non-standard plurals: 1) zero plurals, 2) regular plurals, 3) double plurals, 4) mutation plurals, 5) plurals in -(e)n, and 6) plurals in -(e)r.	
Written rule for regular plurals	If a singular ends in a sibilant that is not followed by -e, add -es. A few nouns ending in -s have a variant in which the consonant is doubled before the inflection. If a sibilant is followed by -e, only -s is added.	
	If the singular ends in a consonant plus y, change the y to i and then add -es. Proper nouns are exceptions. If a vowel precedes the final y, the plural is regular.	
	For some nouns ending in -o, add -es. In some instances there is variation between -os and -oes.	

The problem facing teachers is how to satisfy all these criteria – in particular, how to balance 'truth' and 'demarcation' on the one hand and 'simplicity' and 'conceptual parsimony' on the other. Fortune (1998) explored how six popular grammar practice books handled five grammatical structures (i.e. conditional sentences, the passive voice, verb forms to express future meanings, present simple vs progressive, and countable and uncountable nouns). He found considerable variation in their treatment of these structures and noted that there was a tendency towards oversimplification and misleading explanations. For example, one book for intermediate-level learners only explained how to use articles with countable nouns and 'completely ignored' the zero article with uncountable nouns. Fortune suggested that this might cause learners to form a 'false dichotomy' (p. 78).

Grammar is not just about 'form', however. As we noted in Chapter 3, it is about how a specific grammatical form maps onto a specific meaning or meanings. This is fully recognized in the pedagogical literature. Larsen-Freeman (1995, 2003), for example, distinguished three dimensions of grammatical rules: form, meaning and function/use. 'Form' concerns the phonological, morphological, graphological and syntactic features of language. 'Meaning' refers to the semantic notions that grammatical forms express. 'Function/use' refers to when and why a particular grammatical structure is used in context. Celce-Murcia and Larsen-Freeman (1999) illustrate these three aspects of grammar in a pedagogic rule for English passive voice. The form of this structure consists of a subject, an auxiliary verb (*be* or *get*) with the past participle of the main verb, followed (optionally) by the particle *by* and a noun phrase. The semantic meaning conveyed by this passive construction is that the noun in subject position is the patient rather than the agent. There are several functions/uses of this construction – to avoid the need to specify the agent, to be evasive or tactful, or to provide objectivity. Larsen-Freeman (1995, 2003) makes a strong case for including all three dimensions in a pedagogical grammar. Clearly, this will satisfy the 'truth' criterion but it may also make it difficult to satisfy the 'simplicity' criterion as this account of the passive construction illustrates. The problem of how to balance these two criteria remains a matter of some controversy.

METALANGUAGE

The importance attached to simplicity in explanations of grammatical rules is reflected in the advice that the guides give about the use of metalanguage. In general, they advise against excessive use of metalanguage. For example, Scrivener (2005) suggested that grammar explanation should be 'simple, clear and short' (p. 267) but did not specifically address the use of metalanguage. Harmer (2007) claimed that 'few people are comfortable with grammatical explanations and terminology' (p. 53). Mohammed (1996) suggested that metalanguage poses 'an additional learning burden'. He argued that it constitutes 'a separate body of knowledge that has nothing to do with the way people actually process language' (p. 283).

Teachers themselves, however, vary in their attitude towards the use of metalanguage. Two surveys of English for Special Purposes (ESP) teachers in New Zealand and the UK found that many of the teachers thought metalanguage is useful but also acknowledged that it was difficult for some students. Borg (1998, 1999) reported that one teacher claimed that metalanguage assisted his teaching in a number of ways: (1) it provided an effective means for communicating about language, (2) it facilitated diagnostic work and (3) it helped learners to become autonomous investigators of language. However, another teacher thought that grammatical jargon was unnecessary, could alienate students and did not promote the use of the language. She avoided the use of technical terms but did respond to students' questions about grammatical concepts.

The ambivalent attitudes that some teachers have towards the use of metalanguage may reflect a tension between their 'peripheral beliefs' (often derived from the training they have received) and their 'core beliefs' (based on their own experience). As Phipps and Borg (2009) showed, teachers may believe that they 'should minimise the use of metalanguage when presenting grammatical structures' (a peripheral belief) but also believe that 'it is important to respond to students' expectations' (a core belief). When these beliefs are in conflict, they generally choose to act in accordance with their core beliefs. This study suggests that the pedagogical advice they had received had little effect on the actual use they made of metalanguage.

The guides focus on the teachers' use of metalanguage and have little to say about whether it is useful for the learners to learn metalanguage, although implicit in the advice they give to teachers is that metalanguage is of little value to learners. Teachers, however, often hold a different view. Alderson (1997), for example, reported that university teachers of foreign languages in the UK expected their students to have a sound knowledge of metalanguage and bemoaned the fact that in general they do not have it. Hu (2010) identified four advantages of learners having a good knowledge of metalanguage: (1) it supports the metalinguistic awareness that learners have developed in the process of acquiring L1 literacy, (2) it enables an explicit discussion of the structural and functional features of highly complex structures, (3) it enables the precise explanation and delimitation of metalinguistic generalizations and (4) it enables teachers to help their learners link up newly encountered structures with knowledge of the L2 that has already been acquired.

EXAMPLES

Presentation also involves providing examples of the target structure. Surprisingly, though, the teacher guides we have inspected have relatively little to say about the choice of examples. We will rely therefore on the findings of Ellis's(2002b) and Fortune's (1998) analyses of a representative sample of grammar practice books to discover how examples are handled in grammar pedagogy.

Ellis (2002b) identified three main methodological aspects for what he called 'data' (i.e. examples): 'source', 'text size' and 'medium' (see Figure 4.1). Source refers to whether the examples were 'authentic' (i.e. taken from texts for which there was a real context) or 'contrived' (i.e. the author of the grammar practice book had devised the sentences him or herself to illustrate the grammar point). Text size concerns whether the examples consisted of 'discrete sentences' or 'continuous text'. The medium of the examples can be written or oral.

Teachers are frequently encouraged to use authentic texts (see Chapter 7 for an in-depth discussion of the case for 'authenticity' in language teaching materials). However, Ellis's analysis found that contrived examples were much more common in grammar practice books. Fortune (1998) also found that

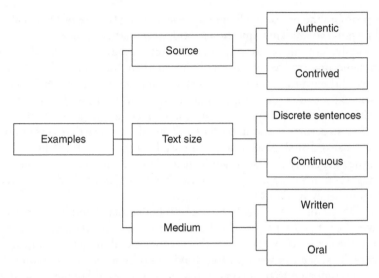

Figure 4.1 Methodological options for presenting examples (from Ellis, 2002b)

only two out of the six grammar practice books he analysed included authentic sources. Presumably, contrived examples are preferred as a matter of convenience (i.e. it is easier to concoct examples than locate them in authentic texts). Fortune (1998) also found that discrete, decontextualized sentences were common in traditional deductive types of grammar presentation. In the practice books, written examples proved more common than oral examples.

Inductive presentation

A common way of presenting a grammar structure inductively involves 'guided discovery'. The aim is to encourage learners to notice the target structure and think about it. Scrivener (2005), for example, offers a range of ways in which teachers can help learners to discover how a particular structure works (e.g. 'offer appropriate examples for analysis and discussion' and 'ask learners to analyse errors'). Scrivener recommends 'Socratic questioning' where the teacher takes the lead in helping learners to understand a new grammar point through a series of structured questions.

Inductive presentation can also take the form of 'consciousness-raising tasks' that students complete individually or in small group work. Ellis (1997: 160) defined a grammar consciousness-raising task as 'a pedagogic activity where the learners are provided with L2 data in some form and required to perform some operation on or with it, the purpose of which is to arrive at an explicit understanding of some linguistic properties of the target language'. The data can be spoken or written and authentic or contrived. Willis and Willis (1996) proposed a number of possible ways learners can be asked to operate on the data. These are summarized in Box 4.1.

Box 4.1 Ways of operating on data in a CR task

1. Identify/consolidate: students are asked to search a set of data to identify a particular pattern or usage and the language forms associated with it.
2. Classify (semantic; structural): students are required to work with a set of data and sort it according to similarities and differences based on formal or semantic criteria.
3. Hypothesis building/checking: students are given (or asked to make) a generalization about language and asked to check this against more language data.
4. Cross-language exploration: students are encouraged to find similarities and differences between patternings in their own language and patternings in English.
5. Reconstuction/deconstruction: students are required to manipulate language in ways which reveal underlying patterns.
6. Recall: students are required to recall and reconstruct elements of a text. The purpose of the recall is to highlight significant features of the text.

(Willis and Willis, 1996: 69)

As Willis and Willis (1996) noted, CR activities have been a part of language teaching for a long time. However, they appear to be becoming increasingly popular in ELT course books. Nitta and Gardner (2005), for example, reported that seven out of nine intermediate-level course books they examined employed grammar consciousness-raising tasks as the initial step in a presentation–practice approach.

Interpretation tasks (Ellis, 1995) are another type of task that can be used to inductively present a new grammatical structure. These differ from CR tasks in that they aim to help learners construct a form-function mapping but without formulating an explicit rule. That is, the emphasis is placed on simply inducing learners to pay attention to a particular feature in the input. They try to achieve this by enhancing occurrences of the feature in a text and by requiring some non-verbal or minimally verbal response from learners, to show they have successfully processed the target feature. Again, such tasks can constitute an alternative to the traditional production-based approach to teaching grammar (see Chapter 5) but can also be used in the first phase of a present–practice lesson. Nitta and Gardner found that interpretation tasks were frequently used in the course books they examined in the presentation stage.

PRACTICE

Practice is viewed as an essential component of a grammar lesson. Ellis (2002b) distinguished a number of options found in grammar practice books as shown in Figure 4.2. Production practice requires learners to produce sentences containing the target structure. In reception practice, learners are required to perform some activity to demonstrate they have understood sentences containing the target structure. Activities involving judgement ask learners to identify whether sentences containing the target structure are grammatical or ungrammatical. Each of these basic types of practice involves further options. Production can be 'controlled' or 'free': controlled activities provide students with a text of some sort (usually discrete sentences) and require them to manipulate it in some way (e.g. by simply repeating it or by filling in blank), while free production activities give the students the opportunity to construct their own sentences using the target structure.[1] Reception can be controlled (i.e. students are able to control the speed at which they have to process the sentences containing the target structure) or automatic (i.e. students are required to process the sentences in real time). Judgement tasks can simply ask learners to state whether a sentence is or is not grammatical or require them to correct the sentences judged to be ungrammatical.

An analysis of grammar practice materials shows that controlled practice activities dominate. Fortune's (1998) survey of six grammar practice books, for example, found that the two main types of practice were 'sentence completion' and 'gap filling'. Ellis's analysis of a similar range of textbooks found that all of them included controlled practice activities. Nitta and Gardner (2005) also found that what they called 'grammar exercises' figured in all but one of the nine books they investigated. Many of the books these authors examined also included free production activities. Almost invariably the controlled practice materials precede the free production materials.

The teacher guides recommend learners should first practice production of a target structure in a controlled manner before attempting to use it in free production. The aim is 'to get students to learn structures so thoroughly that they will be able to produce them correctly on their own' (Ur, 1996: 83).

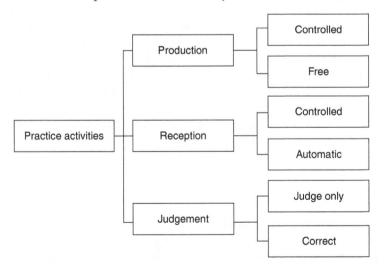

Figure 4.2 Methodological options in grammar practice activities (from Ellis, 2002b)

Learners need a 'bridge' to help them make the 'leap from form-focused accuracy work to fluent, but acceptable, production' (ibid.). This is very clearly the mainstream view of how to organize practice activities. However, there are dissenters. Tomlinson (2011), for example, argued that 'materials should not rely too much on controlled practice' (p. 22).

Explicit vocabulary instruction

The preceding discussion of how explicit language instruction is addressed in language pedagogy has focused exclusively on grammar. We will conclude with a few comments about explicit vocabulary instruction. We find a similar emphasis on present–practice–produce. Various proposals for how to group words for presentation can be found. McCarten (2007), for example, proposed three possible ways: real-world groups (e.g. body parts), language-based groups (e.g. part of speech, words with the same prefix or suffix) and personalized groups (e.g. students' favourite food). Presentation can again be deductive (e.g. the teacher provides a definition of the target words or uses pictures to show their meanings) or inductive (e.g. the learners are invited to infer the meanings of words from examples of their usage in sentences or longer texts). Another alternative is to invite learners to use a dictionary to find the meanings of the target words. As with grammar teaching, practice involves both controlled and free production activities. Again we see that controlled practice activities are dominant (see, for example, Yates, 2006). However, in contrast to grammar teaching, there is greater emphasis on receptive forms of practice (e.g. matching words with their definitions or identifying the word that does not belong in a group). Receptive practice typically precedes production practice, reflecting the belief that receptive knowledge of words precedes productive knowledge.

SLA perspectives on explicit language instruction

In this section we will consider in some depth theoretical positions and research relating to the explicit teaching of grammar. Then, more briefly, we will examine research on explicit vocabulary instruction.

Explicit grammar instruction

In SLA, the key issue concerns the role of explicit language instruction in assisting the development of implicit knowledge of L2 grammar. In Chapter 1, we provided definitions of implicit and explicit knowledge and also considered a number of 'interface positions'. We will begin this chapter with a brief review of these positions and point out their implications for instruction. We will then consider how Sociocultural Theory views the role of explicit instruction. Finally, we will examine the findings of research that has investigated the effect of explicit instruction on L2 acquisition.

The interface issue

The interface issue concerns the relationship between explicit and implicit L2 knowledge. We briefly considered the different positions in Chapter 1. Here we examine them in greater depth and also consider their relevance to explicit instruction.

THE NON-INTERFACE POSITION

This is the position promulgated by Krashen (1981), who views explicit and implicit knowledge as entirely distinct and thus dismisses the possibility of the former transforming into the latter. 'Learning', a conscious, intentional process, results in explicit knowledge; 'acquisition', an unconscious, incidental process results in implicit knowledge. Krashen acknowledges only a limited role for explicit instruction – to help learners 'learn' a few simple grammatical rules that they can then use to monitor their production when they are focused on form and have time to do so. In effect, the non-interface position rejects any major role for explicit grammar instruction in L2 acquisition.

THE STRONG INTERFACE POSITION

This claims that acquisition (especially by adult learners) commences with explicit, declarative knowledge which is then transformed into implicit knowledge through practice (DeKeyser, 1998). This position draws on skill-acquisition theory (see Chapter 5). It constitutes the primary theoretical justification for PPP as it claims that explicit instruction can 'bridge' the gap between explicit and implicit knowledge. It should be noted, however, that DeKeyser sees little merit in controlled practice activities. He argued that learners need to use their explicit knowledge as a 'crutch' while struggling to use the target structure in communication.

THE WEAK INTERFACE POSITION

This makes two claims. The first is that explicit knowledge evolves into implicit knowledge but only if the learner is ready to acquire the targeted feature. The second is that even if this does not occur immediately, explicit knowledge can facilitate cognitive processes such as noticing and noticing-the-gap (Schmidt, 1990; see Chapter 7) and so facilitate the long-term development of implicit knowledge. Ellis (1993) has drawn on the weak interface position to argue that explicit instruction should be restricted to helping learners form explicit knowledge and left it to the learner to use this knowledge to assist subsequent development of implicit knowledge. According to the weak interface position, then, PPP will only be effective if it is timed to coincide with the learners' readiness to acquire the target structure, which is impractical in most teaching contexts (Lightbown, 1985a). It supports the use of consciousness-raising tasks and interpretation tasks, deployed without any supporting practice activities, to assist learners to develop explicit knowledge of target features and notice them in the input.

These different positions support radically different views about explicit language instruction. The non-interface position proposes that explicit instruction is of little value. The strong interface position supports the view dominant in language pedagogy, namely that a grammatical structure should be first presented explicitly and then practised until it can be used accurately in free production. As we saw in Chapter 3, the underlying assumption of a grammatical syllabus aimed at implicit knowledge is that a strong interface is possible. The weak interface position supports an approach based on teaching explicit knowledge to assist learners to attend to grammatical forms in the input and thus facilitate the acquisition of implicit knowledge over time.

The discussion of the interface positions, however, does not take account of the different senses of 'acquisition': (1) the initial incorporation of a 'new' feature in the learner's interlanguage, (2) progress along a developmental sequence and (3) increased control of a grammatical feature that has already been partially acquired. By and large, the positions address only (1). However, even if instruction is powerless to ensure implicit knowledge of an entirely new feature – as claimed by the non-interface position – it may still be effective in assisting learners to progress along a developmental sequence and to achieve greater control over a feature that is already partially acquired. In other words, explicit instruction aids the *rate* of L2 development. Explicit instruction may also help learners to overcome premature fossilization (De Graaff and Housen, 2009).

Explicit grammar instruction and Sociocultural Theory

We introduced Sociocultural Theory in Chapter 1. Here we will see how it has been applied to the teaching of grammar. It emphasizes the importance of developing 'conceptually organized grammatical knowledge' (i.e. descriptions of grammatical features that explain in detail the link between form and semantic/functional concepts). It disputes the usefulness of 'rules-of-thumb' on the grounds that these may actually impede effective development of the target language. As Negueruela (2003) put it, simplified and reductive rules of the kind found in a pedagogic grammar 'depict language as a sedimented entity that appears to have a life of its own independent of people' (p. 83), and, thus, are potentially harmful for learners.

In 'concept-based instruction' (Lantolf and Thorne, 2006) the aim is to develop learners 'scientific knowledge' of a grammatical structure. This draws on the three principles of Systemic-Theoretical Instruction (STI) (Galperin, 1989, 1992): (1) instruction needs to be organized around coherent theoretical units, (2) the grammatical constructs should be presented in material form to learners by means of charts and diagrams and (3) to achieve full understanding learners need to verbalize the concept-based explanation as they try to apply it in practice activities. The latter principle is of special importance. It is through verbalizing explicit information about a grammatical structure that learners are able to internalize it and thus use it freely in communication. Lantolf and Thorne do not frame their theory of explicit grammar teaching in terms of implicit/explicit knowledge, but their proposal can be seen as compatible with a strong interface position.

Research studies investigating explicit grammar instruction

There is now an enormous body of research that has investigated the effects of 'form-focused instruction' (see Ellis, 2012 for a recent review). Our concern here is with a subset of this research, namely that which has investigated the effects of explicit instruction defined as instruction that involves 'explanation' with or without 'practice. We will not attempt an exhaustive review but rather consider the main findings and illustrate these through reference to a few key studies.

The role of metalanguage

Explanation involves metalanguage, so a good starting point is to consider what research has shown about the value of metalanguage for L2 learning. This has been investigated in correlational studies. The results of the research are somewhat mixed but in the case of adult learners there is clear evidence that an increase in the breadth and depth of explicit knowledge goes hand in hand with the acquisition of metalanguage (Ellis, 2004). The obvious explanation is that linguistic labels help sharpen learners' understanding of linguistic constructs.

Roehr's (2008) study illustrates this finding. She gave a German language test and a metalanguage test to sixty university students taking Advanced German at a British university. The language test had forty-five gap-fill and multiple-choice items testing grammar and vocabulary features commonly taught in German instruction for English speakers. The metalanguage test had fifteen items requiring the learners to correct, describe, and explain L2 features matching the language test and fifteen items requiring identification of the grammatical role of highlighted parts in sentences. Roehr found a strong correlation ($r = .81$) between the language and metalanguage tests.

Another finding is that knowledge of metalanguage correlates positively with general language proficiency. Elder and Manwaring (2004) investigated university students in Chinese courses in Australia and investigated the relationship between knowledge of grammatical terms and learners' subsequent performance on both continuous assessment tasks and end-of-semester Chinese language examinations. Knowledge of metalanguage was a better predictor of learning success than the ability to explain rules. This led Elder and Manwaring to suggest that it is the ability to understand and apply rules that knowledge of metalanguage assists, rather than the ability to articulate rules that is important. In another study, Elder (2009) reported a strong correlation between knowledge of metalanguage as measured by a Metalinguistic Knowledge Test and the scores on standard proficiency tests (e.g. TOEFL) for adult ESL learners in New Zealand.

These studies suggest that at least for some learners knowledge of metalanguage is useful. However, as always, care must be taken in interpreting correlational studies. We cannot be certain that it is metalanguage that contributes to depth of explicit knowledge and proficiency. It is also possible that learners' knowledge of metalanguage increases as a result of gains in explicit knowledge and proficiency.

Explicit explanation only

Several studies have investigated consciousness raising (CR) – that is, explicit explanation without any practice activities. CR can be direct (as in the case of deductive grammar teaching) or indirect (as in the case of inductive grammar teaching). Indirect CR involves asking learners to complete CR tasks. Such tasks are designed to assist learners' understanding of grammatical structures (i.e. their explicit knowledge) not their implicit knowledge. However, in accordance with the weak interface hypothesis, it is assumed that explicit knowledge will assist noticing and thus contribute to the acquisition of implicit knowledge over time.

In a series of studies, Fotos (1993) investigated the extent to which CR was effective in developing Japanese university students' explicit knowledge and whether this then helped them to notice the target features in subsequent input. Fotos and Ellis (1991) compared the effects of direct and indirect CR (involving CR tasks) on learners' explicit knowledge of dative alternation in English. They found both teacher-provided metalinguistic explanation and a CR task resulted in significant gains in understanding of the target structure, although the former seemed to produce the more durable gains. In a follow-up study that investigated the effects of the two types of CR on three grammatical structures (adverb placement, dative alternation and relative clauses), Fotos (1994) reported that both types were equally effective.

Three other studies suggest that CR tasks are an effective way of developing explicit knowledge. Mohamed (2001) compared direct grammar instruction and CR tasks. Her study involved fifty-one adult ESL learners in a New Zealand tertiary institution. Direct grammar instruction took the form of hand-outs explaining the target structures and giving examples. Indirect instruction involved the performance of CR tasks in small groups. Mohamed found that the majority of learners were successful in performing the CR tasks. Both groups gained in learning but the gains achieved through the CR tasks were significantly greater. Pesce (2008) compared the effects of direct instruction and CR tasks on learners' acquisition of Spanish past tenses (imperfect/preterit). Both groups of learners completed a pre-test, immediate post-test and delayed post-test. The group that completed the CR tasks outperformed the teacher-instructed group in both the immediate and the delayed post-tests.[2] Finally, Eckerth (2008) measured the effects of learners performing two CR tasks (a text reconstruction task and text-repair task) by means of a sentence-assembly test, which he considered provided a valid measure of explicit knowledge. An interesting finding of this study is not only that learners manifested significant gains of the structures targeted in the CR tasks, but also that 'non-predicted learning' took place of structures that were not targeted by tasks but that were attended to incidentally, when the learners performed the tasks interactively.

Fotos (1993) also investigated whether the explicit knowledge that learners had gained from completing CR tasks assisted 'noticing' of the target features. Several weeks after the learners had completed the CR tasks, they completed a number of dictations that included exemplars of the target structures and were asked to underline any particular aspects of language that they paid special attention to as they did the dictations. Fotos found that they underlined exemplars of the target structures much more frequently than other features.

These studies suggest that asking learners to complete CR tasks helps them to develop explicit knowledge of target grammar rules and that the knowledge they gain in this way can lead them to pay attention to exemplars of the rules in subsequent input. However, the studies did not demonstrate that the learners subsequently acquired implicit knowledge, as there was no subsequent test of learners' ability to use the target features in free communication. Thus, they do not constitute clear evidence in favour of the weak interface hypothesis. The studies also showed that direct CR without any practice can also contribute to learners' explicit knowledge.

Practice only

'Practice' can be defined as intentional and persistent activity involving production of a specific target feature with awareness and with the aim of mastering the use of the feature.[3] The Audiolingual Method (see Chapter 2) is premised on the assumption that practice of the controlled kind is sufficient for 'habit-formation' and that there is no need for explicit explanation. Only a few studies have investigated the effects of controlled practice by itself. These can be divided into studies that examine 'error-avoiding' and 'error-inducing' practice. The aim of the former is to prevent learners from making errors while the aim of the latter is to induce errors so they can then be corrected.

There is little evidence that error-avoiding controlled practice has much effect. Ellis (1984b) investigated whether there was any relationship between the number of times a group of ESL learners practised producing 'when' questions in a controlled teacher-led activity and their development of this structure. Somewhat surprisingly those students who had the fewest practice opportunities manifested greater development than those who received the most. Sciarone and Meijer (1995) investigated the effects of students' engaging in computer-based controlled practice exercises on learning. They found no difference in the test results of students who completed the exercises and those who did not. They noted that even the 'good' students in their sample did not appear to benefit from the practice.

In contrast, error-inducing practice combined with corrective feedback has been found to be effective. Tomasello and Herron (1988, 1989) compared the effects of error-avoidance and error-inducing instruction directed at helping students overcome problems resulting from overgeneralization or L1 transfer. In the former, the problems were explained and illustrated (i.e. explicit explanation plus examples). In the latter, learners were induced to make errors in controlled practice drills and then received immediate correction. The results showed that leading learners 'down the garden path' was the more effective. Tomasello and Herron suggested that the error-inducing practice was effective because it led to learners carrying out a cognitive comparison between their deviant production and the correct target-language utterances and also because it might have been more motivating.

All these studies investigated controlled practice without any explicit explanation. Another possibility is free practice without explicit information. This can still be considered a type of explicit instruction providing learners are made aware of what they are supposed to practise.[4] However, we have been unable to locate any studies that have investigated this option. All the studies where the treatment included free practice also provided explicit information about the target structure.

Explicit explanation with practice

The majority of explicit instruction studies in SLA have investigated the effects of a combination of explicit explanation and various types of practice activities but predominantly those of the free kind. We will consider a representative sample of these studies and then review a rather different study that investigated 'concept-based instruction'.

Two studies that investigated the effects of 'functional-analytic teaching' are worth considering in some detail, because they constitute excellent examples of how to implement this kind of teaching. Harley (1989) devised a set of functional-grammar materials to teach French immersion students the distinction between *passé composé* and *imparfait*. An introduction to the materials provided the learners with a description of the linguistic functions of the two verb tenses. There followed eight weeks of mainly free practice activities designed to focus attention on the uses of the tenses. Examples of these activities are:

> *Proverbes.* The activities...provided an opportunity to learn French proverbs along with opportunities for sustained oral production in referring to the past.
> (p. 341)

> *Souvenirs de mon enfance.* A series of activities designed to draw on students' personal experience in the creation of albums of childhood memories and in tape-recorded interviews.
> (p. 342)

The learners demonstrated significant improvement in the accurate use of the two verb tenses in a written composition, in a rational cloze test and in an oral interview. However, a control group subsequently caught up with the experimental group. Harley suggested that this group might also have subsequently received explicit instruction directed at the target features.

The functional grammar-teaching materials in Day and Shapson's (1991) study involved students planning an imaginary space colony. The learners were 315 Grade 7 early French immersion students. The instruction was extensive, covering three weekly 40–60 minute lessons over a six-week period. It included an introductory session where the various uses of conditional verb forms were summarized (i.e. there was some direct consciousness-raising) followed by practice in the use of the conditional in hypothetical situations and in polite requests. Day and Shapson listed the kinds of activities involved as follows:

> Presentation of an oral report describing and justifying the students' plan; making a model of the plan; preparation of a written report describing each part of the colony and its importance; and preparation of a newspaper article describing the life of the space pioneers.
>
> (p. 35)

Learners were tested by means of oral interviews which prompted them to rephrase what they had said more politely and a written composition with prompts. In both an immediate and a delayed post-test the difference between the experimental and control groups was not significant in the oral interview but it was significant in the written composition.

Both these studies were designed to overcome a limitation of immersion programmes (i.e. immersion learners' failure to achieve high levels of grammatical accuracy). Other studies have examined the effects of explicit instruction on the acquisition of various grammatical features by learners in intensive ESL classes in Canada. The instruction included explicit explanation but was primarily designed to provide opportunities for the learners 'to use language in meaningful and creative ways' (White et al., 1991: 420). We will consider one of these studies.

White et al. (1991) studied the effects of instruction on question formation (WH–and 'yes/no'). Five hours of instruction over a two-week period was provided. The first week consisted of explicit instruction on question formation. In the second week, learners engaged in various free production activities. The teachers were also encouraged to provide corrective feedback. Acquisition was measured by means of a cartoon task, a preference grammaticality judgement task and an oral communication task. In comparison to a control group, the experimental group showed substantial gains in accuracy on all the measures.

Further evidence of the effectiveness of explicit instruction can be found in Negueruela's (2003) study. As we saw earlier, concept-based instruction involves providing learners with a 'scientific description' of a target structure which they then verbalize in a practice activity. Negueruela (2003) taught a group of learners in a university Spanish language course. The class met three times a week for fifteen weeks. The explicit instruction involved a 'Schema for the Complete Orienting Basis of Action' for each grammatical area. For grammatical aspect, this consisted of a flow chart that led the learners through a series of questions to an understanding of when to use the *preterit* and *imperfect* tenses in Spanish.

Negueruela asked the students to verbalize the schema while carrying out a number of oral and written activities both in class and for homework. Altogether the students completed six verbalizations of the aspect schema. Learning was measured in two ways. One involved analysing the verbal explanations the learners produced as they performed the activities. Negueruela found that their initial explanations were simplistic and incomplete, reflecting the rules of thumb that appeared in the students' textbooks but later their explanations became more coherent and accurate. The second way of measuring learning involved inspecting the learners' oral and written production at the end of the course. Negueruela reported that the learners' could use the target features more accurately but this was more evident in writing than in speaking.

Spada et al. (2006) also found that asking learners to verbalize the explicit information they had been given assisted learning. In this study, francophone learners were asked to refer to an explicit explanation of the use of English possessive determiners (i.e. 'his' and 'her') while completing a cloze passage and then discussed their answers in class. This study, however, also involved other types of practice activities, including those based on input-processing.

The studies that we have considered indicate that explicit instruction, especially when it includes free practice activities, assists acquisition. This conclusion is also supported by the results of Norris and Ortega's (2000) often-cited meta-analysis. This examined a total of eighteen studies of explicit instruction involving twenty-five separate treatments, consisting mainly of explicit explanation with free production practice. It reported a large effect size (d = 1.22), which was substantially larger than the effect size reported for implicit instruction (d = 0.31). This is not surprising for, as Norris and Ortega pointed out, a typical explicit treatment involved rule presentation, focused practice, corrective feedback and rule review, whereas a typical implicit treatment consisted only of a single type of exposure. Thus, it is premature to conclude that explicit instruction is superior to implicit instruction.

Nevertheless, the studies we have considered and Norris and Ortega's meta-analysis do clearly demonstrate the efficacy of explicit instruction and thus appear to challenge the conclusion we reached in Chapter 3, namely the instruction based on a grammatical syllabus is unlikely to provide a sound basis for a language course because it does not accord with how learners learn grammar. To address this challenge we need to consider a number of issues concerning the research that has investigated explicit instruction.

Issues in explicit grammar instruction research

THE MEASUREMENT OF ACQUISITION

CR tasks only aim to promote learners' explicit knowledge. The studies that have investigated CR tasks have typically used grammaticality judgement tests to measure learning, on the grounds that these are likely to tap learners' explicit knowledge. The other forms of explicit instruction, however, have implicit knowledge (i.e. the ability to deploy grammatical forms accurately in communicative language use) as their goal. A crucial issue, then, is whether explicit instruction with or without practice does result in implicit knowledge. To assess this we need to examine the way that acquisition was measured in these studies.

Norris and Ortega (2000) distinguished four kinds of measures of acquisition: (1) metalinguistic judgements (e.g. grammaticality judgement tests), (2) selected responses (e.g. multiple choice questions), (3) constrained constructed responses (e.g. fill-in-the-gap items) and (4) free constructed responses (e.g. tasks eliciting spontaneous oral production). They report the effects of instruction for each of these measures. The effect size for free constructed responses ($d = 0.55$), which Norris and Ortega considered the best measure of implicit knowledge, was much lower than effect sizes for the other three measures. In other words, explicit instruction has much less effect on learners' ability to use the target structures accurately in spontaneous oral production, the best measure of implicit knowledge. Nevertheless, it does have some effect. Ellis (2002a) examined eleven studies that included a measure of learning based on free constructed responses and found that six of them reported accuracy gains in oral production. A reasonable conclusion is that explicit instruction has a strong effect on explicit knowledge but also contributes to implicit knowledge. But in what sense does it contribute to the acquisition of implicit knowledge? To answer this question we will return to the definitions of 'acquisition' we gave earlier in this chapter and consider whether explicit instruction has any effects on the sequence of acquisition.

THE EFFECT OF EXPLICIT INSTRUCTION ON THE SEQUENCE OF ACQUISITION

In Chapter 3, we saw that the acquisition of implicit knowledge of a grammatical structure is a gradual, dynamic process involving transitional stages. It follows that if explicit instruction is to have an effect, it must do so by assisting learners to progress along an acquisition sequence. The studies that we have examined in this chapter, however, measured acquisition in terms of accurate language use rather than in terms of whether learners advance along a developmental sequence. Two studies (Pienemann, 1984; Spada and Lightbown, 1999) have shown that there are developmental constraints on whether explicit instruction is effective but also that it can help learners move on to a new stage if they are developmentally ready to do so.

Perhaps, though, the problem of developmental readiness only arises if the instruction is directed at an entirely 'new' structure. It may be less of a problem if the instruction addresses a structure that learners have begun to acquire, as they will already have gained a foothold on the acquisition ladder and the instruction can help them climb higher. In fact just about all the studies we have considered have examined the effect of instruction on partially acquired structures. The increases in accuracy that they reported may have arisen because the learners were developmentally ready to advance to the final target-language stage. We know of no studies that have investigated whether explicit instruction enables learners to acquire a completely new grammatical structure.

THE DURABILITY OF THE EFFECTS OF EXPLICIT INSTRUCTION

If explicit instruction is to be truly useful, its effect must be durable. This is why many of the explicit instruction studies included delayed as well as immediate post-tests. Norris and Ortega's (2000) meta-analysis of twelve studies that reported results for both immediate and delayed post-tests showed there was a decrease but that this was relatively small. They also noted that the decrease was less in studies with longer-term treatments (i.e. three hours or more in duration) than in studies where the instruction lasted less than two hours. Clearly, then, the effects of instruction are often durable and in some cases (e.g. Harley, 1989) become even stronger over time. Again, though, this applies only to structures that learners had already begun to acquire.

Also sometimes the effects of instruction atrophy over time. For example, White (1991) found that gains in the correct positioning of adverbs were largely lost five months after the instruction. Lightbown (1983) suggested that the durability of instructional effects depends on whether the instruction includes communicative activities and also on whether there is continued exposure to the target feature in communication after the instruction is over. Implicit knowledge is not easily lost once acquired whereas explicit knowledge of grammar, like other declarative facts, is easily forgotten. This suggests that in some cases at least the type of knowledge that results from explicit instruction is of the explicit kind.

The length of the instruction

The length of the instructional treatment in the studies we have considered varies considerably. The studies that investigated CR tasks were of relatively short duration (less than an hour). Some of the studies involving explicit explanation and practice activities lasted for weeks (e.g. in Harley's study the instruction continued for eight weeks). Does the length of the instruction have any impact on its effect? It is reasonable to suppose that the longer the instruction is, the more effective it will be. In fact Norris and Ortega's meta-analysis found the opposite. The effect sizes of 'brief' treatments (i.e. less than an hour) and 'short' treatments (between one and two hours) were considerably greater than effect sizes of 'medium' treatments (i.e. three to six hours) and 'long' treatments (i.e. seven hours or longer). However, Norris and Ortega cautioned against concluding that short treatments are better. They suggested that various factors such as the nature of the target structures investigated moderate the effect that the length of the instruction has on learning. For example, simple structures such as plural-s may benefit from a 'brief' treatment whereas complex structures such as relative clauses may not benefit much even from a 'long' treatment. Day and Shapson (1991), for example, found that their lengthy instruction directed at hypothetical French verb forms did not result in improved accuracy in free oral production.

Choice of target structure

In other words, the effectiveness of explicit instruction may depend on the choice of target structure. Some structures are inherently more difficult to teach than others. This was investigated in another meta-analysis carried out by Spada and Tomita (2010). They examined the target structures in a number of studies and attempted to distinguish them in terms of their complexity (see Table 4.4). Surprisingly, they found that explicit instruction directed at complex forms had the largest effect on measures based on free construction.

It is not easy, however, to decide what constitutes a simple or a complex structure. Spada and Tomita classified structures according to the number of transformations involved but this would seem a doubtful metric. It inevitably results in syntactical features being classified as more complex than morphological features. In fact, though, many of the morphological features they labelled 'simple' in Table 4.4 are late acquired and so can be considered 'complex'. Even advanced learners, for example, have continuing problems with prepositions. It is also possible that what constitutes a simple or complex structure will differ for explicit and implicit knowledge as Ellis (2006) suggested. He pointed out, for example, that third person-*s* is easy to learn as explicit knowledge but difficult to acquire as implicit knowledge.

Some conclusions

It is not easy to reach clear conclusions from the research that has investigated explicit grammar instruction. Determining whether explicit instruction 'works' requires considering whether it is directed at learners' implicit or explicit knowledge. With this in mind, we propose the following tentative conclusions:

* Explicit instruction can help learners develop explicit knowledge of grammatical features. All the interface positions acknowledge this. Also, both CR studies and explicit-explanation-plus-practice studies provide clear evidence of it.

Table 4.4 Simple and complex features (Spada and Tomita, 2010: 273)

Simple features	Complex features
Tense	Dative alternation
Articles	Question formation
Plurals	Relativization
Prepositions	Passives
Subject–verb inversion	Pseudo-cleft sentences
Possessive determiners	
Participial adjectives	

- There is also evidence that explicit instruction plus practice – especially when this includes opportunity to use the target structure in communicative tasks – can contribute to the development of implicit knowledge. However, the research only shows that this occurs if the target features had already been partially acquired prior to the instruction. This is demonstrated in the gains in accuracy evident in 'free construction responses'. It is also demonstrated by studies that show explicit instruction can help learners progress along a developmental sequence. However, it is less clear that explicit instruction results in implicit knowledge of those grammatical features that are entirely new to learners.
- Whether the effects of explicit instruction are durable may depend on the extent to which learners have continued exposure to the feature and opportunity to use it subsequent to the period of instruction. This suggests that explicit instruction may be insufficient to ensure 'full' acquisition, even when directed at features that have been partially acquired prior to the instruction.
- Knowledge of metalanguage may be useful – at least for older learners. It can assist the learning of explicit knowledge.
- It may also be helpful if learners are asked to verbalize the grammatical explanation they have been given while performing a communicative task. Sociocultural theorists claim this aids 'internalization'.
- Explicit instruction consisting only of controlled practice has not been found to be effective.
- Some grammatical features are more 'teachable' than others and the effect of explicit instruction varies according to the choice of grammatical target. To date, however, there is no *a priori* metric for determining which structures are amenable to instruction and which ones are not. The extent to which a grammatical feature is teachable may also depend on whether the aim is to develop explicit or implicit knowledge. Some structures may have to be learned implicitly.
- There is currently no clear evidence to show what effect the length of the explicit instruction has on learning. Many of the studies have involved instruction that is both extensive and intensive. It is reasonable to suppose that instruction directed at developing implicit knowledge will need to be more extensive than that aimed at explicit knowledge.

Explicit instruction clearly helps learners to acquire grammar. It contributes to their explicit knowledge and, if a learner is 'ready', can also lead to implicit knowledge. However, there is no clear evidence that teaching entirely 'new' structures results in implicit knowledge and given what is known about the gradual, dynamic nature of L2 acquisition (see Chapter 3) it is doubtful that it can do so.

Explicit vocabulary instruction

There is a broad consensus among L2 vocabulary researchers that explicit vocabulary instruction is desirable and that implicit instruction by itself may be insufficient to enable learners to build a large lexicon. Laufer (2005), for example, identified a number of limitations of implicit instruction: learners may not pay attention to new words if they can understand the overall message, they do not engage sufficiently with new words even if they succeed in guessing their meanings from context, and they may not meet new words a sufficient number of times to remember them. As Elgort and Nation (2010) pointed out, 'deliberate learning can be used to quickly learn the 2,000 most frequent word families in English' (p. 101) and can also at more advanced stages promote depth of knowledge of words that were first encountered incidentally.

Explicit vocabulary instruction involves deciding which lexical items to teach, which aspects of these items are amenable to explicit instruction, and which kinds of instructional activities to employ. We will consider a number of theoretical positions and research relating to each of these.

Choice of items

One of the key issues is whether or not to teach words in lexical sets (e.g. *apple*, *pear*, *banana* in a 'fruit' set). Interference Theory (Anderson, 2003; Baddeley, 1997) suggests that teaching words in a lexical will not be effective. The theory assumes that 'as similarity increases between targeted information and other information learnt either before or after the targeted information, the difficulty of learning and remembering the targeted information also increases' (Papathanasiou, 2009: 313). In other words, it will be easier to learn a set of unrelated words than a set of semantically related items. In general, research has supported the theory. For example, Erten and Tekin (2008) found that fourth grade learners demonstrated shorter response times and better learning of words in an unrelated set. Papathanasiou (2009), however, suggested that it might depend on the proficiency level of the learner. If learners had no prior knowledge of words in a semantic set, they were likely to experience problems in learning them. However, if they already knew a number of the words, they would be able to add the new words to their existing store. In other words, interference only arises if learners have not yet established a mental set.

Another possibility is teaching words in a thematically related set (e.g. *blackboard*, *chalk*, and *get into groups* in a 'classroom set'). In this kind of set words belonging to different parts of speech can be included. Tinkham (1997) reported a study that showed that teaching words in thematically related sets facilitates learning. Al-Jabri (2005) compared four conditions – presenting words (1) in a semantic set, (2) in an unrelated set, (3) in a thematic set and (4) contextually (i.e. thematically unrelated words were presented in a reading passage). Learning was greatest in the case of (2) and (3), followed by (1), and least effective in the case of (4). However, the learners' proficiency was again a factor. There were no statistically significant differences in the most advanced group of learners.

The above studies indicate that: (1) for beginner learners, semantic clusters are more difficult to learn than thematic clusters or unrelated words but (2) for more advanced learners it makes little difference how words are grouped. However, it is not yet clear how well established a mental set needs to be to provide a foundation for the addition of new related items.

Focus of instruction

There are various types of word knowledge. Nation (2001) identified eight aspects of word knowledge relating to the form, meaning and use of a word. These concern both 'breadth' of knowledge (i.e. how many words a learner knows) and 'depth' of knowledge (i.e. how many aspects of a word a learner has mastered). Schmitt (2008) considered that the 'form-meaning link is the first and most essential lexical aspect which must be acquired' (p. 333) and argued that explicit instruction was best equipped to achieve this. He suggested that the more 'contextualized' aspects of vocabulary (e.g. collocation) cannot be easily taught explicitly and are best learned implicitly through extensive exposure to the use of words in context. In other words, he saw explicit and implicit approaches for teaching vocabulary as complementary.

There is plenty of evidence to suggest that explicit teaching of the form-meaning link is effective. Laufer (2005) reviewed a number of studies. These showed that an explicit focus on vocabulary led to gains ranging from 13 per cent to 70 per cent, depending on whether receptive or productive knowledge was tested and whether the instruction also involved meaning-related tasks as well as exercises. This level of learning is much higher than that reported from studies of incidental vocabulary learning from context.

Effective learning activities

There is some evidence that deliberate paired-associate learning of the kind supported by behaviourist learning theory is an efficient and effective way of learning new words (Elgort, 2011). However, there is also evidence to suggest that learning is more effective when it involves deeper engagement with new words. Laufer and Hulstijn (2001) proposed the Involvement Load Hypothesis to explain the differential effect of different kinds of instructional activities on word learning. This proposes that the effectiveness of instruction depends on 'need' (i.e. whether the instructional activity creates a need to learn the word), 'search' (whether the activity involves learners searching for the meaning of a word as opposed to being just given it) and 'evaluation' (whether the activity requires learners to assess the appropriateness of a word for a particular context). They then examined a range of studies to determine the relative effectiveness of different learning techniques. They concluded that activities that involved more need, search and evaluation were more effective. For example, Hulstijn et al.'s (1996) study showed that learning was greater if learners had to look words up in a dictionary (involving 'search') than if the meanings of the words were provided in a gloss (no 'search'). This hypothesis emphasizes the importance of 'engagement'. It can explain why receptive activities by themselves may not be sufficient to ensure productive knowledge of L2 words. To develop productive knowledge learners need to engage in production activities.

Psycholinguistic processing studies (e.g. Jiang, 2002) have shown that the learners' L1 vocabulary is active when processing L2 vocabulary. This suggests that presenting the meanings of new L2 words through their translation equivalents is an effective way of teaching them. Schmitt (2008) reviewed a number of other studies that have investigated comparative ways of presenting new words to learners and concluded that using the L1 is a 'sensible way' of establishing an initial form-meaning link. We will explore the role of the L1 in L2 learning more fully in Chapter 9.

Evaluating the pedagogical claims

We return now to examine the pedagogical issues outlined earlier, in the light of what we have found out about the role of explicit language instruction in the L2 acquisition of grammar and vocabulary. By and large, the teacher guides have taken no account of the SLA research that has investigated the effects of explicit instruction. Their recommendations reflect what seems to have become 'received opinion' about how to teach grammar and vocabulary.[5]

Which type of grammatical description is appropriate?

As we have seen, the teacher guides favour simplified explanations of grammatical rules based on pedagogical grammar rather than full explanations based on descriptive grammar. An inspection of many of the studies that have investigated explicit instruction shows that, in general, they have also favoured presenting pedagogical rules. This is true of both the CR-task studies and the studies that have investigated explicit explanation combined with practice.

There is much to be said in favour of pedagogical rules if the aim is to develop explicit knowledge or provide a declarative basis for attempting to proceduralize knowledge through practice. However, we have seen that sociocultural theorists take a very different view, arguing that learners should be given 'scientific descriptions' and then be encouraged to verbalize these as they perform communicative tasks. Negueruela's study suggests that for some learners – for example, university students taking foreign language classes – such an approach is both viable and effective. It is doubtful, however, whether concept-based language teaching of the kind advocated by Lantolf and Thorne is appropriate for all learners, although the idea of asking learners to verbalize whatever type of explanation they are given is a powerful one and worth experimenting with. There is no consideration of this possibility in the guides.

More research is needed to probe the possibilities of using scientific descriptions with different types of learners. Research that investigates the effect of explaining rules with varying degrees of truthfulness/usefulness would also be helpful. At the moment there is little hard evidence to show whether the type of explanation affects learning.

Is there a role for metalanguage?

Many teacher educators suggest that metalanguage should be used sparingly on the grounds that it plays no role in 'real language use'. SLA studies, however, have shown that knowledge of metalanguage correlates with learners' L2 proficiency. Support for the use of metalanguage also comes from sociocultural theorists' claims about the need for scientific descriptions.

It would seem, then, that there is a role for teaching metalanguage. However, its role needs to be clearly defined and understood. Clearly, teaching metalanguage as an end in itself is of little value. However, if it is taught to help the development of learners' explicit knowledge of grammatical rules, it is likely to be useful. Knowledge of technical terms can help learners construct clear and accurate declarative rules. Ultimately, the case for or against metalanguage depends on whether explicit knowledge is seen as playing a part in the learning process. We have seen that both cognitive and sociocultural theories claim that explicit knowledge can contribute to the acquisition of implicit knowledge – by providing a 'crutch' to aid proceduralization (DeKeyser), by fostering noticing and noticing-the-gap (Ellis), or as a tool for mediating internalization (Lantolf and Thorne). It also can enhance target-like performance by enabling learners to monitor their production for accuracy (Krashen). Perhaps, then, metalanguage deserves a more thoughtful treatment in the pedagogic literature. As we saw from Borg's (1988, 1999) studies, some teachers and learners recognize that metalanguage is both needed and helpful.

Should explicit explanation be inductive or deductive?

Both teacher educators and SLA researchers recognize the value of inductive grammar presentation. Teacher guides often recommend providing learners with opportunities to induce grammatical rules rather than the teacher simply explaining them. Many grammar practice books employ consciousness-raising tasks in the 'presentation' stage of PPP. SLA studies investigating consciousness-raising tasks suggest that CR tasks are as – and sometimes more – effective than direct grammar instruction.

In pedagogic accounts of grammar teaching, inductive activities are largely seen as one way of implementing the presentation stage in a PPP lesson. In contrast, in SLA research, inductive activities in the form of CR tasks are seen as comprising an effective teaching strategy by themselves. Ellis (1991) drew a clear distinction between instruction based on CR tasks and practice, arguing that practice activities frequently fail in their goal of eliciting accurate production of the target feature and that, therefore, an approach that focuses on the inductive learning of explicit rules is preferable. It is, of course, premature to dismiss practice activities (see the following section) but there is surely room for an approach that emphasizes understanding of a grammatical feature rather than insisting on premature production.

There are, of course, limitations to the use of CR tasks, which Ellis (1991) acknowledged:

- CR tasks do not guarantee acquisition of targeted features as implicit L2 knowledge (that is not its aim).
- Some rules may be too complex to be learned explicitly.
- CR tasks are better suited to older learners (but there is the possibility of constructing CR games for children).
- Completing CR tasks is time-consuming; direct explanation may be more efficient.
- While CR tasks are likely to appeal to learners with an analytic/field independent style, they may not appeal to learners with a more experiential/ field dependent learning style.

There is, however, growing interest in the use of CR tasks as an alternative to PPP and they deserve greater consideration in mainstream discussions of grammar teaching.

There is a need for more research investigating not just the product of inductive and deductive presentations of grammatical rules but also the processes involved in both. As Shulman and Keislar (1966) pointed out:

> Just because teaching is inductive, it does not follow that the learner is discovering. Conversely, simply because the teacher is instructing didactically, discovery experiences on the part of the learner are not precluded.
>
> (p. 28)

Eckerth's (2008) study demonstrated the importance of examining the interactions that learners engage in when they perform CR tasks as well as the learning that results. Similar studies examining inductive presentation are needed.

How useful is practice?

We have seen that there is very little evidence to support the use of controlled practice activities although they continue to find a place in pedagogic accounts of grammar teaching and in grammar practice materials. Lightbown (1985a), in her own review of what SLA research offers language pedagogy, concluded that practice does not make perfect. Later (Lightbown, 2000), however, she modified this claim by noting that she was thinking exclusively of controlled practice activities such as those that figure in the Audiolingual Method. She went on to state that 'when "practice" is defined as opportunities for meaningful language use (both receptive and productive) and for thoughtful, effortful practice of difficult language features, then the role of practice is clearly beneficial and even essential' (p. 443). In other words, what is termed 'free practice' in pedagogic circles is not only helpful but also necessary. There is plenty of research evidence to support such a claim. Perhaps, some thought could be given to modifying the traditional PPP sequence by eliminating the central 'P' (i.e. moving directly from presentation to free production practice). In effect, this would amount to 'task-supported language teaching' (see Chapter 6).

There are two important caveats, however. Even free, meaningful practice has its limitations, as Lightbown (2000) acknowledged, because it does not always ensure high levels of fluency and accuracy in the use of the target structure. One reason for this is 'developmental readiness'. Any type of grammar teaching will only be effective if learners are developmentally primed to incorporate the target structure into their interlanguage systems. The difficulty of determining whether learners are developmentally ready is one of the reasons why some SLA researchers (e.g. Long, 1988) have argued against grammatical syllabuses and explicit instruction. The second caveat, which is closely related to the first, is that presentation combined with meaningful practice may not be very effective in teaching 'new' grammatical structures. No amount of meaningful practice will absolve learners from having to progress through developmental sequences. At best, it can only help learners advance along them. One conclusion that might be drawn from this is that practice should not be directed at new structures but rather in helping learners achieve greater accuracy in the use of structures that they have already begun to acquire. It was this reasoning that led Ellis (2002a) to suggest that the teaching of grammar should be delayed until 'learners have developed a sufficiently varied lexis to provide a basis for rule extraction' (p. 23). In other words, it might be better to focus on lexis (including formulaic chunks) with beginners. This position, which is clearly in opposition to the advice found in the teacher guides, was the conclusion reached in Chapter 3.

How should vocabulary be taught?

The teaching of grammar holds a central place in most accounts of language pedagogy. However, there is increasing recognition of the importance of teaching vocabulary as reflected in both the teacher guides (see, for example, Hedge, 2000) and the growing number of vocabulary textbooks on the market (e.g. Redman, 2003; McCarthy and O'Dell, 2010). The research indicates that explicit instruction of vocabulary is helpful but that it needs to be supported by continued contextual exposure to the words taught. The research also supports a number of other points not generally reflected in the textbooks:

- Words are best taught in unrelated or thematic sets rather than in semantic clusters unless learners already have a well-established lexicon.[6]
- An effective way of building initial form-meaning connections is through L1 equivalents.

The research also points to the kind of practice activities that are most likely to foster learning. While paired-associate learning activities can be helpful, activities that involve 'engagement' with the target words in terms of need, search and evaluation are also needed. As was found to be the case with grammar teaching, meaningful practice is more likely to be effective than controlled practice. Practice must also be intensive. Learners need repeated opportunities to encounter and use new words. Finally, the research suggests that explicit instruction cannot handle some aspects of vocabulary such as collocation and thus needs to be complemented with plentiful opportunity for incidental learning – for example, through extensive reading materials (see Chapter 7).

Conclusion

The teacher guides suggest the following about explicit grammar teaching: (1) the explanation of grammar points should be based on pedagogic grammar rather than descriptive grammar, (2) use of metalanguage should be limited, (3) guided discovery is an effective way of presenting a grammatical structure, (4) class time should be spent mainly on practice and (5) there should be a progression from controlled to free practice. However, grammar practice textbooks do not always follow this advice. For example, they favour deductive presentations of grammar points rather than guided discovery and they give greater emphasis to controlled than to free practice. As for explicit vocabulary instruction, the guides recommend teaching different aspects of words in semantic sets and do not clearly set limits on what aspects of vocabulary can be taught explicitly.

SLA research gives clear support to the explicit instruction of both grammar and vocabulary. Explicit instruction serves as one way of implementing Principle 3 – 'Instruction need to ensure that learners focus on form'. However, the research also challenges much of the received opinion found in the teacher guides. It suggests that there is merit in teaching explicit knowledge of grammar as an end in itself and in supporting this with teaching some metalanguage. It casts doubt on the value of the second P (controlled practice) in the PPP sequence. The research also suggests that explicit instruction is much more likely to be effective if it is directed at grammatical features that learners have partially acquired, rather than at new features. Thus, the conclusion reached in the previous chapter – namely that a grammatical syllabus is incompatible with how implicit knowledge of an L2 is acquired – remains intact as such a syllabus assumes the teaching of new structures. Explicit grammar instruction has a place in language teaching but not based on a grammatical syllabus. Instead it should draw on a checklist of problematic structures and observational evidence of their partial acquisition. In the case of vocabulary, however, explicit instruction can usefully draw on predetermined lists of words.

We have used the word 'challenge' advisedly in reaching these conclusions: we do not wish to recommend the abandonment of received opinion. We recognize that the research has produced mixed results and does not support unequivocal positions. But we would like to see the assumptions that underlie some of the established opinions about how to teach grammar and vocabulary questioned and some of the instructional options the research lends support to given consideration.

Notes

1 Finer grained distinctions for 'controlled' and 'free production' are possible. For example, Ur (1996) distinguished six types on a continuum from 'controlled drills' to 'free discourse' (see Ur, 1996: 84).
2 Pesce measured learning of both syntactical and morphological aspects of the Spanish verbs. The advantage for the CR group was evident for both aspects in the immediate and delayed post-tests. However, in the case of the syntactical features it was only evident in the immediate post-test.
3 This definition of 'practice' is overly narrow. We recognize that practice can also be receptive. However, we have elected not to consider this type of practice in this chapter for two reasons. It does not figure in the pedagogic guides and we deal with it in Chapter 5 when we discuss comprehension-based approaches to language teaching.
4 'Free practice' activities need to be distinguished from 'focused tasks' (see Chapter 6). The crucial difference is the instructional purpose. Free practice activities are directed at intentional learning – the learner is aware of what they are supposed to be practising. Focused tasks are directed at incidental learning – the learner is not made aware of the target feature. Focused tasks constitute a form of implicit instruction as defined by De Graaff and Housen (2009).
5 Hedge (2000) is an exception to this generalization. She did preface her own comments about grammar teaching with an account of how learners learn grammar through reference to such constructs as 'noticing', 'sequence of acquisition' and 'automatizing'. She also drew on ideas about 'consciousness-raising' in SLA.
6 Nation (2000), however, argued that it may not be realistic to expect teachers to avoid teaching words in semantic sets totally and suggested a number of ways in which the interference that this might cause could be mitigated (e.g. by presenting the items at different times and in different contexts).

DISCUSSION QUESTIONS

1. What are the major differences between implicit knowledge and explicit knowledge? Which type of knowledge do you think should be the ultimate goal of language teaching?
2. Which teaching approaches, deductive or inductive, do you support? Why?
3. What are the advantages and disadvantages of using a 'descriptive grammar' and 'pedagogic grammar' in grammar teaching?
4. What are the major differences between the perspectives of teacher educators and SLA researchers regarding the value of metalanguage in L2 learning?
5. Choose a particular type of students you are familiar with (e.g. secondary school students in your country) and discuss to what extent metalanguage would be of value for these students. Give your reasons.

6. What differences are there in the views about the value of 'controlled practice' between the teacher guides and SLA researchers? What is your own view about controlled practice activities?

7. Which of the three interface positions would you support? Why?

8. What is 'consciousness raising (CR)'? In what ways can this contribute to L2 acquisition?

9. What has SLA research shown about the effects of 'practice only' (i.e. with no grammar explanation or free production activities) on L2 acquisition?

10. This chapter discusses a number of different deductive approaches for teaching grammar (i.e. 'explicit explanation' combined with 'practice'). What are these different approaches? Which approach do you favour? Why?

11. This chapter discusses a number of issues that need to be considered when designing studies investigating the effects of explicit instruction. What are these issues and how can they be addressed?

12. How does the length of instruction or choice of target structure influence the effect of explicit instruction on L2 acquisition?

13. Why is it necessary to distinguish the effect that explicit instruction has on grammar and vocabulary learning?

14. Consider the pros and cons of 'teaching words in set'.

15. Discuss the kinds of activities that you consider most appropriate for explicit vocabulary teaching.

5 Comprehension-based and production-based approaches to language teaching

Introduction

In the last two chapters we examined to what extent linguistic syllabuses and explicit instruction are compatible with how learners learn a second language (L2). In this chapter we switch attention to the methodology of language teaching. As we have seen, linguistic syllabuses are traditionally implemented by means of a production-based methodology (i.e. the specific linguistic items listed in the syllabus are taught by means of activities that require learners to produce them). However, it is also possible to implement such syllabuses by means of activities that require learners to comprehend input that has been especially designed to help them process a specific target feature. We will ask whether such an approach accords with the way in which learners acquire an L2 and whether it is more effective than a production-based approach.

Comprehension-based instruction (CBI) and production-based instruction (PBI) can figure in the teaching of any aspect of language (e.g. grammar, vocabulary, pronunciation or notions/functions), although by and large they have been used to teach grammar. An inspection of course books and the teacher education literature (e.g. Ur, 1996), however, show that PBI is the dominant approach (see Ellis 2002b). We will examine whether this is justified.

This chapter first provides definitions of CBI and PBI. It then examines the historical contexts of the two types of instruction and considers them from a pedagogical perspective. This will include a detailed account of the major ways in which the two types of instruction are currently realized – Processing Instruction in the case of CBI and present–practice–produce (PPP) in the case of PBI. This section of the chapter concludes with a summary of the key pedagogical issues surrounding the two approaches. We then move on to consider the SLA theories that inform CBI and also review the empirical research that has compared the effects of CBI and PBI on L2 acquisition. The chapter concludes by revisiting the key pedagogical issues from the perspective of the SLA theories that inform these methodologies.

Definition of CBI and PBI

CBI and PBI are two different ways of intervening directly in interlanguage development. The essential difference between them rests on whether production is or is not required. Comprehension-based activities are designed to provide learners with input only. However, they do not proscribe production: learners are free to engage in both social and private speech when responding to the input. Production-based activities also provide learners with input but in addition they require a response involving production. CBI can be implemented solely through one-way interaction (i.e. teacher to students) or it can also involve two-way interaction if students elect to respond verbally to the input. PBI invariably involves two-way interaction between teacher and students or between students working in pairs or groups.

CBI and PBI can be realized in a number of different ways. For example, Total Physical Response (Asher, 1969) and Processing Instruction are both types of CBI, as both require learners to demonstrate comprehension of the input they receive and both avoid requiring any production of the target features. The Audiolingual Method is production-based as its drill activities (e.g. repetition, substitution and transformation drills) involve intensive production practice. Present–practice–produce (PPP) is also production-based as it involves controlled production in the second phase and free production in the last phase. Task-based teaching, however, can be either comprehension-based (i.e. involving input-based tasks) or production-based (i.e. involving output-based tasks). We will discuss task-based teaching and these two types of tasks in detail in Chapter 6.

CBI and PBI can entail 'focused' and/or 'unfocused' instruction. Focused instruction involves the pre-selection of target language features in accordance with a linguistic syllabus, whereas in unfocused instruction there is no pre-selection of target features. Unfocused CBI and PBI require a task-based syllabus and activities designed to expose learners to general samples of the target language in the case of CBI, or elicit free production of the target language in the case of PBI. For example, unfocused CBI can be implemented through listening and reading activities involving texts that have not been selected to teach specific target features. Extensive reading materials can be considered a type of CBI (see Chapter 7). In the case of unfocused PBI, production tasks provide learners with opportunities to practise communicating in the target language using the linguistic (and non-linguistic) resources at their disposal. In unfocused CBI and PBI, learning occurs incidentally when learners 'pick up' particular linguistic forms from the input or 'notice-the-gap' between their own L2 production and the target L2 forms.

Focused CBI and PBI both draw on a linguistic syllabus (see Chapter 3). In focused CBI, a specific target feature is embedded in the input in such a way that learners are induced to process it (i.e. to establish a form-meaning mapping) in order to comprehend the input. Total Physical Response and Processing Instruction both require this. In focused PBI a target feature is elicited by means of either text-manipulation or text-creation activities. Text-manipulation activities supply learners with sentences illustrating the target structure and require them to operate on these in some way as in, for example, the kinds of exercises found in the Audiolingual Method (i.e. they constitute controlled-production activities).

Text-creation activities require students to compose their own sentences (i.e. they involve free-production activities). Finer distinctions can also be made. For example, drawing on Ur's types of practice, text-manipulation activities can consist of 'controlled drills', 'meaningful drills' and 'guided, meaningful practice' while text-creation activities can involve 'free sentence composition', 'structure-based discourse composition' or 'free discourse'. As we saw in Chapter 4, in PPP, the 'practice' stage involves text-manipulation activities and the 'produce' stage text-creation activities.

The distinction between focused and unfocused instruction is an important one. Focused instruction is designed to cater to intentional language learning whereas unfocused instruction caters to incidental language learning. Hulstijn (2003) provides a very clear statement of the significance of the intentional/incidental distinction for language pedagogy:

> There are two popular views on what it means to learn a second language. One view holds that it means months and years of 'intentional' study, involving the deliberate committing to memory of thousands of words (their meaning, sound and spelling) and dozens of grammar rules. The other, complementary, view holds that much of the burden of intentional learning can be taken off the shoulders of the language learner by processes of 'incidental' learning, involving the 'picking up' of words and structures, simply by engaging in a variety of communicative activities, in particular reading and listening activities, during which the learner's attention is focused on the meaning rather than the form of language.
>
> (p. 349)

However, it is not quite as simple as this for even focused language instruction provides opportunities for incidental learning as well as intentional learning. This is because materials designed to teach a specific linguistic feature (say, a grammatical structure) will also, inevitably, expose learners to a variety of other linguistic features which may be acquired incidentally. The theoretical premises of incidental and intentional learning will be examined in detail in Chapter 7.

Table 5.1 details the methods, kinds of instruction (i.e. CBI or PBI), types of activity (i.e. focused or unfocused) and kinds of learning (i.e. intentional or incidental) associated with linguistic and task-based syllabuses. In this chapter we will be concerned only with focused CBI and PBI. Thus, we will only be concerned with how linguistic syllabuses can be implemented through CBI and PBI.

Historical context

Traditionally, language instruction has emphasized the importance of learning through producing sentences in the target language. This is true of traditional ways of teaching grammar such as grammar translation (e.g. L1 → L2 translation exercises) and the Audiolingual Method (which sought to develop

Table 5.1 Types of syllabus, instruction, learning and methods

Syllabus	Methods	Type of instruction	Type of activities	Type of learning
Linguistic	TPR	CBI	Focused	Intentional
	Processing Instruction	CBI	Focused	Intentional
	Audiolingualism	PBI	Focused	Intentional
	PPP	PBI	Focused	Intentional
Task-based	Input-based TBLT	CBI	Primarily unfocused	Incidental
	Output-based TBLT	PBI	Primarily unfocused	Incidental

habits by having learners mechanically produce exemplars of specific structural patterns – see Chapter 2) and contemporary ways such as present–practice–produce (PPP), which differ from traditional methods mainly because they incorporate opportunities for free as well as controlled production in the L2.

However, there have been times when comprehension-based instruction challenged the emphasis on production-based pedagogy. The first occasion was in the 1960s when James Asher developed a method called Total Physical Response (TPR). The main features of TPR are: (1) production should be delayed until learners are ready to speak, (2) exposure to the language should be maximized by introducing grammatical structures through oral commands and (3) the teaching of abstract language should be postponed until learners have developed sufficient knowledge of the L2 to enable them to infer meaning from context. It should be noted that Asher's aim was not to develop listening proficiency but rather to use listening comprehension as a means for teaching the linguistic properties (mainly grammatical but also lexical) of the target language. Asher and associates (see Asher, 1977) conducted a number of studies that compared the effects of Total Physical Response (TPR) and other methods (in particular the Audiolingual Method) on learning. Asher's studies showed that comprehension-based instruction not only developed students' abilities to comprehend the L2 but also to speak it. He also claimed that it resulted in increased motivation, reduced language anxiety and that there was a greater likelihood that students would continue with their study of the language.

The rationale for comprehension-based language teaching received a theoretical boost from a seminal article published by Newmark in 1966. Newmark argued that L2 learning would proceed more smoothly if teachers stopped trying to 'interfere' in the learning process. Interference occurred when learners were forced to produce specific target features. A comprehension-based approach was more clearly compatible with a pedagogical theory that emphasized the need to assist learners to learn 'naturally' (i.e. incidentally). In a later article, Newmark (1981) identified a number of positive features of comprehension-based language teaching: (1) it presents input in a manner that was likely to command the learners' attention, (2) it emphasizes meaning over form and (3) it removes the need for the two aspects of teaching that Newmark was most opposed to – namely, drilling and explicit analysis of language. However, he also identified a number of deficiencies. He saw it as only of value in the beginning stages of learning a language and he was critical of the fact that comprehension-based materials at that time were still typically based on an inventory of grammatical structures and lexical items to be taught (i.e. involved focused instruction).

The growing interest in comprehension-based teaching was clearly reflected in the collection of papers in Winitz's *Comprehension Approach to Foreign Language Instruction*. In his introduction to this book, Winitz (1981) emphasized that 'language acquisition is viewed as non-linear' (p. xvii) and that CBI should therefore not be tied to a structural syllabus. However, the contributors to Winitz's book varied considerably on this point. Some saw CBI as a methodology for teaching predetermined linguistic items (usually grammatical) while others saw it as a means of delivering unfocused instruction. The decoupling of CBI from a traditional, linear syllabus can be most clearly seen in Krashen and Terrell's (1983) Natural Approach. In accordance with Krashen's views about L2 acquisition (see Krashen, 1981), the aim of the Natural Approach was to supply learners with plentiful comprehensible input that would enable them to learn implicitly and incidentally. The essential tenets of this approach were that the goal of language teaching was to develop communication skills and that this could be achieved by recognizing that comprehension always precedes production, that the ability to produce in an L2 emerges only after learners have acquired some language through comprehending input, that 'acquisition activities' (i.e. activities catering to incidental acquisition) are central, and that classroom activities must ensure a low 'affective filter' (i.e. not arouse learners' anxiety).

In the 1990s, however, the advocacy of CBI once again addressed the teaching of specific linguistic (grammatical) features. However, the theoretical grounding had changed. Schmidt (1990, 1993) argued – contra Krashen – that acquisition was not an entirely implicit process and that learners needed to 'notice' linguistic forms in the input for acquisition to take place. VanPatten (1990) reported a study that showed that meaning and form compete for learners' attention and that when learners prioritize meaning they are unlikely to notice specific forms in the input. In his 1996 book, he outlined a number of 'Processing Principles' that explained how learners typically process input and that prevented them from acquiring target features. He then went on to outline a form of comprehension-based instruction called 'Processing Instruction', which aimed to help learners overcome these natural ways of processing input by directing their conscious attention to those grammatical forms that they typically overlook. Like earlier advocates of the comprehension approach, VanPatten argued that the acquisition of grammatical form originates in input. Unlike Winitz and Krashen, however, he rejected the view that learning will always occur 'naturally' and automatically if learners are exposed to comprehensible input. He argued that what was needed was an approach that focused learner's attention on the meanings realized by specific grammatical forms. VanPatten also provided a set of guidelines for designing input-processing teaching materials (e.g. 'Teach only one thing at a time' and 'Learners must do something with the input').

Despite the interest in comprehension-based approaches, production-based teaching has remained the preferred approach in both teacher guides and language course books.

Present–practice–produce (PPP)

PPP can be seen as a development of Audiolingualism (Harmer, 2007). One of the criticisms levelled at Audiolingualism was that controlled drills do not result in the kind of language behaviour found in real-life contexts and thus fail to develop communicative ability. In contrast, Communicative Language Teaching (CLT), which became popular in the 1980s, emphasized the importance of communicative activities. PPP includes the kinds of controlled production activities found in Audiolingualism but also incorporates the kinds of communicative activities promoted in CLT in the free production stage. PPP also reverted back to the deductive explicit instruction found in grammar translation and the Cognitive Code Method (see Chapter 2).

Thus, PPP involves three distinct phases: (1) the presentation of the target feature by means of explicit instruction, (2) the provision of 'practice' in the form of controlled production activities, and (3) the inclusion of free-production activities in the form of situational grammar activities. Teacher educators have provided guidelines for each phase of PPP (see Chapter 4). The overall aim is to get students to learn the L2 features so thoroughly that they will be able to produce them correctly without thought (i.e. to develop their implicit knowledge).

There are some variations in the basic PPP format. Byrne (1986), for example, suggested that the stages involved in PPP should occur cyclically rather than in a linear fashion. He proposed that the teacher plays the role of 'informant' in the presentation stage, a 'conductor' in the practice stage and a 'guide' in the production stage, but that the teacher should be ready to return to an earlier stage if it becomes clear that the students need further information or more controlled practice. To this end, Byrne argued that the teacher needed to carefully monitor the learners' production in the practice or production stages.

Harmer (1998), focusing on learners' affective needs, proposed an approach he called ESA (engage, study, activate). In the engage phase, the teacher attempts to arouse the students' interest and engage their emotions. This might be realized through a game, the use of a picture, audio recording, video sequence, or a news/story/anecdote. In the 'study' stage, the focus is moved onto the target feature. The teacher explains the meaning and form of the feature, presents models and conducts practice of it. In the activate stage, students do not focus on the target language pattern, but employ their full L2 resources to complete a task designed to elicit use of the target feature. Harmer's 'study' phase can be seen as an amalgamation of the 'presentation' and 'practice' phases of PPP while the 'activate' stage represents the 'production' phase of PPP.

Harmer also suggested that the ESA sequence could be varied. For example, in EAS the activate stage precedes the study stage. Asking learners to participate in a communicative activity can reveal the linguistic problems that the learners are having. These could then become the targets in the study stage. This proposal corresponds to the 'deep end' strategy proposed by Brumfit (1978). It has the advantage of ensuring that explicit language work is only undertaken when learners demonstrate a need for it. Harmer pointed out that learners can also be asked to repeat the activate stage after the study stage to see if they are now able to use the features targeted (i.e. ESAS). From this perspective, then, PPP is just one way of implementing ESA (Harmer, 2007: 67).

Harmer's distinction between ESA and EAS is not dissimilar to Ellis's (2003b) distinction between 'task-supported language teaching' and 'task-based language teaching' (see Chapter 6). In 'task-supported language teaching', the target feature is first presented (as in the study stage of the ESA sequence) and then a task is introduced in the apply stage of the sequence. There is opportunity in the post-task phase of a lesson (as in the apply stage) for the direct study of those features that learners found problematic while performing a task.

What PPP, ESA, EAS and task-supported language teaching have in common is a presentation or study stage at some point in the sequence. That is, they all draw on a structural syllabus and they all validate the inclusion of explicit information about the target feature at some point in a lesson. In other words, they constitute forms of explicit grammar instruction.

Processing Instruction

Processing Instruction (PI), proposed by VanPatten (1996), aims at altering the processing strategies that hinder learners' accurate processing of L2 input. It has three key components: (1) provision of explicit information about the target form, (2) information about how to implement a particular processing strategy in order to process input incorrectly and (3) 'structured input' (SI) activities, where the input is manipulated to help learners to abandon their less-than-optimal strategies and to construct form-meaning connections. The first component resembles the first stage of a PPP grammar lesson. It typically involves providing learners with a metalinguistic explanation of the target structure together with some illustrative sentences. The second and the third elements are unique to PI. The second element – information about processing strategies – involves: (1) an explanation of the non-appropriate strategies that learners tend to employ when processing the L2 and (2) some sample activities that enable the learners to try out the appropriate strategies. Sometimes (1) is repeated to remind the learners about the problem they tend to have. The third element – structured input – consists of activities that require learners to process the target structure in a series of sentences but without any need for them to produce the structure. The input sentences are designed in such a way that they can only be understood if the learners are successful in constructing a form-meaning connection for the target feature. The structured input activities are of two different types: 'referentially oriented activities' and 'affectively oriented activities'. The former consist of input sentences that require objective decisions (e.g. indicating whether a statement is right or wrong or answering a simple multiple choice question). The following is an example from VanPatten (1996).

1. *Mi hermana me llama frecuentemente.*
Who calls whom?
a. I call my sister. b. My sister calls me.

In the 'affectively oriented activities', the learners indicate their opinions, feelings, beliefs or their personal circumstances as in this example from VanPatten:

1. Read each statement and select the ones that you think are typical.
Los parientes...
a. nos molestan.
b. nos critican.
c. nos anyuden (help).
d. nos visitan.
e. nos quieren (querer = to be fond of).

According to VanPatten, affectively oriented activities are desirable because they require meaning-focused and communicative use of the L2 in a way that personalizes the instruction for the learners.

VanPatten (1996: 67–70) proposed a set of guidelines for structured input activities:

- Teach only one thing at a time. VanPatten argued that it is important to break down a grammatical structure into specific points. For example, he recommended that Spanish regular past tense should be taught by introducing each of the three verb conjugations in different lessons rather than all three together.
- Keep meaning in focus. The activity needs to ensure that the learners attend to the meaning of the input. In other words, it is not sufficient for learners to simply comprehend the input using top-down strategies. They need to process the target form in order to comprehend. Only in this way will the learners be induced to construct a form-meaning mapping.
- Learners must do something with the input. The learners need to demonstrate that they have processed the information by responding to the input. This involves a non-verbal (or minimally verbal) response to the input sentences.
- Use both oral and written input. In order to cater to individual differences in learners' preference for the medium of instruction, the input should involve both the oral and the written mode.
- Move from sentences to connected discourse (i.e. conversations or monologues). The rationale is that it is easier to start with activities that cater to the learners' limited capacity to process input. Processing discrete

sentences is easier than processing connected discourse, which affords the learners less time to process the target form and also includes 'noise' (i.e. other elements of the language than the target form).

- Keep the psycholinguistic processing strategies in mind. The activities should be designed in such a way that they create the need to alter the learners' processing strategies. For example, requesting a response to the sentence 'He played the violin yesterday' does not induce attention to the *-ed* morpheme of the verb as learners can obtain the meaning of the sentence from the adverb 'yesterday'. This sentence, then, does not induce learners to abandon their default processing strategy (i.e. focusing on content words rather than on grammatical functors). To induce this it would be necessary to request a response to 'He played the violin at the concert' and ask whether the sentence refers to a past or present event.

Ellis (2005) built on VanPatten's account of structured input to propose what he called 'interpretation tasks' (see Chapter 4). These include both referential and affective tasks, as proposed by VanPatten, but also error-noticing tasks (i.e. activities where learners have to spot and correct the errors that result from default processing).

VanPatten (1996) emphasized that Processing Instruction is fundamentally different from other comprehension-based approaches such as Total Physical Response (TPR) and the Natural Approach or input enhancement (see Chapter 7) because it is designed to push learners to construct form-meaning mappings. VanPatten argued that simply comprehending the content of the input (as in TPR or the Natural Approach) or directing the learner's attention to the form by emphasizing the target feature (as in input enhancement) does not guarantee that the particular linguistic form is processed accurately.

CBI and PBI in language pedagogy

The teacher education literature shows production-based language teaching as dominant. Of the eight methods that Richards and Rodgers (1986) described, five of them are production-based. The Audiolingual Method relies on oral pattern drills and performance of memorized dialogues. Situational Language Teaching emphasizes the importance of the use of context to elicit guided production of specific grammatical forms. Communicative Language Teaching introduces 'tasks' to provide opportunities for free production. The Silent Way is only silent for the teacher: learners are expected to produce. Community Language Learning invites learners to first produce in their L1 and then, with the assistance of the teacher, in the L2. Ur (2011) listed six options for teaching grammar, the first three of which involve production (Option 1: Task plus focus on form; Option 2: Grammar explanation plus practice; Option 3: Communication). Also, an inspection of some of the popular grammar books of the last two decades demonstrates the importance attached to learner production. Ellis's (2002b) analysis of popular grammar practice books found that they all included copious production activities but only two provided any comprehension-based activities. Teacher guides also tend to emphasize production. Ur (1996) described a number of different types of 'practice' designed to assist the learner to 'make the "leap"' from form-focused accuracy work to fluent communication: all the types involve production of one kind or another.

There are obvious reasons for this emphasis on production. First, the goal of most language courses is to enable students to speak and write in the L2 and it would seem self-evident that this can best be achieved by having students speak and write. Second, teachers frequently evaluate the success of their lessons in terms of student participation and view 'participation' as necessarily involving production. Students' production, when erroneous, provides opportunities for corrective feedback and 'errors' are generally only conceived as problems with production not comprehension. To examine whether these reasons have any validity, we will now take a look at SLA to see what theories and research have to say about CBI and PBI.

SLA perspectives on CBI and PBI

In this section we examine two theoretical positions that provide support for PBI and CBI: Input Processing and Skill Acquisition Theory. We will also review a number of studies that have compared the effects of the two types of instruction.

Input Processing

VanPatten's (1996) Input Processing Theory claims that L2 acquisition is primarily input-driven but that simply exposing learners to input does not guarantee successful learning. This is because the learners' internal processors act on the input in such a way that only part of the input makes its way into the developing system of the second language.

Figure 5.1 shows the two learning processes in VanPatten's model. In (1) – 'input processing' – that portion of the input that is processed by the learner constitutes 'intake'. Processing requires that the learner establish a connection between a linguistic form and its meaning or function. However, 'input processing' is often difficult for L2 learners because of their limited attentional resources. VanPatten (2004: 7) claimed that during interaction L2 learners are focused primarily on the extraction of meaning from the input but that noticing (i.e. attention to specific linguistic forms in the input) is necessary for intake to occur. However, such noticing is constrained by working memory, which limits the amount of information learners can process online during comprehension (e.g. Just and Carpenter, 1992). VanPatten then went on to propose that input processing is facilitated when learners successfully detect forms in input and this might result in the second of the processes shown in Figure 5.1 – accommodation or restructuring of the developing L2 system.

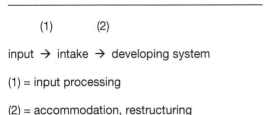

(1)   (2)

input → intake → developing system

(1) = input processing

(2) = accommodation, restructuring

Figure 5.1 VanPatten's model of input processing (see VanPatten 1996: 7)

VanPatten identified a number of default input-processing principles that explain how learners allocate their attention during online processing of L2 input. These principles constrain how learners process input. They need to be overridden in order for acquisition to take place. VanPatten (1996) initially proposed two major principles and three subprinciples for principle 1. Later, however, he expanded the principles (VanPatten, 2004). Box 5.1 presents the full list of processing principles.

Box 5.1 VanPatten's input processing principles

Principle 1. The Primacy of Meaning Principle. Learners process input for meaning before they process it for form.

Principle 1a. The Primacy of Content Words Principle. Learners process content words in the input before anything else.

Principle 1b. The Lexical Preference Principle. Learners will tend to rely on lexical items as opposed to grammatical form to get meaning when both encode the same semantic information.

Principle 1c. The Preference for Non-Redundancy Principle. Learners prefer processing 'more meaningful' morphology before 'less meaningful' morphology.

Principle 1d. The Meaning-Before-Non-Meaning Principle. Learners are more likely to process meaningful grammatical forms before non-meaningful forms irrespective of redundancy.

Principle 1e. The Availability of Resources Principle. For learners to process either redundant meaningful grammatical forms or non-meaningful forms, the processing of overall sentential meaning must not drain available processing resources.

Principle 1f. The Sentence Location Principle. Learners tend to process items in sentence initial position before those in final position and those in medial position.

Principle 2. The First Noun Principle. Learners tend to process the first noun or pronoun they encounter in a sentence as the subject/agent.

Principle 2a. The Lexical Semantics Principle. Learners may rely on lexical semantics, where possible, instead of word order to interpret sentences.

Principle 2b. The Event Probabilities Principle. Learners may rely on event probabilities, where possible, instead of word order to interpret sentences.

Principle 2c. The Contextual Constraint Principle. Learners may rely less on the first noun principle if preceding context constrains the possible interpretation of a clause or sentence.

To sum up, VanPatten (2007) argued that input processing (defined as the process by which a form-meaning connection is established) in conjunction with other cognitive processes (such as 'restructuring') leads to changes in the learner's internal grammar, which will subsequently become manifest in both receptive and productive language use. In other words, VanPatten viewed comprehension and production as drawing on a single knowledge store, which is developed as a result of processing input. However, VanPatten emphasized that his theory of input processing is not a complete model of acquisition but rather addresses only the 'first hurdle' (p. 25) of language acquisition. He saw it as explaining how learners acquire new grammatical features and thus of particular relevance to beginner or intermediate level learners. He acknowledged that production-based instruction may also be needed for learners to achieve full control over the features they had acquired.

There have been a large number of Processing Instruction studies that have compared the effects of comprehension-based and production-based instruction. Many of them (e.g. VanPatten and Cadierno, 1993; Benati, 2005) lend support to the superiority of comprehension-based instruction in developing receptive and sometimes also productive knowledge of the target grammatical features. These studies typically compared two groups – a processing instruction (PI) group and a traditional instruction (TI) group – using a quasi-experimental methodology. In an early study, VanPatten and Cadierno (1993) compared the effectiveness of PI and TI on the acquisition of the placement rule for Spanish direct pronouns. In the processing instruction, the presentation stage first contrasted the grammatical concepts of object and subject of a verb and then identified subject and object pronoun forms. This was followed by an explanation of the important points to keep in mind about pronoun position in Spanish. Two types of activities followed the presentation stage. One type required the learners to listen or read sentences and then demonstrate that they had correctly assigned argument structure to the string. This typically involved selecting the drawing that best represented what they heard or read or selecting the best English translation of the Spanish sentence. The second type of activity had learners respond to the content of a series of sentences by checking 'agree' or 'disagree', 'true for me' or 'not true for me', and so on. In several activities the participants read a very short passage in which the object pronouns had been highlighted. The participants were asked what those particular utterances meant. At no point were the learners asked to produce sentences containing the object pronoun forms. The traditional instruction also began with an explicit account of the target feature. The practice stages involved moving from mechanical form-oriented practice, consisting of oral and written transformation and substitution drills to meaningful practice involving oral and written questions, simple sentence formation and finally to more open-ended communicative practice (i.e. oral and written question-and-answer activities). In other words, the traditional instruction followed a standard PPP sequence with the focus on eliciting production of the target forms from the learners.

Two tests – an interpretation test and a production test – were used for the pre-test and post-tests. For the interpretation tests, the learners were asked to match each sentence they heard with one of two pictures that were simultaneously presented on an overhead projector. The two pictures represented the same action, the difference between them being who the agent was and who the object of the verb was. The production task was based on activities used in the traditional instruction and included five items, each of which consisted of an incomplete sentence. The learners' task was to complete the sentence according to a visual clue. The post-test results showed that in the production test, there were no significant differences between either the PI group and the control group or the PI and the TI group. Only the PI group showed a significant gain compared to the control group. On the other hand, for the interpretation test, the PI significantly outperformed both the TI and the control groups in the post-tests, while there was no significant difference between the TI and the control group.

VanPatten and Cadierno's study has led to a number of further studies that either replicated it or extended it in various ways. Many of them (e.g. Benati, 2005) replicated the comparison of PI and TI for different target languages. Those studies generally reported similar results. However, some studies compared PI with meaning-based production practice (MOI) (Farley, 2001). The production treatment typically consisted of explicit instruction of the target form followed by activities involving communicating one's opinions, beliefs, or feelings about a designated topic. There are also some studies that have shown that PI is beneficial even when there is no explicit information about the target feature (VanPatten and Oikkenon, 1996). This led VanPatten to claim that the crucial element of Processing Instruction is 'structured Input' and that explicit explanation may not be necessary. However, some recent studies (e.g. Fernandez, 2008) suggest that at least for some structures, processing instruction is more effective if the structured input is preceded by explicit explanation.

There are also some studies that have challenged the superiority of PI (Allen, 2000; Collentine, 1998; DeKeyser and Sokalski, 1996; Salaberry, 1997). In many of these studies, the production practice involved meaning-based rather than just controlled production practice suggesting that the form-meaning mapping which VanPatten saw as crucial to acquisition can also occur in PBI. However, the advocates of Processing Instruction (e.g. Wong, 2001) have argued the difference in the results might be due to the fact that the Processing Instruction in those studies was not designed in such a way as to enable learners to overcome their default processing strategies. VanPatten has also pointed out that Processing Instruction will only be effective for those grammatical structures that are influenced by his Processing Principles (i.e. not all structures are governed by these).

Skill Acquisition Theory

Skill acquisition refers to a form of learning where 'skilled behaviours can become routinized and even automatic under some conditions through repeated pairings of similar stimuli with particular responses' (Speelman and Kirsner, 2005: 26). Skill acquisition draws on Anderson's (1983, 1993) ACT theory – a kind of 'cognitive S–R (stimulus–response) theory' (Anderson, 1983: 6). ACT theory distinguishes declarative knowledge (i.e. the representation of facts) and procedural knowledge (i.e. the representation of actions in particular situations). Procedural knowledge is developed by storing condition–action memories in memory. The theory also proposes that declarative knowledge can be proceduralized through domain-specific production (i.e. practice). As the need to refer to declarative knowledge is reduced when proceduralization occurs, the load on working memory is similarly reduced. In other words, acquisition takes place by (1) proceduralization of declarative knowledge and (2) automatization of access to information in working memory through practice.

Skill Acquisition Theory provides the rationale for the strong-interface position we considered in Chapter 4. DeKeyser (2007) emphasized the importance of 'practice' in transforming declarative into procedural knowledge. He pointed out that the power law of practice leads to qualitative changes in the learners' knowledge system over time, but only 'in the basic cognitive mechanisms used to execute the same task' (DeKeyser, 2007: 99). This is because the kind of knowledge that characterizes the later stages of development (i.e. the automatization stage) is highly specific and so does not transfer to tasks that are dissimilar from those used to develop the knowledge. From this theoretical perspective, then, the knowledge that results from comprehension-based instruction is only available for use in receptive tasks while that which results from production-based tasks is only available for use in productive tasks. In other words, Skill Acquisition Theory claims that there is no single knowledge store – as claimed by VanPatten – but rather different knowledge stores that support receptive and productive language skills.

DeKeyser (2007) defined 'practice' broadly as 'specific activities in the second language, engaged in systematically, deliberately, with the goal of developing knowledge of and skills in the second language' (p. 1). In his 1998 article, he emphasized the importance of transferable production practice. Drawing on Paulston's (1970, 1972) three types of drills – that is, mechanical, meaningful and communicative – he pointed out that studies have shown that mechanical drills have only a very limited effect on acquisition. He argued that 'good practice needs to involve real operating conditions as soon as possible, which means comprehending and expressing real thoughts, and this necessarily involves a variety of structures, some of which will be much further along the declarative-procedural-automatic path than others' (p. 292). DeKeyser (2007) argued that the transfer of declarative knowledge to procedural knowledge is likely to occur, to the extent that the cognitive operations involved in the practice activity match those in a natural communicative context.

A key prediction of Skill Acquisition Theory is that effects of instruction are skill-specific. That is, input-based instruction will benefit receptive skills and output-based instruction production skills. This prediction contrasts directly with Input Processing Theory. In an attempt to challenge VanPatten's theory, DeKeyser and Sokalski (1996) replicated the procedures of VanPatten and Cadierno's (1993) study, in a study that investigated the effects of comprehension and production practice on the acquisition of two structures that differed in terms of grammatical complexity. The Spanish direct object clitic pronoun was chosen as a simple rule and the conditional form was chosen as a complex rule. Eighty-two university students in Spanish courses were allocated to the input group, the output group and the control group. All three groups received a grammatical handout before receiving instruction. The input group performed comprehension tasks that required the learners to respond to structured input containing the target structures. The output group performed production tasks that required the learners to fill in the blanks, translate sentences and answer questions. The control group received their regular lessons (i.e. they were not taught either structure). The activities for the input and output conditions progressed from mechanical to meaningful as VanPatten and Cadierno (1993) suggested. Both groups received feedback in the form of teacher-based discussion and corrections. The immediate test results showed that the input group significantly outperformed the control group only in the comprehension tests for both structures, while the output group outperformed the control group in the production tests for both structures and the comprehension test for the conditional form. However, the significant differences disappeared in the delayed post-test conducted one week later. DeKeyser and Sokalski claimed that the results largely supported the predictions of Skill Acquisition Theory but that 'both testing time and the morphosyntactic nature of the structure in question favour one skill or the other' (p. 615).

DeKeyser (1997) attempted to address both the interface between declarative and procedural knowledge and skill specificity by examining the effects of the amount and type of practice on L2 development of a miniature computerized linguistic system, Autopractan – an artificial agglutinative language with flexible word order. Three groups of sixty-one participants received grammar explanation for four grammatical rules. Then Group A received comprehension exercises for two of the grammatical rules and production exercises for the other two rules. Group B received the opposite and Group C practised all four rules in both comprehension and production exercises. DeKeyser reported that the reaction times and the error rates for performance of both the single-task and the dual-task conditions, indicated that gradual automatization of the target grammar rules had taken place. The results also conformed to the Power Law of Practice (Newell and Rosenbloom, 1981); that is, the practice, whether through comprehension or production tasks, had exactly the same effects on grammar learning as it has been shown to have on the acquisition of other cognitive skills. There was also support for the skill-specific effects of practice. Acquisition of comprehension or production skills was less apparent if only the opposite skill was practised. DeKeyser argued that the skill-specific effects of the instruction were more clearly evident in this study than in either DeKeyser and Sokalski (1996) or the Processing Instruction studies, because it examined the long-term effects of instruction and thus was able to show what effect instruction had when learners reached more or less full automatization of the target structures. A limitation of this study, which might invalidate it for some researchers, is that it did not investigate a natural language. Teachers, in particular, might be sceptical of it for this reason. In contrast, VanPatten's studies were conducted in a classroom context.

Ellis (2009) criticized Skill Acquisition Theory by pointing out that it does not account for two established aspects of second language acquisition. First, it does not provide an explanation for the order and sequence of acquisition (see Chapter 3). Second, he argued, that it is difficult to accept that the acquisition of all L2 features begins with declarative knowledge, as the acquisition of both vocabulary and grammar in an L2 must involve incidental learning to a considerable extent and such learning does not require a declarative stage.

Relative effectiveness of CBI and PBI

The studies we have considered so far have produced mixed results. Many of the PI studies produced results that indicate that CBI is more effective than PBI in developing receptive knowledge and is as or more effective in developing productive knowledge. These results support the model of L2 learning shown in Figure 5.1. However, DeKeyser's studies suggest that instruction is skill-specific; that is, PBI benefits productive knowledge and CBI receptive knowledge, as predicted by Skill Acquisition Theory. One way of resolving the apparent contradiction is to conduct a meta-analysis of those studies that have compared the two types of instruction.

Shintani et al. (2013) carried out such a meta-analysis of studies that have compared CBI and PBI. It included thirty-five experimental studies in thirty articles published between 1990 and 2010. Many of these studies involved PI but some also involved other forms of CBI. The results showed that: (1) overall both types of instruction had large effects on both receptive and productive knowledge, (2) for receptive knowledge, CBI had a greater effect than PBI when the acquisition was measured within one week but the difference diminished in the delayed tests (i.e. post-tests administered between one week and seventy-five days after the treatment), (3) for productive knowledge, CBI and PBI had similar effects in short-term measurements but PBI was more effective in the delayed tests, (4) the initial advantage found for CBI was evident primarily in Processing Instruction studies and (5) PBI involving text creation is more effective than PBI involving text manipulation.

Shintani et al. suggested that the differences in the effects of the two types of instruction can be explained in terms of whether the target features were 'new' or 'partially acquired', with CBI more advantageous for the former and PBI for the latter. This conclusion lends support to VanPatten's claims; namely, input-based instruction that induces processing of the target features is likely to be especially beneficial in the case of 'new' features, but output-based instruction helps learners to develop greater control over those features that have already entered the learners' L2 system. The findings of the meta-analysis, however, do not support DeKeyser's claims about the skill-specific nature of instruction; that is, both CBI and PBI lead to development in both learners' receptive and productive skills. However, they do support his claim that production practice that includes communicative activities (i.e. text-creation activities) is superior to practice consisting of text-manipulation activities.

The pedagogic issues revisited

We will now address a number of specific questions relating to the role of CBI and PBI and L2 acquisition in the light of what SLA theory and research has shown about these two types of instruction.

Is production practice necessary for the development of production skills?

Contrary to the general position evident in both language course books and teacher guides, it is clear that although production practice can lead to acquisition, it is not necessary. Also, as we saw in Chapter 4, its effectiveness is constrained by the learner's developmental level. Input Processing Theory claims that CBI is effective in developing not just receptive knowledge of new grammatical features but also productive knowledge. While the results of studies that have compared CBI and PBI are somewhat mixed, they do very clearly show that CBI benefits production as well as comprehension of grammatical features. Thus, we conclude that grammar teachers should not worry that CBI will not help their learners to develop productive skills.

Which type of instruction is more effective?

We have seen that SLA theory lends support to both CBI and PBI. While the Processing Instruction studies have attempted to show that CBI is more effective overall, there is in fact plenty of evidence to suggest that production practice – especially if this is combined with explicit instruction and includes text-creation activities – assists acquisition (see Chapter 4). It may be, then, that this question is ill-advised: both types of instruction can be effective. The meta-analysis conducted by Shintani et al. (2013) suggests that CBI may be preferable for low-proficiency learners and for 'new' grammatical structures, while PBI may be more beneficial for helping more advanced learners achieve greater control over 'partially acquired' structures.

Which types of CBI and PBI are more effective?

Neither CBI nor PBI are monolithic types of instruction: each can be implemented in a variety of ways. SLA theory points to the specific characteristics of both types that are important for acquisition. In the case of CBI, structured input that focuses learners' attention on the target features and assists them in constructing form-function mappings has been shown to be effective. In the case of PBI, Skill Acquisition Theory stresses the importance of engaging learners in production activities that involve real-time processing. This is best achieved by means of text-creation activities. Both types of instruction also seem to be effective if they are accompanied by explicit instruction.

Conclusion

This chapter has examined the effectiveness of comprehension-based instruction (CBI) and production-based instruction (PBI). We have seen that present–practice–produce (PPP) – a type of PBI – has been given prominence in teacher manuals and in grammar teaching materials. In contrast, CBI has been largely neglected despite the strong case made for it by Asher (1977), Winitz (1981) and Krashen and Terrell (1983). SLA has a role to play in addressing the imbalance evident in current language pedagogy. It provides theoretical support and empirical evidence for CBI. Thus, while both PBI and CBI have been found effective in developing learners' grammatical systems, it is worthwhile considering giving greater emphasis to the use of CBI in the future.

Can CBI, then, overcome the limitations of a grammatical syllabus discussed in Chapter 3? Principle 5 of instructed language learning stated 'Instruction needs to take into account the order and sequence of acquisition'. However, these concern how productive knowledge is acquired. The sequence of acquisition we considered in Chapter 3 addresses how learners gradually acquire the ability to *produce* target language structures. Pienemann's Processability Theory accounts for the processing constraints that govern the acquisition of productive knowledge of grammatical structures, not receptive knowledge. Overall, the results of the PI studies have shown that PI is much more effective in developing receptive than productive knowledge and thus might be best seen as a means of achieving this. It is possible then that a grammatical syllabus provides a basis for systematically teaching 'new' grammatical structures if it is implemented through PI and aimed at developing receptive rather than productive knowledge.

However, to establish the viability of such a proposal, it will be necessary to show that PI is effective in developing learners' implicit receptive knowledge (not just their explicit knowledge). In fact, the receptive and productive tests used to measure learning in the PI studies have been primarily of the discrete point kind and thus do not convincingly demonstrate that the instruction resulted in implicit knowledge. Two PI studies (VanPatten and Sanz, 1995; Marsden, 2006) did include measures based on free production but neither provided entirely convincing evidence that either CBI or PBI enabled learners to use the target features in the real operating conditions of actual communication. The receptive tests used in the PI studies also do not convincingly show that learners developed the ability to process target features rapidly and effortlessly in communication. It is possible then that PI – like the explicit language instruction we considered in Chapter 3 – results in explicit knowledge rather than implicit receptive or productive knowledge. If this is the case, it functions in much the same way as the consciousness-raising tasks we considered in Chapter 3 and a grammatical syllabus can still serve only (but usefully) as a basis for developing this type of knowledge.

It is possible, of course, that grammar instruction will be most effective if it involves a combination of comprehension-based and production-based activities within the same lesson. However, we know of no research that has compared a combined approach to teaching grammar with an approach consisting of just CBI or PBI. However, given what is known about the gradual way acquisition takes place, it is unlikely that target-level accuracy in the production of a new target feature can be achieved within a short period of time. Nor is a combined approach likely to fare any better where implicit receptive knowledge is concerned.

These continuing doubts about basing instruction – whether CBI or PBI – on a grammatical syllabus led some SLA researchers to propose a radically different approach to teaching an L2 – one that abandoned the attempt to intervene directly in interlanguage development and instead aimed to create the conditions for acquisition to take place naturally. We turn to consider this approach in the next chapter.

DISCUSSION QUESTIONS

1. See Table 5.1: types of syllabus, instruction, learning and methods. How do 'focused' CBI and 'unfocused' CBI differ in terms of the learning processes involved? What is the difference between 'focused' and 'unfocused' PBI? Why is the issue of 'focused' vs 'unfocused' an important one.
2. What are the main arguments in support of CBI?
3. Harmer has proposed a variation on traditional PPP – ESA (engage, study, activate). How does this differ from PPP? Which of these two types of PBI do you prefer? Why?
4. Which approach, CBI or PBI, do teacher educators generally support? Why?
5. How does Processing Instruction differ from TPR or comprehension practice?
6. What do the studies that have investigated Input Processing indicate about the effects of CBI and PBI?
7. What are the pros and cons of Skill Acquisition Theory? What does this theory tell us about the effects of CBI and PBI?
8. What does SLA research show about the relative effectiveness of CBI and PBI?

6 Task-based language teaching

Introduction

Task-based language teaching (TBLT) was developed as an alternative to traditional methods such as grammar translation, the Audiolingual Method or present–practice–produce (PPP). It has received increasing support from a number of SLA researchers. A number of books – Candlin and Murphy (1987), Crookes and Gass (1993), Skehan (1998, 2011), Ellis (2003b), Mayo (2007), Eckerth and Siekmann (2008) and Samuda and Bygate (2008) – have expounded the theoretical and research basis for TBLT. It has also received strong support from teacher educators such as Prabhu (1987), Estaire and Zanon (1994), Willis (1996) and Nunan (1989, 2004).

TBLT, however, has not been without it critics, who view it as an approach advanced by SLA theorists but unsupported by the practical experience of language teachers. Critics such as Bruton (2002) and Swan (2005) have questioned what they see as the theoretical advocacy of TBLT. Other critics (e.g. Seedhouse, 2004) have challenged the claim that 'tasks' lead to the kinds of interactions that promote acquisition and have suggested that 'task' is an inadequate construct on which to base a language course because it is not possible to predict how learners will actually perform a task. Still other critics (e.g. Littlewood, 2007) have questioned the feasibility of introducing TBLT in classroom contexts where both teachers and learners have traditionally seen language as an 'object' to be studied rather than as a 'tool' for communicating. It should be noted, too, that even advocates of TBLT (Samuda and Bygate, 2008; East, 2012) acknowledge that teachers may experience problems in introducing TBLT into their classrooms. In short, TBLT continues to be an approach that arouses both fervent advocacy and determined resistance.

'Task' is both a pedagogical and theoretical construct (Pica, 1998). Thus it is ideally suited to this book which seeks to explore pedagogic positions in terms of SLA theory and research. However, as Skehan (2011) noted 'those attached to a task-based approach are largely (but not exclusively) researchers' (p. 413). For this reason, in this chapter, we have not taken as our starting point how task-based teaching is viewed in language pedagogy. Instead, we begin by outlining what task-based teaching consists of, drawing on the work of both teacher educators such as Willis and researchers such as Skehan. We explore TBLT from two points of view: (1) the design of tasks and task-based courses and (2) their implementation. We first consider what is meant by a 'task' and then consider different types of tasks and how tasks can be incorporated into a task-based syllabus. We then consider proposals for implementing tasks in language classrooms. This provides the context for examining what SLA has had to say about TBLT by drawing, in particular, on the work of Long, Skehan and Robinson. We will conclude by considering the various criticisms that have been levelled against TBLT and attempt to address them in the light of SLA theory and research. Finally, we will consider a number of studies that have sought to compare the effects of TBLT and traditional language teaching (e.g. PPP) on L2 learning.

Task-based language teaching

Task-based language teaching aims to develop learners' communicative competence by engaging them in meaning-focused communication though the performance of tasks. As Johnson (1979) put it, 'fluency in the communicative process can only be developed within "task-oriented teaching" – one which provides "actual meaning" by focusing on tasks to be mediated through language, and where success or failure is seen to be judged in terms of whether or not these tasks are performed' (p. 200). However, TBLT is not just concerned with developing 'fluency in the communicative process'. It also aims to develop learners' linguistic competence (i.e. to help them acquire new language) and their interactional competence (i.e. their ability to use the target language to participate in discourse). A key principle of TBLT is that even though learners are primarily concerned with constructing and comprehending messages, they also need to attend to form for learning to take place.

Defining 'task'

Various definitions of a 'task' have been provided (e.g. Bygate et al., 2001; Ellis, 2003b; Samuda and Bygate, 2008; Willis, 1996).[1] Summarizing these various definitions, Ellis (2003b) proposed that for an instructional activity to qualify as a 'task' it must satisfy the following criteria:

1 The primary focus should be on 'meaning' (i.e. learners should be mainly concerned with encoding and decoding messages not with focusing on linguistic form).
2 There should be some kind of 'gap' (i.e. a need to convey information, to express an opinion or to infer meaning).
3 Learners should largely rely on their own resources (linguistic and non-linguistic) in order to complete the activity. That is, learners are not 'taught' the language they will need to perform a task, although they may be able to 'borrow' from the input the task provides to help them perform it.
4 There is a clearly defined outcome other than the use of language (i.e. the language serves as the means for achieving the outcome, not as an end in its

own right). Thus, when performing a task, learners are not primarily concerned with using language correctly but rather with achieving the goal stipulated by the task.

These four criteria then are directed at ensuring that a task results in language use where learners treat the language as a 'tool' for achieving a communicative outcome rather than as an 'object' to be studied, analysed and displayed.

As Widdowson (2003) pointed out, the term 'meaning' in criterion (1) is ambiguous. It can refer to both semantic meaning and pragmatic meaning. The former refers to the specific lexical and grammatical meanings encoded by words and grammatical structures. The latter refers to the functional meanings that arise when language is used to describe, request, apologize and so on. Larsen-Freeman (1995, 2003) referred to this aspect of meaning as 'use'. Widdowson pointed out quite correctly that many exercises require attention to semantic meaning. For example, an exercise that requires learners to choose the correct verb form to complete a blank in a sentence will require learners to attend to the meaning of the form of the verb. However, such activities do not require learners to give attention to the pragmatic meaning of a sentence (i.e. to 'use'). Thus, criterion (1) in the definition above refers to activities that require learners to use language pragmatically and indexically for purposes of communicating their own meaning intentions. In other words, in claiming that a 'task' requires a primary focus on meaning, we are stating that it must require learners to attend to both semantic and pragmatic meaning. For example, a Spot-the-Difference Task that requires learners to find the differences in two pictures will necessitate attention both to the physical properties of the objects in the pictures and their spatial location (i.e. semantic meaning) and to encoding utterances in such a way that learners are able to relate what they say and hear to the pictures and to their interlocutor's utterances (i.e. pragmatic meaning) and to deal with any communication problems that may arise.

These criteria help to distinguish a 'task' from an 'exercise'. Exercises are activities designed to practise specific language items. Thus, they do not require a primary focus on meaning, there is no 'gap', learners manipulate the language provided in the exercise rather than use their own linguistic resources, and there is no other outcome than that of practising language. Tasks do not aim to practise language but to create communicative contexts for using language.[2] From this perspective, a distinction can be drawn between a task and a situational grammar exercise of the kind used in the free production stage of PPP (Ellis, 2003b): in the former, the learners are not informed of any specific linguistic focus and therefore pay primary attention to message content and engage in language use, whereas in situational grammar exercise, learners are told what the linguistic focus is, and thus are likely to make efforts to use it correctly.

Teacher educators often emphasize the importance of authentic use of language in TBLT (e.g. Nunan, 2004). The question that arises is how authentic tasks should be. Ellis (2003b) distinguished situational and interactional authenticity. A task achieves situational authenticity when the context it creates mirrors a real-life context (e.g. an information gap task that requires a learner to find out whether it is possible to reserve a hotel room on the dates needed and at a cost that is affordable). A task achieves interactional authenticity when it results in the kinds of language use that occur in non-pedagogic communication (e.g. conversation). Willis and Willis (2007) drew finer distinctions, suggesting that the 'authenticity' of a task can be viewed as involving three different levels:

> Level 1: it gives learners the opportunity to engage in producing meanings which will be useful in the real world (e.g. using vocabulary to do with a topic of general interest).
> Level 2: it results in the kind of discourse which is very common in everyday life (e.g. expressing opinions and constructing arguments to support those opinions).
> Level 3: it involves an activity which could easily occur in the real world.

Views differ with regard to the whole question of the importance of 'authenticity' in language teaching materials, an issue that we revisit in Chapter 7.

Task types

There are a number of different ways of classifying tasks. Willis's (1996) pedagogic classification was based on an analysis of the kinds of tasks commonly found in textbook materials. The types reflect the kind of operations learners are required to carry out in performing tasks:

- Listing (i.e. tasks where the completed outcome is a list).
- Ordering and sorting (i.e. tasks that involve sequencing, ranking, categorizing or classifying items).
- Comparing (i.e. tasks that involve finding differences or similarities in information).
- Problem-solving (i.e. tasks that demand intellectual activity as in puzzles or logical issues).
- Sharing personal experiences (i.e. tasks that allow learners to talk freely about themselves and share experiences).
- Creative tasks (i.e. projects, often involving several stages that can incorporate the various types of tasks above and can include the need to carry out some research).

Prabhu (1987) identified three types of tasks according to whether they involved an information-gap, an opinion-gap, or a reasoning-gap. An information-gap task requires the learners to share information that one person has that the other does not. Information-gap tasks can be one-way (i.e. one student possesses all the information that needs to be communicated) or two-way (i.e. the information needed to achieve the outcome of the task is divided among the students). In a one-way task, therefore, one student functions as the speaker and the other as a listener, whereas in a two-way task both (all) the students participate as both speakers and listeners. Jigsaw tasks where the information needed to perform the task is split among three or more learners constitute one kind of two-way task. For example, in the Heart Transplant Task, which requires students to exchange information about candidates for a heart transplant operation, each student will have information about just one of the candidates. Only when all the information is shared do the students have a complete picture of the four candidates. Information-gap tasks can be designed to involve the exchange of very simple information (as, for example, in a Spot the Difference Task) or much more complicated information (as, for example, in the Heart Transplant Task).

An opinion-gap task requires the participants to exchange opinions usually on an issue that is controversial and thus likely to arouse different viewpoints. For example, the Heart Transplant Task could evolve into an opinion-gap task if the students were asked to decide which of the four candidates was the most deserving of the transplant once they had exchanged information about the candidates.

A reasoning-gap task requires the learners to derive some new information by inferring it from the information they have been given. In reasoning-gap tasks the learners engage in synthesizing information and then deducing new facts. Prabhu (1987) argued that reasoning-gap tasks are more likely to result in sustained engagement with meaning than information- or opinion-gap tasks.

Tasks can also be distinguished in terms of whether they are focused or unfocused. Unfocused tasks are tasks designed to provide learners with opportunities for using language in general. Focused tasks are tasks designed to provide opportunities for communicating using some specific linguistic feature (typically a grammatical structure). However, focused tasks must still satisfy the four criteria for tasks stated above. For this reason the target linguistic feature of a focused task is 'hidden' (i.e. learners are not told explicitly what the feature is). Thus, a focused task can still be distinguished from a 'situational grammar exercise', as in the latter learners are made aware of what feature they are supposed to attend to. Focused tasks serve as 'proactive form-focused instruction' (Lyster, 2007); that is, as 'preplanned instruction designed to enable students to notice and to use target language features that might otherwise not be used or even noticed in classroom discourse' (p. 44).[3] They provide opportunities for using specific linguistic features under 'real operating conditions' (i.e. in the same conditions as occur when language is used outside the classroom). Focused tasks are valuable because they can elicit the use of language features that learners might otherwise not attend to and avoid using.

A final important distinction is between input-based tasks and output-based tasks. A common misunderstanding is that TBLT consists of asking learners to perform production tasks – in particular speaking tasks. This misunderstanding has arisen because both teacher educators and SLA researchers have tended to refer only to production-tasks. However, while production-tasks are central to TBLT, they are not essential. TBLT can also make use of input-based tasks. These are tasks that do not require learners to produce in the target language. They take the form of either listening or reading tasks. However, input-based tasks do not prohibit learners' production; they simply do not require it. In fact, when learners perform input-based tasks, they frequently do engage in L2 production, both as private speech (e.g. as when they repeat silently or *sotto voce* a word or phrase they have heard) and as social speech (e.g. when they seek clarification of something they have not understood). Input-based tasks, then, are one-way tasks where the teacher is in charge of the information to be communicated but the learners have the opportunity to negotiate for meaning when they need to.[4]

Input-based tasks must also satisfy the four criteria for a 'task' stated above. It is worth noting that in the case of the third criterion (i.e. learners use their own resources), learners need to use both their linguistic and their non-linguistic resources (i.e. context and world knowledge) to process the input. In input-based tasks, learners' attention to form is achieved through the feedback they receive on whether they have successfully processed the input. However, although they involve listening or reading, their purpose is not just to develop these skills. Like output-based tasks they seek to create communicative contexts in which language can be learned. In task-based instruction, whether involving output-based or input-based tasks, skill development and language learning go hand in hand.

The task-based syllabus

Language teaching involves decisions about: (1) what content to teach and what order to teach it in and (2) how to teach the content. Decision (1) involves syllabus design (see Chapter 3) while (2) involves language teaching methodology. Here we consider the design of task-based courses; in the following section we take a look at the methodology of TBLT.

Distinguishing syllabus design and methodology, however, is controversial in the case of TBLT. Nunan (1989) argued that in task-based teaching the focus shifts from the 'outcomes of instruction' (i.e. the linguistic knowledge or skills to be mastered) towards the 'processes of learning' (i.e. what learners need to do in order to learn) and went on to claim that, in this case, the 'what' and the 'how' of teaching are merged. Kumaravadivelu (1993) also argued that 'methodology becomes the central tenet of task-based pedagogy' (p. 73) since the goal is to allow learners to navigate their own paths and routes to learning. We would argue, however, that a task-based curriculum still involves making decisions about content (i.e. what tasks to include in the syllabus) and methodology (i.e. how the tasks will be carried out in the classroom). Skehan's (1996) distinction between the 'design' and 'implementation' aspects of tasks is premised on a need to distinguish 'syllabus' and 'methodology' in TBLT in the same way as in other approaches to language teaching.

Ellis (2003b) distinguished two types of task-based syllabus: one based entirely on unfocused tasks and one based on focused tasks.[5] In the former, the development of a syllabus requires only a specification of the tasks to be included in the syllabus (i.e. there is no attempt to specify the linguistic content to be taught). In the case of the latter, however, it is necessary to specify both the tasks and the linguistic content to be taught. In a sense, then a syllabus of focused tasks is both a task-based syllabus and a linguistic syllabus. It should be noted, however, that a syllabus consisting of focused tasks still differs from a structural syllabus, as the aim is to promote task-based teaching (where learners are not made aware of what the linguistic focus of a task is) rather than task-supported teaching (where they are made aware). Teachers often ask whether TBLT can incorporate a linguistic syllabus (Samuda and Bygate, 2008). The answer to this is 'yes' providing that the linguistic content of the syllabus does not lead to intentional learning of the target features in the syllabus. It is, of course, also possible to develop a modular syllabus consisting of separate task-based and linguistic components, as proposed by Ellis (2003b). In such a syllabus, the modules are separate (i.e. there is no attempt to integrate the teaching of the linguistic content and the task-based content).

The selection of tasks in a syllabus involves a consideration of the thematic content of the tasks and the types of tasks. The choice of thematic content will depend to a considerable extent on whether the pedagogic purpose of the task-based course is to develop general proficiency or the ability to perform some specific uses of the L2. In the case of the former, the guiding principles in the selection of content for tasks will be: (1) topic familiarity, (2) intrinsic interest and (3) topic relevancy. This will involve predicting the kinds of general situations that learners may later find themselves in.[6] In the Communicational Teaching Project (Prabhu, 1987), many of the tasks involved themes related fairly directly to the school curriculum or aspects of school organization (e.g. the letters of the alphabet, calendars, maps and school timetables). In specific purpose task-based courses it is necessary to first carry out a needs analysis to identify the 'target tasks' that learners will need to perform in real-life situations and then 'translate' these into pedagogic tasks (see Long, 2005).

Once the tasks have been selected they will need to be sequenced. This will involve 'grading' the tasks so that they pose a steadily increasing challenge for the learners. Widdowson (1990a) noted that sequencing tasks faces several problems, in particular the choice of the grading criteria to be used. He argued that we do not possess a sufficiently well-defined model of cognitive complexity to establish such criteria. In this respect, however, a task-based syllabus is problematic in much the same way as are linguistic syllabuses as there is no accepted model of linguistic complexity either (see Chapter 3). However, a number of criteria for grading tasks have been proposed (Candlin, 1987; Nunan, 1989; Brindley, 1987). Drawing on these Ellis (2003b) suggested that grading should take account of:

- Input (i.e. the information that learners are exposed to in the task work-plan). Ellis suggested that this would involve a consideration of the medium of the input (i.e. whether it was verbal or non-verbal), linguistic complexity in the case of verbal input, the learners' familiarity with the topic, and context dependency (i.e. whether the input was contextually supported by, for example, visual information).

- Task conditions (e.g. a task involving a single operation will be easier to perform than a task involving dual operations).
- Process factors (e.g. a task involving only the conveyance of information is likely to be easier than a task involving giving and justifying opinions).
- Task outcome (e.g. whether the outcome is closed or open and how complex the outcome is – for example, a closed task such as Spot the Difference Task that requires learners to only identify a limited number of differences will be easier than an open task, such as the Heart Transplant Task, which requires learners to decide which candidate should receive the heart transplant).

Such grading criteria, however, only provide general guidelines for the sequencing of tasks. As Prabhu (1987) pointed out 'no syllabus of generalized tasks can identify or anticipate all the sources of challenge to particular learners' (p. 89). Ellis (2003b) concluded his discussion of grading criteria by proposing that course designers should first assess the complexity of tasks intuitively and then use explicit criteria to evaluate the reliability of their assessment.

Implementation of TBLT

The implementation of a task-based syllabus involves a consideration of a number of factors: (1) the design of a lesson, (2) the participatory structure of the lesson and (3) the roles adopted by the teacher and the students.

While various designs for a task-based lesson have been proposed (e.g. Estaire and Zanon, 1994; Lee, 2000; Prabhu, 1987; Skehan, 1996; Willis, 1996), they all have in common three principal phases: a pre-task phase, a main-task phase and a post-task phase. In each of these a number of options are possible (see Ellis, 2003b). Some of the main options are shown in Table 6.1. These options affect how students perform the task. Some are intended to make the task easier (e.g. the pre-task options listed in Table 6.1) while others make it more difficult (e.g. time pressure in the main task phase). A number of options provide for a focus on linguistic form in the pre-task phase (e.g. pre-task planning, which encourages students to think about the language they will need to perform the task) and 'language work' in the post-task phase. A point of controversy, however, is in what phase attention to form should ideally occur, with Willis (1996) arguing that it should be reserved to the post-task phase and Ellis (2003b) proposing that it can occur in all phases of the lesson. Some versions of TBLT allow for the pre-teaching of linguistic features in the pre-task phase but, as we have already noted, this may result in learners treating the task as requiring them to focus on the linguistic form they have been taught rather than on communicating to achieve the task outcome.

Table 6.1 Implementation options in the different phases of a task-based lesson

Phase	Options	Description
Pre-task phase	1. Modelling performance of the task	Students listen or watch the task being performed by 'experts'.
	2. Pre-teaching language	The teacher presents language that will be useful for performing the task.
	3. Schema-developing	The teacher elicits and extends students' knowledge of the topic of the task.
	4. Strategic planning	The students are given time to prepare to perform the task before they actually perform it.
Main-task phase	1. Time pressure	Students are given only a limited amount of time to perform the task.
	2. Contextual support	Students are allowed to access the input data when they perform the task.
	3. Explicit instruction	The teacher takes time out from the performance of the task to explicitly teach a linguistic feature that is useful for performing the task.
	4. Surprise element	Additional information relevant to the task is provided after the students have started to perform the task.
Post-task phase	1. Repeat performance	Students are asked to repeat the task.
	2. Report	Students are asked to report the outcome of the task to the whole class.
	3. Language work	Students complete language exercises related to linguistic problems that they experienced when performing the task.

The participatory structure of a lesson concerns how the teacher's and students' contributions to the performance of the task are organized. A basic distinction can be made according to whether the type of participation is individual (i.e. each student works by him or herself) or social (i.e. interaction occurs between the participants). In the case of social organization, various options are possible: the teacher can conduct an activity in lockstep with the whole class, a student can take on the role of 'teacher' and perform the task with the rest of the class or the students can be asked to interact among themselves in small groups or pairs. Differences exist regarding the type of participatory structure favoured by different advocates of task-based teaching. Willis and Willis (2007) emphasize social activity in small group work and TBLT is frequently associated with this type of participatory structure. Prabhu (1987), however, rejected group work in favour of the teacher performing the task in lockstep with the whole class and the students subsequently performing a similar task individually. Input-based tasks necessarily involve a teacher–class participatory structure.

TBLT, like Communicative Language Teaching, sees language classes as social events (Breen, 2001) and language learners as active agents of their learning (Breen, 1987). Therefore, the teacher's role needs to shift from that of knowledge-provider to that of facilitator (Gatbonton and Segalowitz, 2005) while the students' role changes from that of 'language learner' to that of 'communicator'. The nature of the teacher's role will vary according to whether the task is to be performed in lockstep with the teacher or in pairs or small groups. Shintani (forthcoming) suggested how a teacher can facilitate learners' performance of input-based tasks carried out in a whole-class context. The teacher can:

- Scaffold learners' participation in the interactions that arise out of the performance of a task through the use of gesture and repetition.
- Orientate learners to focus on meaning by making the task outcome clear from the beginning, and then making it clear when the outcome has been reached.
- Make use of the L1 to support the learners' comprehension but gradually shift to the use of the L2 as learners' confidence and ability to comprehend the L2 increases.
- Encourage learners to negotiate when they fail to comprehend the teacher's commands.
- Encourage learners to initiate use of the L2 (i.e. do not position them always as respondents to the teacher's questions or statements).
- Give clear feedback to learners' verbal and non-verbal responses.

Other teacher educators (e.g. Samuda, 2001) have argued that teachers can sometimes usefully adopt a more didactic role in task-based teaching – for example, by taking time out from the performance of a task to explicitly explain points of language. Other teacher roles are also needed when the learners perform tasks in groups. Jacobs (1998) mentions modelling collaboration, observing and monitoring the students' performance, and intervening in group work when learners are clearly experiencing difficulty. Also a teacher can function as a task participant, sitting with students to do the task.

For tasks to work as they are intended, students need to function primarily as 'communicators' rather than as 'learners'. However, as many commentators have noted, it is unlikely that students (especially older ones) will totally abandon the learner role when performing a task, as they recognize that ultimately the aim is to improve their L2 proficiency. Perhaps, then, what is needed is for learners to move backwards and forwards between these two roles. This can occur when students work collaboratively in groups, assisting each other with linguistic problems when they arise, but orienting primarily to achieving the task outcome. Educators see collaborative activity in group work as a key feature in the successful implementation of task-based teaching (Storch, 2001).

SLA theories and research

We turn now to examine the SLA theories that have informed – and been used to promote – TBLT. These theories address many of the key pedagogic issues – what types of tasks to include in a syllabus, how to sequence them and the options for implementing them in ways that will promote learning. All the theories we will consider are based on the assumption that acquisition requires learners to pay attention to form as well as meaning (see Principle 3 in Chapter 1). They differ, however, in how they think this can be best achieved in TBLT. These theories have generated a large number of studies. However, we will not attempt a full survey of the research but instead consider a few key studies.

Focus on form in interaction (Long, 1991; Lyster, 2001)

As we have seen, tasks require a primary focus on meaning. However, for acquisition to take place learners also need to pay attention to form. Long claimed that L2 acquisition is best promoted when learners are led to attend to form in a context where they are endeavouring to express their meaning intentions. He coined the term 'Focus on Form' (FonF) to refer to the occasional shifts in learners' attention from meaning to a linguistic form that can occur while the overriding focus remains on communicating (Long, 1991). This shift can be triggered by perceived problems with either comprehension or production and it can be initiated either by the teacher or by the learners themselves. A key feature of FonF is that it emphasizes form-function mapping. That is, it draws attention not just to a linguistic form but also to the semantic or pragmatic meaning realized by that form in the specific context in which it is used. As Doughty (2001) put it, attention to form facilitates acquisition in the 'window of opportunity' that arises when learners are struggling to decode or encode a message that is communicatively important to them.

Long claims that Focus on Form is compatible with how learners acquire an L2. In Chapter 3 we referred to research that has shown learners acquire grammatical features in well-defined orders and sequences and we saw that such a finding cannot be easily reconciled with an approach to language teaching based on a structural syllabus (what Long refers to as 'Focus on Forms'). It is for this reason that Long argues that attention to form needs to occur at a time the learner is ready to acquire it and that this can be best achieved by drawing attention to those specific features that the learner is attempting to use in communication, but is using incorrectly.

Long's views about the importance of FonF derive from his earlier work on the role of interaction in L2 acquisition. These are considered fully in Chapter 8 (see also Chapter 1) so we will only briefly outline them here. The Interaction Hypothesis (Long 1983b, 1996) claims that interaction promotes acquisition when 'negotiation of meaning' occurs; that is, when learners experience a problem in comprehending something or when they are unable to clearly say what they want to say. In such situations, their interlocutors resort to various discourse strategies such as recasts or clarification requests. Recasts are utterances that reformulate the problematic utterance in a target-like way as in this example:

Learner: I visit doctor.

Teacher: You visited your doctor yesterday?

Learner: Yes, yesterday.

Clarification requests are utterances that prompt the learner to reformulate the problematic utterance so it can be understood as in this example:

Learner: I visit doctor.

Teacher: Sorry?

Learner: Yesterday I visited doctor.

Such strategies help learners make the link between meaning and form: it induces learners' attention to the linguistic form required to convey the message the learner is trying to understand or to produce. It achieves this in three ways: (1) by means of 'negative evidence' (i.e. signalling to learners that something they have said contravenes target language norms), (2) by providing learners with 'positive evidence' that enables them to notice the gap between their existing L2 system and the target language system and (3) by pushing learners to modify their own erroneous output (Pica, 1998).

For Long, FonF works for acquisition when there is negotiation of meaning in the context of face-to-face interaction arising from the performance of a task. Long (2008) also argued that negotiation involving recasts is especially facilitative of acquisition because they provide learners with both negative and positive evidence. Lyster (2001) adopted a different position. First, he argued that what he called 'negotiation of form' (i.e. the attention to form that arises even when there is no communication problem) can also facilitate acquisition. For example, if a learner says 'I go cinema yesterday' the teacher is unlikely to have a problem understanding but may still 'negotiate' by saying 'Oh you went to cinema yesterday'. In this case, the focus is on a linguistic problem not a communicative problem. Second, he challenged Long's claims about the importance of recasts. He argued that recasts are often ineffective because learners do not notice they are being corrected and also fail to 'uptake' the correct form in their subsequent utterance. He claimed that prompts (e.g. clarification requests) are more likely to assist learning by helping learners to obtain greater control over these forms they have already partially acquired. The debate concerning which type of negotiation strategy – recasts or prompts – is best equipped to assist acquisition, however, can be easily resolved if it is acknowledged that acquisition involves both the learning of new forms (for which recasts may be needed) and the increase of control of partially acquired forms (for which prompts may be more effective). Lyster is justified, however, in arguing that negotiation of form is just as effective as the negotiation of meaning as it also serves to draw learners' attention to linguistic form in the context of communication. There does not always have to be a communication breakdown. We will revisit the debate between Long and Lyster in Chapter 10 when we consider the role of corrective feedback in L2 acquisition.

One of the most extensive studies of FonF in classroom interaction is Ellis et al.'s (2001) study of what they called 'form-focused episodes'. This study examined the occasions and the various ways in which teachers drew learners' attention to form, while tasks were being performed in a whole-class context in a private language school in New Zealand. The study also investigated the extent to which the learners successful repaired their errors in these episodes. The main findings of this study are summarized in Table 6.2. This study did not investigate whether the form-focused episodes led to learning but in a follow-up study Loewen (2005) was able to show that learners who participated in such episodes were subsequently able to use the same forms accurately over 50 per cent of the

Table 6.2 Summary of the main findings of Ellis et al.'s (2001) study of form-focused episodes in task-based classrooms

Main finding	Comment
There was a total of 448 episodes (one every 1.6 minutes)	This constitutes a remarkable high level of attention to form. However, it did not disturb the 'communicative flow' of the tasks.
Reactive and pre-emptive FFEs evenly balanced	Ellis et al. investigated occasions when FonF occurred when the teacher attempted to pre-empt a linguistic problem (i.e. attempted to prevent a linguistic error occurring) as well as reactively in negotiation sequences. Thus, they extended the definition of FonF to cover any occasion in a task performance where the teacher drew attention to form.
Episodes arising out of a need to just attend to form outnumbered those where a communication problem occurred 3 to 1	This reflects the fact that when primary attention is directed at meaning as required in TBLT, teachers and learners are also likely to take opportunities to attend to form even if there is no communication problem.
Over 80% of the episodes were simple	A simple episode was defined as one consisting of no more than four turns. The form-focused episodes were typically simple and therefore transitory.
Explicit and implicit episodes evenly balanced (but responding episodes were mainly indirect)	Many of the episodes were quite explicit (i.e. form was addressed in a direct and clear fashion). Implicit episodes often involved recasts.
Grammar and vocabulary accounted for 75% of all episodes	The study also investigated pronunciation and discourse/ sociolinguistic aspects of language use but these received little attention.
The overall level of successful uptake of the target form by the learners was high	The learners responded by making efforts to self-correct and were generally successful.
Teacher-initiated episodes were less likely to result in successful uptake than learner-initiated episodes	Learner-initiated episodes were those where a learner either posed a question about a linguistic form or said something that created a communicative or linguistic problem which the teacher responded to. Teacher-initiated episodes occurred when the teacher attempted to pre-empt a linguistic problem.

time, suggesting that learning had taken place. This research, then, showed that the negotiation or meaning of form occurred frequently in task-based lessons involving adult learners and that it appears to facilitate learning.

A cognitive theory of L2 learning (Skehan)

Skehan has been in the forefront of theorizing about the role that tasks can play in language learning and together with Pauline Foster and others, conducted a number of studies investigating how various task design and implementation variables impact on L2 production. His theoretical position was outlined in his 1998 book and further developed in subsequent publications (see his 2011 book which provides a collection of his articles on tasks and task-based teaching).

His theory involves the following premises:

1 A dual-mode linguistic system
Skehan (1998) proposed that speakers (native speakers and learners) possess a dual-mode linguistic system and that much of language is exemplar rather than rule-based – a position compatible with the importance that many SLA researchers attach to formulaic sequences (see Chapter 3). Learners are able to draw on their exemplar-based system in real-time language processing. However, a memory-based system is limited and not all language use involves real-time processing. There are times when language users need to formulate precise and novel propositions. This requires a rule-based system. When users are not under pressure to perform rapidly online, they have the time to access such a system.

2 Attention capacity is limited
Skehan argued that learners' have limited processing capacity and this therefore restricts what they can attend to. He commented: 'I take it to be natural for human beings to prioritize meaning, and in the case of second language speakers it follows that when there is communicative pressure of any sort, meaning will be the priority, and form will be something of a luxury' (2011: 398). In other words, learners have difficulty in attending simultaneously to both meaning and form and, as a result, will need to prioritize one or the other. Prioritizing form is only possible if they do not have to devote all their efforts to communicating meaning. Skehan proposed the Trade-Off Hypothesis, according to which attention to one aspect of L2 production (e.g. meaning) has a detrimental effect on another aspect (e.g. form).

3 Tension between acquisition and performance
Performance requires learners to prioritize meaning; however, acquisition necessitates attention to form in order for linguistic material to be transferred from working memory to long-term memory. Also, the aspects of form attended to need to lead to 'cumulative and patterned development' (p. 398). The tension between performance and acquisition constitutes the major challenge facing TBLT.

4 Focus on form
   Thus, focus on form is essential for acquisition but not for performance. Tasks that simply prioritize achieving the outcome will not work for acquisition: 'for any task-based approach to work, conditions have to be created so that form is not forgotten' (p. 398). This necessitates ensuring that the task conditions are not excessively demanding so that processing capacity is freed to attend to form. Focus on form can be promoted if learners are given an opportunity to plan before they perform a task.

5 Complexity, accuracy and fluency
   Skehan argued that the performance of a task needs to be examined in relation to three dimensions of production: complexity, accuracy and fluency. Fluency requires learners to draw on their memory-based system, accessing and deploying ready-made chunks of language and, when problems arise, using communication strategies to get by. Accuracy and complexity are achieved by learners drawing on their rule-based system and thus require syntactic processing. Complexity is distinguished from accuracy in that it is related to the 'restructuring' that arises as a result of the need to take risks, whereas accuracy reflects the learner's efforts to control existing resources and to avoid errors.

6 Levelt's model of speaking
   Skehan drew on Levelt's model of speaking to provide a well-established theoretical basis for his different premises. A key distinction in Levelt's (1989) model is 'conceptualization' and 'formulation'. The former concerns the propositional content that a speaker wishes to convey and the communicative intent. The latter involves developing a linguistic plan for encoding the message by accessing both lexis and grammar. Skehan argued that conceptualization links with complexity (i.e. the more detailed the conceptualization, the more complex the language needed) and formulation with accuracy and fluency, both of which depend on the degree of control that speakers are able to exercise over their linguistic system. L1 and L2 speakers do not differ with regard to conceptualization but they do with regard to formulation. Frequently, L2 speakers find themselves experiencing difficulty in formulating messages to encode the messages they have conceptualized.

7 Interlanguage development
   Skehan suggested that the three dimensions of language production can also account for how interlanguage development takes place. That is there is a natural sequence consisting of:

   Complexity → accuracy → fluency

   Learners first acquire new L2 features but cannot use them accurately or fluently. They achieve control over them by first slowing down to avoid error and then by speaking more rapidly. This pattern of development accords with skill-learning theory as propounded by Anderson in his ACT-R model (Anderson, 1983: 15; see Chapter 4). However, Skehan does not consider that this pattern of development can be accomplished through explicit instruction of the PPP kind. Rather it requires using tasks that create communicative contexts in which it can occur naturally.

Skehan's research has both fed off his theory and helped to develop it. In a series of experimental studies conducted in conjunction with Foster, he has systematically investigated a range of design and implementation variables, measuring their effect on learners' performance of different tasks in terms of the complexity, accuracy and fluency of their production. For reasons of space we consider only one study here – the study that, in fact, began it all. Foster and Skehan (1996) investigated thirty-two pre-intermediate ESL learners' performance of three different tasks (a narrative task, a personal task and a decision-making task). The learners performed these tasks under three conditions – detailed strategic planning, undetailed strategic planning and no strategic planning. The difference between detailed and undetailed planning rests in the extent to which the learners are guided to attend to form. Various measures of complexity, accuracy and fluency were calculated. They found that planning aided fluency and complexity with more detailed planning having a greater effect than undetailed planning. Detailed planning also resulted in greater variety of past tense usage. However, somewhat surprisingly, undetailed planning led to greater overall accuracy. There were also differences in the performance of the three tasks. The personal task resulted in the greatest fluency while the effects of undetailed planning on accuracy were much greater in the decision-making task.

Summarizing the results of such studies, Skehan (2011) proposed a number of relationships between task variables and the processes involved in conceptualization and formulation. He distinguished task variables that complexify/pressurize performance of a task and those that ease performance and so encourage learners to focus on form. Strategic planning, for example, is seen as an implementation variable that assists conceptualization and thus leads to greater complexity in production. In contrast, a task that involves concrete, static information eases the pressure on conceptualization and thus encourages a focus on form. In the case of formulation, requiring learners to perform the task in a limited period of time pressurizes learners, while including a post-task condition encourages a focus on form. In short, as Skehan put it 'One needs to distinguish the complexity of a pre-verbal message from the difficulties that arise from the expression of the message subsequently' (p. 530). The extent to which TBLT is successful in promoting acquisition will depend on the skill of the task designer and the teacher in manipulating the design and implementation variables of different tasks to achieve a balance between complexity, accuracy and fluency.

The Cognition Hypothesis (Robinson)

Probably the most ambitious attempt to formulate a theory of task-based teaching and learning is Peter Robinson's Cognition Hypothesis (Robinson,

2001, 2003, 2005). The basic claim of Robinson's theory is that complex tasks will promote more accurate and complex, though less fluent, language than simpler tasks. Robinson also proposed that complex tasks lead to more interaction, greater attention to form, and more uptake of information from the input than simpler tasks.

Drawing on the Cognition Hypothesis, Robinson (2007; 2011c) proposed the Triadic Componential Framework (TCF) for L2 task classification. The three components are: (1) task complexity, (2) task conditions and (3) task difficulty. Robinson identifies key variables relating to each of these. In the case of task complexity, he distinguishes 'resource directing' and 'resource-dispersing' variables. Resource-directing variables govern the demands made on the learner's attention and, thereby, the extent to which the learner focuses on specific linguistic forms. Thus, potentially, they influence interlanguage development. Task variables that are resource-directing include whether the task requires: (1) reference to events happening in the 'here-and-now' or to events that took place in the past elsewhere (in the 'there-and-then'), (2) reference to a few easily distinguishable features or to many similar features, (3) reference to easily identifiable locations or to locations where no support is available and (4) transmission of simple information or provision of reasons for intentions, beliefs or relations. Resource-dispersing variables govern the procedural demands made on the learners' attentional and memory resources, but they do not affect the extent to which they attend to specific linguistic forms and, thus, Robinson claims they enhance automaticity but do not promote the acquisition of new L2 forms. Examples are: (1) providing or not providing strategic planning time, (2) providing or not providing background knowledge prior to performance of the task, (3) a task with or without a clear structure, (4) a task involving a few or many steps to complete it and (5) a task that requires just one or several operations to be performed.

The second component, task conditions, includes variables that affect the demands made on learners when they perform a task. Robinson distinguishes two kinds of demands. Participation variables influence what he calls 'interactional demands'. Examples are: (1) open solution (i.e. whether the task has many possible outcomes or just one or a limited number), (2) one-way vs two-way flow (i.e. whether the task allocates all the information to one learner or splits it among both or several learners) and (3) convergent vs divergent solution (i.e. whether the task requires students to agree on a solution/outcome or allows them to disagree). Participant variables make 'interactant demands'. For example, the demands made on the participants will vary depending on the proficiency level of the learners, whether they are of the same or different gender, their familiarity with the topic of the task and whether or not they have shared cultural knowledge.

The third component is 'task difficulty'. This concerns learner factors rather than task factors and so, Robinson claims, affect learners' perceptions of task difficulty, which contribute to between-learner variation in how successful a particular task is performed. Robinson distinguishes two sets of learner factors

– those relating to the individual learners' ability (e.g. working memory or reasoning skills) and those relating to learners' affective response to a task (e.g. task motivation and anxiety). Robinson proposes that such factors will play a bigger role in influencing how learners perform complex tasks than simple tasks.

At the heart of the Complexity Hypothesis is Robinson's attempt to predict the complexity level of different tasks. Robinson argues that 'L2 pedagogic tasks should be sequenced for learners on the basis of increases in their cognitive complexity' (2011b: 9). He gives an example of how this might be achieved. Thus before asking learners to perform a highly complex task they should be asked to perform a series of lead-in tasks that are less complex. The complex task involved a number of cognitive operations – complex reasoning, reporting what happened and providing an explanation for an event. The lead-in tasks involved gradually complexifying the demands made on the learners in terms of +/-planning time, +/-reasoning and type of reasoning (i.e. simple vs complex). Thus the Complexity Hypothesis constitutes an attempt to address Widdowson's (2003) critique of TBLT, namely that there is no theory of cognitive complexity that can be used to grade and sequence tasks.

The Cognition Hypothesis affords a number of predictions:

- Increasing the conceptual demands of a task by manipulating resource-directing variables will have an effect on *both* the accuracy and the complexity of learners' production when they perform a task. This prediction contradicts Skehan's Trade-Off Hypothesis as it sees accuracy and complexity as clearly linked.
- Complex tasks will lead to more interaction and negotiation of meaning than simple tasks.
- In contrast, resource-dispersing variables ease the pressure on learners and so help them to use the L2 with greater fluency.
- There will be less variation among learners when they perform simple tasks than when they perform complex tasks.

These predictions have led to a host of studies (see, for example, the studies in Robinson, 2011c) but with somewhat mixed results. We will give one example here. Kim (2009) asked thirty-four adult learners enrolled in an intensive English programme in the US to perform a number of tasks during regular class periods. These tasks differed in complexity with regard to whether or not reasoning was required in the narrative tasks and the number of elements in the Spot the Difference tasks. Kim investigated the effect of task complexity on the extent to which the learners' clearly focused on form when they performed the tasks interactively, which she measured in terms of 'language related episodes' (LREs). These are episodes where learners focus on some aspect of form (i.e. analogous to the Form-Focused Episodes discussed earlier). The main prediction of the Cognition Hypothesis (the first one listed above) was only partially supported. For example, the group of high-proficiency learners engaged in more LREs in the Picture Narration task and were more linguistically accurate when performing the complex version (in line with the Cognition Hypothesis). However, the low-proficiency learners participated in more LREs when performing the simple narration task. In the case of the Spot the Difference Task, the low proficiency group's performance of the simple version conformed to the prediction of the Complexity Hypothesis. However, different results were obtained for the high-proficiency group, where no difference was evident in their performance of the simple and complex version of the tasks.

It should be noted that many of the studies testing the Cognition Hypothesis have been laboratory based (Kim's study being a notable exception), casting some doubt on the relevance of their findings to the L2 classroom. In this respect, the research differs from that based on Skehan's Cognitive Theory, which, in the main, was carried out in actual classrooms.

Summing up

These three theories provide a clear basis for explaining how task-based teaching can contribute to L2 acquisition. Central to all three is the notion that attention to form in the context of meaning-focused language is necessary for acquisition to take place. They differ only in how they propose attention to form should occur and how tasks can ensure that it does. According to Focus on Form, tasks promote acquisition through the negotiation of meaning or form. According to Skehan's cognitive theory of L2 learning, tasks promote learning when they create the conditions that favour either complexity or accuracy. According to Robinson's Complexity Hypothesis, task complexity promotes acquisition by inducing attention to form that results in both increased complexity and accuracy and in the kinds of interaction (e.g. negotiation of meaning) that facilitate acquisition. These theories have spawned numerous studies investigating how specific task design and implementation variables affect learners' performance of different tasks. They do not always afford consistent results but they have demonstrated conclusively that it is possible to manipulate learners' attention to form while they are communicating in ways that are likely to promote acquisition. However, there is still only limited evidence that such manipulation actually results in acquisition. In general the studies have focused on task performance (i.e. production), not on learning and have been cross-sectional rather than longitudinal. This has allowed room for critiques of task-based teaching to emerge. We will now turn to these.

Critiques of TBLT

Criticisms of TBLT have been advanced by both researchers (e.g. Seedhouse, 1999, 2005) and by teacher educators and course book writers (e.g. Bruton, 2002; Sheen, 2003; Swan, 2005). The essential difference between these two groups is that whereas the first based its criticisms on evidence, the latter rely on opinion derived from their own experience of teaching. Norris (2007) referred to the former as 'critics' and the latter as 'pundits'.

Ellis (2009) examined ten criticisms of TBLT and provided responses to them. He pointed out that in many cases the pundits had misunderstood what TBLT involves, setting up 'aunt sallies' to attack. Here we will address a number of the major criticisms and examine them in terms of the theoretical positions advanced in the previous section and the research they have spawned (i.e. we will attempt an evidence-based response).

TBLT neglects the teaching of grammar

The pundits have argued that a task-based syllabus does not offer any grammar teaching. Sheen (2003), for example, claimed that in task-based language teaching there is 'no grammar syllabus', and Swan (2005) argued that TBLT 'outlaws' the grammar syllabus. As we noted earlier, this is also an issue for teachers, who commonly question when grammar can be taught in task-based teaching (Willis and Willis, 2007; Samuda and Bygate, 2008).

First, it should be noted that grammar can be incorporated directly into a task-based syllabus through focused tasks. However, not all proponents of TBLT advocate this. Skehan, for example, seeks to induce a broad focus on form (including grammar) by designing unfocused tasks that encourage the use of clusters of grammatical features rather than specific predetermined features. Studies have shown that it is also quite difficult to design tasks that make the use of a specific grammatical feature essential (Loschky and Bley-Vroman, 1993). For this reason it may be easier to induce focus on grammatical form methodologically rather than through task design – for example, by providing opportunities for strategic and online planning, or through the negotiation of meaning and of form, or, in the post-task phase of a lesson by the direct (and even traditional) teaching of linguistic features that were shown to be problematic for learners in the main-task phase. In short, TBLT provides for the teaching of grammar in a variety of ways. What it seeks to avoid is the explicit, itemized, linear approach to grammar teaching that the pundits clearly favour.

TBLT does not cater for the acquisition of 'new language'

Another common criticism of TBLT is that it 'provides learners with substantially less new language than "traditional" approaches' (Swan 2005).

One of the main premises of TBLT is that L2 acquisition takes place when learners notice or pay selective attention to form while engaging in communication. Thus, tasks aim to create communicative situations where the learners are encouraged to use their own linguistic resources freely. However, TBLT can also offer a variety of opportunities for learning new language through the input that the performance of tasks provides. Studies have shown how 'listen-and-do tasks' can be enriched with 'new' vocabulary in ways that foster acquisition (e.g. Loschky, 1994; Ellis et al., 1994; Ellis and Heimbach, 1997; Shintani, 2011, 2012). Other studies have shown that such tasks can also be seeded with grammatical features with positive effects on acquisition

(Shintani and Ellis, 2010; Shintani, 2013). These studies have shown that such tasks are effective both for developing listening comprehension and as a means for exposing learners to new linguistic material in ways that foster acquisition. Reading tasks afford similar opportunities. Indeed, extensive reading activities can be viewed as tasks. Studies (e.g. Dupuy and Krashen, 1993) have shown that incidental vocabulary acquisition occurs as a result of extensive reading. In short, tasks can provide much greater exposure to the target language, including 'new' language, than the kinds of activities typically found in course books of the kind Swan favours.

TBLT neglects aspects of language other than grammar

Swan (2005) claimed that the 'theoretical rationale for TBLT is typically limited to the acquisition of grammar and that vocabulary and phonology are ignored'. However, all the theoretical positions outlined in the previous section cater to all levels of language, not just to grammar. 'Focus on Form', for example, involves attention to phonological, lexical and discourse features as well as grammatical. Ellis et al. (2001), in the study referred to earlier, reported that out of 429 focus-on-form episodes in some twelve hours of TBLT in two adult ESL classes, 159 addressed lexical problems and 76 pronunciation problems. In fact, in this study, the combined number of focus-on-form episodes for vocabulary and pronunciation exceeded that for grammar. In a follow-up study, Loewen (2005) found an even greater emphasis on vocabulary and pronunciation: in twelve adult ESL classes involving thirty-two hours of TBLT, 43 per cent of the form-focused episodes addressed vocabulary and 22 per cent pronunciation, while only 33 per cent addressed grammar.

TBLT limits the role of the teacher

Earlier in this chapter we noted that the teacher's main role in TBLT is that of facilitator. Reflecting this, Swan (2005) argued that task-based language teaching promotes learner-centredness at the expense of teacher-directed instruction. Swan comments: 'the thrust of TBLT is to cast the teacher in the role of manager and facilitator of communicative activity rather than an important source of new language' (p 391). This criticism, however, is based on an over-narrow view of what the facilitator role involves. It entails far more than just setting learners to work on a task in groups, as Shintani's (forthcoming) list of roles a teacher can perform when conducting input-based tasks with learners illustrates. Shintani argued that a teacher needs to act as a 'resource provider' as well as a 'navigator' when performing input-based tasks with young beginner learners. Even in production-based tasks, the need to direct learners' attention to form during the performance of the task requires the teacher to engage in various types of pre-emptive and reactive focus on form. Prabhu (1987), for instance, argued that it was only the teacher who could ensure the 'good models' of English needed to promote interlanguage development. Samuda (2001) noted that 'central to the role of the teacher in TBLT must be ways of working *with* tasks to guide learners towards the types of language processing believed to support L2 development' (p. 120, emphasis in original).

Tasks result in very limited learner outputs

A more serious potential problem with TBLT is that tasks result only in samples of impoverished language use that are of little value for acquisition. Seedhouse (2004) provided some evidence of this. He compared the interactions that occurred when learners performed tasks in pairs with those that arose in what he called 'meaning and fluency oriented contexts' (i.e. classroom contexts where interaction arises out of a real communicative need). He found that the performance of tasks was characterized by indexicalized and pidginized language, because the learners had limited linguistic resources and were over-reliant on context. In contrast, the interactions in the meaning and fluency context were linguistically richer and more naturalistic. Seedhouse argued that task-based interactions may lead to fossilization rather than acquisition.

However, as the theories discussed in the previous section make clear, the nature of the interactions that take place in TBLT will depend on the individual students, the design features of the task and the method of implementation. More advanced learners performing more complex tasks will engage in more linguistically rich interactions, especially if they are given the opportunity to engage in pre-task and online planning (Yuan and Ellis, 2003). Robinson's Cognition Hypothesis suggests that what determines the language used in performing a task is task complexity and that it is possible to sequence tasks that will scaffold increasingly complex production.

TBLT is not suitable for beginner learners or foreign language contexts

A commonly held view (see Swan, 2005) is that beginner learners need to be taught grammar because without it they will not be able to communicate. A corollary of this belief is that TBLT is only suited to 'acquisition-rich' environments (e.g. where learners have access to the target language in the wider community) and is not suited to 'acquisition-poor' environments (such as many 'foreign' teaching contexts), where a more structured approach is required to ensure that learners develop the grammatical resources needed for communicating.

There are a number of problems with this line of argument. First, it assumes that TBLT always involves pair-work or group-work tasks. Such tasks are only possible for students who have sufficient communicative skills in the L2. If the learners do not have these skills, they will need to use their mother tongue to complete the tasks and, as a result, might produce very little L2. It seems evident that such tasks are not suitable for beginner learners. However, as we have pointed out, tasks can also be input-based. There is plenty of evidence (see e.g. Ellis, 1999 for a review of studies) to show that input-based tasks enable learners to develop not only the ability to comprehend input but also the grammatical resources they will need to speak and write.

It is also important to recognize that learners do not need grammar to perform simple tasks. As we saw in Chapter 3, natural L2 acquisition does not begin with 'grammar' but with a basic variety that is essentially lexical. Grammaticalization takes place only very gradually. So there is no need to delay task-based teaching until learners have been taught some grammar. An assumption of TBLT is that the acquisition of the grammar of a language is a slow, organic process which the learner – not the teacher – is in charge of.

It can also be argued that TBLT is ideal for situations where there are only limited communicative opportunities outside the classroom (as in most foreign language contexts). The absence of such opportunities makes it even more important to ensure they are made available inside the classroom. TBLT provides a means for achieving this.

Studies comparing TBLT and PPP

Given the dysfunctional relationship that frequently holds between researchers and teachers (Clarke, 1994), it is perhaps not surprising to find that it is those language teaching professionals not engaged in research who are the most critical of SLA researchers' promotion of TBLT. But, as Skehan (2011) pointed out, there really is no justification for rejecting research in favour of personal experience as a basis for deciding how a language should be taught. Perhaps, though, there is a need to subject the rival claims of TBLT and more traditional approaches to direct empirical scrutiny, as Sheen (2003) has called for.

In fact, there have been relatively few studies that have compared TBLT and traditional approaches. Sheen (2006) conducted a longitudinal comparative study of the effects of focus on form (involving TBLT with corrective feedback) and focus on forms (involving PPP) on the acquisition of question forms and adverb placement by French grade six elementary students. The results of an aural written comprehension test, a grammatical judgement test and an oral interview showed that the FonFs group improved significantly on all the tests while the control group did not. The FonFs group also outperformed the FonF group. However, the design of the study clearly favoured the FonFs group as there was no attempt to ensure that the target features were systematically attended to in the FonF group. In effect, then, the task-based instruction was not implemented in accordance with the key principle of TBLT – the need to ensure a focus on form.

De la Fuente (2006) compared PPP with production-based TBLT with and without a post-task explicit explanation of the lexical forms that were the target of the instruction. The participants were university students in an elementary Spanish class. The PPP learners received 50 minutes of instruction consisting of the three phases of the PPP – explanation of the new words (presentation), controlled oral and written production exercises (practice) and a role play performed in pairs (free production). The students in the two TBLT conditions worked on a restaurant task in pairs where students needed to negotiate the meaning of the target words to complete the task (i.e. ordering food). After completing the task, the '+explicit' instruction group received explicit explanations of the words whereas the '-explicit' instruction group simply repeated the same task. Acquisition was measured by means of a discrete-item oral production test. The results showed that the three conditions were equally effective in the immediate post-test. However, in the delayed post-test, conducted one week after the treatment, both TBLT groups outperformed the PPP group. There was no significant difference between the two TBLT conditions. Examining the interactions that occurred in each group, de la Fuente found that the TBLT instruction provided more opportunities for the negotiation of meaning, production of the target words, and online retrieval of target words than the PPP. This study shows that FonF can lead to better vocabulary acquisition than FonFs. However, as de la Fuente pointed out, a limitation of the study was that acquisition was only measured by discrete-point test.

Other studies have also shown that, in some respects, TBLT is superior to PPP. Shintani (2013) compared TBLT involving input-based tasks with PPP for young beginner learners. The target features were a set of English concrete nouns and adjectives. The input-based groups performed a set of listen-and-do tasks which required the learners to identify the target nouns. The participants in this group did not receive any explicit information about the meanings of the target words. The production-based group, on the other hand, did receive explicit instruction in the 'present' phase of PPP, which was followed by oral production practice and game-like activities that required the learners to produce the target nouns. Interestingly, Shintani found similar levels of productive knowledge in the two groups' acquisition of the nouns, despite the significantly fewer opportunities for output in the input-based group. In the case of adjectives, however, the input-based group outperformed the PPP group. Shintani explained the results in terms of differences in the nature of the interactions that occurred in the two groups. While the interactions in the production-based group consisted of IRF (i.e. initiate–respond–feedback) exchanges (Sinclair and Coulthard, 1975), the interactions in the input-based group involved negotiation of meaning which was often initiated by the students.

Shintani (2013) also looked at the effects of the same two types of instruction on the incidental acquisition of plural-s and copula *be*. The two grammatical features were not directly taught to either the PPP or the TBLT groups but opportunities for their acquisition occurred through exposure in the classroom interactions.[7] The study examined: (1) the interactional differences in the two instructional contexts, (2) the different opportunities for noticing the two grammatical features that arose in the interactions and (3) the learners' acquisition of the two structures. The main findings were that the two contexts were characterized by clear interactional differences, incidental acquisition took place when opportunities for 'noticing' occurred, the task-based context led to greater acquisition than the form-oriented context, plural-*s* was acquired but not copula *be*, and the key factor determining acquisition was whether there was a functional need to attend to the structures, which only occurred in the task-based classroom. Overall, then, this study suggested that where incidental acquisition is concerned, a task-based learning environment is more favourable than a PPP environment but that it may not guarantee the acquisition of grammatical features, such as copula *be*, that are communicatively redundant.

As we noted in Chapter 2, method-comparison studies are problematic because of the difficulty of controlling the variables involved. Clearly, both TBLT and PPP can be implemented in a variety of ways and with differing levels of success depending on the teachers and students involved. Nevertheless, given the intensity of the debate that surrounds TBLT, it is desirable to attempt the kind of comparative method studies referred to above. The better designed studies that have been conducted to date provide evidence that: (1) TBLT is effective in promoting acquisition and (2) in some respects it is superior to PPP.

Conclusion

In this chapter we have provided a description of task-based language teaching, drawing on both the pedagogic and the research-based literature. We then turned to work in SLA and examined three theoretical positions that have informed TBLT. While, it is not just SLA researchers who advocate task-based teaching, it is probably true to say that they have played the major role in bringing TBLT to prominence in language pedagogy. It is, therefore, not surprising that some teachers and teacher educators who favour more traditional approaches involving the direct teaching of language have resisted TBLT and sought to discredit it. We have considered a number of their critiques and found them wanting, based often on fundamental misunderstandings of TBLT. However, we have acknowledged the need for the controversy to be addressed through empirical enquiry and have discussed a number of studies that have attempted this.

The Principles of Instructed Language Learning in Chapter 1 make frequent reference to the need to incorporate tasks into teaching, reflecting the fact that a task-based approach is clearly compatible with what we currently know about how learners acquire an L2. However, it is also clear that TBLT is not always easy to implement. Ellis (2009) identified a number of very substantial difficulties teachers face in implementing this approach. For example, educational systems often emphasize knowledge-learning rather than skill-development and a task-based approach to language teaching is not readily compatible with such a philosophy: a structural approach based on teaching discrete items of language accords more closely with an educational philosophy that emphasizes knowledge transmission. Also, TBLT calls for the use of performance-based testing but in many educational contexts examinations test knowledge rather than skills and, understandably, teachers will feel the need to tailor their teaching to such examinations and thus resist a switch to TBLT. Arguably, then, if TBLT is to be successfully introduced, it is not just the support of SLA researchers that is needed but also that of educators and language testers.

Notes

1 Breen (1987) states that a 'task' can be a 'brief practice exercise' or a 'more complex workplan that requires spontaneous communication of meaning'. However, other definitions of 'task' seek to distinguish it from 'exercises' and it is these that informed the definition we provide in this chapter. We prefer to use 'activity' as a generic term and then distinguish between 'task' and 'exercise'.

2 However, the distinction between a 'task' and an 'exercise' can be seen as continuous rather than dichotomous. That is, some activities may satisfy some of the criteria of a 'task' but not all. For example, cued card activities that specify the specific functions that learners must perform in order to construct a dialogue, do not have any outcome other than simply 'practice' but do have a gap and do require, to some extent at least, that learners use their own linguistic resources.

3 The terms 'pre-emptive' and 'proactive' need some explanation. Pre-emptive focus on form occurs when the teacher attempts to prevent an error occurring – for example, by advising students to take care in using the past tense in a narrative task before they start speaking. Proactive focus on form is when the task has been designed to focus attention on a specific linguistic form (i.e. it is a focused task) and the teacher provides feedback on learners' attempt to use this form.

4 Input-based tasks, like output-based tasks, can be unfocused or focused. Focused input-based tasks can be distinguished from the structured-input tasks that figure in Processing Instruction (see Chapter 5) in that they do not make the linguistic focus explicit to learners.

5 Another possibility is a syllabus that consists of a combination of focused and unfocused tasks.

6 See Estaire and Zanon (1994) for an example of how to choose thematic content for a task-based syllabus.

7 Incidental acquisition can potentially occur in any classroom, irrespective of the type of instruction. Thus even in a classroom where intentional learning is prioritized (as in PPP), opportunities will arise for incidental acquisition of linguistic features other than those targeted in the lesson.

DISCUSSION QUESTIONS

1. Examine the four criteria for 'tasks'. Give examples of typical language teaching activities that would satisfy these criteria and thus can be considered 'tasks'. Also, give examples of activities that do not meet these criteria and thus constitute 'exercises'. Can you think of any activities that seem to fall halfway between 'tasks' and 'exercises'?
2. A key criterion for deciding whether an activity is a 'task' is whether there is a 'primary focus on meaning'? What is meant by 'meaning' here?
3. Look at Willis and Willis's three levels of 'authenticity'. Imagine that you are designing a course for L2 learners working in a tourist agency. Suggest activities for each level.
4. Consider the three types of tasks proposed by Prabhu (1987) – information-gap, opinion-gap and reasoning gap. Make sure you are clear about the differences. Which of these types do you consider the most difficult and the easiest? Give your reasons.
5. What is the difference between a 'focused task' and an 'unfocused task'? Think of a particular teaching context you are familiar with. Which type of task would be best suited to this context? Give your reasons.
6. What factors need to be taken into account when sequencing tasks? Devise a set of guidelines for grading and sequencing tasks.
7. Look at Table 6.1: Implementation options in the different phases of a task-based lesson. Which options are best suited to: 1) young beginner learners and 2) adult advanced learners? Are there some options that would suit learners of any age?
8. What are the different roles of a teacher in TBLT?
9. Look at Table 6.2: Summary of the main findings of Ellis et al.'s (2001) study of form-focused episodes in task-based classrooms. What do these findings indicate about the nature of 'focus on form' in task-based classrooms?
10. What are the main differences between Skehan's cognitive theory of L2 learning and Robinson's Cognition Hypothesis? What are the implications of each theory for TBLT?
11. How can grammar be addressed in TBLT?
12. How can TBLT ensure that learners are exposed to ample 'new language'?
13. How can pronunciation be taught in TBLT? Describe a task that could be used to teach pronunciation.
14. How can vocabulary be taught in TBLT? Describe a task that could be used to teach new vocabulary.
15. How can TBLT be effectively implemented with learners who are complete beginners?
16. To what extent is TBLT suited to an EFL context where there is very limited opportunity for using the L2 outside the classroom?

Part III

Language pedagogy and SLA: an internal perspective

When we adopt an internal perspective on language teaching, we need a very different set of terms from those used to talk about the external perspective. We will no longer use standard pedagogic terms such as 'method', 'syllabus' or 'PPP'. Instead we need to talk about 'speech acts', 'turn-taking', 'questioning behaviour', 'negotiation', 'exchange structure', 'topic control', 'scaffolding' and 'language mediating language' (Swain, 2000). Such terms help us describe how interactional events are constructed as teachers actually teach and how learning opportunities are shaped. They provide a language for talking about teaching as a *process* of classroom communication or what Douglas Barnes (1976) has called the 'hidden curriculum'. However, it is not a language with which teachers are generally familiar.

There are, however, good reasons for adopting an internal view of teaching. One is that ideas about teaching that seem different when viewed externally may in fact turn out to be very similar when examined internally. Also, ideas that are apparently similar may turn out to be very different in classroom-process terms. When we employ external constructs (such as 'task'), we make assumptions about the kind of activity they will give rise to (e.g. message-focused language use) but, in fact, the actual activity that arises from a task may or may not be that which was intended. In other words, the constructs that inform an external view of teaching may lack validity when viewed from an internal perspective.

The teacher guides have much less to say about 'teaching as interaction'. However, they do stake out positions regarding the kind of input learners should be exposed to and they also discuss key aspects of pedagogy related to 'interaction' – the teaching of speaking, learner participation, small group work and classroom management. There is also an ongoing debate about the role of the L1 in the L2 classroom. One aspect of interaction – corrective feedback – does receive considerable attention. The chapters in this section examine the pedagogical positions relating to these issues and examine relevant SLA research.

7   Teaching as 'input'

Introduction

Teaching, however defined, involves 'input'. No matter which approach or method is adopted, learners are exposed to the input provided by the teacher, other students and in the instructional materials. Input can be oral or written. Oral input is provided in comprehension-based language instruction, in task-based language teaching, and, more generally, in the classroom talk that arises no matter what the teaching approach. Written input is provided in textbook practice materials and through reading.

The distinction between 'focused' and 'unfocused' tasks was considered in Chapter 6. The same distinction can also be applied to input. Focused input caters to intentional language learning whereas unfocused input caters to incidental language learning. However, it is not as simple as this, for even focused input provides opportunities for incidental learning as well as intentional learning. This is because input materials designed to teach a specific linguistic feature (say, a grammatical structure) will also, inevitably, expose learners to a variety of other linguistic features. For this reason, in this chapter, we will treat input generically, irrespective of whether it has been designed to present specific linguistic features or to expose learners to meaningful samples of language. In other words, we see input as providing learners with the data that, potentially, they can process for learning. The key question, then, becomes what kinds of input under what conditions are most likely to foster learning.

The starting point, as in earlier chapters, will be to examine pedagogic positions first. We will then examine what SLA has to say about the role of input in L2 learning before returning to the pedagogic issues.

Pedagogic issues

An inspection of the indexes of some popular methodological handbooks for language teachers (e.g. Hedge, 2000; Nunan, 1991; Ur, 1996) reveals that for the most part they do not include 'input' as an entry. Also two recent books devoted to language teaching materials (Tomlinson, 2011; Harwood, 2010) provide only scant references to 'input' in their indexes. Even Savignon's (1997) book on communicative language teaching, where one might expect 'input' to figure as a key concept, does not mention the term in either the glossary or the index. It would seem then that 'input' is not a term that belongs to mainstream thinking about language pedagogy. The teacher guides do not conceptualize teaching in terms of 'input' perhaps because this construct is viewed as belonging to the discourse of SLA. However, this is not to say that the authors of these guides do not recognize the importance of input. Rather they prefer to address it in relation to constructs that are viewed as having greater direct significance for language teaching, in particular 'authentic materials', 'teacher-talk' and 'teacher questions', all of which figure in the indexes of the teacher guides. There is also recognition of extensive reading as a source of input for learners.

Authentic materials

It is useful to distinguish the terms 'authentic materials' and 'authenticity', if only because it is somewhat easier to define the former than the latter. Morrow (1979) defined an authentic text as a 'stretch of real language produced by a real speaker or writer for a real audience and designed to convey a real message of some sort' (p. 13). In other words, authentic materials contrast with 'contrived materials' (i.e. materials consisting of input that has been specially designed for L2 learners to teach the language). However, Morrow's definition raises problems. What does Morrow mean by 'real speaker' and 'real audience'? One interpretation is that he is referring to the language produced by native speakers for native speakers of a particular language, as in the definition offered by Porter and Roberts (1981). Another interpretation, however, is broader, giving recognition to the fact that communication between speakers (including non-native speakers) can also be 'authentic' provided that it is involves conveying a 'real message of some sort'. This broader interpretation accords more with current views about the ownership of a language not resting solely with native speakers. It also circumvents the difficulty of pinning down concepts such as 'native speaker' and 'non-native speaker' (Carter and McCarthy, 2003).

'Authenticity' is even more problematic. The issue here is whether authenticity is seen as a property that resides in texts or whether it is treated as something that arises in the way discourse is processed. Widdowson (2003; see also 1978) preferred the term 'genuine discourse' to refer to the first of these senses of authenticity, reserving the term 'authentic' for the 'specific ways in which language is made communicatively appropriate to context' (p. 93). Widdowson argued persuasively that it is the process of authentication that is important, not whether a text is genuine:

> People make a text real by realizing it as discourse, that is to say by relating to specific contexts of communal cultural values and attitudes. And this reality does not travel with texts.
>
> (p. 98)

Bachman (1990) makes a very similar distinction in his discussion of language tests. He distinguishes 'situational authenticity' and 'interactional authenticity'.

The former pertains when a test elicits a performance which can be assessed in relation to the extent it mirrors the 'reality' of non-test use. The latter pertains when the test elicits a performance that is assessed in terms of whether it demonstrates interactional competence. Thus, 'authenticity' may refer to the 'genuine' language seen to occur in real-life situations, or to the 'authentic' use of language that occurs when learners/test-takers authenticate pedagogic or test materials in actual language use.

This difficulty of defining authentic materials and authenticity will be of relevance when we come to consider what SLA has to say about input. However, it has been largely ignored in the pedagogic literature, where the consensual view is that authentic materials are those based on 'genuine' (i.e. native speaker) texts and authenticity is a quality inherent in the texts, not in how a text or task is processed by a reader or listener. Authentic materials, then, are texts taken from such real-life sources as TV commercials, cartoons, news clips, comedy shows, movies, soap operas, radio ads, songs, advertisements, sports reports, obituary columns, advice columns, restaurant menus, street signs, cereal boxes, sweet (candy) wrappers, tourist information brochures, TV guides, comic books, and bus and train schedules.

The kinds of claims made on behalf of the use of such texts can be seen in Box 7.1. What is striking is the provenance of these claims, spanning a period from 1981 to 2010. In other words, while there have been notable developments in language pedagogy over this period, commitment to the use of authentic materials has been maintained throughout. The authors of these claims identify a number of advantages of authentic materials. The main one is that they expose learners to features of language use that are not typically found in contrived ('artificial' texts) and that unless learners are exposed to them they will not be able to handle 'real' texts (Harmer; Nunan; Tomlinson). An associated claim is that authentic materials, unlike contrived materials, come with a 'communicative context' (Willis). Authentic materials are also seen as beneficial because they are more interesting and motivating than contrived materials (Grellet; Nunan). It should be noted, however, that Harmer also suggests that 'simulated-authentic' materials might have a place in language teaching.

Box 7.1 Pedagogic claims about authentic materials

'It is important to use authentic texts whenever possible...Authenticity means that nothing of the original texts is changed and also that its presentation and layout are retained...By standardizing the presentation of texts in a textbook, one not only reduces interest and motivation, but one actually increases the difficulty for students' (Grellet, 1981: 7–8).

'[T]he material designed to foster the acquisition of receptive skills must be at least simulated-authentic...If they are artificial...they will not serve this purpose since students will be unlikely to encounter anything like them in real life' (Harmer, 1983: 150).

'Contrived simplification of language in the preparation of materials will always be faulty, since it is generated without the guide and support of a communicative context. Only by accepting the discipline of using authentic language are we likely to come anywhere near presenting the learners with a sample of language which is typical of real English' (Willis, 1990: 127).

'Exposing learners to authentic materials is important for two reasons. Firstly, non-authentic listening texts differ in certain ways from authentic texts. They usually contain linguistic features more usually found in written rather than spoken language. There are few of the overlaps, hesitations, and false starts found in authentic texts, and there is very little negotiation of meaning. These differences do not always adequately prepare learners for dealing with genuine communication either inside or outside the classroom because some of the features of authentic communication that rarely appear in non-authentic texts (such as repetition, requests for clarification, and so on) actually facilitate comprehension. Also, the use of authentic sources leads to greater interest and variety in the material that learners deal with in the classroom' (Nunan, 1999: 212).

'Make sure that the language the learners are exposed to is authentic in the sense that it represents how the language is typically used. If the language is inauthentic because it has been written or reduced to exemplify a particular language feature, then, the learners will not acquire the ability to use the language typically or effectively' (Tomlinson, 2010: 87).

Numerous studies have demonstrated the gap that exists between authentic language and the kind of language typically found in textbooks (see Gilmore, 2007 for a survey of these studies). This research has flourished since the advent of corpus-based analyses of language. There are marked differences in the linguistic, pragmalinguistic and discourse features found in native-speaker corpora such as the British National Corpus, the Cambridge and Nottingham Corpus of Discourse in English (CANCODE) and the Lund Corpus on the one hand and those found in language teaching textbooks on the other hand. Williams (1988), for example, found almost no correspondence between the language used in authentic business meetings and that presented in thirty business English textbooks. However, while such gaps are not in dispute, the relevance of the highly detailed information about actual usage available from analyses of native-speaker corpora is debated. One view is that this information needs to be fed directly into the development of materials:

With a more accurate picture of natural discourse, we are in a better position to evaluate the description upon which we base our teaching and teaching materials, what goes on in the classroom, and the end products of our teaching, whether in the form of spoken or written output.

(McCarthy, 1991: 12)

Widdowson (2003), however, takes issue with this position. He argued that the corpus-based analyses only provide 'stretches of inert language' which only become meaningful if they are activated 'by some kind of appropriate contextual connection' (p. 104). He maintained that the contextual conditions of the classroom are such that it is easier to make 'unreal' samples of language 'real' than 'real' samples. In other words, classroom communication is inherently different from real-world communication, making it difficult and perhaps impossible to co-opt so called authentic language into it.

The claim that authentic materials come with a 'communicative context' (Willis, 1990) is difficult to justify. It presumes a very structural view of 'context'; that is, the context is seen as determining the features of language that are used. While to a degree this might be true, 'context' needs to also be viewed as dynamic – constructed by the participants as and in the communication that takes place. This is Widdowson's point: it is simply not possible to import the context associated with a particular discourse into the classroom, because the classroom is itself a configuration of social and psychological facets that influence how a particular discourse is constructed.

It is quite possible that authentic materials will be motivating and interesting for *some* learners, but it is difficult to see how texts produced by native speakers for native speakers will motivate learners with very limited L2 proficiency. This point has been recognized by some authors (e.g. Williams, 1983), who argue that the difficulty of authentic texts makes them demotivating for learners. Thus, the claim that authentic materials are intrinsically stimulating and interesting is clearly one that needs investigating empirically. It is, of course, extremely difficult to investigate a general claim such as 'authentic materials are more interesting and motivating than artificial materials' because so much depends on how both types of materials are used in the classroom. This may be why there has been very little attempt to do so. Peacock (1997), however, reports an interesting small-scale experiment in which he compared Korean learners' responses to lessons involving artificial and authentic materials on alternate days. His main finding was that authentic materials did elicit more motivated on-task and self-reported behaviour but only after the eighth day of their use. Initially, the students preferred the artificial materials. Peacock claimed that his students were beginners but this seems doubtful as the materials included poems, television listings, two short articles and an advertisement – all of which would require considerable knowledge of English.

The major problem with authentic materials lies in the linguistic and cultural difficulty they pose for learners, especially those of low proficiency. There are a number of ways of addressing this problem. One way is to ignore it on the grounds that such materials encourage a tolerance of partial comprehension and the use of inferencing strategies (McRae, 1996). Another is to limit the use of authentic materials to advanced level learners. A third solution is to select authentic texts that are at a level suitable for a particular group of learners but locating such texts is likely to be a time-consuming process. A fourth way is to simplify the texts. Of course, this is likely to remove those features from the text that make it 'authentic'. However, Widdowson (1978) suggested that one way round this was 'gradual approximation' (i.e. learners first read or listen to a series of simplified versions of a text before graduating to the authentic version). The fifth way, proposed by many advocates of authentic materials, is to design tasks which will assist learners to comprehend them. In Widdowson's terms, this amounts to assisting learners to 'authenticate' an authentic text in the context of a pedagogic activity. The process of 'authentication', however, applies equally to contrived texts, so one wonders what the advantages are in insisting on 'real' texts.

We have seen, then, that considerable controversy surrounds the use of authentic materials in language teaching. By and large, the debate has been conducted without reference to SLA, although Gilmore (2007), in this comprehensive review of authentic materials and authenticity in foreign language teaching, does touch on a number of key issues (e.g. the importance of comprehensible input and 'noticing'). We will consider these later. We will turn now to another construct relevant to the role of input that has figured in both the pedagogic and SLA literature.

Teacher-talk

'Teacher-talk' is a term used to refer to the language used by a teacher when addressing students in a classroom. Teacher educators recognize the importance of teacher-talk and seek to identify those characteristics that constitute 'good teaching'. Nunan (1991), for example, commented:

> Teacher talk is of crucial importance, not only for the organization and management of the classroom but also for the processes of acquisition. It is important for the organization and management of the classroom because it is through language that teachers either succeed or fail in implementing their teaching plans. In terms of acquisition, teacher talk is important because it is probably the major source of comprehensible target language input the learner is likely to receive.
>
> (p. 189)

This comment is interesting because it emphasizes the dual function of teacher-talk – as a tool for carrying out pedagogic activities and as a source of input for acquisition. However, an inspection of popular teacher guides indicates that it is the first of these functions that receives the most attention. The focus is on the various roles that teachers can play in the classroom. There is scant mention of how teacher-talk relates to acquisition.

A common view expressed in these guides is that teachers should minimize the amount of time they talk in order to maximize student talk time. When teachers adopt the roles of 'controller' or 'assessor', they regulate when students speak and what language they use and as a result dominate the classroom talk (typically speaking for 70 per cent or more of the time). Harmer (1983) considered that this may sometimes be necessary in the 'accurate production stage' of a lesson but that the teacher will subsequently need to relinquish control in order to provide opportunities for students to talk more and use language more creatively. To address this, teachers need to adopt different roles, for example as a 'prompter', 'participant' or 'resource'. The perceived importance of reducing teacher-talk time is reflected in an interesting action research project carried out by Warren-Price (2003). He set about investigating his own use of teacher-talk and reported that becoming more aware of his classroom actions enabled him to reduce the amount of teacher-talk time.

The view that teachers talk too much rarely goes unchallenged. There are, however, some dissenting opinions. O'Neill (1994), for example, commented:

> I, personally, have grown more and more suspicious of the assumption that teacher-talk is automatically bad. I accept that some, perhaps many teachers talk too much, but I also believe that many teachers do not talk enough. I believe it is wrong to judge or assess teacher-talk only by reference to its quantity. It is just as important to assess its quality.

He argued that the crucial issue was not how much teacher-talk there was but whether it was of the right kind and went on to specify the conditions that need to be met for teacher-talk to be effective (see Box 7.2). Prabhu (1987) also rejected the view that teacher-talk needed to be restricted, arguing that in large classes of beginner learners in an Indian secondary school, students needed access to the best models available and these were better provided by listening to the teacher than to other students.

Box 7.2 A teacher educator's perspective on teacher-talk

Teacher-talk is useful when the following conditions are met:

It is broken into sense groups.

It is simplified but not unnatural.

It is more redundant than 'ordinary speech' and words and structures are naturally repeated or 'recycled' at regular intervals.

It is broken into 'short paragraph' segments to encourage or invite students to interrupt, comment, and ask questions.

When new vocabulary or structure is taught, typical examples are given.

The teacher gets regular feedback through questions – especially 'open questions'.

The teacher uses other devices to get feedback such as student physical responses.

A variety of elicitation and explanation techniques are used (e.g. use of context, enactment, illustration).

> A variety of correction techniques are employed, including both covert and overt types.
>
> It is between 85 per cent and 95 per cent comprehensible.
>
> (O'Neill, 1994)

The question of the quality of teacher-talk, however, has not been entirely neglected in the pedagogical literature. It is most clearly addressed in the views expressed about teachers' use of questions. Ur (1996), for example, has a section in her teacher guide called 'effective questioning'. She elects to deal with this in the context of IRF exchanges (i.e. classroom discourse consisting of initiate–respond–feedback sequences) where questions serve as the primary means of initiating such exchanges. She identifies a number of criteria for effective questioning: (1) clarity (whether students grasp the meaning of a question and the kind of answer required), (2) learning value (whether the question stimulates thinking and responses that will contribute to learning), (3) interest (whether learners find the question interesting and challenging), (4) availability (whether most of the students can try to answer it), (5) extension (whether the question invites extended and/or varied answers) and (6) teacher reaction (whether students are confident their responses will be treated with respect). She then discusses a number of examples of teacher questions in terms of these criteria. These are clearly sensible criteria but, in some cases, may be difficult to apply – for example, how will teachers know if a question has 'learning value'?

The general picture that emerges from this brief account of how teacher-talk is addressed in the pedagogical literature is that there is awareness that it is an important aspect of language pedagogy. It is, however, dealt with largely in terms of opinions about what constitutes effective practice, based largely on educators' own experience. Not surprisingly, then, there are differences in opinion – for example, regarding teacher-talk time. There is a conspicuous absence of any reference to the SLA research that has investigated teacher-talk or to L2 learning theories that might inform what kinds of teacher-talk are likely to foster learning.

Extensive reading

Richards et al. (1992) defined extensive reading as follows:

> Extensive reading means reading in quantity and in order to gain a general understanding of what is read. It is intended to develop good reading habits, to build up knowledge of vocabulary and structure, and to encourage a liking for reading.
>
> (p. 133)

It contrasts with 'intensive reading' in terms of both quantity and, in part, purpose. Whereas intensive reading aims at full comprehension of a text, extensive reading is more concerned with 'general understanding' and promoting 'good reading habits'. Extensive reading is also a source of input for developing L2 proficiency, especially vocabulary.

Extensive reading has held an important place in language pedagogy for a long time. Palmer (1917) is credited as the first person to advocate extensive reading. Early teacher guides (e.g. Bright and McGregor, 1970; Ellis and Tomlinson, 1980) included detailed accounts of how to plan and implement an extensive reading programme. Both these guides were designed for second language teaching in Africa. In contrast, early teacher guides for foreign language teaching (e.g. Rivers and Temperley, 1978) dealt with extensive reading more cursorily. More recently, however, extensive reading has been viewed as equally important for both second and foreign language settings. There is now a website devoted entirely to it (http://extensivereading.net/), providing information about how to set up a programme, examples of model programmes, resources available and copies of papers documenting the value of extensive reading and reporting studies of its implementation, including in foreign language settings (e.g. Powell, 2005).

The pedagogic literature proposes a number of benefits of an extensive reading programme. Hedgcock and Ferris (2009) claim that it:

- improves comprehension skills;
- develops automaticity;
- enhances background knowledge (schemata, both content and formal);
- builds linguistic knowledge (i.e. linguistic schemata);
- improves production skills (speaking and especially writing);
- promotes confidence and motivation.

(p. 211)

In other words, extensive reading programmes are seen not just as a means of improving reading skills but also of developing linguistic proficiency (i.e. both learners' linguistic resources and their ability to deploy these in communication). Thus, a key argument underlying the advocacy of extensive reading programmes is that learners can acquire an L2 incidentally as they read to understand. Krashen (2004) has consistently made the case for the 'power of reading' as source of input for acquisition. Pointing out that 'language is too complex to be deliberately and consciously learned one rule or item at a time' (p. 11) and therefore learners need to 'acquire' the language incidentally through exposure to input they can understand. He argued that simplified readers are ideally suited to ensure this happens.

Not everyone agrees with Krashen, however. Folse (2004), for example, argued that 'learning new words from context' is a 'vocabulary myth' given the difficulty that many L2 readers experience in inferring the meanings of unfamiliar words from context. Hulstijn (1992) found that L2 readers had great difficulty in using context to guess the meanings of new words and were prone to make errors. Drawing on such research, Folse concluded 'what ESL students need is *not* just exposure to reading materials; they need reading with explicit, planned vocabulary work' (2004: 7).

There are also impediments to implementing an extensive reading programme. Ferris and Hedgcock (2005) reported that extensive reading is frequently underused and suggested a number of reasons why this was so. They noted that it is much easier to carry out an extensive reading programme in a context where the same teacher spends sustained time with a class, as in primary schools, and much more difficult in contexts where the teacher only meets with the class a few times each week, as in university language classes. Teachers also face the problem of student resistance. Students in academic settings may resent having to spend time on reading books not directly related to their field of study. In some cases, such learners may have had very little experience of extensive reading in either their L1 or the L2 and thus find the effort of reading widely for general understanding difficult and unrewarding. Such readers adopt a word-by-word processing strategy which makes it very difficult for them to read for pleasure.

There is also the problem of locating suitable resources for an extensive reading programme. Nation (2006) pointed out that in order to read easily for comprehension (the aim of an extensive reading programme), readers need to already know 95–98 per cent of the words that occur in a text. Huckin and Bloch (1993) noted that 'that a lack of vocabulary knowledge is the largest obstacle for second-language readers to overcome' (p. 154). L2 learners will also need the grammatical knowledge to process sentences. Thus, if extensive reading is to contribute to L2 learners' linguistic development, they will need access to books that lie within their existing level of proficiency. This is not easily achieved using authentic reading materials (i.e. books written for native speakers). Once again, then, the issue of authentic materials and of authenticity needs to be confronted. Nuttall (1996) was of the view that 'authentic material is ideal' for extensive reading and that 'however good a simplification is, something is always lost' (p. 178). In contrast, many advocates of extensive reading are committed to the provision of non-authentic, simplified materials. Day and Bamford (1998), for example, argued that the materials need to be at the 'i minus 1' level (i.e. below the linguistic ability of the learners). They are critical of the 'cult of authenticity' and the 'myth of simplification'. They make the obvious point that simplified texts are essential because low-proficiency readers need them.

Simplified texts come in a number of forms. Widdowson (1978) distinguished 'simple accounts' (i.e. texts that have been completely rewritten in a simple form) and 'simplified versions' (i.e. texts where the difficult language has been replaced and, where necessary, difficult concepts have been elaborated). Hill and Thomas (1988) point to a third possibility – 'simple original' (i.e. an original text written especially for L2 readers). Most graded reading series (e.g. Oxford University Press' *Bookworms*) adopt a mixture of these approaches to simplification, to ensure that the books are matched to the learners' proficiency levels. They are premised on Widdowson's view that what matters is not authenticity but ensuring that L2 readers are able to 'authenticate' the materials they are asked to read. Day and Bamford argued further that a simplified text can be considered 'authentic' because it has not been written to teach language but with a communicative objective in mind. They cite Alderson and Urquhart (1984) who commented: 'If simplification is defined as making a text appropriate to the audience, then perhaps any text can be considered a simplification' (p. 196).

The use of simplified texts in an extensive reading programme raises a number of points. The first is whether it is possible for such texts to provide learners with interesting, worthwhile reading materials. Day and Bamford argued that it is and, indeed, an inspection of graded reading series such as *Bookworms* shows that creative readers can be designed for even very low proficiency readers. The second point concerns whether simplified reading materials are, in fact, so lacking in authenticity even if this is defined in the traditional way (i.e. as texts produced by native speakers for native speakers). Allan (2008) set about comparing the linguistic features in the British National Corpus with those found in a corpus of graded readers. Although she did find some differences, she also reported that the readers exposed learners to many of the features found in the native-speaker texts. She concluded that 'the data may not be authentic but it does contain authentic features' (p. 30). The final point – perhaps the most crucial – concerns the criteria for preparing simplified reading materials. Traditionally, these have involved the compilation of the vocabulary and the grammatical structures to be used at each level in a graded reading series. This, however, constitutes a very narrow view of what simplification entails as we will see when we turn to examine the SLA research.

We have examined the pedagogic positions evident in three key aspects of language teaching – authentic materials, teacher-talk and extensive reading. We have seen that in each case there are notable differences in the opinions expressed by commentators. These all involve the problematic issues of authenticity and simplification. Should materials be 'authentic' or are 'contrived' materials also of value? Should teachers simplify their language in teacher-talk? Does their tendency to talk too much impede learners' access to 'natural' discourse? How can extensive reading materials be designed in such a way as to ensure an 'authentic' reading experience for L2 learners? What kinds of simplification are needed to foster language learning? We will now turn to a consideration of what SLA has to say about 'input' before returning to these pedagogic questions.

Input in SLA

Gass (1997) considered input the 'single most important concept of second language acquisition' (p. 1). We will begin by examining a number of SLA theories that address the role played by input in L2 acquisition and then consider some of the descriptive and experimental studies that have investigated input, comprehension and learning. We will conclude by proposing a number of generalizations about the kinds of input that theory and research suggest will foster learning.

Theoretical perspectives

Input is addressed in just about every theory of L2 acquisition reflecting the general assumption that no learning can take place unless learners have access to input.[1] We will limit our discussion of theoretical perspectives on input to four theories that directly address the role of input: the Incidental Learning Hypothesis, the Frequency Hypothesis, the Input Hypothesis and the Noticing Hypothesis.

Incidental Learning Hypothesis

In its most basic form, the Incidental Learning Hypothesis claims that learners can learn new linguistic features without any intention of doing so. In other words, they can 'pick up' L2 forms simply through exposure to input. Schmidt (1994) points out that incidental learning can occur when learners' primary attention is focused on one linguistic feature (e.g. they are engaged in intentional learning of this feature) but acquire some other feature that is present in the input. However, prototypically incidental acquisition refers to the learning of formal features when learners are primarily engaged in the effort to comprehend input.

When learners acquire forms incidentally, they may do so with or without consciousness. The idea that incidental learning can be conscious may seem counter intuitive and, for this reason, there is a common misunderstanding that it necessarily implies unconscious or subconscious processing. However, allocating primary attention to one feature or to comprehending the input does not preclude the possibility of peripheral attention being paid to some other linguistic feature. As we will see later, when we consider the Noticing Hypothesis, there are reasons to believe that all learning, whether intentional or incidental, involves some degree of consciousness. In fact, it is more controversial to claim that learning can be entirely unconscious. Arguments abound in the SLA literature as to whether implicit learning (i.e. learning that occurs without any awareness whatsoever) can occur. Incidental acquisition is therefore not synonymous with implicit learning. As Hulstijn (2003) put it 'implicit learning entails more than what is meant by incidental learning' (p. 360).[2]

Like all theoretical propositions, the Incidental Acquisition Hypothesis is only valid if it can be tested empirically. It has been investigated by exposing learners to input and then without any pre-warning testing them on some of the features contained in the input. For example, they might be asked to read a passage for general understanding and then tested on whether they have learned a set of words in the text. This is precisely the approach that has been adopted in investigating whether vocabulary learning takes place in extensive reading.

Ortega (2009) claimed that 'it is unanimously agreed in SLA that incidental learning is possible' (p. 94). However, no claim is made that incidental acquisition is superior to intentional learning. Indeed, studies that have compared incidental and intentional language learning generally find the latter more effective, as we saw in Chapter 4 when we considered explicit vocabulary instruction. The Incidental Acquisition Hypothesis is important for two reasons. First, it acknowledges that much of the learning that takes place is associative in nature (e.g. learners are able to map form onto meaning, when acquiring new words of grammatical structures simply through exposure). Second, there are limits to how much of a language can be learned through deliberate effort.

Frequency Hypothesis

This hypothesis was initially formulated by Hatch and Wagner-Gough (1976) as an explanation for the order of acquisition (see Chapter 3). They proposed that the order in which learners acquired different grammatical morphemes reflected the frequency with which these items occurred in the input. The hypothesis applies to the acquisition of vocabulary in the same way: learners learn words that occur frequently in the input before those that occur less frequently.

More recently, the Frequency Hypothesis has been couched within connectionist accounts of L2 learning. These view language not as an inventory of items and rules but as a labyrinth of connections between linguistic elements (sounds, syllables, words, morphemes) that combine into 'constructions' or 'collocations'. These connections have different strengths. Learning occurs when exposure to input leads to new connections being formed or to changes in the strength of existing connections.

A key claim of the Frequency Hypothesis is that learning is primarily exemplar-based rather than rule-based. That is, learners learn associatively by identifying and then storing sequences of sounds, syllables and words that occur in the input, as suggested in the discussion of formulaic sequences in Chapter 3. From this perspective, grammatical development 'is a process of assembling knowledge about distributional and semantic-distributional relationships between words' (N. Ellis, 1996: 98). For example, in acquiring third person-s, the learner does not acquire a rule that states 'add-s to the verb in the third person of the present simple tense' but rather, through exposure internalizes a construction consisting of 'he/she/it + Verb(s)' which is associated with the meaning realized by this tense. Evidence showing how this grammatical feature is learned comes from a study by R. Ellis (1988), who reported that the learners he investigated were much more likely to add-s to the verb following third person pronouns (*he/she/it*) than following a noun subject. The Frequency Hypothesis provides a ready explanation for this as exemplars of pronoun + verb(s) occur much more frequently in the input than any particular noun + verb(s) combination. Learners supply third person-s when the verb follows a pronoun, but are likely to continue to omit it in complex nominal constructions even at advanced levels.

An implication of the Frequency Hypothesis is that learners need access to large amounts of input to fine-tune their developing linguistic knowledge. N. Ellis (2002) argues that learners are naturally sensitive to the frequencies of sequences of sounds and words in the input and respond to them, sometimes with awareness but often without. He saw input frequency as 'an all pervasive causal factor' and then, punning on the meaning of 'count', went on to claim 'in the final analysis of successful language acquisition and language processing, it is the language learner who counts' (p. 179).

'Frequency' is, however, not a straightforward concept. In Chapter 3, we noted an important distinction between 'token frequency' and 'type frequency'. N. Ellis (2007) proposed that learners respond differently to them. Token frequency concerns how often specific linguistic forms appear in the input. It promotes entrenchment and the conservation of irregular forms (e.g. irregular past tense forms). Type frequency refers to the items that can occur in a slot in a construction. It facilitates the development of a general category governing the items that occur in a particular slot (e.g. regular past tense-*ed*).

The Frequency Hypothesis cannot provide a full explanation of L2 acquisition. An obvious example of where frequency fails to account for learning is English definite and indefinite articles. These are the most frequently occurring items in any input learners of English are exposed to, but they pose enormous problems, especially for learners whose L1 does not include articles (e.g. Japanese). Responding to N. Ellis's claims about the centrality of input frequency as a causative factor, Gass and Mackey (2002) noted 'an issue of central importance that remains to be addressed relates to exactly how frequency interacts with other aspects of the L2 acquisition process' (p. 257).

The Input Hypothesis

The Input Hypothesis was introduced briefly in Chapter 1. Here we consider it in greater depth. It is the key hypothesis in Krashen's theory of L2 acquisition. As this theory has had considerable influence on language pedagogy, the five hypotheses that comprise it are summarized in Table 7.1. Note should be taken, however, of the fact that it has been subjected to substantial criticism over the years and, as a theory, no longer figures in current thinking in SLA. Ortega (2009), for example, in her survey of SLA, makes no mention of it. In particular, the claim that acquisition takes place 'subconsciously' has been challenged, on the grounds that attention to linguistic form is needed even in incidental and implicit learning (see the account of the Noticing Hypothesis that follows).

Krashen summarizes his basic position in terms of a single claim: 'people acquire second languages only if they obtain comprehensible input and if their affective filters are low enough to let the input in' (Krashen, 1985: 4). There is no direct role for output in Krashen's theory – the ability to speak in an L2 develops only as a result of the acquisition that takes place through comprehensible input.

Table 7.1 Summary of Krashen's theory of L2 acquisition

Hypotheses	Description
The Acquisition-Learning Hypothesis	We learn second languages in two different ways: through 'acquisition', which is a subconscious process resulting in implicit knowledge, and 'learning', which is a conscious process resulting in explicit knowledge.
The Natural Order Hypothesis	Learners acquire the rules of grammar in a predictable order which is independent of the order in which the rules are taught.
The Monitor Hypothesis	Learners use the implicit knowledge resulting from 'acquisition' to produce utterances but under certain conditions are able to use the explicit knowledge resulting from 'learning' to edit their output.
The Input Hypothesis	This claims that 'humans acquire language in only one way – by understanding messages, or by receiving "comprehensible input"' (Krashen, 1985: 2)
The Affective Filter Hypothesis	For 'acquisition' to take place, learners need to be 'open' to input; if learners are unmotivated, lacking in self-confidence or anxious, input, even if comprehensible, does not reach the learner's language acquisition device.

According to the Input Hypothesis, then, it is not just any input that works for acquisition, the input has to be comprehensible. Krashen suggested two key ways in which input is made comprehensible. First, situational context can make the meaning of the input clear when learners can relate what is said to objects and actions they can see. Second, input becomes comprehensible when it is simplified, as occurs naturally in the simplified codes that learners are exposed to (i.e. caretaker-talk in L1 acquisition and foreigner and teacher-talk in L2 acquisition). There is no need to 'fine-tune' the input to the learner's current level of development as matching will occur naturally, as long as efforts are made to ensure learners comprehend what they hear and read.

Clearly learners do need access to input that is comprehensible. There is plenty of evidence to show that simplified input aids comprehension, although as we will see later in this chapter simplifying input does not guarantee that it is comprehended (see, for example, Leow, 1993). The main problem with the Input Hypothesis rests in the claim that acquisition will automatically take place if learners comprehend input. Learners can comprehend input through top-down processing, using contextual clues to process what they hear or read. When this happens, there is no need for them to attend (even subconsciously) to the actual linguistic forms in the input and, as a result, no learning can take place. In other words, the processes involved in comprehension and acquisition are not identical and, as Gass (1988) pointed out, what is important is not comprehensible input but rather comprehended input. Færch and Kasper (1986) argued that only when learners perceive that there is a gap between the input and their existing interlanguage and also recognize that this is due to a gap in their L2 knowledge does comprehensible input lead to acquisition. The

Input Hypothesis, therefore, has serious flaws as it takes no account of the role of 'attention' in processing input.

The Noticing Hypothesis

One of the most contentious issues in SLA is whether acquisition entails consciousness and, if so, what kind of consciousness (see the introductory comments on this in Chapter 1). The Frequency Hypothesis is neutral as to whether frequency works by itself or in consort with conscious attention. The Input Hypothesis rejects any role whatsoever for conscious attention in 'acquisition', seeing it as a defining characteristic of 'learning'. Schmidt (1990, 1994, 2001), however, argues that even incidental and implicit learning involve consciousness.

'Noticing' is the conscious registration of formal features in the input. Learners, for example, may notice that the noun in the phrase 'three little balls' has an 's' on it. They may also notice that it signals a particular meaning – 'more than one'. In his 2001 article, Schmidt is careful to point out that learners do not notice 'rules' but rather 'exemplars' of forms and form-meaning mappings. That is, noticing does not involve awareness at the level of understanding, although it may subsequently lead to this deeper level of consciousness. For example, learners may notice that a noun sometimes has an 's' on it and may or may not go to construct an explicit rule to explain the use of 's' (i.e. 'put an "s" on a noun to convey the meaning 'more than one'). Noticing involves working memory: learners 'intake' an exemplar of a form they have attended to and may rehearse this, for example, by repeating it out aloud or silently to themselves.[3] Intake, however, is not acquisition. It is part of the process that can lead to acquisition. Acquisition takes place only when a form that has been activated in working memory results in a change in the learner's long-term memory. Noticing makes acquisition possible but does not guarantee it.

Schmidt also discusses 'noticing-the-gap'. This draws on a case study of his own learning of Portuguese while in Brazil (Schmidt and Frota, 1986). He reported that in nearly every case, new forms appeared in his spontaneous speech after they had been consciously attended to in the input to which he had been exposed. This involved registering the difference between what he attended to in the input and his own output. In other words, he became aware of a gap between his existing L2 knowledge and the input. He hypothesized that it was noticing-the-gap that led to change in his interlanguage system.

Although, there is little disagreement that attention is needed for acquisition to take place, theorists disagree over whether it needs to be conscious or whether it can occur below a conscious threshold. In contrast to Schmidt, Tomlin and Villa (1994) argued that what they called 'detection' can occur outside of either focal or selective attention. Both Schmidt and Tomlin and Villa acknowledge that attention is not an all-or-nothing affair; rather, there is a continuum ranging from low-level, automatic attention to high-level, controlled attention when a learner becomes subjectively aware of a linguistic form in the input. The difference between Schmidt and Tomlin and Villa lies in what kind of attention they claim is needed for learning. Schmidt argued that a relatively high level of attention is needed, whereas Tomlin and Villa claimed that focal attention is not necessary for detection to occur. N. Ellis (2002) proposed that both low-level and focal, subjective attention contribute to acquisition but in different ways. Noticing (i.e. focal attention) is needed for the initial registration of a new, difficult element but once this element has been incorporated into long-term memory, low-level attention is sufficient to consolidate what has been acquired. He commented 'once a stimulus representation is firmly in existence, that stimulus need never be noticed again; yet as long as it is attended to for use in the processing of future input for meaning, its strength will be incremented and its associations will be tallied and implicitly catalogued' (p. 174). Schmidt appears to have changed his position over time. In his early articles he claimed 'that there is no learning whatsoever from input that is not noticed' but in his 2001 article he argued that noticing was necessary for learning to take place but in his 2001 article he acknowledged that some learning might be possible without noticing but that the more learners notice, the more they learn.

The Noticing Hypothesis raises two other issues. The first is whether successful acquisition requires awareness at the level of understanding (i.e. do learners need to construct some kind of explicit representation of a form they have attended to in the input?). The Incidental Acquisition Hypothesis is premised on the understanding that awareness at the level of understanding is not necessary for acquisition and this is the position taken by Schmidt and N. Ellis, among others. In other words, 'noticing' suffices. However, it still remains a possibility that acquisition will be facilitated if learners have developed a more explicit representation of what they have attended to. This is the position that Leow (1997) adopts: learners learn better if they engage in conscious rule-formation. Truscott and Sharwood-Smith (2011), however, point out that it is very difficult, perhaps impossible, to draw a clear boundary between noticing and conscious understanding. They comment 'a pure case of noticing or apperception, with no understanding, is difficult to imagine' (p. 503).

The final issue concerns what it is that is attended to in the data. Schmidt (1995) argued that nothing is free in L2 learning. That is, to acquire a phonological feature, learners need to attend to that feature, to acquire a new word they must attend to that particular word, and to acquire a grammatical morpheme they must notice it. In other words, one does not acquire element x by attending to element y. Again though, if detection does not involve consciousness (Tomlin and Villa's position), it would be possible for learners to acquire x while attending to y.

The Noticing Hypothesis addresses the role of consciousness in L2 learning. However, as should be clear from the preceding discussion, 'consciousness' is a slippery concept involving very different cognitive operations. The key questions are 'Is subconscious learning possible?' as claimed by Krashen and 'If consciousness is required, what level is needed for acquisition to take place?' The debates that surround these questions may lead teachers to conclude that the Noticing Hypothesis is of little relevance to language pedagogy. Such a conclusion is unwarranted, however. Teachers do need to consider how learners can be made conscious of elements in the input.

Research on input and L2 acquisition

Now we have considered various theoretical perspectives we will examine some of the research that has investigated input to L2 learners and its relationship to L2 acquisition. There is now a very substantial body of such research. No attempt will be made to provide a complete review. Instead, we will focus on specific studies in areas of particular relevance to language pedagogy. The starting point will be the descriptive research that has examined teacher-talk. This leads into a consideration of the role played by simplified input and then of studies that have investigated incidental acquisition through extensive reading. We conclude with an account of research that has investigated 'noticing'.

Teacher-talk

Research on teacher-talk was motivated by earlier studies of caretaker-talk and foreigner-talk. These showed that proficient speakers of a language make a number of 'modifications' to the way they use language when addressing learners with limited proficiency (i.e. children or non-native speakers). The modifications affect all levels of language – pronunciation, lexis, grammar and discourse – and serve a number of different functions, the main one being to facilitate effective communication by making it easier for the interlocutors to understand. Starting in the 1970s, researchers asked whether teachers likewise modify the way they speak to L2 learners in classrooms.

The descriptive research which investigated this question was carried out in the 1970s and 1980s and surveyed by Chaudron (1988) in his book *Second Language Classroom Research*. A typical study involved recording lessons, preparing transcripts and then documenting qualitatively or quantitatively different features of the teachers' talk. Chaudron's survey identified a number of general characteristics of teacher-talk that emerged from the studies. These are summarized in Table 7.2. Teachers adjust their input in the ways shown in Table 7.2 quite naturally (i.e. they do not consciously set out to modify the way they talk). However, the research also shows that there is considerable variation among teachers; some teachers are much better than others in modifying how they speak to suit the proficiency level of their students.

Is teacher-talk optimal for acquisition and if so what are the features of teacher-talk that make it optimal? Krashen (1981) claimed it is optimal because it helps to make input comprehensible to learners. Wong Fillmore (1985) identified a number of features of teacher-talk that she claimed were facilitative of acquisition in kindergarten classrooms with both L1- and L2-speaking children: avoidance of translation, an emphasis on communication and comprehension by ensuring message redundancy, the avoidance of ungrammatical teacher-talk, the frequent use of patterns and routines, repetitiveness, tailoring

Table 7.2 General characteristics of teacher-talk

Characteristic	Brief description
Amount of talk	In general, the research showed that the teacher takes up about two-thirds of the total talking time.
Functions of talk	While there is variability among teachers and programmes, the general picture is one of teacher explaining, questioning and commanding. In contrast, learners mainly respond.
Speed of talking and pausing	Teachers tend to slow down their rate of speech and use longer pauses when talking to classroom learners as opposed to other native speakers and also do so to a greater extent with less proficient learners.
Volume of talk	Teachers tend to speak more loudly and to make their speech more distinct when addressing L2 learners.
Vocabulary	Teachers tend to use high-frequency words resulting in a lower type–token ratio and vary their use of vocabulary in accordance with the learners' proficiency level. However, this does not happen, or not to the same extent, in some contexts (e.g. university classes).
Grammar	Teachers are likely to use shorter utterances and less subordination with less proficient learners. Teachers also tend to avoid the use of marked structures such as past tense.
Ungrammatical speech	Teachers rarely resort to ungrammatical teacher-talk. In this respect, teacher-talk differs from foreigner-talk where ungrammatical input is quite common.
Repetitions	Teachers use more self-repetitions with L2 learners, in particular when they are of low-level proficiency.

questions to suit the learners' level of proficiency, and general richness of language. However, there are some reasons to believe that teacher-talk is not always ideal. As noted in Table 7.2, teachers tend to underuse past tense and also tend to use very few words outside the most frequent word families (see Meara et al., 1997). The crucial point is whether teachers are able to adjust their input in relation to the learners' proficiency (i.e. simplifying less as learners acquire the language). There is evidence that at least some teachers automatically do this. Owen (1996), for example, found that the teacher he investigated adapted her spoken language depending on the level of the student (e.g. he spoke more rapidly and used more polysyllabic words with the more advanced learners).

An aspect of teacher-talk that has received special attention from SLA researchers is teacher questions. One reason for this is that teachers ask a lot of questions! Long and Sato (1984), for example, observed a total of 938 questions in six elementary level ESL lessons. Most of these were display question (i.e. questions designed to test whether a student has knowledge of a particular fact or can use a specific linguistic item correctly, as in the question 'What does x mean?'). Teachers typically ask few referential questions (i.e. questions that are genuinely information-seeking, as in the question 'Why didn't you do your homework?'). Long and Sato reported that display questions outnumbered referential questions in their study by more than three to one. Such questioning behaviour contrasts with the way questions are used in everyday communication, where referential questions predominate. Display questions have been shown to elicit shorter responses from students than referential questions (Brock, 1986). Teachers have also been found to be reluctant to wait for a student to respond. White and Lightbown (1984), for example, reported that the shorter the wait-time, the fewer and the shorter the students' responses were. However, there is considerable variation in both teachers' questioning behaviour and the kinds of response their questions elicit. Display questions can lead to extended sequences of talk when the teacher and students jointly negotiate their meaning over several turns (Lee, 2006). More important than the type of questions may be the strategies teachers employ when asking questions. Wu (1993) observed a number of different strategies used by Chinese teachers of English in Hong Kong secondary schools: (1) rephrasing by expressing a question in a new way, (2) simplifying an initial question, (3) repeating the question, (4) decomposing an initial question into two or more parts and (5) probing by following up a question with one or more other questions. Wu reported that (5) was the most effective way, encouraging the students to elaborate on an initial response.

There are, however, no studies that have investigated how teacher-talk (including teachers' questioning behaviour) facilitates acquisition, probably because of the difficulty – ethical and methodological – of designing experimental studies that compare classes where there is 'optimal' teacher-talk with those where no input modifications have been made. One exception is Nassaji and Swain's (2000) study of teachers' corrective feedback, which reported that feedback that was systematically tuned to learners' ability to self-correct their errors, was more effective than feedback that consisted of randomly applied corrective strategies (see Chapter 10).

Simplified input, comprehension and L2 acquisition

Krashen (1981) claimed that simplified input serves as one of the main ways in which input is made comprehensible. This led researchers to investigate whether simplified input does in fact assist comprehension.

There is clear evidence that speech rate has an effect on comprehension. Native speakers are able to process input at speeds of 320 words per minute (Conrad, 1989) but even relatively advanced learners have difficulty at such a speed. Griffiths (1990) found that lower intermediate-level adult learners' comprehension was adversely affected at rates around 200 wpm. However, they comprehended equally well at both slow speeds (94–107 wpm) and medium speeds (143–54 wpm). Zhao (1997) reported a study in which he compared learners' comprehension of computerized oral texts in conditions where they had no control over the speed at which they listened to them and conditions in which they did. He found that when given the chance, the learners elected to slow down the speech rate and that this resulted in higher levels of comprehension. Zhao noted 'as more and more audio materials are digitized, a computer program can be developed to allow the learner to change the speed of any message at any time' (p. 62). In many instructional contexts, however, computer control over speech rate will not be possible.

Other studies have investigated the effect of input modifications on comprehension. Parker and Chaudron (1987) in a review of twelve studies concluded that although linguistic modifications assist comprehension, they do not do so consistently. They found that what they called 'elaborative modifications' had a more consistent effect. They distinguished two types of elaborative modification: (1) those contributing to redundancy (e.g. repetition of constituents and paraphrases) and (2) those that helped to make the thematic structure of sentences clearer. Subsequent studies, however, produced mixed results. Oh (2001) found elaborative input effective but Long and Ross (1993) found a linguistically simplified text resulted in higher levels of comprehension than an elaboratively modified text. Ellis et al. (1994) reported two studies. One showed that elaborative modified input resulted in better comprehension than entirely unmodified input. The other showed no difference. Some studies (e.g. Leow, 1993) have found that simplified input has no effect on comprehension.

There is an obvious reason for the mixed results of these studies – the extent to which learners are successful in comprehending input will depend on a myriad of factors, including the learners' linguistic proficiency, their ability to process input in working memory and their familiarity with the topic. In other words, the nature of the input (i.e. whether and how it is modified) is just one factor out of many. For example, elaborative modifications may well be effective if the learners' proficiency is such that they can process the resulting input, but will not be effective if the result is more complex language that they cannot handle.

While it is helpful to understand whether simplified input assists comprehension, it is perhaps much more important to find out whether it promotes acquisition. This has been investigated in two ways. The first involves examining the relationship between comprehension and acquisition on the assumption that when input is simplified and leads to comprehension, it will also assist acquisition. The second entails investigating the direct relationship between simplified input and acquisition.

Even if simplified input aids comprehension, it does not follow that comprehended input leads to acquisition. R. Ellis (1995), for example, reported a study that showed only a very weak relationship between learners' comprehension of input and their acquisition of vocabulary. Clearly, the relationship between comprehension and acquisition is a complex one. If learners rely on top-down processing to comprehend input, they will not process the linguistic input and so no language learning is likely. In other words, some level of bottom-up processing is needed for acquisition to take place as claimed by the Noticing Hypothesis. This might be why learners in immersion programmes, who have been exposed to massive amounts of L2 input, often fail to achieve high levels of grammatical competence (Swain, 1985). They become adept at comprehending input using top-down strategies and, as a result, do not process the input linguistically. Simplified input may even have a negative effect in this respect if it enables learners to comprehend without the need to attend to linguistic form.[4] In other words, the input needs to 'stretch' learners to some extent, forcing them to apply bottom-up strategies to achieve comprehension. In Chapter 5 we considered VanPatten's (1996) claims that learners process input in accordance with a number of default strategies that prevent them from attending to crucial data in the input and need to be pushed to attend to these data in order for acquisition to occur. Despite these caveats, 'it is clear that some sort of comprehension is necessary' (Gass, 1997: 77).

There is evidence, however, that simplified input aids acquisition. Ellis et al. (1994), in the study mentioned above, found that learners exposed to premodified input (i.e. input that had been simplified) in oral commands acquired more new words than those exposed to baseline input (i.e. unsimplified input). Han (2010) reported that learners who read a premodified version of a text demonstrated greater receptive learning of vocabulary than learners who read a baseline version of the same text. R. Ellis (1995) examined the characteristics of oral premodified input that assisted learning. He found two input factors that were significantly correlated with vocabulary scores: (1) range (i.e. the number of different commands that a word appeared in) and (2) length of the commands (i.e. the number of words in a command). Learners remembered best those words that occurred in many different commands and in longer commands – that is, in input that had been elaboratively simplified. However, the most convincing evidence that simplified input assists acquisition is to be found in studies that have investigated extensive reading.

Extensive reading and acquisition

As we noted earlier, extensive reading is claimed not just to develop reading skills but also linguistic competence. A number of studies lend support to this argument. One of the earliest was Elley and Mangubhai's (1981) report of a 'book flood' programme in Fiji. They found that the programme had an effect on grammar as reflected in the students' ability to 'recite complex English sentences correctly' (p. 25). Many other studies (e.g. Hafiz and Tudor, 1990; Dupuy and Krashen, 1993) have since documented the vocabulary learning that takes place through extensive reading. In some cases, learners learn more vocabulary through reading than they do as a result of direct language teaching. Rodrigo et al. (2004), for example, found that a reading programme consisting of graded books led to greater gains in vocabulary than a traditional grammar and composition programme. However, not all studies have reported that extensive reading leads to significant gains in vocabulary. Hafiz and Tudor (1989), for example, found no statistically significant gains in vocabulary in ESL students in England. Swanborn and de Glopper (2002) reported that the low-ability readers they studied learned hardly any words incidentally. One reason why learners fail to acquire new vocabulary from extensive reading may be they are not exposed to the same words a sufficient number of times. Nation

(2009) pointed out that 'it is important to make sure that there are repeated opportunities to meet the same vocabulary in reading, and these repeated opportunities should not be delayed too long' (p. 51).

Another reason that inhibits vocabulary acquisition from extensive reading is the difficulty that some learners experience in inferencing the meanings of words from context. Success in contextual inferencing depends on the linguistic complexity of the text and the learners' ability to make use of inferencing strategies. We have already noted that learners need to know 95 per cent of the words in the text to comprehend it. They may well need to know closer to 98 per cent to be able to infer the meanings of those words they do not know. This may explain why low-proficiency learners have sometimes failed to demonstrate any learning. Also, even if the general linguistic complexity of a text makes inferencing possible, there is no guarantee that learners will be successful in doing so, as the context in which a word appears often fails to make its meaning transparent. Learners have also been found to lack the inferencing skills needed to make effective use of context. Huckin and Coady (1999), following an extensive review of incidental L2 acquisition research from reading, pointed out that 'effective word guessing requires the flexible application of a variety of processing strategies, ranging from local ones such as graphemic identification to global ones such as the use of broader contextual meanings' and then went on to note that 'some strategies arise naturally but others need to be taught' (p. 190). Finally, it cannot be assumed that the guessing from context that assists comprehension will necessarily result in the acquisition of new words. If the meaning of a word can be guessed easily, little attention to its form is needed with the result that it may not be retained. Learning vocabulary involves attending to both the form and the meaning of words.

To conclude this section, there is plenty of evidence to support the claim that learning (especially of vocabulary) does occur through extensive reading. But learning is not a foregone conclusion. It depends on a number of factors. One of these is whether learners actually pay attention to words they do not know.

Noticing and acquisition

One way in which learners can be induced to pay attention to linguistic forms in the input is by enriching the input – that is, by seeding the input with the target feature(s) (i.e. particular words or grammatical structures) so that learners are exposed to a high frequency of them over a period of time. A second way is by enhancing the input in some way (Sharwood-Smith, 1993). In oral input this can be achieved by means of emphatic stress on specific lexical or grammatical forms. In written input, it can be achieved by boldfacing, italicizing, underlining, colouring or enhancing the font size of specific forms. A third way is through text-elaboration (e.g. providing the meanings of unknown words through glosses or paraphrases). These ways of modifying the input can be seen as a kind of 'noticing instruction' aimed at making target forms salient to learners.

A number of studies have investigated the effects of such input modifications on both 'noticing' and acquisition. A good example is Kim (2006). She asked university-level learners of English to read a magazine article in both an unmodified, baseline version and in a number of different modified versions involving lexical elaboration and/or typographical elaboration. She then measured acquisition in terms of the learners' ability to recognize previously unknown word forms in the text and understand their meanings. She reported that typographical enhancement by itself did not assist acquisition of either the forms or meanings of the words. Explicit lexical elaboration (i.e. learners were explicitly told they were being given the meaning of a word) was effective. So too was implicit lexical elaboration (i.e. the meaning of a word was provided by means of an appositive) but only when combined with typographical enhancement. This study then indicates that text-elaboration can be effective in drawing learners' attention to unknown words and in helping learners learn them. Other studies (e.g. Shook, 1994; White, 1998) have investigated the effects of textual modifications on the acquisition of grammatical features, providing evidence that modified input helps learners to both notice the target features and learn them. Many of these studies, like Kim's, also investigated the effects of different types of textual modifications.

These studies varied considerably in the methodology they employed to investigate the effects of textual modifications and, not surprisingly, reported mixed results. However, overall they suggest the following conclusions:

- Modified input, whether enriched, enhanced or elaborated, can help learners to notice and acquire both unknown words and grammatical features and to use partially acquired features more accurately.
- In general, modified input is more effective if learners' attention is explicitly drawn to the target items. Enriched input alone is less effective as it results in only low-level awareness of the items.
- Noticing appears to be related to learning; learners learn when 'detection' of the target items has taken place.

The purpose of textual modifications is to provide affordances for learning by making key features salient to learners. It does not follow, of course, that learners will take advantage of these affordances. What learners notice and learn from the input will depend partly on the noticeability of features in the input but also, crucially, on how they orientate to the input.

Some conclusions

There has been an enormous amount of research investigating input and its role in L2 acquisition reflecting the importance that SLA attaches to input. The preceding sections have only sampled this research. More detailed accounts can be found in Gass (1997: chapter 4) and R. Ellis (2008: chapter 7). The theories and research we have considered point to the following conclusions:

1   Learners need input to learn. To achieve high levels of competence in an L2 they need exposure to massive amounts of input.

2 Much of the learning that takes place through exposure to input is incidental. Incidental acquisition can involve conscious attention to linguistic forms and their meanings but, according to some SLA theorists, can also take place without consciousness.

3 Learners are naturally responsive to the frequency of linguistic forms in the input; in general, they will acquire those features that occur frequently more easily and more quickly those features that are less frequent.

4 At least some level of comprehension of the input is required for acquisition to take place. Thus the provision of comprehensible input is likely to facilitate acquisition. However, it does not guarantee it even if the learners' affective filter is low.

5 Those linguistic forms in the input that are noticed (i.e. consciously attended to) are more likely to be acquired than those that are not noticed. Acquisition is also enhanced when learners notice-the-gap (i.e. pay attention to the difference between the input and their own output).

6 Awareness at the level of understanding is not necessary for acquisition to take place but increases the likelihood of forms attended to in the input entering long-term memory.

7 Much of the input that learners are exposed to is simplified in various ways. This can occur naturally in the modifications that characterize teacher-talk or by design in, for example, graded readers in an extended reading programme.

8 Teacher-talk is not a 'register' (i.e. a variety of language use with fixed linguistic properties); rather, it is highly variable, as shown by the way teachers vary the strategies they use when asking questions. Teacher-talk is tailored to the proficiency of the learner. Thus, the level and type of simplification varies. Over time, learners will be exposed to input that increases in linguistic complexity.

9 While the results of different studies are somewhat mixed, there is sufficient evidence to claim that simplified input aids both comprehension and acquisition. The clearest evidence of this can be found in studies that have investigated extensive reading.

10 Simplified input is more likely to result in learning if the modifications induce noticing by making linguistic forms salient to learners. This can be achieved by seeding texts to artificially increase the frequency of specific forms in the input, by enhancing the input (phonologically or typographically) or by elaborating the input to show the meanings of specific forms. Some SLA researchers have argued, paradoxically, that elaboration is the most effective way of simplifying input.

Evaluating pedagogical claims

We return now to examine the pedagogical issues outlined earlier, in the light of what we have discovered about the role of input in L2 acquisition. We will address a number of specific questions relating to these issues and then conclude with some general proposals for how language pedagogy can take better account of what is known about input and L2 acquisition.

Should language teaching materials be authentic or is learning better served through simplified materials?

We saw that there were conflicting pedagogic views about authentic materials. In general, language educators have promoted the use of authentic materials, on the grounds that they expose learners to the kinds of language use they will experience in non-pedagogic contexts. However, some commentators have recognized that authentic materials may be too linguistically complex for some learners, especially those of low proficiency. Research on input in SLA emphasizes the need to ensure that input is comprehensible to learners and thus does not lend support to the use of authentic materials if these are beyond their linguistic capacity. Instead, the research shows the importance of providing learners with simplified input. From an SLA perspective, then, fully authentic materials will only be of value to learners if they have reached a level of development that makes them processible. As such, they are likely to have only a limited role in a complete language programme.

There is, however, the danger that simplified input will deprive learners of exposure to the wide range of linguistic features needed for full development. The research suggests two ways in which this can be addressed: (1) by ensuring that the modifications made to the input are carefully graded to match the learner's level of development and (2) by making use of elaborative rather than linguistic modifications (e.g. by providing implicit or explicit paraphrases of low frequency words and difficult structures). A number of researchers have advocated elaborative rather than linguistic simplification and this approach allows for the use of authentic materials. However, arguably, once modified in this way the materials are no longer authentic!

Widdowson (1978) argued that it is 'authentication' rather than 'authenticity' that is important. Authentication must necessarily involve the ability to process a text for meaning and in many cases some form of simplification will be needed to achieve this. However, a simplified text may deprive learners of the kind of data they need to develop their interlanguages. 'Gradual approximation' (pp. 91–93) may provide a way around this conundrum as it marries learners' need for a simple text that learners can read authentically, with their need for text that is linguistically rich enough to promote learning.

Simplification is a *process* no matter whether it involves the preparation of a 'simple account', a 'simplified version' or a 'simple original'. Brumfit (1993) described this process in this way:

> processes of simplification, whether linguistic, discoursal, or conceptual, involves tacit or explicit judgements about the salience of particular features in relation to the purpose of the discourse, which in turn is responsive to the nature of the audience being addressed.
>
> (p. 4)

Simplification involves questioning what aspects of the input might impede comprehension and the achievement of a communicative purpose and then making appropriate adjustments. This is a process that the writer of a simplified text must engage in by him or herself. In this respect, it contrasts with the simplification that occurs in teacher-talk, where input is simplified as part of the ongoing process of negotiation between the teacher and the learners. For this reason, teacher-talk is potentially an ideal source of simplified input.

Is teacher-talk helpful for acquisition?

The dynamic nature of teacher-talk, then, is well-equipped to provide learners with comprehensible-input. Potentially, too, the discourse adjustments that arise in teacher-talk (e.g. the online repetitions and paraphrasing that studies have shown regularly occur), can help to make specific linguistic forms prominent in the input and thus encourage the noticing that Schmidt argued is required for learning to take place. Teacher-talk, then, can facilitate the kind of input processing that SLA research has shown to be important for learning. For this reason, perhaps, the fact that teachers tend to dominate talk-time in a classroom is less of a problem than some educators have claimed. As O'Neill (1994) pointed out, it is the quality of teacher-talk that is important, not its quantity. Beginner learners, in particular, can benefit from well-adjusted teacher-talk, as Prabhu (1987) argued. More advanced learners, however, will need opportunities for production (see Chapter 8).

Teacher-talk, however, does have limitations as a source of input for learning. In whole-class situations, for example, teachers may find it difficult to ensure that the adjustments they make are well suited to individual learners. Hakansson (1987) speculated that teachers may aim their talk at some hypothetical average learner with the result that it is not well tuned to individual learners. Another problem lies in the fact that teacher-talk has been shown to be lacking in the full range of grammatical features and is characterized by low-frequency vocabulary. Thus, there is a danger that the input remains oversimplified. In other words, teacher-talk may be ideal for lower proficiency learners but inadequate as a source of input for more advanced learners. A final problem concerns teachers' reliance on display questions and their reluctance to allow time for students to respond. Some studies have shown that this limits opportunities for learner output.

Teacher education programmes typically do not provide training in how teachers might overcome these limitations, reflecting a general tendency to view teaching in terms of materials, instructional activities and teaching procedures (i.e. what we called the 'external' view of language pedagogy). The importance of teacher-talk and its potential problems point to a need for educators to address teacher-talk directly. One way in which this can be achieved is by encouraging teachers to reflect on their own practice of teacher-talk by preparing transcriptions of lessons and then examining them in terms of pre-determined features of teacher-talk (such as amount of teacher-talk, rate of speech, linguistic and discourse modification and types of questions). Thornbury (1996) and Walsh (2006) reported studies that investigated the use of such training practices with teachers.

How can language pedagogy ensure that learners are exposed to the kinds of input needed to foster language learning?

SLA theory and research can help answer this question. It suggests four conditions that have to be met for input to work effectively for acquisition:

1 Learners need access to large amounts of input.
2 The input needs to be comprehensible.
3 The input also needs to be sufficiently linguistically rich to provide affordances for learning.
4 Learners need to not just comprehend the input but also pay attention to linguistic forms in the input that they have not yet acquired.

It is unlikely that condition (1) can be met through a course book and teacher-talk. It is, for this reason, that extensive reading is important. A carefully graded set of readers can ensure that learners are exposed to the quantity of input needed to achieve high levels of L2 proficiency. It will also ensure that the input that learners are exposed to is comprehensible. Graded reading materials provide learners with an input that is incrementally richer. In this way, learners will be exposed to a wide range of grammatical structures and to low-frequency as well as high-frequency vocabulary.

Extensive reading, then, serves as a major (perhaps, for foreign language learners, the primary source) of data for incidental acquisition. However, an extensive reading programme cannot guarantee that learners will pay attention to those linguistic forms they have not yet acquired (condition (4)). SLA research indicates a number of ways in which this can be addressed. These involve going beyond purely linguistic modifications to the input by making key items salient to learners. This can be done by enriching the input so that these items occur with a high level of frequency, an approach supported by the Frequency Hypothesis. However, studies of enriched input indicate that this may not always be successful. A better approach, therefore, might be to enhance the input typographically and a better approach still would be to elaborate the input by providing implicit or explicit glosses, that make the meanings of the key items clear and thus enable learners to construct the form-meaning mapping that is central to L2 acquisition. These methods of modifying the input cater to incidental acquisition. They do not preclude the possibility of supplementing extensive reading programmes with direct pre-teaching of key items or the use of post-reading language activities aimed at intentional learning as Folse (2004) argued is needed. Such practices are frowned on by some advocates of extensive reading but are likely to enhance learning.

An alternative approach for encouraging learners to attend to linguistic forms in written input, is to provide training in the strategies learners need to successfully inference the meanings of words and structures. Jenkins et al. (1989) proposed a 'SCANR procedure' that could serve as a basis for such training (see Table 7.3). However, the effectiveness of such training remains

Table 7.3 Jenkins et al.'s (1989) SCANR for inferencing the meanings of words from context

Step	Description
Substitute	a word or expression for the unknown word, e.g. pride or arrogance could be substituted for hubris.
Check	the context for clues that support your idea, e.g. prompts in the proximate text that shows the meaning, as in this excerpt: Hubris was considered a crime in ancient times not because it was not only proof of excessive pride, but also resulted in violent acts by or to those involved.
Ask	if substitution fits all context clues. The teacher may provide one more sentence to check whether the new item fits meaningfully or not, e.g. Hubris is a disease of the aristocrats.
Need	a new idea? More example sentences could be elicited at this stage.
Revise	your idea to fit the context. Teacher, colleagues, or a dictionary could be consulted at this stage.

uncertain. Fraser (1999), for example, found that the strategy training she provided did not have any direct effect on vocabulary learning.

Conclusion

Principle 6 of instructed language learning (see Chapter 1) stated: 'Successful instructed language learning requires extensive L2 input'. In this chapter we have seen that teacher manuals do not typically view teaching in terms of 'input'. In line with SLA theory and research, however, we have argued that 'input' is an essential construct for thinking about language pedagogy and have identified the types of input and the processing conditions involved in incidental acquisition. The insights provided by SLA have enabled us to examine a number of pedagogic issues and controversies and to suggest ways in which these insights might be utilized pedagogically, to ensure that learners have access to the quantity and quality of input they need and are able to make effective use of the data it affords them.

Input can be interactive or non-interactive. In the case of teacher-talk, the input is interactive; in extensive reading it is non-interactive. However, in this chapter we have not made a clear distinction between these two sources of input. In the next chapter, we will turn to look at the role played by interaction in L2 acquisition, focusing not just on the input that interaction provides, but also on the ways in which interaction can induce noticing and scaffold learners' production of new linguistic forms.

Notes

1 There are, however, some theories that propose that L2 learning is not entirely dependent on input. The Projection Hypothesis (Zobl, 1985) claims that exposure to a 'marked' linguistic feature can trigger access to an

associated 'unmarked' feature, even though learners have not been exposed to this feature. For example, if learners are exposed to the marked use of relative pronouns with prepositions, as in sentences such as 'The house *in which they lived for three years* has been demolished', they may also be able to learn the unmarked use of relative pronouns as the subject of a clause, as in the sentence 'The house *that was for sale* has been demolished'.

2 Hulstijn (2003) also proposed that intentional and explicit learning can be distinguished. Intentional learning involves a 'deliberate attempt to commit new information to memory' whereas explicit learning 'involves awareness at the point of learning' (p. 360).

3 Robinson (1995) defined 'attention' as involving general alertness to input, orientation to a stimulus, and detection of a feature it contains (i.e. 'noticing' in Schmidt's terms). He defined 'noticing' as involving both detection and rehearsal in short-term memory.

4 This is why some SLA researchers (e.g. Long, 1996) have argued that elaborative simplification is preferable to linguistic simplification. The former enriches texts by providing learners with the meanings of unknown words rather than by removing them from the text.

DISCUSSION QUESTIONS

1. In this chapter we treat input 'generically'. What do we mean by this? Why is it important to consider input in this way?

2. We point out that 'input' is not a term that belongs to mainstream thinking about language pedagogy and that the teacher guides we inspected do not conceptualize teaching in terms of 'input'. Why do you think this is? To what extent do you – as a teacher – conceive of teaching in terms of 'input'?

3. Why is the term 'authenticity' problematic? After reading this chapter, what definition of 'authenticity' do you favour?

4. Consider the different claims about the value of authentic materials in Box 7.1. After reading this chapter, how valid do you find each of these claims?

5. Do teachers talk too much? What are the differing views about this in the pedagogic literature?

6. Nuttall (1996) considered that 'authentic material is ideal' for extensive reading. Do you agree? What arguments have been advanced in support of simplified reading materials?

7. What is 'incidental learning'? Why do SLA researchers place considerable emphasis on this type of learning?

8. 'Frequency' is, however, not a straightforward concept. Explain why this is.

9. 'The Frequency Hypothesis cannot provide a full explanation of L2 acquisition.' Explain what else is needed to explain L2 acquisition.

10. What are the limitations of Krashen's Input Hypothesis?

11. A major point of debate in SLA is whether acquisition can take place subconsciously or whether it involves consciousness at least at the level of 'noticing'. Review the debate as it is presented in this chapter. Then consider its significance for language pedagogy. In other words, should teaching be directed at subconscious or conscious learning?

12. How might 'teacher-talk' assist L2 acquisition?
13. In what ways has 'simplified input' been shown to assist acquisition?
14. How can learners be induced to 'notice' linguistic forms in the input? Can you think of any pedagogic strategies that will induce 'noticing'?
15. Instructed Language Learning Principle 6 stated: 'Successful instructed language learning requires extensive L2 input'. This chapter has reviewed SLA research that supports this but it also shows that acquisition requires more than just 'extensive input'. What else is needed to make input work for acquisition?

8 Teaching as 'interaction'

Introduction

In the last chapter, we noted that 'input' is not a construct that figures widely in teachers' or teacher educators' thinking about language pedagogy. However, 'interaction' is much more widely accepted as an important aspect of language teaching. Teacher guides (e.g. Hedge, 2000; Nunan, 1991; Ur, 1996) all include an entry for 'interaction' in their indexes and in some cases deal with it at considerable length. They also pay some attention to SLA research on interaction. Hedge, for example, considered the 'role of interaction in the classroom' (2000: 13) in terms of constructs taken directly from SLA (e.g. 'comprehensible output' and 'negotiation of meaning'). Nunan included numerous transcripts of classroom interactions and drew from time to time on SLA research in his commentaries on them. Ur drew attention to one of the key findings of research that has investigated classroom interaction – the ubiquity of the initiate–respond–feedback (IRF) exchange – and invited readers to consider the appropriateness of this type of interaction for different learners and learning activities. However, in general, the teacher guides pay little attention to how interaction facilitates (or sometimes impedes) language learning.

In this chapter we will see that the role of interaction in SLA has been investigated from two different theoretical perspectives. As we noted in Chapter 1, interaction can be viewed as a source of input and opportunities for output, which foster the internal processing that results in acquisition. Block (2001) refers to this as the 'Input–Interaction–Output Model'. Social theories, however, view interaction as a site where learning takes place 'in flight'. In such theories, the distinction between 'participation' and 'acquisition' (Sfard, 1998) becomes blurred. Thus, we can distinguish theories in terms of whether they view learning as occurring *from* interaction or *in* interaction. By and large, where teacher guides pay attention to SLA research, they draw only on the Input–Interaction–Output Model and do not consider social accounts of interaction and learning.

We will begin by examining four aspects of teaching in which 'interaction' has figured in teacher guides. These are: (1) the teaching of speaking, (2) learner participation in the classroom, (3) small group work and (4) classroom management. We will then consider how SLA has viewed the role of interaction in L2 learning, first from the perspective of the Input–Interaction–Output Model and then from that of sociocultural theory.

Pedagogic perspectives

Teacher guides frequently view interaction in terms of the various participatory structures that are possible in a classroom. Scrivener (2005), for example, distinguished individual work, pair work, small groups, large groups, whole class (where the teacher and students move around and mingle) and whole-class (plenary). Each of these affords different types of interactions and also different management requirements. Harmer (1983) discusses the advantages and disadvantages of some of the main types of participatory structures. For example, he noted that whole-class interaction provides the learners with a 'good language model' but restricts opportunities for student talk.

Teacher guides also consider the kinds of interactions that arise in these different participatory structures. Ur (1996) listed the following types of interaction, indicating the level of activity manifested by the teacher and the students in each:

TT = Teacher very active, students only receptive

T = Teacher active, students mainly receptive

TS = Teacher and students fairly equally active

S = Students active, teacher mainly receptive

SS = Students very active, teacher only receptive

Ur did not define what she means by 'active' but it would seem that what she has in mind is the extent to which the students contribute to the discourse. The only specific type of interaction Ur mentioned is initiate–respond–feedback (IRF), where the teacher typically dominates by assuming responsibility for the initiate and feedback moves. An assumption commonly held by teacher educators is that the IRF exchange restricts students' contributions to classroom interaction by positioning the teacher as the source of expertise (Hedge, 2000) and, as a result, limits opportunities for learning. Ur, however, adopted a somewhat different position, implying that different interaction patterns are appropriate for achieving the objectives of different activities. What is missing, however, is any clear formulation of how these different types of interaction cater to actual learning.

A common theme in discussions of interaction in the classroom is the significance of cultural norms (Choudhury, 2005; Tsui, 1996). Asian students' lack of involvement in classroom interactions is seen as deriving from a cultural predisposition to avoid being conspicuous or appearing different from others and a fear of losing face in public by performing poorly in the L2 (e.g. through committing linguistic errors). In Asian classrooms, too, teachers are seen as favouring a transmission style of teaching which constrains the type of interaction. This raises an important question: should teachers simply accept that classroom interaction will be limited as a result of these cultural predispositions or should they look for ways of increasing learners' opportunities to learn through interaction? As we will see when we consider what teachers and educators have had to say about the role of learner participation in the classroom, there is a strong belief that while teachers need to be sensitive to their students' cultural norms, students need to participate actively.

Teaching speaking

Chapters on 'teaching speaking' in the teacher guides invariably lead to a discussion of 'interaction', especially in terms of how to develop students' conversational skills. Such skills can be tackled directly or indirectly (Hedge, 2000). Direct approaches involve the systematic analysis and teaching of the elements that comprise speaking. Traditionally, these have involved micro-linguistic elements (i.e. the phonological, lexical and grammatical aspects of spoken language). Increasingly, however, direct approaches also figure for teaching aspects of interactional competence such as turn-taking, repairing problems in conversations, and recognizing the boundaries in speaking events (Kasper, 2006). Direct approaches typically involve both an awareness-raising component (e.g. through the analysis of transcripts of interactions) and practice exercises such as cloze activities as in Barraja-Rohan (2011). They constitute an extension of the 'linguistic' approaches we considered in Chapter 3 and are essentially 'accuracy' oriented. In contrast, indirect approaches are experiential and 'fluency' oriented: they aim to develop speaking skills not by presentation, analysis and practice but by engaging learners in holistic activities such as role play and 'discussion'. They draw on the design and methodology of task-based teaching (see Chapter 6).

Hedge considered achieving a balance between accuracy and fluency-based activities an 'essential criterion' for developing a programme to teach speaking. For example, she saw merit in designing tasks to practise the patterns of interaction that occur in service encounters. She also recommended teaching students the language they will need for the negotiation of meaning and the 'rules' involved in, for example, the openings and closings of conversations and in interrupting politely. But she also recognized the importance of 'fluency'-based activities – free discussion, role play and gap activities.

In contrast, Ur wished to restrict accuracy-based work to the teaching of pronunciation, vocabulary and grammar (i.e. language-as-system) and saw the teaching of the four skills (including speaking) as requiring a fluency orientation. She identified four characteristics of a 'successful' speaking activity: (1) learners talk a lot, (2) participation is even, (3) motivation is high and (4) language is at an acceptable level. She then discussed ways of overcoming the problems that she claimed learners have with speaking activities. She recommended using group work, basing the activity on easy language, choosing topics that stimulate interest, giving clear instructions about how learners are supposed to participate in an activity, and keeping students speaking in the target language. Ur's recommendations are clearly based on her personal experience and probably reflect the views of many teachers. However, they are all challengeable. Not all teacher educators see merit in group work (see, for example, the position adopted by Prabhu (1987) discussed in the previous chapter). Nor is there complete agreement that speaking tasks should be based on 'easy language', especially if such tasks are seen not just as a means of developing communicative fluency but also of enhancing linguistic competence. Nor would all educators agree that it is essential to insist that students only use the target language (see Chapter 9).

Perhaps the major problem in these accounts of how to teach speaking is the uncritical acceptance of the separateness of 'knowledge-getting' and 'skill-using activities' (Rivers and Temperley, 1978). As we will see when we examine what SLA has to say about interaction, such a separation is neither necessary nor desirable. The development of 'fluency' and 'accuracy' co-occur through or in interaction and may in fact need to do so, if learners are to acquire linguistic knowledge that is deployable in communication.

Learner participation

There is a simple axiom that appears to underlie teachers' views about learners' participation in language classrooms – the more they participate, the better. As Weaver and Qi (2005) put it 'students who actively participate in the learning process learn more than those who do not' (p. 570). This has led teacher educators to emphasize the importance of student participation in classroom interaction as illustrated in the extracts from the teacher guides in Box 8.1.

More often than not, however, 'active participation' is not clearly defined. By and large, the comments in Box 8.1 suggest that it is perceived purely in quantitative terms, although exactly what is meant by 'talk a lot' is not clear (i.e. it could refer simply to the number of turns a student takes or to the number of words spoken). Qualitative aspects of participation are not considered. The comments also reveal an interesting difference in opinion. Whereas Ur and Scarcella saw a need for all students to participate actively and recommend that students are given equal opportunities to participate, Mohr and Mohr recognized that participation levels can be allowed to vary to take account of differences in students' language proficiency. Also other commentators (e.g. Allwright and Bailey, 1991) have warned against forcing students to participate when they are not ready. Choudhury (2005) also noted that 'some learners may wish to be quiet and listen in order to learn'. Czerwionka (2009) also noted that many introverted students who participate little in class are often high achievers. In other words, the belief that learners need to speak to learn has not gone entirely unchallenged.

Box 8.1 Sample quotations from teacher guides about the importance of participation

'Teachers need to show students that they expect them to participate in oral activity by constantly inviting every member of the class to participate' (Scarcella, 1990: 101).

'Learners talk a lot. As much as possible of the period of time allotted to an activity is in fact occupied by learner talk. This may seem obvious, but often most time is taken up with teacher talk or pauses' (Ur, 1996: 120).

'Participation is even. Classroom discussion is not dominated by a minority of talkative participants; all get a chance to speak, and contributions are fairly evenly distributed' (Ur, 1996: 120).

'All students are encouraged to participate, and teacher uses a variety of strategies to arrange for participation of all. However, the teacher does not exclusively determine who talks and students are encouraged to influence speaking turns' (Scarcella and Oxford, 1992: 33).

'Increase opportunities for STT (Student Talking Time)' (Scrivener, 2005).

'In order to be proficient and productive students, English-language learners (ELLs) need many opportunities to interact in social and academic situations. Effective teachers encourage their students' participation in classroom discussions, welcome their contributions, and motivate them by such practices. However, many educators often allow their less proficient students to remain silent or to participate less than their English-fluent peers' (Mohr and Mohr, 2007).

Overall, students' failure to participate actively in classroom interaction is perceived as a problem. Tsui (1996), for example, reported that ESL teachers working in Hong Kong identified the need to increase student participation as the major problem they faced in their teaching. Aubrey (2011) likewise saw students' willingness to communicate as an essential feature of effective language teaching in Japan. While this problem is frequently discussed in relation to Asian learners, it is by no means restricted to them. As noted above, the prevalence of the IRF exchange in classrooms throughout the world is seen as inhibiting learner participation.

Thus the focus of much discussion of student participation is on identifying the factors that inhibit it and proposing ways of increasing it. Tsui reported on the reasons that the teachers she investigated gave for students' reticence in speaking. The main reason was the students' low English proficiency but Tsui noted that students' self-confidence and willingness to take risks were just as important. Tsui's teachers did not see the problem as entirely due to the students' limitations. They acknowledged that teachers contributed to it by their intolerance of silence in the classroom and by their tendency to ask only the brighter students to respond to questions. Tsui asked the teachers to experiment with strategies designed to alleviate students' anxiety, which she considered to be the underlying cause of their reluctance to participate. These included lengthening wait time, improving questioning technique (e.g. by asking more referential questions), accepting a variety of answers, allowing students to check their answers with their peers before speaking to the whole class, focusing on content rather than form, and establishing good relationships with the students. Not all of these strategies were effective, however. For example, extending wait time led to increased anxiety and had a negative effect on participation whereas peer support prior to public performance proved effective. Aubrey (2011), in a discussion of how to promote greater willingness to communicate among Asian students, went a step further and suggested that one way of avoiding communication anxiety was by not requiring students to expose themselves in speaking to the whole class, but just allowing them to address the teacher's questions when they were working in small groups.[1] Small group work is seen as one of the main ways of enhancing both the quantity and the quality of student participation.

Small group work

Small group work is recommended in all the teacher guides we have inspected. It is seen as advantageous in a number of different ways. In particular it provides greater student talk-time than lockstep teaching and thus is of particular value for developing oral fluency (Ur, 1996). Here again, then, we see an emphasis on the quantity rather than the quality of learner talk. In this respect, the guides contrast with the pedagogical arguments advanced by some researchers. Long and Porter (1985) in a detailed discussion of group work emphasized its value in improving the quality of student talk (e.g. by requiring them to perform a wide range of language functions and engaging more fully in self- and other-correcting).

The guides also tend to emphasize the socio-affective advantages of group work. Ur (1996) pointed out that it helps to foster independence, feelings of cooperation and student motivation. Harmer (1983) also emphasized its value in developing self-reliance on the part of learners. Hedge (2000) noted that it promoted collaboration amongst students. In contrast, how group work contributes to learning receives almost no attention. Ur (1996) commented 'there is some research that indicates that the use of group work improves learning outcomes' (p. 232) but does not comment on what this research has shown or how group work assists learning.

All the guides also point out the disadvantages and dangers of group work. Ur noted that the advantages of group work are not always realized because the teacher loses control, the learners overuse their L1, and it is disliked by some learners. Hedge also commented that group work does not accord with the 'educational ethos' of some students and that students who find it difficult to assert themselves may not benefit. Ewald (2004) describes a number of problems she found arose in group work with her students – they sometimes failed to find the correct activity in their workbook, they looked bored, they pretended to comprehend even when they did not, they engaged in off-task behaviour, and attempted to hide this when the teacher approached. Ewald addressed these problems by video-recording the groups and then discussing the recordings with the students and encouraging them to engage in personal reflection about their behaviour. She found that this led to the students working more collaboratively and staying on task.

As befits the practical aims of teacher guides, the focus of much of the commentaries on group work is on how to set up groups. Ur stressed the importance of 'effective and careful organization' and offered detailed advice about how to ensure this in terms of 'presentation' (e.g. reviewing the language that students will need to perform the group activity), 'process' (i.e. the roles the teacher needs to perform when the group work is in progress), 'ending' (i.e. concluding the activity while the students are still enjoying it) and 'feedback' (i.e. reviewing the outcome of the group work in full-class interaction). Scrivener (2005: 56–57) offered a very similar plan for organizing group work involving a lead-in activity followed by performance of the activity and a post-activity. Hedge pointed to the importance of ensuring group cohesiveness. She discussed the logistics of setting up a group in terms of the roles that can be assigned to the different group members (i.e. chair, scribe, spokesperson and timekeeper). Harmer (1983) and Lynch (1996) considered the composition of groups, with the former seeing advantages in both mixed and homogenous groups and the latter drawing on research that pointed to the advantages of heterogeneity in terms of proficiency, L1 background and cultural background.

These guides do acknowledge some of the research that has investigated interaction in small group work. Hedge, for example, referred to Pica and Doughty's (1985) study that compared how communicative tasks were performed in lockstep with the teacher and in small groups. By and large, though, there is no consideration of the SLA theory and research that has addressed the contribution that small group interactions can make to learning.

The management of interaction in the classroom

Teachers are managers of the interactions that take place in their classrooms and the importance of this is fully recognized in the teacher guides. At one level, management entails deciding which type of participatory structure to select for a particular activity and how to ensure this works effectively. This is the level that figures most strongly in the guides. There are other levels, however. The management of classroom activities involves interactional routines for starting, proceeding and concluding instructional activities and for handling interpersonal issues. These routines through their sheer repetitiveness afford opportunities for language learning. Through managing teaching-as-interaction, teachers and students jointly construct patterned ways of acting and interacting, which constitute the 'culture' of the particular classroom in which they work.

The importance attached to managing classroom interaction is most clearly evident in Scrivener (2005). He devoted a whole chapter to 'classroom management' addressing such issues as seating, giving instructions, using the board, eliciting and students' use of language. He illustrated the role played by management in brief descriptions of four different lessons. Summaries of these can be found in Table 8.1. The teachers manage the interactions that occur in these classes in very different ways, in some cases directing it, in other cases intervening minimally. Although Scrivener does not directly say so, it is clear that he considers the four lessons examples of effective teaching. He commented that they involve little 'teaching in the traditional manner' but 'a lot of management' – of seating and grouping, of the teaching activities, of the learners' participation levels and of the 'flow of conversation and work'. However, in general, Scrivener's treatment of classroom management reflects Wright's (2005) observation that it has been reduced to a 'series of procedures and techniques' for organizing classrooms and groups and is seen as 'part of the craft knowledge and skills of the profession' (p. 1). At no point did Scrivener consider how opportunities for language learning arise out of these management activities.

Wright provided the most comprehensive account of classroom management and its importance in language education. He views 'managing' classrooms in terms of relationships involving: (1) learning opportunity (i.e. 'what a person may consciously or unconsciously encounter'), (2) learning (i.e. 'what learners do – behaviourally or cognitively – as they internalize new knowledge and skills') and (3) helping ('what another person can do to assist another engaged in learning'). Talk is seen as the primary means by which the relationships among all these elements are established:

> Classroom talk is the most obvious indicator of classroom management in action at the local level and by examining the texts of classroom talk we can discern patterns of participation which exemplify different management practices.
>
> (p. 255)

Table 8.1 The management of four different types of lessons (based on Scrivener, 2005: 11–15)

Teacher	Participatory structure	Student behaviours	Teacher behaviours
Andrea	Small group work based on decision-making task	Students engage in active and noisy discussion	Non-interventionist; answers questions when asked; offers quick suggestions
Maia	Teacher-class; circle formation	Chatting 'naturally'	No overt correction; 'managing the class' involves encouraging quieter students to speak, asking questions, recasting
Lee	Teacher-class; lockstep grammar class	Students attempt sentences using 'going to'; repeat incorrect sentences; choral repetition	Introducing 'going to' by eliciting sentences based on a picture; speaks little except for brief instructions and short corrections
Paoli	Pair work based on information-gap task designed to practise new vocabulary	Lot of talking but uneven participation – some pairs silent and one pair using L1	Moves around room monitoring and encouraging students to complete the task

It is through the 'discoursal possibilities' afforded by classroom talk that contexts for teaching and learning arise.

Hall (2011) discussed these 'discoursal possibilities' in terms of what he called 'high and low structure approaches' to classroom management. The former emphasize the teacher's role in organizing learning and the latter arise when the learners are involved in deciding what and how to learn. High structure approaches typically result in 'instructional discourse' (e.g. in the prevalence of IRF exchanges and a focus on accuracy), whereas low structure approaches are more likely to lead to 'natural discourse' (where roles are negotiated and there is a focus on meaning and fluency). Hall proposed that 'what kind of talk is both appropriate and best facilitates L2 learning will vary according to context' (p. 30) but does not elaborate on how this might occur.

Interaction and L2 acquisition

We have seen that teachers and teacher educators recognize the importance of interaction in a number of aspects of language teaching. However, the crucial issue – how language learning arises out of interaction – has received little attention. We will now turn to what SLA has to say about this issue.

Ortega (2009) sums up her account of the role of the linguistic environment in learning with this comment:

> What matters in the linguistic environment is not simply 'what's out there' physically or even socially surrounding learners, but rather what learners make of it, how they process (or not) the linguistic data and how they live and experience that environment.
>
> (p. 8)

This is why interaction is seen as so important. It is mainly through interaction, especially conversational interaction, that learners 'make something' of their linguistic environment. How this occurs has been addressed in two very different theoretical paradigms in SLA.

The cognitive–interactionist paradigm is based on the claim that internal (cognitive) and external (environmental) factors combine to make language learning possible. The environment affords learners the data they need for acquisition but acquisition itself occurs inside the learner's mind (brain) as a result of internal processing. As we will see, interaction plays a number of roles in providing learners with data, in activating the cognitive processes responsible for acquisition and affording opportunities for speaking. In contrast, the sociocultural paradigm rejects the separateness of environment and mind and sees interaction not as a source of data but as a site where learning occurs. Acquisition occurs 'in flight', so to speak, as speakers mediate each other's attempts to use the L2. As Artigal (1992) put it, the 'language acquisition device' lies not in the heads of learners but in the social interactions they participate in. We will explore these two ways of viewing the role of interaction and the research they have motivated separately.

The cognitive–interactionist paradigm

Two theoretical hypotheses have proved enormously influential in this paradigm: Long's (1983b, 1996) Interaction Hypothesis and Swain's (1985, 1995) Comprehensible Output Hypothesis.

The Interaction Hypothesis

The Interaction Hypothesis (IH) addresses how incidental acquisition takes place. It claims that incidental learning is facilitated through the negotiation of meaning. This occurs when interlocutors seek to prevent or address a communication problem. We provided an example of a negotiation of meaning sequence in Chapter 1, where we saw that they have a definite structure. They are accomplished by means of a variety of conversational strategies, such as comprehension checks (which can serve to head off potential problems) and confirmation checks, recasts and requests for clarification (which are used to deal with problems that have arisen) and often result in modified input (i.e. input that has been adjusted to facilitate the interlocutors' comprehension).

In its original formulation (Long, 1983b), the IH was quite limited as it focused on how negotiation helps to make input comprehensible. In the updated version, Long (1996) extended its reach in some important ways. First, he drew on Schmidt's Noticing Hypothesis (see Chapter 7) to explain how interaction facilitates the cognitive operations involved in acquisition:

> it is proposed that environmental contributions to acquisition are mediated by selective attention and the learner's developing L2 processing capacity, and that these resources are brought together more usefully, although not exclusively, during 'negotiation for meaning'.
>
> (p. 414)

In other words, Long proposed that negotiation facilitates acquisition when: (1) it leads to learners selectively noticing linguistic forms in the input and (2) the forms attended to lie within the learner's 'processing capacity' (i.e. are learnable in terms of where a learner has reached in the order and sequence of acquisition). The central claim of the IH, then, is that negotiation of meaning promotes learning because it enables learners to map the correct form onto the meaning that they wish to convey. This arises because negotiation provides an opportunity for learners to carry out a cognitive comparison between their own, erroneous use of a linguistic form and the target language form.

The updated IH also drew on research by Pica (1992), who proposed that the negotiation of meaning promotes acquisition not just by affording learners comprehensible input but also by showing them how to segment utterances into their constituent parts, by providing negative evidence (i.e. correcting them when they make an error) and by pushing them to modify their own output to make it more target-like. The role that negotiation plays in assisting segmentation is illustrated in this sequence:

NS: with a small pat of butter on it and above the plate
NNS: hm hm what is buvdaplate?
NS: above
NNS: above the plate
NS: yeah

(p. 225)

Here the learner initially fails to segment 'above the plate', hearing it as a single item ('buvdaplate') but when the NS responds by emphasizing 'above' the learner is able to distinguish the separate constituents. We will deal with the role that negotiation plays in providing negative evidence in Chapter 10 when we consider corrective feedback. The importance of modified output is examined when we consider the Comprehensible Output Hypothesis in the following section.

Research based on the IH has focused on whether the negotiation of meaning helps comprehension, what factors increase the likelihood of negotiation taking place, and whether negotiation actually results in acquisition. A number of studies have shown that input does become more comprehensible when learners have the chance to negotiate meaning. Pica et al. (1987), for example, conducted a study that compared learners' comprehension of directions under a baseline condition (which involved listening to directions of the kind native speakers address to other native speakers), a premodified condition (where baseline directions were simplified in accordance with the kinds of modifications native speakers make when they address non-native speakers) and an interactionally modified condition (where the learners were given the opportunity to negotiate the directions if they did not understand them). The learners comprehended the directions best in the interactionally modified condition (as claimed by the IH) and worst in the baseline condition. This finding has been replicated in other studies. However, as we noted in Chapter 7, comprehensible input does not guarantee learning; it merely increases the likelihood of it occurring. Also, interactionally modified input is not always advantageous. Ehrlich et al. (1989) found that native speakers sometimes have a tendency to over-elaborate when negotiating meaning and that this can have a detrimental effect on comprehension.

Other studies have investigated how best to induce the negotiation of meaning. A key finding of importance for language pedagogy is that negotiation is more likely to occur when learners perform tasks that involve required information exchange (e.g. two-way information-gap tasks). Gass et al. (2005), for example, reported a much higher incidence of negotiation of meaning in a required-information exchange task than in an optional-information task.

Later studies investigated whether the negotiation of meaning assisted acquisition. Mackey (1999), a key study, is summarized in Table 8.2. This study demonstrated that interactionally modified input enabled learners to progress along a developmental sequence (i.e. to produce questions indicative of a more advanced stage of development). It established a clear link between negotiation and 'acquisition' as this has been defined in studies of naturalistic

Table 8.2 Mackey's (1999) study of interactionally modified input

Participants	Target structure	Design	Tests	Results
34 adult ESL learners in a private school in Sydney	WH and SVO questions	Five groups completed the same communicative tasks with a NS. The groups varied in terms of: (1) whether they received interactionally modified or premodified input, (2) whether they participated in meaning negotiation or not and (3) their developmental readiness to acquire question forms. The interactionally modified input consisted of feedback made up of a mixture of recasts and clarification requests.	The participants completed tasks similar to those used in the treatment immediately after the final treatment, two weeks later and again five weeks later. Acquisition was measured in terms of ability to produce developmentally more advanced questions.	Only the learners who received recasts and clarification requests demonstrated clear evidence of development – they advanced along the developmental sequence and produced more developmentally advanced questions.

acquisition – see Chapter 3. Mackey's study, however, was laboratory- not classroom-based. The extent to which it is possible to extrapolate from such studies to the classroom is a matter of some debate (see Ellis, 2012). Also, it could be argued that this study involved the negotiation of form rather than meaning as the feedback learners received was not triggered by problems in communication. Clearer evidence of the role played by the negotiation of meaning in a classroom context can be found in the input-based studies referred to in Chapter 6 (e.g. Shintani, 2012).

The Interaction Hypothesis has been enormously influential in SLA, giving rise to a large number of studies. However, it is not without its critics (e.g. Foster and Ohta, 2005) and, in many respects, it provides a very limited account of how interaction serves as a source of acquisition. One limitation lies in Long's insistence that it is *meaning* that is negotiated. As we noted in Chapter 6, negotiation of *form* (rather than meaning) is more common in many classrooms. That is, in whole-class interaction negotiation sequences occur even though no breakdown in communication has occurred, as in this example:

T: What were you doing?

S: I was in pub   Trigger

(2)

S: I was in pub   Trigger (repeated)

T: In the pub?   Indicator

S: Yeh and I was drinking beer with my Response
friend.

This sequence has the same structure as a negotiation of meaning sequence but it seems likely that the teacher understood the student's utterance ('I was in pub') but still chose to indicate there was a problem with it by recasting and providing the missing definite article ('In the pub?'). Arguably such negotiation of form sequences also foster noticing and form-meaning mapping in the same way as negotiation of meaning sequences. There is no reason why the IH cannot be extended to include them.

The IH is better equipped to explain how vocabulary and syntax is acquired than grammatical morphology. This is because communication breakdown are more likely to occur as a result of a lexical or word order problem, rather than because a morphological error has been committed which is less likely to interfere with intelligibility. Satos's (1986) longitudinal study of two Vietnamese children provided evidence of this. She found that the interactional support the learners were given obviated any need for them to attend to past tense features so they did not acquire them. Pica (1992) also reported that there were few instances of morphological modifications in her data.

Perhaps the most serious criticism of the IH from the perspective of language pedagogy is that negotiation sequences constitute only a small part of the total interaction in the classroom. Nakahama et al. (2001) pointed out that there are other aspects of interaction that may be just as or more important. They found that the negotiation resulting from an information exchange task was very mechanical and suggested that the interaction resulting from a discussion task might be more beneficial for acquisition. They showed that even though the discussion task did not result in much negotiation of meaning, it generated significantly longer and more complex turns and greater use of discourse strategies such as paraphrase. IH researchers such as Pica (1996), however, always acknowledged that negotiation is not the only source of data for acquisition, although they also claimed that learners' data needs can be best met through negotiation.

As we noted above, many of the IH studies were laboratory based, where interaction was one-on-one (as in Mackey's study) and negotiation was induced by the type of task used to elicit interaction. Two studies suggest that negotiation of meaning is limited in a classroom setting. Foster (1998) found relatively few instances in the adult ESL classroom she investigated. She suggested that rather than engage in the painstaking, frustrating and face-threatening nature of extensive negotiation when performing information or opinion-gap tasks in groups, the learners opted for a 'pretend and hope' rather than a 'check and clarify' approach. Slimani-Rolls (2005) investigated adult learners of L2 French performing communicative tasks. She found that there was considerable individual variation in the amount of negotiation, with 25 per cent of the learners producing 60 per cent of the meaning negotiation and 20 per cent producing none at all.[2] These studies suggest that negotiation is much less frequent in a classroom setting and also that when it does occur not all learners contribute to it.

The Comprehensible Output Hypothesis

Research based on the later version of the IH acknowledged the importance of the modified output that learners produce as a result of negotiating meaning. Swain (1985) proposed the Comprehensible Output Hypothesis as a complement to Krashen's Input Hypothesis. It was motivated by the fact that studies had shown that although immersion learners become confident in using the L2 and develop considerable discourse skills, they fail to achieve a high level of grammatical competence. Swain argued that this could not be explained by a lack of comprehensible input, as immersion classrooms are rich in this. She speculated that it might be because the learners had limited opportunity to talk in the classroom and were not 'pushed' in the output they did produce. Evidence for this came from a study by Allen et al. (1990), which showed that immersion students' responses were typically 'minimal' (i.e. less than 15 per cent of students' L2 utterances were more than a clause in length).

In a later article, Swain (1995) discussed three ways in which output could contribute to grammatical competence. First, it serves a consciousness-raising function by triggering 'noticing'. That is, producing language helps learners to notice their problems. Second, producing language enables learners to test out hypotheses about the L2. One way in which this occurs is through the modified output that learners produce following negative feedback. Third, output allows learners to reflect consciously about L2 forms. This can occur in the context of communicative tasks when learners negotiate for meaning and grapple with a grammar problem. De Bot (1996) also pointed a fourth way in which output assists acquisition – by helping learners to increase control over linguistic forms they had already partially acquired.

The Comprehensible Output Hypothesis has been investigated in a number of ways. Pica (e.g. Pica, 1988; Pica et al., 1989) was interested in whether learners modify their output as a result of meaning negotiation. She found that this depended on whether the indicator move consisted of a recast or a request for clarification, with modified output much more likely following a request for clarification. Subsequently, Lyster and Ranta (1997) investigated what they called 'uptake with repair' in French immersion classrooms, reporting that it was much more likely to occur following what they called 'prompts' (which included requests for clarification) than recasts (see Chapter 10).

These studies investigated other-initiated modified output but, as Shehadeh (2002) noted, learners' sometime self-initiate by repairing their own errors. Shehadeh examined learners' 'hypothesis-testing episodes' when performing a picture-description task with a native-speaker partner. These episodes involved learners in monitoring and modifying their initial output as in this example:

You have two chairs (0.8) one near of the bed (0.8) near of the bed (0.9) near to the bed (1.0).

Shehadeh reported that in 87 per cent of such episodes the native speaker did not provide any feedback on the learners' output and speculated that in such cases the learners would be likely to assume that the hypotheses represented by their self-corrections were confirmed.

There are different positions regarding the role played by output in language acquisition. Krashen has consistently argued that output plays no role in the acquisition of grammar (see, e.g. Krashen, 1998). Both Long and Pica, however, have claimed that modified output contributes significantly to acquisition. Long (1996) argued that it is 'facilitative, but not necessary' (p. 448). Pica (1992) claimed that modified output helps learners to analyse and break a message into its constituent parts and also to produce forms that may lie at the cutting edge of their linguistic ability. These conflicting positions can only be resolved through empirical studies of the effects of output modification on acquisition.

A number of studies suggest that pushed output does assist acquisition. In a small-scale study involving just three learners, Nobuyoshi and Ellis (1993) found that two of the learners they investigated were able to improve the accuracy of their use of past tense forms in oral narratives, as a result of being 'pushed' by means of requests for clarification and that their improvement was sustained in narratives produced one week later when they were not pushed. The third learner, however, neither modified his output initially nor showed any later gains in accuracy. Van den Branden (1997) found that 11–12-year-old children who had been pushed to modify their output in the context of a two-way communicative task produced significantly more output, more essential information and a greater range of vocabulary in a similar communicative task performed later, than did children who had not been initially pushed. Loewen (2005) found that learners' uptake involving repair in classroom-based communicative lessons was a strong predictor of their ability to subsequently correct their errors in tailor-made tests administered to individual students. De la Fuente (2002) found that negotiated interaction that included pushed output promoted productive acquisition of new words to a greater extent than either premodified input or negotiated interaction without pushed output. Finally, Izumi et al. (1999) conducted a study that showed that groups of learners who performed a task that required them to produce the target structure (English relative clauses) outperformed those groups that just received input. In line with Swain's Comprehensible Output Hypothesis, Izumi et al. suggested that the output was more effective because it induced a cognitive comparison between the target language form and the learners' interlanguage (IL) form, leading them to eradicate the IL form.

The Comprehensible Output Hypothesis was formulated as part of the input–output model of L2 acquisition. Swain herself, however, subsequently preferred to conceptualize the role played by output in terms of a Sociocultural Theory of L2 acquisition, which we will examine shortly.

General comment

Gass and Mackey (2007) warned that the direct application of what they called the 'interaction approach' to the classroom may be premature. For a start, there is still quite limited evidence to show that interaction leads to acquisition. These hypotheses take little account of the specific contextual factors that determine why classroom participants interact in the way they do, when they do, and what they take from interaction. Nevertheless, the Interaction Hypothesis and the Comprehensible Output Hypothesis offer a number of very specific ways in which interaction can facilitate acquisition, which are of potential value to teachers. We summarize these ways in Box 8.2.

Box 8.2 Cognitive–interactionist SLA – the contributions of interaction

Interaction assists incidental language acquisition by providing input and opportunities for output that facilitate L2 development.

Input

- Interaction provides learner with comprehensible input through the negotiation of meaning or form.
- Interaction induces attention to linguistic forms when learners negotiate either meaning or form.
- Interaction helps learners to segment chunks into their constituent parts.
- Interaction provides learners with feedback on their efforts to use the L2 and causes them to notice-the-gap between their own erroneous utterances and their target language equivalents.

Output

- Output requires 'bottom-up processing' and thus is likely to make learners aware of gaps in their competence.
- Learners can be prompted to produce 'pushed output' (i.e. output that is more comprehensible and/or more linguistically accurate).
- Learners have an opportunity to produce long as well as short turns.
- Learners have an opportunity to experiment with L2 forms that lie at the cutting edge of their linguistic development.
- Learners can self-correct their own output.

The sociocultural paradigm

In her 2000 article called 'The output hypothesis and beyond: mediating acquisition through collaborative dialogue', Swain announced her intention to reinterpret the role of output in L2 acquisition in terms of Sociocultural Theory. Swain questioned the input–output model which had informed her earlier work and argued that 'participation' (Sfard, 1998) serves as a better metaphor for investigating the role played by interaction in L2 learning. In line with this theoretical re-orientation, she proposed a switch in terminology from 'output' to 'collaborative dialogue'. Swain now accepted the Vygotskian view of learning, namely that psychological processes originate in external activities and are subsequently transformed into mental ones through the mediation of semiotic tools.

Sociocultural Theory was briefly introduced in Chapter 1. Here we will outline the key constructs of Sociocultural Theory (SCT) as these have been applied to SLA and also examine a number of studies that have investigated 'collaborative dialogue'. Readers interested in concrete instantiations of the key constructs might like to refer to Swain et al.'s (2011) book which reports a number of 'narrative tellings' of teachers' and researchers' experiences of working with L2 learners.

Mediation

According to Vygotsky (1987), humans are equipped at birth with a biological inheritance that allows for simple lower mental functions to be performed. Higher-order mental functioning involving memory and rational thinking, however, arise as a result of sociocultural experiences with the world. Thus, learning is not something that goes on exclusively inside the head of the learner but also in the world the learner inhabits. SCT brings the social and the psychological into contact through the notion of mediation, defined by Lantolf and Thorne (2006) as 'the process through which humans deploy culturally constructed artefacts, concepts, and activities to regulate (i.e. gain voluntary control over and transform) the material world or their own and each other's social and mental activity' (p. 79).

Language is the most powerful semiotic tool available for mediating thought. In the case of language learners, the L2 serves as both the object of their attention and the tool for mediating its acquisition. As Swain (2000) put it, L2 acquisition involves learning how to use language to mediate language learning. This can occur in two ways. First, language serves as a tool for engaging in social interaction, enabling learners to construct utterances in the L2 that are beyond their individual abilities. One of the most obvious ways in which this can occur is through 'vertical constructions' (Scollon, 1976), as in this example from Ellis (1984b):

T: Take a look at the next picture.

S: Box

T: A box, yes.

S: A box bananas.

The learner's final utterance ('A box bananas') can be seen as a repetition of the first part of the preceding utterance ('A box') with a noun ('bananas') added. Second, learners can mediate their own learning through private speech (i.e. the speech that we sometimes direct at ourselves). Lantolf (2000a) argued that private speech is a kind of social interaction as it constitutes 'talking to yourself'. However, Lantolf and Thorne (2006) acknowledged that learners (even quite advanced ones) may have difficulty in using the L2 for private speech. In other words, the L2 is able to serve as a tool for mediating social activity but is perhaps not so readily available for mediating mental activity.

Zone of proximal development (ZPD)

To understand the ZPD it is necessary to distinguish two levels of development. Vygotsky (1978) distinguished 'the actual developmental level, that is the level of development of the child's mental functions that has been established as a result of certain already completed developmental cycles' (p. 85) and the level of potential development as evidenced in problem solving undertaken with the assistance of an adult (an expert). These two levels are referred to as 'development' and 'learning'. The ZPD relates to the second of these levels: the level of potential development (i.e. 'learning'). It is important to understand that the ZPD is not a psychological construct – it does not lie inside the mind of the learner. Rather it is a sociocognitive construct – it involves the psychological contributions that learners make to the social interactions they participate in. As Newman and Holzman (1997) put it 'the ZPD is not a place at all; it is an activity' (p. 289).

There is a third level often ignored by sociocultural theorists. This is the level that lies beyond the learner, where the learner is unable to perform the task even if assistance is provided. The existence of such a level is compatible with research on the order and sequence of acquisition (see Chapter 3), which suggests that learners are constrained in what they can learn and follow a pre-determined developmental trajectory (i.e. they can only learn what they are ready to learn). Lantolf (2005), however, rejected this account of acquisition, arguing that it is incompatible with the SCT view that learning is 'revolutionary' and 'unpredictable'.

The ZPD has frequently been invoked by both L2 researchers and language teaching methodologists. As Kinginger (2002) pointed out, there is a danger of the construct becoming so stretched as to lose shape and meaning. Researchers have interpreted the construct creatively in support of their own particular views about L2 acquisition and teacher educators have appropriated it to provide a simplistic justification for pair and group work. Kinginger proposed that it is most justifiably used to provide a rationale for 'collaborative dialogue'.

Internalization

What starts out as 'learning' becomes 'development' as 'external activities are transformed into mental ones' (Swain, 2000: 103). This process is referred to as 'internalization' and, in many respects, constitutes the least theorized aspect of SCT in SLA. As Vygotsky (1978) put it, 'learning is not development' but 'properly organized learning results in mental development and sets in motion a variety of developmental processes that would be impossible apart from learning' (p. 9). More simply, Ohta (2001) described internalization as 'the movement of language from environment to brain' (p. 11). The question that arises is exactly how and under what conditions this movement takes place.

One way of characterizing internalization is as progress from object or other regulation to self-regulation. An example will clarify what this involves. Imagine a learner obtains an electronic dictionary and feels compelled to use it to check the meaning of every difficult word in a reading text; this is object-regulation. The teacher then discusses and practices with the learners the strategy of 'selective dictionary use'; this is other-regulation. Finally, the learner is able to vary his/her use of the dictionary according to whether the goal is to learn new vocabulary or to comprehend a text efficiently; this is self-regulation. As this example suggests, the primary means by which a learner moves from object/other-regulation to self-regulation is through social interaction. However, claiming that object/other-regulation leads to self-regulation simply restates the claim that 'learning' becomes 'development' and does not explain how.

The closest SCT comes to explaining internalization in L2 acquisition is by drawing on Vygotsky's account of 'imitation'. As Vygotsky (1986) put it, 'to imitate, it is necessary to possess the means of stepping from something one knows to something new' (p. 187). Thus imitation is not a mechanical process of repeating what someone else has said but a creative, transformative activity. Lantolf (2005) illustrates this with an example taken from Saville-Troike (1988), which shows how imitation can arise in communicative speech:

> Teacher: You guys go brush your teeth. And wipe your hands on the towel.
>
> Child: Wipe your hand. Wipe your teeth.

The child first imitated the teacher's utterance ('wipe your hand') and then extended it to a novel utterance ('wipe your teeth'). The process is analogous to that involved in vertical constructions described above (i.e. the learner repeats part of an utterance and then adds something new). What is interesting about this example is that it results in the kind of lexical overgeneralization that has been observed to occur in L2 acquisition. Lantolf argues that this is important because it demonstrates that such errors do not reflect purely internal, mental processes as claimed in cognitive accounts of L2 acquisition. Imitation is both social and cognitive in nature. Lantolf (2006) also claimed that 'deferred imitation' (i.e. imitation of a pattern some time later) may help learners to analyse the pattern 'off line' and may be especially beneficial for internalization. The 'vicarious responses' that Ohta (2001) observed classroom learners make when another student is answering a teacher's question can also be seen as a kind of imitation.

Assisted performance

Interaction is central to SCT accounts of L2 acquisition. It is the primary way in which a ZPD is created (i.e. it helps learners to perform a specific feature which is not yet part of their self-regulated L2 system). Various terms have been used to refer to the types of interaction claimed to construct ZPDs and thereby foster 'learning' – 'scaffolding' (Wood et al., 1976), 'collaborative dialogue' (Swain, 2000) and 'instructional conversation' (Donato, 2000). As a cover term for all of these, we will employ the term 'assisted performance' (Ohta, 2001).

We can distinguish three broad approaches to identifying the important features of assisted performance. One is to identify in very general terms what teachers need to do to scaffold learners' contributions to an interaction. Often cited is Wood et al.'s (1976) list. Teachers can assist learning through:

1 Recruiting interest in the task.
2 Simplifying the task.
3 Maintaining pursuit of the goal.
4 Marking critical features and discrepancies between what has been produced and the ideal solution.
5 Controlling frustration during problem solving.
6 Demonstrating an idealized version of the act to be performed.

The second approach is to examine actual interactions in order to identify the specific aspects of discourse that assist the learner. The third approach is to examine how interaction mediates joint problem solving, where learners explicitly address their linguistic difficulties. We will consider these last two approaches in greater depth.

We have already noted one specific discourse strategy that enables learners to construct utterances that lie 'beyond their competence', as Swain (2000) put it. Learners 'borrow' from their interlocutors' utterances in order to construct their own utterances vertically. What motivates vertical constructions is the learners' desire to express what they want to say in order to make an ongoing contribution to an interaction. In this way, learning language is part and parcel of learning how to interact in the L2. Linguistic development, in other words, occurs concurrently with the development of interactional competence in an L2. Ohta (2001), for example, in her study of Japanese foreign language classrooms in the United States, showed that classroom interaction consists to a large extent of 'interactional routines'. She illustrated how learners 'acquire facility in L2 interaction through progressively expanded involvement' in such routines, moving from 'peripheral participation to more and more active involvement' (p. 187) and how as they do so they appropriate linguistic forms.

Sociocultural studies of L2 classrooms have also led to a reconsideration of the role played by initiate–respond–feedback exchanges in learning. Such exchanges have been shown to be dominant in many classrooms. Consolo (2000), for example, in a study of English classes in Brazil, found that 'most of the time, teachers and students rigidly observe their part in the socially defined classroom roles' (p. 105) imposed by IRF. Berry (1981) explains why IRF is so prevalent. It arises because the teacher takes on the role of both 'initiator' and 'primary knower'. Only when the teacher either abandons the role of 'primary knower' or allocates the initiating role to the students do different discourse patterns occur.

SLA researchers in the cognitive–interactionist tradition have seen the IRF exchange as limiting because it affords learners few opportunities for extended utterances, limits the range of language functions to be performed and provides few occasions for negotiating meaning as communication breakdown is infrequent. As Van Lier (1996) put it, 'in the IRF exchange, the student's response is hemmed in, squeezed between a demand to display knowledge and a judgment on its competence' (p. 151). In other words, classrooms where the IRF dominates have been considered less than ideal for L2 acquisition.

Sociocultural theorists, however, have re-evaluated the potential of IRF for learning. For example, Nassaji and Wells (2000) pointed out that richer contributions from students are likely if the initiation move involves teacher questions that 'introduce issues as for negotiation' (p. 400). Ohta (2001) found that the Japanese learners she investigated appropriated the language they were exposed to in IRF exchanges for use in subsequent group work. For example, she showed how IRF exchanges helped learners of L2 Japanese to develop the interactional competence involved in producing appropriate listener responses (e.g. the use of *ne* as an aligning expression), which occur frequently in ordinary Japanese conversation. Antón (1999) suggested that IRF plays an important part in prolepsis (i.e. where the teacher anticipates a difficulty learners may experience and attempts to deal with it). The teacher she investigated employed open-ended questions in IRF exchanges designed to help the learners to reflect on form and to lead them to verbalize a rule. Antón argued that this kind of proleptic teaching constitutes 'effective assistance (i.e. a scaffold)' (p. 308).

There has also been a re-evaluation of some of the traditional techniques of language teaching and the interactions they give rise to. Guk and Kellogg (2007), for example, drew on Vygotsky's (1978) own suggestions regarding the techniques that teachers can use to other-regulate learners to illustrate how demonstration, requests for repetition, leading questions and initiating solutions can assist learning:

1. T: Repeat after me. Dahye is stronger than Yeseul.

2. Ss: Dahye is stronger than Yeseul.

3. T: Than Yeseul.

4. Ss: Than Yeseul.

5. T: Keokkuro hamyeon mueorahuyo?

(How would you say it the other way?)

Yeseul is......

6. Ss: Yeseul is weaker...

7. T:...Weaker than Dahye.

8. Ss: Yeseul is weaker than Dahye.

Like researchers in the cognitive–interactionist tradition, sociocultural researchers consider that group work affords rich learning opportunities. But whereas the former view group work as desirable because it enables students to engage in more negotiation of meaning sequences than in teacher-led lessons, the latter are interested more broadly in how novice–novice interactions assist learning. Ohta (2001), for example, noted how listeners would give their partner time to complete an utterance, or prompt him/her by repeating a syllable, or co-construct the utterance by providing a syllable, word or phrase that contributed towards its completion or, sometimes, provide an explanation in the L1. These techniques were also used when a learner made an error. Ohta emphasized the reciprocal nature of assisted performance: 'this is the key to peer assistance – that both peers benefit, the one receiving assistance and the one who reaches out to provide it' (p. 125).

A limitation of much of this research on assisted learning is that it has focused more or less exclusively on 'assistance' and much less on 'learning'. In fact, sometimes 'assistance' is naively equated with 'learning'. To demonstrate that classroom interaction leads to 'learning', it is necessary to show that interaction assists learners to perform some aspect of language that they were unable to perform independently. Researchers often fail to show this. Another limitation of the research is that it has failed to demonstrate whether 'internalization' took place. That is, it does not show that 'development' has occurred. To investigate development, a longitudinal investigation is needed but, by and large, studies informed by SCT have been short term. An exception is Markee (2008). He examined the occurrence of a specific lexical item in the interactions that took place in a classroom over a whole language course and was able to show how assisted use of this item transformed into independent use. The studies involving Swain and her co-researchers, which we will now examine, also made efforts to investigate 'development'.

These studies illustrate the third approach to investigating assisted performance. They examined how learners address the linguistic problems they experience when performing a task in small group work and how the talk they engage in while doing this mediates learning. These studies drew on the idea of a 'language related episode' (LRE).[3] Swain (1998: 70) defined this as 'any part of a dialogue in which students talk about the language they are producing, question their language use, or other- or self-correct'. Thus LREs include negotiation sequences but they also include sequences where there is no communication breakdown (i.e. where the talk about language is focused explicitly on linguistic form), as in this example from Kim (2009: 258):

Learner A: She find the money.

Learner B: No...It should be...she found the money...past.

Learner A: Ah...sorry...she found the money.

Such episodes can result in: (1) a correct resolution to the linguistic problem (as in the example above, (2) an incorrect resolution, or (3) they can remain unresolved. Researchers have investigated both the extent to which LREs occur in small group or pair work and their effect on 'development' (i.e. whether they lead to subsequent self-regulated behaviour). Swain and Lapkin (2007) also proposed the term 'language units' to refer to occasions where an individual learner identified a linguistic problem and then sought to resolve it him or herself through private speech.

One of the earliest studies to investigate LREs was Donato's (1994) study of group work interactions in university French classes. In a detailed analysis of an exchange involving the construction 'tu t'es souvenu', Donato showed how the learners' collective scaffolding enabled them to produce the correct form of the verb even though no single learner knew this prior to the task. Altogether Donato identified thirty-two instances of such collective scaffolding involving a range of linguistic structures and then showed that individual learners were able to produce the structures that had figured in their collective scaffolding independently in a subsequent task. This study provides clear support for the central claim of Sociocultural Theory, namely that the genesis of language learning can be observed in the interactions that learners engage in when addressing a problem-solving task.

Swain's studies differed from those we have considered so far in that they were quasi-experimental, reflecting perhaps the research methodology she had become familiar with in her cognitive–interactionist period. The typical design of these studies was as follows:

1 Learners complete a task (e.g. a dictogloss) in pairs of groups.
2 Their performance of the task is recorded and transcribed and all the language related episodes identified.
3 These episodes were coded as successfully resolved, unsuccessfully resolved or unresolved.
4 Individual learners take tailor-made tests or complete new tasks to see whether they are now able to use the features targeted in the LREs correctly.

We will not attempt to review all of Swain's studies. Instead we provide a summary of one (Swain and Lapkin, 2002) in Table 8.3. This study demonstrates a clear relationship between the LREs that the two learners participated in and the changes they made to their written texts. Such studies show how learners mediate their learning when a linguistic problem arises. It also provides some evidence of 'development' by including tests or post-tasks. However, arguably, these studies still do not convincingly demonstrate that full internalization has taken place as the post-tasks typically involved performance of the same kind as in the initial task. Thus, we cannot be certain that the learners were able to generalize their learning to new tasks and new contexts.

Swain's studies all involved pair or small group work. Adopting a similar approach to Swain, Storch (2002) investigated to what extent the effectiveness of group work depends on the learners' collaborative engagement in a task. She examined the relationship between different patterns of dyadic interaction and language development, measured in terms of the extent to which 'learning', as

Table 8.3 Summary of Swain and Lapkin's (2002) study

Participants	Design	Data analysis	Results
Two adult learners of L2 French	1. Video-tape of mini-lesson on French reflexive verbs 2. Learners write a story collaboratively (audio recorded) 3. Story is reformulated by a native speaker 4. Stimulated recall where learners comment on the differences they have noticed 5. Learners rewrite original story	1. Comparison of initial and final learner texts (functioning as pre- and post-test) 2. Relationship between changes made to text and LREs	1. 80% of the changes that the learners made were correct 2. The changes they made were directly traceable to the LREs

evidenced in the interactions, led to 'development', as evidenced in subsequent tasks. She analysed these patterns in terms of two intersecting dimensions: (1) mutuality (i.e. 'the level of engagement with each other's contribution') and (2) equality (i.e. 'the degree of control or authority over a task') (p. 127). She found that the most collaborative dyad (i.e. the dyad manifesting high mutuality and high equality) achieved more instances of transfer of knowledge than both the dominant/passive and the dominant/dominant dyads, with the expert/ novice group intermediate.

'Languaging'

In her 1990 article, Swain struggled to find a label for the kind of dialogic activity that she considered important for learning and development. More recently, Swain (2006) coined the term 'languaging' to refer to the role that language production (oral or written) plays in making meaning when learners are faced with some problem (i.e. in a language-related episode). As Swain et al. (2011) pointed out, 'languaging' can also take place in private speech as well as in social talk. It serves two functions. One of these we have already discussed. It mediates learning by enabling learners to jointly construct a ZPD and perform a linguistic feature that is beyond any single learner. Swain also claimed that languaging gives learners the opportunity to reflect on problematic forms (i.e. it leads to metalinguistic understanding). In other words, the type of 'learning' that Swain considered important occurs when learners endeavour to make a linguistic feature an artefact that they can consciously think about. In this key respect, then, 'languaging' is not synonymous with 'speaking' or 'writing', which often serve to simply convey a message: 'languaging' only occurs when learners use language as a cognitive tool to mediate thinking.

General comment

Sociocultural theorists generally do not discuss learning in terms of the explicit/implicit distinction but it is clear from Swain's account of 'languaging' that they do view it – in part at least – as an intentional process involving explicit representations of linguistic features. In this respect, then, Sociocultural Theory differs from cognitive–interactionist theories, which emphasize the role of interaction in incidental learning and see no need for metalinguistic understanding. In one other major respect, however, these two paradigms share a common view about the kind of instructional activity that will create the interactional space for learning to occur – it requires 'tasks', where language serves as a tool for making meaning and achieving outcomes, rather than 'exercises' that just require the display of correct language (see Chapter 6). The main ways in which interaction contributes to learning and development according to SCT are summarized in Box 8.3.

Box 8.3 summarizes how SCT views the role of interaction in L2 learning

1. A distinction can be made between 'learning' (i.e. the external manifestation of a new linguistic feature) and 'development' (i.e. the internal representation of the feature).
2. 'Learning' precedes 'development'. That is, in the first instance performance of a new linguistic feature is assisted. Only later does the learner develop independent control over it.
3. Learning takes place *in* interaction (not inside the learner's head). It is mediated by interpersonal interaction (social talk) or intrapersonal interaction (private speech).
4. Mediated learning occurs when a zone of proximal development is constructed.
5. Subsequently, as a result of such social and psychological processes as imitation, internalization occurs. At this point the learner achieves self-regulation (i.e. is able to deploy new forms independently without interactional assistance).
6. Learning can be mediated in both expert–novice (e.g. teacher-learner) interactions and in novice–novice interactions (i.e. small group work).
7. Interaction mediates learning through collaborative activity in a variety of ways (e.g. through vertical constructions, proleptical IRF sequences, and initiating a solution for a linguistic problem).
8. The problem-solving activity that occurs in language-related episodes when learners experience a linguistic problem promotes both the construction and the analysis of new linguistic forms, fostering both learning and development.

Re-examining the role of interaction in language pedagogy

We have seen that 'interaction' is an important construct in language pedagogy and that a number of the teacher guides make specific reference to the SLA research on interaction. However, in general, interaction is viewed in quite limited ways in discussions of language pedagogy. It is treated as something that teachers have to 'organize' in skill-using activities while its role in knowledge-forming receives little attention. By and large, 'interaction' is treated as a means of increasing opportunities for student talk, with an emphasis on the quantity rather than the quality of students' contributions. Classroom management is discussed in terms of how to organize instructional activities and different participatory structures (e.g. pair and small group work) rather than in terms of how the management of interactions creates learning opportunities. In short, as is perhaps natural, the chief focus of the teacher guides is on the external aspects of teaching; interaction, as an internal aspect, receives consideration only in relation to the implementation of the external techniques of instruction and, then, only in quite limited ways.

What then can the theory and research on interaction in SLA offer language pedagogy? As we noted in Chapter 1 (see Principle 8), creating the right kind of interaction for acquisition constitutes a major challenge for teachers, especially in teacher-centred classrooms. In this section we will suggest why a consideration of interaction needs to be given a central place in discussions of language pedagogy and point to some ways in which current knowledge about the role of interaction in language learning can feed into pedagogy. In attempting this, we will draw on both cognitive–interactionist and sociocultural theories, treating them as complementary rather than alternative accounts of interaction and learning. We will use these theories to adjudicate some of the assumptions that we see underlying the pedagogic accounts of interaction in the teacher guides.

'Interaction in the classroom needs to provide plentiful opportunities for student talk'

This claim has obvious appeal. However, the SLA theories we have examined do not give it unconditional support. The Interaction Hypothesis, for example, states that one of the major purposes of interaction is not just to provide learners with opportunities to talk but also to provide the comprehensible input that results from the negotiation of meaning. In other words, interaction involves listening as well as speaking and both have a role to play in L2 acquisition. As we noted earlier, Ohta (2001) illustrated how pair work creates opportunities for learners to assist each other because of the different roles performed by speakers and listeners. Speakers struggle to produce utterances in the L2 because of limitations in working memory and the need to process output consciously. Listeners, however, are under less pressure and so can notice errors in their partner's production, anticipate what will come next and formulate their own turn. SLA theory then emphasizes the importance of viewing interaction holistically, not just in terms of 'speaking opportunities'.

Both cognitive–interactionist and sociocultural theories point to the need to consider the *quality* of learner talk not just its *quantity*. The Comprehensible

Output Hypothesis, for example, suggests that learners need opportunities for 'pushed output'. The Interaction Hypothesis proposes that such output can arise when learners modify their own output as a result of the feedback they receive from a teacher or another learner. A limitation of many classrooms is that there is often little opportunity for pushed or modified output. Learner utterances are often very short – a single word or a short phrase or, at most, a single clause. This can also be the case in group work. A key issue, then, is how teachers can create opportunities for pushed output and for longer student turns. Sociocultural Theory also suggests various ways in which learners can 'stretch' their L2 production – for example, through vertical constructions or through imitating (voluntarily) utterances addressed to them. Intrapersonal interaction in the form of private speech – not mentioned in any of the teacher guides we have considered in this chapter – allows learners the opportunity to experiment with and extend their output.

'The more learners participate in interaction, the better'

This assumption is really an extension of the previous one. 'Participation' is defined as student talk. It would follow from such an assumption that those learners who participate more learn more. There is a logical problem here. If some students participate a lot, they will deprive other students of the opportunity to participate so they cannot all 'learn more'. But also there is no evidence to show that learners who participate extensively in classrooms are better learners. Studies that have investigated the relationship between learner participation and learning have produced very mixed results (see Ellis, 2008). While some do report a positive correlation between the amount of participation and learning, others report no relationship at all and some even report a negative relationship (i.e. it is those learners who participate the least who demonstrate greater learning). Allwright (1980), for example, describes how one learner 'stole' turns in the classroom to the point where he dominated the interactions that took place, but in fact was not one of the better learners in the class. Quite often it is the 'silent speaker' (Reiss, 1985) who is the 'good language learner'. The SLA research emphasizes the qualitative aspects of interaction rather than quantitative aspects of learner participation.

'Initiate–respond–feedback (IRF) exchanges restrict learners' opportunity to engage actively in classroom interaction'

IRF serves as one the main ways in which teachers manage classrooms. It enables them to control the interactions that take place by ensuring that communication proceeds smoothly. It has been criticized, however, for affording very limited opportunities for learner talk and language learning. For example, it allocates learners to the responding role and results in very few opportunities for the negotiation of meaning (Pica and Long, 1986). From the perspective of the IH therefore, IRF exchanges are undesirable.

However, as we pointed out earlier, Sociocultural Theory has adopted a different position, arguing that IRF can help construct ZPDs and thus enable learners to perform beyond their existing competence. The apparent contradiction between the claims of the IH and Sociocultural Theory can be resolved if it is recognized that what is important is the nature of the IRF exchange itself – for example, whether the initial teacher question is an open rather than a closed one and whether the follow-up move allows an opportunity for a further contribution from the learner. The SLA research then points to the need for a more discriminating view of the role of IRF exchanges in classroom interaction than is common in the teacher guides. It acknowledges that potentially they can be quite limiting but also points to ways in which they can assist learning.

'Interaction constitutes a source for developing fluency in speaking'

Perhaps the main difference between the perspective on interaction evident in the teacher guides and that found in SLA concerns the role that interaction is perceived as playing in language development. In discussions of pedagogy, interaction is treated as important for developing fluency but not for accuracy. Interaction is seen as providing learners with opportunities for practising the language they have already acquired (i.e. in skill-using activities). A corollary of this position is that learners need to be 'taught' language before they can begin to interact in an L2. This is the assumption that underlies the continued advocacy of linguistic syllabuses (Chapter 3) and the present–practice–produce (PPP) approach to language teaching (Chapter 5). A clear distinction is drawn between 'knowledge-getting', which involves 'teaching', and 'skill-using', which requires 'interaction'. This conception of pedagogy has advantages, which we considered in Chapter 5. But it is fundamentally flawed in that it fails to recognize that teaching involving knowledge-getting activities also entails interaction and that it is the interaction itself rather than the 'teaching' that creates opportunities for learning.

In contrast, SLA views interaction as not just contributing to fluency (i.e. increasing control over existing linguistic resources) but as a source of new language learning. In other words, in SLA interaction has a knowledge-getting as well as a skill-getting function. This is true of both the cognitive–interactionist and sociocultural accounts of interaction, although, as we have seen, they differ significantly in how they see interaction contributing to the learning of new language. Cognitive–interactionist theories claim that interaction facilitates the acquisition of new language by inducing learners to notice new linguistic forms in the input, helping them to map these forms onto the meanings they wish to express, and pushing them to modify their own output to make it more target-like. Thus it assists both the development of fluency and the cognitive processes involved in acquiring new language. Sociocultural Theory sees learning as occurring within interaction. Interaction mediates learning by assisting learners to produce new linguistic forms that they are not yet capable of producing independently. It also prompts development by providing opportunities for rehearsing the new forms that have been learned (e.g. by imitating them). It fosters 'languaging' to solve linguistic problems. Together, these theories afford a rich account of how learning arises in and out of interaction. They provide an alternative way of viewing teaching and have led to proposals for an approach that emphasizes the importance of learning-through-interacting, as in task-based language teaching (Chapter 6).

'Group-work is a means of increasing student participation and self-reliance in the classroom'

All the teacher guides promote small group work. It is seen as important because it affords learners plenty of opportunity for talking in the L2 and also because it fosters learner independence. The main focus in the guides is on how to set up and manage small-group work. Group work clearly can serve these functions and it is obviously important to consider how it can be best organized. There is, however, very little attention given to how group work contributes to learning.

SLA researchers have shown great interest in small group work. In part, this is because much of their research has been conducted by examining the interactions that occur in pairs of speakers or in small groups. The focus has been on how group work affords opportunities for learning. Long and Porter (1985) drew on this research to propose a 'psycholinguistic rationale' for group work by comparing it with lockstep teaching. They argued that in group work:

- there is more opportunity for language practice;
- the practice is more varied because learners have to perform a wider range of language functions;
- learners use language just as accurately as in lockstep teaching;
- learners engage in self- and other corrections to a greater extent;
- they engage in more negotiation of meaning sequences when they perform communicative tasks.

Subsequent research based on the Interaction Hypothesis has shown that when learners interact in pairs or groups and negotiate meaning, they acquire new language. Research based on Sociocultural Theory has shown that learners are capable of constructing new linguistic structures even when no member of the group has knowledge of them. Swain's research has shown that the language-related episodes that arise in group work serve not just for 'learning' but also 'development, as shown in learners' ability to use what they have learned in groups independently at a later time. In short, learners do not always need to be 'taught' new language; they are capable of acquiring it on their own when they interact collaboratively in small groups. What is important, then, is how to organize group work to maximize opportunities for learning. Studies such as Storch (2002) provide valuable insights into how this can be achieved.

Conclusion

Interaction is the *sine qua non* of teaching (Allwright, 1984). Thus the key questions are 'How does interaction foster language learning?' and 'Are some kinds of interaction more likely to foster learning than others?' We have seen that, by and large, these are not questions that figure in mainstream accounts of language pedagogy, where the focus is on 'interaction' as a means of increasing student participation, developing fluency or managing teaching. This, we would argue, is a very restricted view of the role of interaction in language teaching. Teachers need to recognize that ultimately *all* teaching is interaction.

We have examined two different ways in which SLA approaches the role of interaction in language learning. These are quite different but not, we would argue, incommensurate. In cognitive–interactionist theories, the input and output that arises in interaction links with internal processes such as noticing to promote interlanguage development. In sociocultural theories, language development is a social process, mediated by both interpersonal and intrapersonal interaction. Interaction is where 'learning' occurs and is also what prompts the linguistic behaviour needed for subsequent 'development' to take place. Both of these theories have their strengths and their limitations. From the perspective of language pedagogy, we do not consider it necessary to engage in the SLA debate about whether one approach is superior to the other. Rather, along with Foster and Ohta (2005), we would claim:

> Social interactive approaches are important, whether understood from a cognitive perspective as triggering acquisition in the brain, or from a sociocultural perspective as the embodiment of the language development in process.
>
> (p. 426)

Together these two approaches to understanding and investigating interaction and its roles in L2 learning can enrich our conceptualization of language pedagogy.

Notes

1 Aubrey (2011) also points out that the common practice of nominating students to respond to a question can be stressful. Many teachers, however, feel it is essential to nominate students to ensure that at least one student responds and also to distribute speaking turns evenly around the class.

2 However, it may not be necessary for learners to actively participate in negotiation. They may be able to benefit simply by attending to the interactionally modified input provided by other students' negotiation (see Pica, 1991).

3 Ellis et al. (2001) proposed a somewhat similar construct – 'form-focused episode' (FFE) to refer to sequences of talk in teacher-class lessons where there is explicit attention to linguistic form. They distinguished three types of FFE – teacher-initiated, student-initiated and responding. This study was considered in Chapter 6.

DISCUSSION QUESTIONS

1. Explain what is meant by talking about acquisition occurring 'in' and 'through' interaction?
2. Teacher guides address how the 'participatory structure' of a classroom affects the kind of interaction that occurs. What are the typical characteristics of the interactions that occur in each of these participatory structures?
   a. Teacher–whole class
   b. Teacher–student
   c. Student–student
3. Pedagogic accounts of teaching speaking skills often distinguish between 'knowledge-getting' techniques which focus on 'accuracy' and 'skill-using' techniques that focus on 'fluency'. Can you give examples of these different techniques? To what extent do you feel this is a useful distinction?
4. Pedagogic accounts emphasize the importance of 'active participation' on the part of learners and assume 'the more they participate, the better'. What constitutes 'active participation' and do you agree that the more learners participate, the better?
5. What do you see as the main advantages and disadvantages of group work?
6. What is meant by the term 'management of interaction'? How is this dealt with in the pedagogic literature?
7. Briefly explain how these different theories of L2 acquisition view the role of interaction in L2 learning:
   a. Cognitive–interactionist theories
   b. Sociocultural Theory
8. The Interaction Hypothesis views the 'negotiation of meaning' as facilitative of acquisition. Explain what the 'negotiation of meaning' is and in what ways it is claimed to assist language learning.
9. What criticisms can be levelled at the Interaction Hypothesis?
10. What evidence is there to support the role of learner output in L2 acquisition? How convincing is this evidence? Is it sufficient to dismiss Krashen's claim that output plays no role in acquisition?
11. 'The ZPD is not a place at all; it is an activity' (Newman and Holzman, 1997: 289). It what sense is the ZPD an 'activity'? What is the importance of the ZPD for understanding the role of interaction in L2 learning?
12. Sociocultural Theory distinguishes 'learning' and 'development'. What is the difference? What is the relationship between the two?
13. A crucial construct of Sociocultural Theory is 'assisted performance'. Discuss some of the ways in which learners' performance in the L2 can be 'assisted'?
14. What does Swain mean by 'languaging'? In what ways does 'languaging' support language learning?
15. You have been asked to write a short chapter on 'Language Teaching as Interaction' for an introductory guide for pre-service teachers. What are the main points you would want to cover in this chapter?

9 Using the L1 in the L2 classroom

Introduction

We have elected to talk about 'L1 use' in this chapter. However, this is not the preferred term in much of the literature. Macaro (2001), for example, prefers to talk about 'codeswitching' while Hall and Cook (2012) make a case for 'own language' (as opposed to 'new language'), on the grounds that in many contexts the common shared language is not the 'first' language of all the students in a classroom. We have stuck with 'L1 use' because it is the term used in much of the literature and because it accords with the nomenclature in SLA.

Teachers often express uncertainty about the use the learners' first language (L1). This uncertainty arises because of the dominance of monolingual teaching since the beginning of the twentieth century (Hall and Cook, 2012). It is reflected in the responses teachers have posted to the questions posed in the British Council's 'Teaching English' web page (2009). The web page asked whether the respondents agreed with these two statements:

> If we use L1 in language teaching, learners will become dependent on L1, and not even try to understand meaning from context and explanation, or say what they want to say within their limited command of the target language (L2).
>
> A non-threatening environment is essential for L2 learners to learn the target language effectively and the L1 can be used by the teacher to some extent.

The two statements encapsulate two of the reasons frequently given for and against the use of the L1. On the one hand, using the L1 deprives learners of the opportunity to experience communicating in the L2 but, on the other hand, it helps to alleviate the anxiety that arises when communicating with limited linguistic resources. Macaro (2011) claimed that the issue of whether teachers should codeswitch is 'the most important theoretical and pedagogic question facing both the research and practitioner communities today'.

We begin as usual by examining the different pedagogic perspectives regarding the use of the L1, beginning with an examination of the role afforded the L1 in different methods and then considering what teacher educators have proposed and what actual uses teachers and learners put the L1 to. We examine the arguments that have been advanced in support and against the use of the L1 in L2 classrooms. This provides the background for a consideration of how SLA views the role of the learners' L1 in L2 learning.

Pedagogic perspectives

Role of the L1 in different methods

Methods vary enormously in the role they allocate to the L1. This may be one reason why so much uncertainty exists about codeswitching in language pedagogy. Table 9.1 lists the methods which essentially outlaw the use of the L1 (column A) and those where it is given a constitutive place (column B). In the Direct Method and the Audiolingual Method, for example, use of the L1 is prohibited on the grounds that learners need to be maximally exposed to the L2 and use of the L1 may interfere with the development of native-like habits (a point we will consider later). None of the methods in column A place much store on the metalinguistic explanation of target language features. In contrast, such explanation figures in all the methods listed in column B with the exception of two-way immersion programmes. It would seem, then, that whether the L1 is seen as a useful or necessary resource, depends in part on whether the method is inductive or deductive in nature.

There is another important difference in the methods listed in Table 9.1. All the methods in column A can be effectively implemented by a monolingual teacher. In contrast, the methods in column B assume bilingual competence on the part of the teacher. Clearly, if teachers lack knowledge of the students' own language, codeswitching is not possible. However, as we will see, such a situation does not preclude the students themselves making use of their L1 (or of any other language they have previously acquired). In considering the role played by the L1, then, it is important to distinguish the functions that it can usefully serve for teachers and students separately. With the exception of the Bilingual Method, the methods listed in Table 9.1 do not do this. Rather they assume that the issue of which language to use applies equally to teachers and learners.

We have deliberately excluded communicative language teaching (CLT) from Table 9.1. This is because, as Cole (1998) pointed out, advocates of this approach have had little to say about the role of the L1. The general literature on CLT makes no or very little mention of the L1. Rather it assumes that the teacher will use the L2 more or less exclusively not just when performing communicative activities, but also for classroom organization and management. To facilitate teachers' use of the L2 as the medium of instruction, Willis (1990) even provided lists of useful L2 phrases to assist them while also acknowledging 'occasionally L1 may still be useful' (p. xiv). The use of the L1 by the students is also viewed as a problem in CLT. Indeed, one of the commonly voiced objections to both CLT and Task-based Language Teaching is that students become so focused on achieving the outcome of a task that they frequently resort to the use of their L1 to resolve communication difficulties.

Use of the L1 in instructional activities

Some of the most popular handbooks for teachers make scant reference to the use of the L1 in teaching activities. Ur (1996), for example, has no entry for

Table 9.1 The role of the L1 in different language teaching methods

A Methods based on exclusive L2 use	B Methods requiring use of the L1
Direct Method Vocabulary is taught through mime and ostensive definition; grammar is taught inductively. The method was teacher-centred and emphasized the oral use of the L2.	*Grammar Translation* Grammar is taught deductively and practised by means of L1 → L2 translation exercises. L2 vocabulary introduced via L1 equivalents.
Audiolingual Method Grammar taught inductively through drilling and performing dialogues scripted in L2. The aim was to develop correct 'habits'.	*Community Language Learning* The teacher invites students to say something on a topic that interests them in their L1 and then translates it into the L2 and asks the students to repeat it. In this way a dialogue in the L2 is built up through translation.
Total Physical Response (TPR) Grammar and vocabulary taught inductively by requiring learners to demonstrate comprehension of commands by performing actions.	*Bilingual Method* The teacher uses the L1 to support students' repetition of L2 dialogues until they are able to perform them in the L2 without it. The students are only allowed to use the L2.
Situational Language Teaching Grammar taught inductively through situational exercises; vocabulary controlled through reference to frequency counts.	*Translanguaging Approach* The learner receives information in one language receptively and is then asked to produce it in the other language (i.e. input and output are conducted in different languages). It is an approach used for students who are already bilingual.
Silent Way The teacher is totally silent and elicits production in the L2 from learners by means of various artefacts (e.g. Cuisenaire Rods and colour-coded pronunciation charts). No recourse to the L1 is allowed.	*Two-way Immersion Programmes* * Students are taught the same subject content in two languages (i.e. their home language and the L2), which are kept separate. These programmes aim at supporting the students' L1 while developing the L2.
Natural Approach Grammar and vocabulary learned incidentally and subconsciously through comprehensible L2 input supplied by the teacher and teaching materials.	

Note: * There is in fact a marked difference between the English language textbooks produced by Western publishers such as Oxford University Press and Longman Pearson and those produced by local publishers in Japan or China. Rubrics in the former are invariably in the L2 (English) whereas in the latter they are more often than not in the L1.

'L1', 'native language' or 'first language' in the index of her teacher guide. In fact the only reference she makes to the use of the L1 occurs in a warning to teachers' about the danger of learners' over-using it when performing communicative tasks in small group work. Chapters in Celce-Murcia's (1991) *Teaching English as a Second or Foreign Language* also make scant reference to the L1. Larsen-Freeman's excellent chapter on grammar teaching, for example, makes no reference to the L1 as a resource for providing descriptions and explanations of grammatical structures in the presentation stage of a lesson.[1] Seal's chapter on vocabulary teaching in the same book offers a variety of ways in which teachers can convey the meaning of words and check students' understanding but these do not include 'translation'. Seal, however, is supportive of learners' using bilingual (as opposed to monolingual) dictionaries, although he cites Underhill (1985) in suggesting that over time they should be 'weaned' off them. In two recent books on language teaching materials (Tomlinson, 2010; Harwood, 2010), we were unable to find a single reference to the use of the L1.

Harmer (2007), however, did provide an extended discussion of the use of the L1. He argued that 'translating in the head' is natural in the early stages of learning. He saw benefits in using the L1 for comparing the L1 and L2 and for maintaining a positive learning environment. He proposed a number of guiding principles for the use of the learners' L1: (1) teachers should acknowledge the students' L1 even if they themselves cannot speak it, (2) they should vary the use of the L1 according to the learners' level of L2 proficiency, (3) they should discuss when it is appropriate to use the L1 with the students and (4) they should encourage students to use the L2 in communicative activities.

In general, however, the overriding assumption in the published teacher guides that we have inspected is that language teaching activities should be entirely – or almost entirely – L2-based. This assumption, however, contrasts markedly with what we have observed in language textbooks published in China and Japan, where the rubrics for activities are generally in the L1 and where translations equivalents for L2 words are frequently provided.[2]

Beliefs about the use of the L1

In contrast to the relative absence of any reference to the L1 in teacher guides, many teacher educators and teachers have all voiced their support. Surveys by Podromou (2002), Ferrer (2005) and Schweers (1999) all testify to considerable enthusiasm for exploiting the L1 in the classroom. Ferrer, for example, reported that the majority of the teachers and teacher educators that he surveyed considered the use of the L1 both inevitable and desirable. He quoted one teacher educator as saying:

> We have this idea of no L1 in the classroom but L1 is constantly being used in the classroom. Students are, especially at lower levels, always using their knowledge of the world and their L1 to make comparisons with English.

However, as Macaro (2005) pointed out, even though many teachers might view the use of the L1 as necessary, they also see it as undesirable. This is clearly evident in Edstrom's (2006) study. She compared her own beliefs about the use of the L1 and her actual practice in a beginning-level university Spanish class. Although she was broadly committed to maximizing the use of the target language, she found that she resorted to the L1 for grammar instruction, classroom management and to address comprehension problems. She identified three reasons for her use of the L1: the need to establish rapport and solidarity with the students, the impossibility of achieving certain goals (such as cultural awareness) through the target language, and the sheer effort of maintaining communication throughout a lesson in the L2.

Thus, when teachers do express a preference for using the L1, they do so generally not because they see it as of cognitive benefit but as a response to the exigencies of the classroom. Kalivoda (1990) suggested one way of dealing with this problem. He proposed that teachers should maintain a strict separation of the two languages but set aside a special ten-minute slot in a lesson for L1 use where 'learners may confirm or clarify their understanding through questions and discussions with the teacher' (p. 268). Such a suggestion, however, while interesting, does not acknowledge any role for the dynamic use of the L1 implicit in the notion of 'codeswitching'.

L2 learners also hold different views about the teacher's use of the L1. Brooks-Lewis (2009) reported a study of Mexican university students' attitudes to the teacher's use of the L1 in an elementary EFL class. In this class, the teacher began by using the L1 (Spanish) exclusively and then gradually shifted to using English. Overall Brooks-Lewis found the students responded positively to the use of the L1 and gave a number of reasons:

> being able to understand what is being said; being able to participate; making the learning meaningful and easier; dissolving the sense of rupture in knowledge, along with ideas of forgetting or replacing identity of the L1; promoting confidence and a sense of achievement; and inspiring language, learning, culture, and self-awareness.
>
> (p. 234)

However, not all the learners were in favour of the teacher using the L1 so extensively. One learner noted that it deprived them of exposure to English and another disliked the teacher's use of contrastive analysis. Hall and Cook (2012) list a number of other studies which indicate learners' support for the use of the L1 as a means of reducing anxiety.

There is a definite discrepancy between the view of the L1 projected in teacher guides (it is largely ignored) and the value placed on it by many teachers, teacher educators and learners. Teacher guides, perhaps, aim at the 'ideal' – teaching the L2 through the medium of the L2. Teachers too seem to share this ideal to some extent but also recognize the inevitability of using the L1 on occasions. We turn now to look at the actual uses that teachers and learners make of the L1 in the classroom.

Teachers' use of the L1 in the L2 classroom

Teachers' use of the L1 is only possible in contexts where the teacher and the learner share the same L1. Researchers have addressed two issues – the extent to which teachers use the L1 and the functions that they use it for.

In a frequently cited study, Duff and Polio (1990) recorded three sessions in each of thirteen foreign language classrooms in the United States. They distinguished utterances that were entirely in the target language from those that were in English (the L1) or were 'mixed' (i.e. contained both L1 and L2 words). They found that some teachers used the target language exclusively, others used it most of the time, and still others hardly at all (one teacher used the target language exclusively for less than 10 per cent of the time). The teachers were consistent in the extent to which they relied on the L1 across lessons. Other studies (e.g. Macaro, 2001; Kim and Elder, 2005) also found that the teachers they investigated varied considerably in their use of the L1, but reported that they were not always consistent across lessons. These studies identified a number of factors that influence teachers' overall choice of language – institutional policy, the students' proficiency level, the instructional approach (the L1 is likely to be used more in grammar-translation than in communicative language teaching), and teachers' own beliefs about the utility of the L1. Summarizing these and other studies, Hall and Cook (2012) point out that teachers tend to underestimate the extent to which they use the L1 and that this might be because of their 'underlying negative attitudes and beliefs about bilingual teaching' (p. 285).

In a follow-up to their 1990 study, Polio and Duff (1994) identified a number of different uses of the L1. These are described in Table 9.2 together with the main findings related to these different uses. In addition to the functional uses of the L1, it has also been argued that there is a moral case. Edstrom (2006), for example, suggests that there is a 'moral obligation' to recognize learners as individuals and to communicate respect. Using the learners' L1 is one way of acknowledging this. These studies, then, indicate that not only is the L1 a natural part of classroom life but also there is an ethical need for it.

Learners' use of the L1

In general, much less attention has been paid to L1 classroom use by learners. However, a number of studies indicate that learners often do employ their L1 for specific purposes.

Immersion programmes permit students to use their L1 in the beginning stages but assume that over time students will switch to using the L2. However, research has shown that immersion learners continue to speak in the L1 throughout the programme. In fact, older learners (i.e. fifth and sixth graders) in French immersion programmes in Canada have been found to actually increase their use of the L1 over time when interacting with each other. Tarone and Swain (1995) suggested that this might be because they lacked knowledge of vernacular-style French required to perform important interpersonal functions such as play, competition and positioning within their peer group and therefore resorted to English. This situation is likely to arise to an even greater extent in foreign language classrooms, where the learners' limited L2 proficiency

Table 9.2 Functions of teachers' L1 use (based on Polio and Duff, 1994)

Categories of L1 use	Description	Findings
Classroom administrative vocabulary	Use of L1 words to refer to aspects of the culture of the university classroom (e.g. 'review section', 'midterm', 'homework').	The L1 words were typically inserted into TL utterances.
Grammar instruction	Use of the L1 to explain grammatical concepts.	This was very common and involved whole utterances in the L1.
Classroom management	Use of the L1 to set up learning activities.	Some teachers used the L1 exclusively; others code-switched (i.e. used a mixture of English and the TL).
Empathy/solidarity	The use of the L1 for interpersonal and rapport-building purposes.	Some teachers used the L1 to digress from instructional sequences in order to background their role as teachers (e.g. joking in the L1).
Practising English	The use of the L1 by students to help their teacher's non-native English.	Students provided English equivalents for TL items.
Unknown vocabulary/ translation	The use of the L1 to show the meaning of TL items.	Teachers used the TL item first and then gave the L1 translation.
Lack of comprehension	The use of the L1 to resolve students' comprehension problems.	This was 'surprisingly uncommon'.
Interactive effect	The teacher responded to a student using the L1 by using the L1 him/herself.	There appeared to be a reciprocal effect – the use of the L1 by one participant led to its use by another.

makes social interaction with other students in the L2 even more problematic. Interestingly, however, advanced immersion learners rarely use the L1 with their teacher (Broner, 2001) or in group work (Swain and Lapkin, 2000).

Overuse of the L1 is perhaps more likely in a foreign language context. However, Storch and Aldosari (2010) reported that Arabic learners of L2 English used the L1 relatively little (only 7 per cent of the total words used in the interactions and only 16 per cent of the turns were in the L1). However, they noted that the type of activity influenced the extent to which the L1 was used. An editing task, for example, resulted in greater use than a jigsaw story task. Students' use of the L1 is more likely when they are focused on form than when they are focused on meaning.

The L1 can also be seen as a cognitive resource for L2 students in some kinds of lessons. Stapa and Majid (2009) found that Malaysian students who generated ideas for a written essay in Bahasa Melayu, produced essays that were awarded significantly higher marks than those of a comparison group that generated ideas in L2 English. Lally (2000) also reported that planning in the L1 resulted in more elaborate content and better organization. Scott and de La Fuente (2008) found that allowing students to use their L1 when performing oral tasks led to more collaborative talk and greater interactional coherence. However, there is also some evidence to suggest that encouraging learners to think in the L2 can lead to more accurate L2 use (Cohen and Brooks-Carson, 2001).

One of the most common uses of the L1 is for metatalk (i.e. the talk that learners employ to establish what kind of 'activity' to make of an instructional activity and also what operations to employ when performing it). Brooks and Donato (1994), for example, described how third-year high school learners of L2 Spanish used the L1 to establish their goals in a two-way information-gap task, that required them to describe where to draw shapes on a matrix sheet consisting of unnumbered small squares. They found that even though the teacher carefully explained the task goals, the learners often felt the need to discuss these between themselves in their L1.

The use of the L1 is less common in language classrooms where the learners do not share a common language. However, it is still possible to create linguistically homogeneous groups in such classes. Storch and Wigglesworth (2003) investigated the L1 use that occurred in such groups. Initially they found that pairs of students who shared the same L1 hardly used it at all. Even when they were explicitly informed that they could use their L1, only two of these pairs did so, using it between 25 and 50 per cent of the time. Other students declined to use it because they thought that doing so would slow down the activity and also that they should use the L2 as much as possible. This study suggests that second language learners may be more resistant to utilizing their L1 than foreign or immersion language learners but that when they do so they exploit it as a mediational tool in similar ways.

In short, research indicates that learners use their L1 profitably. It is used to perform interpersonal functions that are difficult in the L2 and to enable learners to socialize with each other. It also plays an important role in metatalk, helping learners to establish reciprocity regarding the goals and procedures for carrying out an activity. Finally, it helps learners to address problems associated with their limited L2 resources.

A bone of contention: the pros and cons of using the L1

We have examined what teacher guides, teachers and teacher educators have to say about the use of the L1 and also examined some research that has investigated the actual uses teachers and learners put the L1 to in the classroom. We will now sum up the issues that lie at the heart of the disagreements about the role of the L1.

Table 9.3 on p. 234 presents a number of possible beneficial uses of the L1, drawing on the work of two powerful advocates (V. Cook, 2001, 2005; Macaro, 2005). It summarizes the arguments they present in favour of its use in the 'Pros' column. The 'Cons' column presents the alternative arguments that might be used to counter their advocacy. The arguments, it should be noted, are for the most part theoretical in nature, representing opinion and belief, rather than empirically based findings. It is for this reason that the whole issue of the use of the L1 has become so contentious. While there are studies to demonstrate that teachers and learners do indeed use the L1 for these functions (see previous section), there are almost none to show which of the functions is effective in promoting learning.

In recent years, advocacy of L1 use has grown in strength and it is now clear that the pendulum has swung firmly in its favour at least in applied linguistic circles (see, e.g. Hall and Cook's (2012) review article). To a large extent, this advocacy is based on the rejection of native-speaker models as a basis for language teaching, in favour of a model based on English as a lingua franca. The argument is that the assumption that the learners' goal is to emulate native-speaker proficiency is fundamentally flawed and that the appropriate goal should be the 'development of bilingual and bicultural identities and skills that are actively needed by most learners, both within the English-speaking countries and in the world at large' (Hall and Cook, 2012: 273). Interestingly, however, Hall and Cook do not address what is the central question SLA researchers would ask – namely, whether L1 use in the classroom facilitates L2 acquisition. This, arguably, is the question that would most concern teachers too.

The arguments in support of L1 use are generic in nature: they do not take account of context. It would seem highly likely, however, that arguments regarding L1 use need to be contextually framed. Edstrom (2009), for example, pointed out:

> Decisions about appropriate L1 use are in large part inextricably tied to classroom circumstances and cannot be predetermined nor easily generalized from one context to another.
>
> (p. 14)

Edstrom's comment points to the need to not just consider macro-contexts (second vs foreign language settings) but also the micro-contexts that are dynamically constructed as a lesson takes place. If this is so, it could be argued that L1 use cannot be determined *a priori*.

A key issue is in what way the L1 should be incorporated into teacher talk. Macaro (2011) argued strongly that intra-sentential rather than inter-sentential codeswitching was preferable. In other words, teachers should not produce whole sentences in the L1 but rather use it strategically to make the meaning of essential words or lexical strings clear. In this way, teachers can ensure that the L1 functions as an 'embedded language' and the target language as the 'matrix language'.

A second key issue – one that both V. Cook and Macaro address – is the *extent* to which L1 should be permitted. Kaneko (1991) reported a study of English classes in a Japanese two-year college course where the teachers were using the L1 more than 50 per cent of the total talking time (and in one case

Table 9.3 The pros and cons of using the L1

Use of L1	Pros	Cons
Convey L2 meaning	The L1 serves as a rapid and easy way of conveying the meaning of L2 words and sentences.	There is a danger that using the L1 to convey meaning will result in treating the meanings of the L2 as translation equivalents of the L1.
Maintain discipline	When the teacher uses the L1 to discipline the class or an individual student, it indicates that what they say is for 'real' rather than 'pretend'.	Using the L1 for discipline signals to the students that when 'real' communication needs are at stake, there is no need to use the L2.
To explain tasks and tests	The L1 serves as the quickest and most efficient way of getting a task or test underway and ensures that the students are clear what they need to do.	Using the L1 to explain tasks signals to the learners that when there is a real communicative purpose it is all right to use the L1.
To explain grammar	'If the goal is for students to understand the grammar itself rather than to benefit from the incidental language involved, the teacher has to choose the best vehicle for conveying this, which may be the first language' (V. Cook, 2005: 59).	Grammar explanations are of most use to more advanced learners; such learners benefit from explanations in the L2 as they provide learners with L2 input (Krashen, 1982).
To practise codeswitching	Codeswitching is natural in a classroom where the learners share the same language(s) and should be encouraged as an effective form of communication.	Allowing learners to codeswitch will inevitably result in them using their L1 whenever they have a communicative problem, rather than finding out how to deal with the problem in the L2 and this will inhibit the development of L2 strategic competence.
Building personal relationships with students	Performing a pastoral role requires the use of sophisticated discourse skills that cannot be effectively executed in the L2.	Using the L1 to build personal relationships with students provides one of the most 'natural' contexts for the use of the L2 and helps develop learners' competence to use the L2 for personal expression.
Avoidance of unnecessary input modification	If teachers do not codeswitch, they need to resort to input modifications to make what they say comprehensible. The teacher ends up 'hogging the discourse space' and this results in reduced interaction (Macaro, 2005).	Input modifications serve as an important way of making input comprehensible while maximizing exposure to the L2 and thus promoting L2 learning.
Developing translation skills	Use of the L1 can develop the translation skills that some learners will need outside the classroom.	Use of the L1 encourages learners to always think in the L1 rather than in the L2 and thus impedes the development of L2 communication skills.
Preparing for activities conducted in the L2	The L1 can be used in pre-listening and pre-reading activities (e.g. for schema-raising) and also to plan for a spoken or written task. The L1 will ensure deeper conceptualization of the topic addressed in the task.	Preparation for listening, speaking, reading or writing activities is best carried out in the same language the students will use when undertaking the activities (i.e. the L2) as this will facilitate transfer of training and enhanced accuracy.

| Reduce anxiety in the learner | When the teacher codeswitches, the anxiety learners experience when trying (and often failing) to comprehend L2 input is lessened. Similarly, learners will feel less anxious if they can sometimes use their L1. | There are other ways of ensuring that learners do not experience debilitating anxiety when exposed to L2 input (e.g. modifying the input to suit the level of the learner) and not requiring the learner to speak in the L2 until they are ready. |
| Demonstrating respect for the learner by acknowledging their L1 identity | As Brooks-Lewis (2008) put it 'if the L1 is banished, in essence the learner is also' (p. 227). Recognizing the learner's L1 may be especially important if the L2 is associated with colonial or economic subjugation. | It is not necessary to use the L1 to demonstrate respect for the learner. Respect is displayed through the teacher demonstrating familiarity with individual learners and in the way the teacher interacts with them. |

more than 90 per cent). This is clearly not acceptable. Cook (2005) merely notes that the use of the L1 'should not be taken to an extreme' (p. 59). Macaro seeks to be more precise, suggesting that 10–15 per cent constitutes an acceptable threshold. Again, though, there is no empirical basis for such a decision and the extent of talk in the L1 will also need to take account of context.

The role of the L1 in L2 learning

We turn now to look at what SLA has had to say about the role played by the L1 in L2 learning. First, we consider work on language transfer, documenting the shift that has taken place from an early theoretical position where the L1 was seen as a source of 'interference', to more recent theories where it is seen as a 'resource' that learners can draw on. We will then examine the role that the L1 can play in communication strategies before concluding with an account of how the L1 is seen as a tool for mediating learning in Sociocultural Theory and for alleviating anxiety.

L1 transfer

The term 'L1 transfer' has continued to be widely used in the SLA literature but, in many respects, a better term is 'crosslinguistic influence' as this acknowledges that transfer is not always one-way (i.e. sometimes transfer from the L2 into the L1 occurs) and also that a previously acquired L2 can have an influence on the development of a new target language (i.e. an L3). It also gives recognition to the fact that the influence of the L1 may be evident not just in overt errors but also in subtle ways such as the underuse and overuse of specific L2 features.

In early accounts, the L1 was seen as potentially 'interfering' with the acquisition of the L2. This view was grounded in behaviourist theories of L2 learning which claimed that previously acquired 'habits' have to be overcome to enable 'new' habits to be acquired. Habits, it was claimed, are developed by repeatedly eliciting and reinforcing the correct response to a linguistic stimulus and ensuring that the wrong response (i.e. one based on the L1) is avoided. It followed from such a perspective that the learning of another language might be negatively affected in cases where there are differences between the L1 and the L2 but not in cases where the L1 and L2 features were the same – a position known as the Contrastive Analysis Hypothesis (CAH). Lado (1957) spelled out the implications of this hypothesis for the L2 learner:

> the student who comes into contact with a foreign language will find some features of it quite easy and others extremely difficult. Those elements that are similar to his native language will be simple for him, and those elements that are different will be difficult.
>
> (p. 2)

This hypothesis, then, was based on the assumption that 'difference = difficulty'. It motivated a number of contrastive analyses of two languages (e.g. Stockwell et al., 1965) that could be used by course designers and teachers to decide which features of the L2 needed to be taught (i.e. those that differed from the L1).

The CAH proved unsatisfactory in a two major ways:

1 It soon became apparent that differences between the L1 and the L2 do not automatically lead to learning difficulty. For example, French learners of English do not make errors such as 'I them see' even though French word order requires the object pronoun to be positioned before the verb (i.e. 'je les vois').
2 Research also demonstrated that learners may experience difficulty in learning an L2 structure that is similar to their L1. For example, French learners of English are likely to use non-inverted question forms (e.g. 'She is sick?') at an early stage of L2 acquisition even though French has the same word order for yes/no questions as English (e.g. 'Est elle malade?'). This is because the acquisition of many structures follows a universal pattern (see Chapter 3).

As a result, the strong form of the CAH (namely that differences between the L1 and target language can be used to *predict* all errors that will occur) was abandoned. However, the weak form of the hypothesis (namely, that differences can be used only to *explain* some out of the total errors that actually occur) was still tenable.

It also became clear that some researchers were overestimating the instances of L1 transfer. For example, Spanish learners of L2 English frequently use preverbal negation (e.g. 'No coming today') and as negation in Spanish is also preverbal (e.g. 'No viene hoy'), this would appear to be an example of L1 transfer. However, as we saw in Chapter 4, all learners, irrespective of how negation is formed in their L1, manifest this construction at an early stage of development. In fact, it is not possible to assign a particular error to 'transfer' solely on the grounds that the error reflects an L1 pattern. It is necessary to demonstrate that learners whose L1 has the same pattern as the L2 do not make the same error.

Clearly, L1 transfer is a complex phenomenon. Kellerman (1983) captured this crucial fact in an article entitled 'Now you see it, now you don't'. He pointed out that in order to understand how the L1 influences L2 learning, it is necessary to identify the conditions under which transfer occurs. The research that then began to take place started to uncover a number of conditions that influenced whether transfer occurred. These are summarized in Table 9.4.

These conditions operate in conjunction with the learners' stage of development (i.e. their overall proficiency). Over time the constraining effects of markedness, prototypicality, psychotypology and salience on transfer will change as learners gain more experience with the L2. In some cases, this can lead to a reduction in transfer effects but in others it may lead to an increase. Overall, though, learners are more likely to manifest transfer effects at lower levels of L2 proficiency. For example, avoidance in the use of phrasal verbs is more evident in low-proficiency learners whose L1 lacks such verbs but such avoidance declines as learners gain in proficiency (Laufer and Eliasson, 1993). However, the relationship between proficiency and transfer effects is not straightforward. For example, the extent to which there is a 'crucial similarity measure' between the learners' L1 and the L2 may only become evident to learners who have reached a stage where they are able to detect the similarity (i.e. not typically right at the beginning). Also, certain types of transfer errors do not appear until learners have reached a certain threshold of linguistic proficiency. This is especially the case with pragmatic features. For example, advanced learners of L2 English have been shown to over-elaborate politeness features in speech acts such as invitations (e.g. 'I would be very honoured if you would do me the kindness of...') whereas lower-level learners do not do so because they lack the L2 resources to make such pragmalinguistic errors.

The conditions outlined in Table 9.4 are all 'psycholinguistic' in nature. Of more direct relevance to language pedagogy, perhaps, is the role that social context plays in influencing transfer. However, somewhat contradictory views are evident. Odlin (1990) suggested that negative transfer is less common in classroom settings than in natural settings because, in the former, learners are more likely to treat L1 forms as intrusive and even stigmatized. Tarone (1982), however, argued that L1 transfer is more likely to be evident in learners' careful style (i.e. the type of language use that occurs in formal contexts) than in their vernacular style (i.e. the type of language use associated with informal contexts). She suggested that when learners are paying greater attention to how they speak, they are more inclined to use all their potential resources, including L1 knowledge. By and large, the careful style is typical of classroom discourse, so, if Tarone is right, transfer will be more evident in such a setting than in a natural setting where the vernacular style is likely to predominate.

However, generalizations regarding the effect of macro contexts or settings on L1 transfer in general are dangerous. For a start, such generalizations overlook the possibility that the influence of the setting may vary according to the *type* of transfer that takes place. Pavlenko and Jarvis (2002), for example, found that advanced L2 learners in a natural setting manifested instances of semantic extension and loan translation but not of lexical borrowing. One thing is quite clear, however: transfer effects are evident in both classroom and naturalistic settings.

Table 9.4 Conditions influencing whether L1 transfer occurs

Conditions	Description	Examples
Crucial Similarity Measure	Wode (1983) argued that 'only certain L2 elements are substituted by L1 elements, namely, those meeting specifiable similarity requirements' (p. 185). In other words, transfer works hand in hand with overgeneralization. As Wode put it 'those elements which do not meet the similarity requirements are acquired via developmental sequences similar to (identical with?) L1 acquisition'.[1]	German learners of L2 English only produce utterances with post-verbal negation (e.g. 'Today I am coming not') in accordance with the L1 pattern after they discover that English, like German, allows the same pattern in copula sentences (e.g. 'I am not tired'/'Ich bin nicht mude'). It leads to an error, however, because English does not permit V + neg with lexical verbs.
Markedness	Markedness refers to the idea of whether a particular feature is in some sense 'special' (= marked) or 'basic' (= unmarked). Hyltenstam (1984) proposed that 'unmarked categories from the native language are substituted for corresponding marked categories in the target language' but 'marked structures are seldom transferred, and if they are transferred, they are much more easily eradicated from the target language' (p. 43).	Zobl (1983), for example, claimed that the 'pour + infinitive' structure in French is unmarked (it also occurs in some English dialects and was present in Old English) and this can explain why French learners of English frequently transfer this structure into L2 English (e.g.'They have policeman for stop the bus').
Prototypicality	Kellerman (1978, 1986) argued that a crucial factor determining whether transfer takes place is the learners' perception of the transferability of a specific feature. Learners are likely to believe that some L1 features are more transferable than others.	In a well-known study, Kellerman investigated whether Dutch learners of L2 English were prepared to translate Dutch sentences containing 'breken' ('break') into English. He found that they were ready to translate the sentence 'hij brak zijn been' (= he broke his leg) but resisted translating 'sommige arbeiders hebben de staking gebroken' (= some workers have broken the strike). He concluded that it was these learners' perceptions of the 'coreness' of the meaning of 'breken' that determined their readiness to transfer the different uses of 'breken'.

Language distance and psychotypology	The 'distance' between the native and the target languages can also influence the extent to which L1 transfer occurs. Distance can be viewed as both a linguistic phenomenon (i.e. by establishing the degree of actual linguistic difference between two languages) and a psycholinguistic phenomenon (i.e. by determining what learners think is the degree of difference between their native language and the target language). Kellerman (1977) used the term 'psychotypology' to refer to learners' perceptions about language distance.	Sjöholm (1976) reported that Finnish learners of L2 English make fewer errors than Swedish learners. Swedish is a language that is linguistically much closer to English than Finnish. Evidence of the learners' psychotypology and its effect on transfer comes from Kellerman's (1979) extension of his 'breken' study. Dutch learners were much more likely to accept that 'breken' sentences containing non-core meanings could be translated into German than into English.
Salience	Transfer occurs rarely or not at all in certain types of structure especially those that are very salient (i.e. are easily attended to by the learner). Such structures arouse a high level of awareness that enables learners to monitor their production and so eliminate the effects of transfer.	Odlin (1990) pointed out that learners rarely make word order errors as a result of transfer. Word order is more salient than many morphological features and thus learners become conscious of it and it is less vulnerable to transfer.

Note: 1 In a similar vein, Anderson (1983) proposed his Transfer to Somewhere Principle, which also emphasized the importance of some degree of congruity between the L1 and the target language. However, Kellerman (1995) produced evidence to show that 'there can be transfer which is not licensed by similarity to the L2, and where the way the L2 works may very largely go unheeded' (p. 137) and expressed this in terms of the Transfer to Nowhere Principle as a complement to the Transfer to Somewhere Principle.

As we have seen, it is also clear that transfer operates in conjunction with universal tendencies in L2 acquisition. Thus, transfer cannot provide a complete explanation of the errors that learners make. This realization is central to the notion of 'interlanguage' (Selinker, 1972; see Chapter 2). Interlanguage is the product of a number of different psycholinguistic processes, including simplification, overgeneralization and L1 transfer. All learners are likely to be challenged by some target language features irrespective of their L1 and will manifest the same set of approximations as they construct and reconstruct their interlanguages. The effect of the L1, however, may still be seen in the rate at which learners abandon early interlanguage forms for more advanced ones and also in whether they succeed in achieving the final target-language state. For example, German learners of English, like Spanish learners, manifest the same preverbal negation stage to begin with but rapidly shift to more target-like negative constructions, whereas Spanish learners remain at the early pre-verbal stage for much longer and some, like Schumann's (1978) Alberto,[3] fail to acquire the target language construction. All learners experience difficulty with English articles but those learners whose L1 lacks an equivalent article system (e.g. Japanese or Chinese learners) typically fail to fully acquire native-like competence in this aspect of grammar even after many years of study.

Finally, transfer involves more than just the incorporation of L2 linguistic features into interlanguage. Transfer is also conceptual; that is, the learner's L1-specific worldview affects the acquisition of another language. Conceptual transfer involves the underlying ways in which learners perceive and conceptualize the world. It draws on the notion of linguistic relativity according to which how people view the world is determined wholly or partly by the structure of their mother tongue. Von Stutterheim (1991) showed that languages differ in whether events are seen and encoded as 'bounded' (as in German) or 'unbounded' (as in English), and that German learners of L2 English transfer the conceptual organization of German into English. It follows that learning another language involves developing new ways of conceptualizing reality.

L1 as a resource

So far the L1 has been seen as a source of errors – that is, the focus has been on negative transfer (i.e. how the L1 impedes the acquisition of the target language). This is probably how many teachers view the L1 – as a form of 'interference'. SLA researchers, however, have been at pains to demonstrate that the L1 is not just an impediment to L2 learning but also a resource that learners can draw on to facilitate both the use and the learning of an L2. We will discuss four ways in which this can take place: through positive transfer, through the use of L1-based communication strategies, as a tool for 'mediating L2 learning' and as a means for reducing anxiety.

Positive transfer

Transfer is not always 'negative'; there are clear instances of it having a positive influence on L2 development. This occurs when there are similarities between the L2 and L2. Ringbom (2007) emphasized that 'learners, consciously or not, do not look for differences, they look for similarities wherever they can find them' (p. 1). Odlin (1989) noted that the facilitative effect of the L1 is evident not so much in the total absence of certain errors – as would be expected on the basis of behaviourist notions of positive transfer – but rather in a reduced number of errors and, also, in the rate of learning.

Clear examples of positive transfer can be found in two studies of relative clauses (Gass, 1979; Hyltenstam, 1984). Languages vary in whether they permit pronoun retention in such clauses. English does not. The following sentence, for example, is ungrammatical:

The woman that I gave a book to *her* is my sister.

All learners, irrespective of whether their L1 permits pronoun retention or not, make errors such as this but Gass and Hyltenstam found that their frequency varied according to the language group. In Hyltenstam's study, for example, the Persian learners produced the most copies, followed by the Greek, with the Spanish and Finnish learners producing the fewest. This order corresponded exactly to that predicted on the basis of the structural properties of the learners' native languages.

The facilitative effect of the L1 is evident in other aspects of L2 acquisition. In many cases, this is obvious, as when two languages share a large number of cognates (e.g. English and French), thus giving the learners a head start in vocabulary. Ringbom (1992), noting that 'transfer is at least as important in comprehension as it is in production' (p. 88), showed that Swedish-speaking Finns had an advantage over Finnish-speaking Finns in reading and listening comprehension because of the closer proximity of their L1 to English. He suggested that the positive effect of the L1 may be more clearly evident in 'decoding' than in 'encoding'. This may help to explain why learners' with L1 writing systems which are the same or similar to the L2 (e.g. Japanese learners of L2 Chinese) have an advantage over those learners whose L1 writing system is entirely different. Cummins (1981) advanced the Interdependency Principle, according to which cognitive academic proficiency is in part common to both the L1 and the L2 and therefore literacy skills can be transferred easily from one language to another.

Communication strategies

The L1 can be used as an aid to communication in the L2. Learners are frequently required to communicate messages for which they lack sufficient L2 linguistic resources and so need to fall back on whatever other resources they possess, including their L1. As Tarone (1977) put it 'conscious communication strategies are used by an individual to overcome the crisis which occurs when language structures are inadequate to convey the individual's thought' (p. 195). Færch and Kasper (1980) saw communication strategies as psycholinguistic devices that learners use during the planning stage of a speech act, when they have a problem in expressing what they want to say. In both definitions, communication strategies are seen as: (1) conscious and (2) problem solving. Communication strategies constitute an important aspect of learners' 'strategic competence'.

Various taxonomies of communication strategies have been developed (see Ellis, 2008: chapter 4). A basic distinction can be made between those strategies that involve the use of the L2 (e.g. approximation, word coinage or circumlocution) and those that draw on the L1. Tarone (1977) identifies two L1-based communication strategies:

1 Literal translation (i.e. the learner translates word for word from the native language, e.g. 'He invites him to drink' in place of 'They toast one another').
2 Language switch (i.e. the learner inserts words from another language, e.g. 'balon' for 'balloon'). This subsequently became referred to as 'borrowing'.

Poulisse (1990) added a third L1-based strategy:

3 Foreignizing (i.e. the learner borrows an L1 word and attempts to pronounce it like an L2 word).

Various studies have shown that learners make plentiful use of L1-based communication strategies especially when they experience lexical problems. As might be expected, a general finding is that L1-based strategies figure more strongly with low-proficiency learners. As learners become more competent in communicating in the L2, they draw more heavily on L2-based strategies.

While communication strategies are seen as important for communicating, there is disagreement about whether they facilitate L2 learning. Skehan (1998) argued that they remove the need for learners to develop their interlanguage resources (i.e. strategic competence compensates for lack of linguistic competence). In contrast, Kasper and Kellerman (1997) identified a number of ways in which communication strategies may assist L2 acquisition (e.g. they help to keep the flow of the conversation going and thus increase learners' exposure to input, they increase control over existing L2 resources, and they can result in the acquisition of new linguistic resources when learners incorporate strategic solutions into their interlanguage). Ringbom (1992) also claimed a relationship between transfer in communication and learning:

> Transfer in communication is motivated by the learner's desire to comprehend or produce messages, but it may also have an effect on the process of hypothesis construction and testing, which many scholars see as central to interlanguage development. In other words, transfer in communication may lead to transfer in learning.
>
> (p. 106)

These two views about the role of communication strategies in acquisition need not be seen as contradictory. It is possible that some learners develop their strategic competence at the expense of their linguistic competence, while others exploit communication strategies for their learning opportunities. Thus, L1-based communication strategies might sometimes impede and sometimes facilitate learning in the same L2 learner.

The L1 as a mediational tool

In Sociocultural Theory, the use of the L1 is seen as one of the primary means by which learners can mediate L2 learning. It does so in two ways: through private/inner speech and by serving as a cognitive tool for scaffolding production in the L2.

Learners frequently use their L1 in private speech. Because private speech is intended for the speaker, not the listener, it is not constrained by the same norms that affect social speech. As a result, L2 learners can feel free to resort to the use of their L1 in their self-directed speech. In fact, as Ushakova (1994) pointed out, even those learners who are successful in learning a second language continue to use their L1 as inner speech. Lantolf (2006) cited studies that indicated that advanced-level learners continue to experience considerable difficulty in using the L2 for inner speech to regulate their own thinking. He considered it unlikely that classroom learners would ever succeed in this and suggested that it might only occur when learners possess an intent and a commitment to live their lives as members of a target language community. He drew on Kramsch's (1993) idea of a 'third space' (i.e. a world consisting of hybrid cultural models derived from both the L1 and L2) to suggest that only those learners who inhabit such a space succeed in conducting inner speech in the L2. This being so, it is clearly necessary to accept that the L1 will play a major role in most learners' inner world. This need not be seen as a problem however, as there is ample evidence to show that when the L1 is used for private speech, it can facilitate both communication and learning (see, in particular, Ohta, 2001).

There is also plenty of evidence to show that the L1 plays a facilitative role in social interaction involving L2 learners. Antón and DiCamilla (1999), for example, examined the collaborative interaction of adult learners of Spanish. These learners used the L1 not just for metatalk but also to assist each other's production in the L2, as in the following extract, where the students are composing a text about the eating habits of Americans:

G: I don't know the word for snack

D: Um...

G: Ohm so you just say 'in the afternoon'

D: We we could...in the afternoon

G: So what time in the afternoon

D: Um

Or do we want to just say in the afternoon?

D: Let's say...

G: Por la tarde?

D: Por la tarde...comen...what did they eat?

The learners use their L1 to 'overtly address the problem of accessing the linguistic items needed to express their idea' (p. 237). Antón and DiCamilla noted that this use of the L1 often arose when the students were faced with a cognitive challenge. When there was no problem, the learners created text directly in the L2.

Affect

Nation (2003) claimed 'using the L2 can be a source of embarrassment particularly for shy learners and those who feel they are not very proficient in the L2' (p. 2). In other words, the use of the L1 in the classroom can serve as a means of reducing learner anxiety and creating rapport. Allowing learners to use their L1 can also allay the threat to learners' own cultural identity posed by having to use the L2 (Auerbach, 1993). Schweers (1999), building on Auerbach's (1993) sociopolitical rationale for the use of the L1 in ESL classrooms, argued that when the teacher speaks the students' L1, she is able to show that she respects and values their own culture.

Horwitz et al. (1986) distinguished three sources of situational anxiety in foreign language classrooms: 1) communication apprehension, arising from learners' inability to adequately express mature thoughts and ideas, 2) fear of negative social evaluation, arising from a learner's need to make a positive social impression on others and 3) test anxiety, or apprehension over academic evaluation. Meyer (2008) argued that the L1 can alleviate the anxiety that arises from all three sources. For example, learners may be more prepared to negotiate for meaning by requesting clarification if allowed to do so in the L1. Meyer cites Shimizu (2006: 77), who found that Japanese students rarely asked clarification questions when required to do so in English (the L2) and thus failed to address misunderstandings and consequently progressed more slowly in English.

However, we know of no studies that have actually demonstrated that the use of the L1 leads to lower anxiety. Also the relationship between anxiety and L2 learning is a matter of some controversy. Krashen (1981) argued that 'acquisition' is facilitated when the 'affective filter' is low. Other researchers (e.g. Scovel, 2001) have suggested that anxiety can have a facilitative effect on learning and there is some research that supports this view. Djigunovic (2006), for example, reported that high-anxiety learners produced longer texts in the L2 than low-anxiety learners although they were also less fluent. There is also disagreement as to whether anxiety is to be seen as the cause or the result of poor achievement. Sparks et al. (2000) promulgated the Linguistic Coding Difference Hypothesis, which claims that success in foreign language learning is primarily dependent on language aptitude and that students' anxiety about learning an L2 is a consequence of their learning difficulties. MacIntyre and Gardner (1991) argued that the relationship between anxiety and learning is moderated by the learners' stage of development and by situation-specific learning experiences. Their model hypothesizes that learners initially experience little anxiety so there is no effect on learning. Subsequently, language anxiety develops if learners have bad learning experiences. This then has a debilitative effect on learning. This model suggests that the use of the L1 with beginner learners might help to avoid negative learning experiences and attendant anxiety and thus foster subsequent development. There is, however, clearly a need for studies that investigate what impact use of the L1 has on learners' situational anxiety at different stages of their development.

Final comment

The role that the L1 plays in L2 learning is clearly a complex one. We can distinguish two broad approaches. From a psycholinguistic perspective, researchers have examined how the L1 affects the development of learners' interlanguage. From a social-psychological perspective, other researchers have explored how the use of the L1 in communication facilitates L2 learning. The first perspective informs mainstream work in SLA. It has led to detailed information about the role of L1 transfer, showing that linguistic differences between the L1 and the target language do not necessarily result in negative transfer (as reflected in errors traceable to the L1) and that similarities can facilitate learning by speeding up acquisition. SLA researchers see negative and positive transfer as processes that arise naturally as learners engage with the L2. The second perspective views the L1 as a resource that learners can draw on to facilitate communication and to scaffold learning of the L2. Use of the L1 enables learners to overcome communication problems, to engage in learning behaviours that promote L2 learning and, possibly, to reduce situational language anxiety, which might impede learning.

There is a conspicuous lack of research that has investigated what effect (facilitative or debilitative) use of the L1 has on actual learning. Laufer and Girsai (2008) reported a study that compared the incidental acquisition of a set of words and collocations by Hebrew-speaking learners of L2 English in three instructional conditions: a meaning-focused condition involving tasks that did not focus explicitly on the target items, a non-contrastive condition which involved an explicit focus on the items, and a contrastive analysis and translation condition involving translation tasks followed by explicit contrastive analysis of problematic items. The results of immediate and delayed tests showed a clear advantage for the contrastive analysis and translation condition. However, the method of testing involved translation tasks which clearly favoured this group. In another study, Tian and Macaro (2012) compared the effects of two ways of teaching the new vocabulary in a listening text to first-year majors in a Chinese university. One group of learners were provided with L1 equivalents and the other group with definitions and paraphrases in the target language. Post-tests required students to indicate whether they knew the words and if they did to write down the meaning in either English or Chinese. The results showed that the group that received L1 equivalents learned more new words but, interestingly, they opted to demonstrate the meaning of the words by means of L1 translations.

There is clearly a need for further research on the effects of use of the L1 on learning. Researchers need to demonstrate that use of the L1 results in better productive use of the L2 in tests that do not involve translation. The two studies mentioned above deal with vocabulary; there is also a need to investigate grammar. Finally, studies that investigate child learners as well as adults are needed, as it cannot be assumed that children will benefit from L1 translations in the same way as adults.

Conclusion

In this chapter we have examined the arguments that exist regarding the value of teachers and students using the L1 in the L2 classroom. The view evident in many methods, in teacher guides and in the opinions of a number of educational commentators is that teachers and learners should strive for maximal use of the L2. Turnbull and Arnett (2002), in a review of the research on teachers' use of the target language and L1, claim that there is a 'near consensus' on this issue. Hall and Cook (2012) refer to this as the 'monolingual assumption'.

However, as we have seen, it is also clear that teachers often do make use of the learners' L1 even when they adhere to a 'maximal position' about the use of the target language. Also, V. Cook, Macaro, G. Cook, and Hall and Cook have advanced powerful arguments in support of using the L1 – not just because it helps teachers to meet the practical needs of managing life in a classroom but also because it can help language learning, promote 'multicompetence' and develop learners' bilingual identities. The argument for the use of translation in the L2 classroom is persuasive, eloquently put by G. Cook (2010):

> Humans teach and learn by moving from the familiar to the unfamiliar, by building new knowledge onto existing knowledge. Language learning and teaching is no exception to this rule. Translation is just such a bridge between the familiar and the unfamiliar, the known and the unknown...Learners moreover need that bridge to maintain the links between their languages and identities.
>
> (p. 155)

What light does SLA research throw on this contentious issue? The case for maximal use of the L2 is supported by research that shows the importance of L2 input for learning. Principle 6 stated 'Successful instructed language learning requires extensive L2 input' and in Chapter 7 we examined the research that supports this principle. Clearly, if teachers and learners resort to the L1, there will be less exposure to the L2. Thus, classroom participants need to strive for maximal use of the L2. As we noted in Chapter 1, ideally this means that the L2 needs to become the medium as well as the object of instruction, especially in a foreign language setting. However, as we also noted in Chapter 1, there is also a place for the strategic use of the L1 in the classroom.

SLA research has demonstrated that teachers (and learners) need not fear that the L1 will 'interfere' with the L2 learning process. Research on language transfer demonstrates convincingly that learners do indeed, in part at least, move from the 'known' to the 'unknown', as G. Cook claimed. Learners draw on their L1 naturally and automatically in a manner that teaching should not try to obstruct. This will sometimes result in errors but can also facilitate interlanguage development in the case of positive L1 transfer. The L1 needs to be seen as a communicative resource that both teachers and learners can draw on in various ways that research suggests can facilitate learning. Learners make natural use of the L1 in communication strategies (e.g. 'literal translation' and 'language switch'). When talking in groups, they make effective use of the L1 to solve linguistic problems. Learners are also likely to make cross-linguistic comparisons and this can contribute to the explicit knowledge that we have argued can facilitate acquisition (see Chapter 3).

It is unlikely, however, that the debate regarding the use of the L1 will be easily resolved. As Macaro (2005) recognized the crucial issues are: (1) the specific functions that the L1 serves and (2) the extent of L1 use. While there is a body of descriptive research that provides useful information about what teachers and learners do, there is almost no research that has investigated the actual effects of the classroom use of the L1 on L2 learning. This is, perhaps, why claims and counterclaims continue to proliferate. One thing is clear, however, it is very unlikely that educational or pedagogic promulgations will have much effect on attitudes and practices regarding the use of the L1 (Song and Andrews, 2009). Perhaps the way forward for now is to encourage teachers to reflect on their own practices, as in Edstrom (2009), and develop a critical perspective on their own use of the L1.

Notes

1 It should be noted, however, that in two-way bilingual immersion programmes instruction should be exclusively in the target language, translation should be avoided, and the two languages be kept rigidly separate (Cummins, 2005). In other words, the use of the two languages in the same lesson is not permitted.
2 However, other educators have recommended the contrastive teaching of grammar. James (1980) saw it as catering to the natural tendency of learners to compare the L2 system to their L1 system. It serves to highlight areas where there are clear differences between the two systems and constitutes one way of raising learners' consciousness about features of the L2 grammar that they might otherwise ignore.
3 Schumann (1978) reported that Alberto showed no evidence of acquisition of a range of grammatical structures after many months of living in the United States.

DISCUSSION QUESTIONS

1. There are a number of different terms that can be used to refer to the use of the learners' mother tongue in the L2 classroom – 'L1 use', 'codeswitching', 'own-language use'. Explain the difference in the meanings of these terms. Why are researchers such as Macaro and Cook critical of the term 'L1 use'?
2. Why do teachers often express uncertainty about using the L1 in the classroom?
3. The teacher guides warn against the use of the L1 when performing communicative tasks. On what grounds? What is your own view about this?
4. There would appear to be discrepancy between what teachers believe they should do and what they actually do regarding the use of the L1. What explanation can you give for this?
5. Look through the categories of the teacher's L1 use in Table 9.2. Which of these uses do you consider legitimate? Which ones do you think should be avoided?

6. In what ways can the learners' use of the L1 be viewed as beneficial for L2 learning?
7. Go over the arguments for and against the use of the L1 in Table 9.3. Consider each use and decide on your own view.
8. Hall and Cook (2012) argue that the appropriate goal should be the 'development of bilingual and bicultural identities and skills that are actively needed by most learners, both within the English-speaking countries and in the world at large'. How convincing do you find this argument?
9. In what ways does SLA research on L1 transfer give support to the use of the L1 in teaching?
10. What view does Sociocultural Theory hold about the use of the L1 by teachers and learners? Do you agree with this view?
11. Consider how the use of the L1 might help to alleviate learners' anxiety when learning an L2.
12. We concluded this chapter with this statement: 'Classroom participants need to strive for maximal use of the L2.' Do you agree? Would it perhaps be better to aim for 'optimal use'? If so, how would you define 'optimal use'?

10 Corrective feedback

Introduction

Corrective feedback (CF) takes the form of responses to learner utterances that contain (or are perceived as containing) an error. It occurs in reactive form-focused episodes consisting of a trigger, the feedback move and (optionally) uptake. In this example, taken from Yang and Lyster (2010: 243) the teacher's utterance signals an error has been committed and provides metalinguistic feedback which results in the student's uptake:

Student: I went to the train station and pick up my aunt. (= trigger)

Teacher: Use past tense consistently. (= feedback move)

Student: I went to the train station and picked up my aunt. (= uptake)

CF can be overt as in this example or more covert (e.g. if the teacher had said 'Oh, you picked up your aunt'). It can occur in both task-based language teaching and in more formal teaching involving explicit language instruction. It can also occur in both oral and written form. In the case of writing, 'uptake' takes the form of a revision of the original text that was corrected.

Corrective feedback supplies learners with negative evidence. That is, it signals that something that the learner has said or written does not conform to target language norms. In this respect, it contrasts with other forms of input that provide the learner with positive evidence (i.e. models that conform to target language norms). However, as we will see, CF can provide both negative and positive evidence. In the example above, the teacher's feedback merely signals that something is incorrect and needs modifying. However, if the teacher had said, 'Use the past tense – you must say "picked up"', the feedback would contain both negative and positive evidence. As we will see later, this distinction between negative and positive evidence is an important one when considering the role that CF plays in L2 acquisition.

We will adopt the same approach as in a number of other chapters. First, we will examine how CF is handled in the pedagogic literature and then switch attention to SLA. In both cases, we will consider oral and written CF.

Corrective feedback in language pedagogy

All the teacher guides we have inspected affirm the importance of providing both positive feedback and negative feedback (i.e. CF). Nunan (1991), in fact, devotes more attention to positive feedback than CF. He noted that it serves two functions – 'to let students know they have performed correctly' and 'to increase motivation through praise' (p. 195). Praising students is seen as an important way of fostering positive attitudes to learning. Correcting students may be deemed necessary but it is also seen as potentially dangerous because it can damage learners' receptivity to learning. Therefore it needs to be given 'in an atmosphere of support and warm solidarity' (Ur, 1996: 255). There is a clear recognition in the language of teacher guides of the affective and cognitive dimensions of CF (Vigil and Oller, 1976). Teachers, however, are likely to pay greater attention to the affective dimension.

In a seminal article, Hendrickson (1978) addressed five central questions about corrective feedback:

- Should learners' errors be corrected?
- When should learners' errors be corrected?
- Which errors should be corrected?
- How should errors be corrected?
- Who should do the correcting?

These questions continue to be the central questions addressed in the pedagogic literature so we will base our review on them.

Should learners' errors be corrected?

The value attributed to oral CF in language pedagogy varies in different methods. For example, in audiolingualism 'negative assessment is to be avoided as far as possible since it functions as "punishment" and may inhibit or discourage learning', in humanistic methods 'assessment should be positive or non-judgemental' in order to 'promote a positive self-image of the learner as a person and language learner', while in skill-learning theory 'the learner needs feedback on how well he or she is doing' (Ur, 1996: 243). However, in the post-method era (see Chapter 2), methodologists are less inclined to be prescriptive about CF, acknowledging the cognitive contribution it can make while also issuing warnings about the potential affective damage it can do. Ur, for example, recognized that 'there is certainly a place for correction' but 'we should not overestimate this contribution' because it often fails to eliminate errors. She concluded that she would rather invest time in avoiding errors than in correcting them. Other methodologists, however, distinguish between 'accuracy' and 'fluency' work and argue that CF has a place in the former but not in the latter. Harmer (1983), for example, argued that when students are engaged in a communicative activity, the teacher should not intervene by 'telling students that they are making mistakes, insisting on accuracy and asking for repetition etc.' (p. 44). Hedge (2000) observed that teachers' notes accompanying course books frequently instruct teachers to leave correction until the end of fluency activities. Scrivener (2005) supported a similar position:

> If the objective is accuracy, then immediate correction is likely to be useful; if the aim is fluency, then lengthy, immediate correction that diverts from the flow of speaking is less appropriate.
>
> (p. 299)

However, he did allow for 'brief, unobtrusive, immediate correction' in fluency work. He also suggested that teachers should make a list of the errors their students make in a fluency activity and address them when the activity is over. Ur also considered that it is sometimes appropriate to correct during fluency work ('gentle, supportive intervention' can help the 'floundering' student). She also noted that it was not always desirable to correct during accuracy work (e.g. if a student has contributed an interesting, personal comment that contains an error).

Similar differences in opinion exist where written CF is concerned. Truscott (1996), reflecting the views of teachers who adhere to process theories of writing, acknowledged that correcting learners' errors in a written composition can help them to eliminate the errors in a subsequent draft. However, he argued that written correction has no effect on grammatical accuracy in a new piece of writing (i.e. it does not result in acquisition). Ferris (1999) disputed this claim, arguing that it was not possible to dismiss correction in general as it depended on the quality of the correction – in other words, if the correction was clear and consistent, it would work for acquisition. This debate has run on over several years and, as we will see later in this chapter, has led to a number of studies investigating whether written CF can improve linguistic accuracy in subsequent writing.

Uncertainty about the value of written CF is also evident in the pedagogic literature. Scrivener (2005), for example, pointed out that 'red pen' corrections can discourage students but also noted that most learners expect to have their writing corrected by the teacher. Ur (1996) saw correcting students' written work as a normal part of a teacher's job. Hedge (2000) deemed it 'an expected role for the teacher' in foreign language situations. In general, then, teacher educators recognize the need for written CF and are more concerned with how it should be done. However, all commentators acknowledge that 'corrective feedback' is just one type of 'feedback' on writing. They distinguish feedback aimed at providing formative suggestions to help learners revise the content or organization from corrective feedback intended to address the errors learners have made. An issue of some importance is whether these two types of feedback should be combined or handled separately as proposed by Hall (2011) and advocated in the process writing approach.

When should learner errors be corrected?

We will see later that the timing of CF is an issue that SLA theory has addressed. In the case of oral CF, as we have just seen, teachers have the option of either correcting immediately an error occurs or making a note of the errors and delaying correction until later. Gattegno (1972) came out strongly in favour of not rushing in to correct learner errors even in accuracy-oriented work. He commented:

> Against a common teachers' demand for immediate correctness through so-called imitation, I take upon myself the burden of controlling myself so as not to interfere. By doing so, I give time to a student to make sense of 'mistakes'.
>
> (p. 31)

Gattegno was reacting to one of the requirements of the Audiolingual Method, namely that errors (if they do occur) should be corrected immediately and students asked to imitate the correct form. However, other methods – especially those associated with humanistic language teaching – view immediate correction in particular as potentially damaging.

Written CF is always delayed as teachers need to collect in written work to correct errors. The issue of timing, however, arises in the process approach to teaching writing. Johns (1990) described this as an approach where 'ESL teachers…encourage several drafts of a paper, require paper revision at the macro levels, generally through group work…and delay the student fixation with and correction of sentence-level errors until the final editing' (p. 26). Correction of linguistic errors (i.e. corrective feedback), therefore, occurs only in the draft prior to submission of a piece of writing. Here teachers can provide more substantive error correction or encourage students to self-edit.

Computer-mediated communication offers somewhat different opportunities for the timing of CF. Both immediate and delayed communication are possible. In synchronous chat, opportunity arises to correct written errors as they occur but corrections can also be provided later, asynchronously (e.g. by email) after the teacher has had a chance to view a transcript of the interaction. Bower and Kawaguchi (2011) argued that delayed, asynchronous correction is preferable because it gives time to identify and explain errors and also because learners have plenty of time to consider the corrections to their output.

Which errors should be corrected?

The teacher guides warn against over-correction and propose that teachers should be selective in the errors they correct. As Ur (1996) noted 'learners can only use just so much feedback information: to give too much may simply distract, discourage and actually detract from the value of learning' (p. 255). It should be noted, however, that learners want to be corrected (Cathcart and Olsen, 1976). However, they do not necessarily want all their errors corrected.

Katayama (2007) surveyed Japanese university students' views about corrective feedback and found that only a minority thought the teacher should correct every error they made. Katayama argued that selective correction was both practical and more supportive of students' feelings.

If teachers are to correct some errors and ignore others, ideally, they need to do so in a principled manner. Various proposals have been advanced regarding which errors to address. Corder (1967) distinguished 'errors' and 'mistakes'. An error takes place as a result of lack of knowledge (i.e. it represents a gap in competence). A mistake is performance phenomenon, reflecting processing failures that arise as a result of competing plans, memory limitations and lack of automaticity. One possibility then is for the teacher to correct 'errors' but leave it to the learner to self-correct 'mistakes'. Burt (1975) suggested that teachers should focus on 'global' rather than 'local errors'. Global errors are errors that affect overall sentence organization. Examples are wrong word order, missing or wrongly placed sentence connectors, and syntactic overgeneralizations. Local errors are errors that affect single elements in a sentence (e.g. errors in morphology or grammatical functors). Krashen (1982) argued that CF should be limited to features that are simple and portable (i.e. 'rules of thumb' such as, in English, plural-*s* or past tense-*ed*). Ferris (1999) similarly suggested that written CF should be directed at 'treatable errors' (i.e. errors relating to features that occur in 'a patterned, rule-governed way' (p. 6)). Others, including myself (Ellis 1993), have suggested that CF be directed at marked grammatical features or features that learners have shown that they have persistent problems with. In fact, none of these proposals are easy to implement in practice. The distinction between an 'error' and a 'mistake' is nothing like as clear-cut as Corder made out, while the gravity of an error is largely a matter of personal opinion. Vann et al. (1984), for example, found that some teachers were inclined to view all errors as equally serious – 'an error is an error'.

How should errors be corrected?

Oral and written CF are treated separately in the teacher guides. Various strategies for correcting oral errors are proposed. Scrivener (2005), for example, lists thirteen strategies. Interestingly, though, there is a high degree of agreement in the guides about what the basic strategies are. They include:

- Questioning the learner – for example, 'the teacher may say "Is that correct?"' (Harmer, 1983: 63).
- Direct indication – for example, 'Tell the students that there is an error' (Scrivener, 2005: 300).
- Requesting clarification – for example, 'the teacher looks puzzled and requests clarification' (Hedge, 2000: 291).
- Requesting repetition – for example, 'the teacher simply asks the student to repeat what he has just said' (Harmer, 1983: 62).
- Echoing – for example, 'the teacher may echo what the student has just said with a questioning intonation' (Harmer, 1983: 62).

- Using gesture – for example, 'the teacher moves his or her hand to indicate an error' (Hedge, 2000: 291).
- Modelling – for example, the teacher 'provides a model of the acceptable version' (Ur, 1996: 249).
- Discuss the error – for example, 'Write the problem sentence on the board for discussion' (Scrivener, 2005: 301).

Hendrickson (1978) identified a similar set of strategies in his seminal article many years ago and these seem to have been handed down over time.

Two points stand out about this treatment of CF strategies. First, all the guides simply provide lists. There is no attempt to classify the strategies into general types (e.g. strategies that provide learners with the correct form vs those that prompt them to produce it themselves). Second, there are no examples of these strategies taken from actual classroom interaction: the guides are content to provide simple descriptions of them (but see Omaggio, 1986 for an exception). Ur, however, proposed that teachers use her list of strategies to carry out an observation of how CF is carried out in an actual lesson.

The guides are wary of recommending the use of any particular strategy. Hedge (2000), for example, simply concluded that teachers need to use a variety of strategies. It is, however, possible to see a general preference for those strategies that require learners to correct their own errors. As Harmer (1983) put it, the 'object of using correction techniques is to give the students(s) a chance to get the new language right' (p. 63). Thus, even when using those strategies that involve providing learners with the correct form, the guides recommend that students should be asked to repeat the sentence correctly. This preference for guiding learners to self-correct reflects a general principle that underlies thinking about CF – as Scrivener (2005) put it, 'people learn more by doing things themselves rather than being told about them' (p. 3). Nevertheless, in his specific comments on error correction, Scrivener (2005) noted that simply giving the correct form 'may be the quickest, most appropriate, most useful way of helping' (p. 301).

Of concern to all the guides is the importance of 'encouraging, tactful correction' (Ur, 1996: 249). Ur emphasized that students vary in how they respond to the different strategies and thus there is a need for sensitivity on the part of the teacher. As a follow-up to observing the strategies employed in a lesson, she suggested that teachers consider trying to describe the manner in which the CF was given using adjectives such as 'gentle', 'hesitant' and 'supportive'. Once again, then, we see the emphasis on the affective aspect of CF rather than the cognitive aspect.

The guides also propose a fairly standard set of written CF strategies. Three basic strategies can be distinguished:

- Direct correction. As Ferris (2006) noted, this can take a number of different forms – crossing out an unnecessary word, phrase or morpheme, inserting a missing word or morpheme, and writing the correct form above or near to the erroneous form.

- Indirect correction where the teacher indicates that the student has made an error without actually correcting it. This can be done by underlining the errors or using cursors to show omissions in the students' text or by placing a cross in the margin next to the line containing the error.
- Using an error coding system consisting of abbreviated labels for different kinds of errors (e.g. VT = verb tense error). This constitutes a form of metalinguistic feedback.

Many of the guides are keen on the use of an error coding system and provide examples. This again reflects the importance attached to students working out the corrections for themselves rather than direct correction. Brumfit (1977), for example, proposed a model for correcting written errors that involved both indirect correction and the use of an error coding system. This model consisted of five main stages, starting from underlining a mistake and diagnosing it in the margin and concluding with putting a cross in each line with a mistake but not show where. The underlying idea was to gradually remove the amount of assistance the teacher provided so as to foster self-dependence on the part of the student. Brumfit's model did not include direct teacher correction. In general, the guides also assume that correction will be unfocused (i.e. all or most of the errors will be corrected). However, Scrivener (2005) recommended that the teacher tell the students what aspect of grammar (e.g. verb tenses) will be focused on and correction limited to that aspect.

The key question, of course, is how effective these strategies are. Ferris (2002) suggested that direct CF may be needed if learners do not know what the correct form is (i.e. are not capable of self-correcting the error themselves). In contrast, indirect feedback caters to 'guided learning and problem solving' (Lalande, 1982) and thus may be more likely to lead to long-term learning. In general, however, the guides avoid evaluating the different strategies, preferring simply to describe them. An exception is Ur, who came out firmly in favour of direct CF. She was dismissive of indirect CF, commenting 'I do not see much value in demanding that students focus again on the wrong form and try to work out what is wrong' (pp. 256–57).

One point the guides emphasize is the importance of asking students to revise their writing following CF. As Hedge (2000) commented, the aim is to encourage students 'to see writing as something that can be improved' (p. 316). The guides also stress the need for teachers to comment on the content and organization of the students' writing and not just focus on the errors.

Who should do the correcting?

There are three possible answers to this question – the teacher, the student who made the error, or another student. Nunan (1988) found that the students he surveyed tended to value correction when it was provided by the teacher and gave self-discovery of errors a low rating. Leki (1991) also reported that students wanted and expected the teacher to correct all the errors in their writing. However, students differ in their stated preference. Katayama (2007), for example, reported that the Japanese university students he investigated preferred to have the opportunity to self-correct with the help of a hint from the teacher. Such a view accords more closely with the view expressed by teachers who generally favour making the student responsible for the correction.

This is clearly reflected in the advice given to teachers. Hedge (2000) and Scrivener (2005), for example, advised giving students the opportunity to self-correct and, if that fails, inviting another student to perform the correction. Chaudron (1977) also recommended eliciting the correction from either the student who committed it or another student. He viewed this approach as a viable form of 'successful correction'. However, there is also recognition of the potential dangers of students correcting each other. Ur noted that it can be very time-consuming and also that it can have a negative impact on the student being corrected. The least favoured option in the guides is teacher correction – a reflection of the same general educational principle referred to above. Omaggio (1986), however, approved of teacher correction: (1) if there is no time for other methods, (2) when the frequency of errors within a particular utterance impedes communication and (3) in drills. Irrespective of who does the correction, there is wide agreement that the teacher needs to ensure that the student who initially made the error produces the correct form.

In the case of writing, student correction can again be conducted by the teacher, by the individual student (i.e. each student is asked to edit his own work) or by another student (i.e. in peer correction). The guides all acknowledge that the teacher should take responsibility for correcting learners' written errors. However, they also clearly favour other alternatives. Ferris (2002) emphasized the importance of training learners to self-edit their own work. She commented 'our goal should be to have our students become skilful independent editors who can function beyond the ESL writing class' (p. 334) and proposed a procedure for helping writers to achieve this. This consisted of three basic stages: (1) teaching students to pay attention to errors, (2) training them to recognize different types of errors and (3) providing self-editing practice. Peer correction is also frequently mentioned in the guides. Edge (1989) recommended it on four grounds: (1) it encourages learners to think about what is correct, (2) the teacher can observe the students and thus form an idea of the extent to which students have a clear understanding of specific features, (3) it encourages students to be less dependent on teachers and (4) it helps learners to recognize that they can learn from each other. Brumfit (1977) suggested another reason – detecting errors in another student's work can help a learner to spot errors in his/her own work. Ur noted that peer correction is time-saving as it removes the need for the teacher to correct individual students' writing. She recognized, however, that peer correction has its problems. Students may feel that corrections proposed by another student are not trustworthy and may resist what they see as criticism when correction comes from another student rather than the teacher.

Some concluding comments

There is a large pedagogical literature dealing with corrective feedback and this section has only touched on a small section of it, focusing mainly on the advice provided in some of the major teacher guides. In addition, there are complete books devoted to it – such as Edge's (1989) *Mistakes and Correction* and Mishra's (2005) *Error Correction in English*. A wide range of pedagogical practice is reflected in this literature but it is also clear that there is a broad consensus about what constitutes effective practice. From the preceding review, the following emerge as the main conclusions:

1 Learners' oral errors should be corrected but care needs to be taken to ensure that correction does not arouse a negative emotional response in learners. Thus it needs to be accomplished sensitively.
2 However, in oral fluency work, where the focus is on communicating, correction should be postponed until the activity is completed.
3 The effectiveness of written CF is the subject of debate but, in general, it is seen as desirable especially in the final draft of a composition. Learners should always be asked to revise their written work following correction.
4 There is a danger of over-correcting so teachers need to be selective in the errors they correct. Various proposals for deciding which errors to correct have been put forward but none are easy to implement in practice.
5 A wide variety of strategies for correcting both oral and written errors have been proposed. While teacher educators have shown reluctance in recommending which strategies teachers should use, there is an overall preference for fostering learners' ability to correct their own errors.
6 As far as possible, it is the students who should do the correction not the teacher, although the teacher can provide clues to help students locate their errors.

We have noted that there is a general underlying principle that informs the advice given to teachers, namely that students will benefit most if they assume the role of corrector rather than depend on the teacher to correct them. We also noted, however, that learners themselves often prefer to be corrected. Missing from all the literature we have considered is any consideration of the research that has investigated whether corrective feedback assists learning.

Corrective feedback in SLA

Theories of L2 acquisition differ in the importance they attach to corrective feedback, so we will begin by considering these. We will then move on to look at some studies that have shown both oral and written CF to be effective in promoting acquisition.

Theoretical positions

Universal Grammar-based accounts of corrective feedback

Universal Grammar (UG) consists of a highly abstract set of linguistic principles that do not constitute the actual rules found in any single language but rather act as constraints on the form that these rules can take. UG-based theories of L2 acquisition assume that: (1) human beings possess a highly specific capacity for language learning (as opposed to a more general cognitive apparatus responsible for all types of learning) and (2) this capacity is innate and biologically determined. UG-oriented SLA researchers seek to show how these principles enable learners to acquire grammatical competence (i.e. implicit knowledge of a language). The claim that learners must draw on UG is based on the poverty of stimulus argument. This states that the input that learners are exposed to is insufficient to ensure full acquisition of a target language grammar and thus UG is required to provide an 'explanation of how it is that learners come to know properties of grammar that go far beyond the input' (White, 2003: 20).

Input provides learners with positive evidence (i.e. it demonstrates what is grammatically possible). It is this sense of input that UG-based theories draw on when arguing input is insufficient for acquisition. However, input can also provide negative evidence through corrective feedback. Can this enable learners to overcome the limitations of positive evidence? Here we find a number of different positions in the literature. One position is that negative evidence can play a role in triggering UG principles and, indeed, may be necessary to enable L2 learners to eliminate incorrect grammatical rules from their interlanguage (White, 1991). In contrast, Schwartz (1986) has argued that negative evidence only results in explicit knowledge and thus plays no role in UG-based acquisition which is a theory of how learners acquire implicit knowledge. She claimed that there is no mechanism that can 'translate' this explicit knowledge into input of the type required by UG. A third position is that negative evidence can play a role in certain stages of L2 development but not others. Carroll (2001) proposed that negative evidence is not interpretable at the beginning stages of L2 learning because learners lack the metalinguistic awareness needed to process corrective feedback and that it also plays no role at an advanced stage because learners are not typically corrected then. However, it might be usable by learners in the intermediate stages of development. Overall, however, Carroll concluded that corrective feedback is unlikely to play a central role in a general theory of L2 acquisition.

The view that corrective feedback has no or only a minor role to play in L2 acquisition has been most fully argued by Krashen and Truscott. Krashen (1982) called error correction 'a serious mistake' (p. 74). He argued that error correction only assists the development of 'learned knowledge' (i.e. explicit knowledge) and plays no role in 'acquired knowledge' (i.e. implicit knowledge), although he did accept that correction directed at simple and portable rules (e.g. third person-*s*) was of some value, because it enabled learners to monitor their production when they were focused on form and had sufficient time to access their 'learned' knowledge.

Where Krashen considered the role of oral CF, Truscott critiqued written CF. In an initial article (Truscott, 1996), he claimed that there was neither any empirical or theoretical justification for correcting students' written errors. In a series of further articles (Truscott 1999, 2004, 2007, 2010), he continued to reject any role for CF where grammar is concerned, although he acknowledged that it might be helpful for vocabulary or the mechanics of writing. His main arguments against written CF are as follows:

1 Those CF studies that have been well designed (i.e. included a control group) have failed to show that CF is effective and, in some cases, have even shown that it is damaging.
2 Even studies that have investigated absolute gains (i.e. gains over time) as a result of CF have in general failed to demonstrate that it is effective.
3 Learners' affective response to CF together with the fact that they are often confused by the corrections they receive is likely to result in avoidance (i.e. students will try to avoid using those grammatical features that have been corrected).
4 CF will not have any effect on the development of the type of knowledge (implicit knowledge) needed to engage in writing or speaking for communicative purposes. One reason for this is the impossibility of knowing which grammatical features learners are developmentally ready to acquire. Writing practice without any correction has a better chance of assisting the natural processes of L2 acquisition.
5 However, CF may have an impact on the kind of knowledge (explicit knowledge) needed for monitoring when completing grammar tests or revising a written text that has been corrected.

Truscott's position is clearly based on the view that written CF (and also explicit instruction) only benefits metalinguistic knowledge but does not contribute to what he called 'genuine knowledge of a language' (1998: 120). Like Schwartz and Krashen, he saw 'true' acquisition as dependent on positive evidence only. As we will shortly see, his position has been challenged both theoretically and on the grounds that the empirical evidence does not support it.

To sum up, in general UG-based accounts either dismiss CF on the grounds that there is no role for negative evidence or view it as of minor importance in fostering acquisition. Both oral and written CF are seen as contributing only to learners' explicit L2 knowledge.

Cognitive–interactionist accounts of CF

Cognitive–interactionist theories emphasize that CF is most likely to assist acquisition when the participants are focused primarily on meaning in the context of producing and understanding messages in communication, commit errors and then receive feedback that they recognize as corrective. That is, CF contributes to 'acquisition', not just to 'learning'. Correcting learners while they are trying to communicate activates the cognitive mechanisms involved in intake, rehearsal and restructuring and thereby fosters interlanguage development. Such feedback helps learners to see how a particular linguistic form realizes a particular meaning in context. It is for this reason that the majority of the studies that have investigated CF, which we consider in a later section, have involved task-based language instruction.

CF can facilitate the processes responsible for acquisition in two ways – by providing learners with positive evidence of target language forms or by pushing learners to self-correct their errors (i.e. through output). In Extract 1 below, the learner fails to use the past tense to refer to a completed action in the past and the teacher responds with a recast (i.e. she reformulates the learner's utterance correcting the error). Recasts such as this provide learners with input. Learning occurs when the learner notices the correction and carries out a cognitive comparison (i.e. attends to the difference between his/her own erroneous production and the target-like input provided by the feedback). This view of the role played by CF emphasizes the importance of noticing and noticing-the-gap in L2 acquisition (Schmidt 1994, 2001; see Chapter 8).

Extract 1

T: When were you in school?

L: Yes. I *stand* in the first row? (trigger)

T: Oh, you *stood* in the first row. (corrective move)

L: Yes, in the first row.

In Extract 2, however, the teacher's response to the error does not provide the learner with positive evidence concerning the target form. Instead, it prompts the learner to self-correct. This learner also makes an error in the use of the past tense. The teacher corrects by requesting clarification ('Pardon?') and this causes the learner to repair his error in the uptake move that concludes the sequence.

Extract 2

S: Why does he fly to Korea last year? (trigger)

T: Pardon? (corrective move)

S: Why did he fly to Korea last year? (uptake)

(Yang and Lyster, 2010: 235)

The relative effectiveness of these two types of feedback has become an issue of controversy. Long (2006) and Goo and Mackey (2013) have argued that recasts are more effective because they provide learners with both negative and positive evidence. They point out that unless learners receive positive evidence it will be impossible for them to acquire 'new' linguistic forms. However, Lyster (2004) evoked skill-learning theory (see Chapter 5) to argue that prompting learners to self-correct is more effective because it helps learners to gain greater control over those linguistic features that they have partially acquired. Lyster drew on earlier research (Lyster and Ranta, 1997), which showed that immersion learners often fail to repair their errors following teacher recasts but were much more likely to do so following prompts such as clarification requests. Lyster suggested that recasts may be ineffective because learners often fail to recognize that they are corrective and thus do not notice the target form.

In some respects, however, the argument over whether recasts or prompts are more effective is pointless. For one thing, as we pointed out in Chapter 4 when we discussed explicit language instruction, 'acquisition' involves both internalizing new forms and gaining control over existing forms, so the two types of CF can both be seen as facilitative but in different ways. Also, it is possible to combine prompts and recasts as in the 'corrective recasts' proposed by Doughty and Varela (1998). These are illustrated in Extract 3. They consist of an initial prompt (in this case a repetition of the learner's erroneous utterance), which is then followed by a recast if the learner fails to self-correct.

Extract 3

L: I think that the worm will go under the soil.

T: I *think* that the worm *will* go under the soil?

L: (no response)

T: I *thought* that the worm *would* go under the soil.

L: I *thought* that the worm *would* go under the soil.

Another controversial issue concerns the relative effectiveness of implicit as opposed to explicit corrective feedback. Extracts 1 and 2 illustrate implicit types of feedback. However, for feedback to have any effect, it must be perceived as corrective (i.e. seen as constituting negative evidence). Learners may interpret implicit feedback as simply indicating that there is some kind of communication problem that needs solving rather than showing them they have made a linguistic error. In other words, they may see it as signalling the need for the negotiation of meaning (see Chapter 8), which may lead to noticing the linguistic error but does not always do so (Hawkins, 1985). Extract 4 illustrates explicit feedback. The teacher responds to the past tense error by directly signalling an error has been committed and by also supplying a metalinguistic clue ('past tense'). This makes the corrective force of the feedback very clear to the learner, who responds by repairing the error.

Extract 4

L: He kiss her

T: No, kissed past tense.

L: He kissed her.

The case for implicit types of CF is based on the claim that they do not interrupt the communicative flow of an interaction to the same degree as explicit types. Explicit CF, however, has the advantage of being more likely to be attended to by the learner.

In the main, cognitive–interactionist theories have addressed the role of oral CF. However, they are also relevant to written CF. As we have already seen, written CF can be direct (i.e. provide the learner with positive evidence) or indirect (i.e. only provide negative evidence). Also written CF may or may not lead to 'repair' of the errors, depending on whether the learners are required to revise their original piece of writing. Written CF differs from oral CF in two important ways. First, it is typically delayed (i.e. learners' errors are not corrected immediately after they have made them). This is of potential significance as some researchers (e.g. Doughty, 2001) have argued that for feedback to be effective it needs to occur in a 'window of opportunity' (i.e. at that moment when the learner is struggling to express him/herself). Second, written CF is necessarily explicit in nature as irrespective of whether the feedback is direct or indirect it will be clear to learners that they are being corrected.

Sociocultural Theory and corrective feedback

Like interactionist–cognitive theories, Sociocultural Theory (SCT) views language learning as interactionally driven. However, whereas cognitive–interactionist theories see CF as triggering the mental processes responsible for acquisition, Sociocultural Theory claims that CF mediates learning not by providing learners with 'data' which they then process internally, but by affording them opportunities to collaboratively produce new linguistic forms. In other words, learning occurs *in* rather than *as a result of* interaction (Lantolf, 2000b). Thus, correction is not something done to learners but rather something carried out with learners. It enables the joint construction of a zone of proximal development – a sociocognitive state manifest in interaction, where learners are helped to use linguistic features that they are not yet able to employ independently. It constitutes a form of other-regulation directed at helping learners to self-regulate (i.e. access and use the L2 independently). See Chapter 8 for a fuller account of Sociocultural Theory.

The key claim of SCT is that corrective feedback needs to be 'graduated' – that is, it must provide the learner with the minimal level of assistance needed to achieve self-correction. In a key article, Aljaafreh and Lantolf (1994) developed a 'regulatory scale' to reflect the nature of the graduated assistance when a tutor helped learners to identify and self-correct their written errors in an oral conference. This scale was based on a continuum of corrective strategies employed by a tutor, reflecting how explicit or implicit the strategies were. Extract 5 provides an example of how a teacher tailored his feedback by systematically employing more explicit corrective strategies. He began by drawing attention to a sentence containing an error. When the learner initially failed to identify the error, the teacher again prompted him. The learner was now able to identify the error but when he still failed to self-correct, the teacher finally provided the correction, which the learner then successfully uptakes.

Extract 5

T: um 'the man wish to change the boy opinion'...do you see anything wrong with that sentence?

S: 'the man wish to change the boy...er is it maybe the boy to changed changed?

T: nnno

S: the boy is opinion

T: yy say again?

S: the boy apostrophe s opinion

T: so how do you say that wi when it's apostrophe s

S: er the boy was

T: no you say the *boy's* opinion

S: boy's opinion

T: hmm

S: yes

From the perspective of Sociocultural Theory, development is evidenced if the learner is successful in self-correcting, as occurred in Extract 5. Further evidence of learning can be obtained by showing that the assistance needed for self-correction to take place diminishes over time. In other words, development is evident when a learner can be shown to self-correct in response to implicit CF where previously more explicit CF was needed, even though this learner may still not be able to demonstrate independent use of the target feature.

These different theoretical perspectives are summarized in Table 10.1. In the next section we will examine some of the research that has investigated these different claims. First though we will take a closer look at the different types of oral and written corrective feedback.

Types of corrective feedback

In this section we will examine the different types of oral and written CF. Common to both, the strategies can be applied in either an unfocused or a focused way. In the case of the former, the teacher corrects all (or most) of the errors the learner makes. In the case of the latter, the teacher elects to correct just one (or perhaps a few) of the errors, focusing on errors that relate to a specific linguistic feature.

Oral CF

Much of the early work on corrective feedback (Allwright, 1975; Chaudron, 1977) was descriptive in nature, directed at identifying the various strategies that teachers use when correcting learners' errors in classroom interaction. The typologies of feedback strategies that resulted from these studies were very

Table 10.1 Corrective feedback in UG-based theories, cognitive–interactionist theories and Sociocultural Theory

	UG-based theories	Cognitive–interactionist theories	Sociocultural Theory
Conceptualization	Corrective feedback is viewed as providing learners with negative evidence. In this respect it contrasts with other forms of input that provide only positive evidence.	Corrective feedback is viewed as an activity that arises when a learner makes an error and another person (usually the teacher) performs a corrective act, which may or may not lead to self-correction by the learner.	Repair is viewed as a joint activity that is negotiated by the participants with a view to helping a learner to identify a linguistic error and to remedy it him/herself.
Theoretical stance	Acquisition depends on innate principles that govern the acquisition of specific grammatical rules. The role of input is to provide learners with data that activates these principles.	CF prompts internal linguistic processing by drawing learners' attention to form-meaning mappings in the context of interaction and enabling them to 'practise' them through uptake.	CF enables the construction of a Zone of Proximal Development through assisting learners to produce a linguistic form that they do not yet have independent control over.
Acquisition	CF may result in explicit knowledge but does not contribute to 'acquisition' (i.e. implicit knowledge.	Acquisition is evident if it can be shown that learners are subsequently able to demonstrate greater accuracy in the use of linguistic features following CF.	Acquisition is demonstrated if learners succeed in self-correcting as a result of CF and if they need less assistance to self-correct over time.

complex. However, later research distinguished a smaller set of more general strategies which served as the basis for experimental studies designed to investigate the relative effectiveness of the different strategies (see next section). Lyster and Ranta (1997) identified six basic strategies based on their analysis of the different ways teachers corrected students in an immersion classroom:

1 Explicit correction (i.e. the teacher clearly indicates that what the student said was incorrect and also provides the correct form).
2 Recasts (i.e. the teacher reformulates all or part of the student's utterance replacing the erroneous part with the correct target language form).
3 Clarification requests (i.e. the teacher indicates that a learner utterance has been misunderstood or is ill-formed in some way).
4 Metalinguistic comments (i.e. the teacher comments on or questions the well formedness of the learner's utterance without explicitly providing the correct form).

5 Elicitation (i.e. the teacher (1) elicits completion of his/her own utterance, (2) uses a question to elicit the correct form, (3) asks a student to reformulate his/her utterance).

6 Repetition (i.e. the teacher repeats the student's erroneous utterance with or without emphasis on the erroneous part).

These six strategies differ in the two key ways we discussed above: (1) they can be input-providing (i.e. they provide the learners with the correct target form) or output-prompting (i.e. they 'push' learners to self-correct their own errors) and (2) they can be implicit (i.e. the corrective force remains covert) or explicit (i.e. the corrective force is made clear to the learners). Based on these two dimensions, Ellis (2012) proposed the classification of CF strategies shown in Table 10.2. These strategies are not always used in isolation. Teachers often employ multiple strategies to correct an error.

As we have seen, the distinction between implicit and explicit strategies is important in sociocultural accounts of CF. Aljaafreh and Lantolf (1994) developed a 'regulatory scale' to reflect the extent to which the oral feedback provided by a writing tutor was implicit or explicit. This contained a number of fine gradations of implicitness/explicitness. For example, 'prompted or focused reading of the sentence that contains the error by the learner or the tutor' constitutes a high level of implicitness, whereas 'tutor provides examples of the correct pattern when other forms of help fail to produce an appropriate responsive action' (p. 471) is very explicit . An example of an intermediate strategy in the scale is 'tutor indicates the nature of the error, but does not identify the error'.

Table 10.2 A classification of CF strategies

	Implicit	*Explicit*
Input-providing	Recasts	Explicit correction
Output-prompting	Repetitions	Metalinguistic comments
	Clarification requests	Elicitation

Written CF

Three basic strategies for providing written corrective feedback have been distinguished by researchers, corresponding quite closely to those discussed in the teacher guides – direct CF, indirect CF and metalinguistic CF. There are also other possibilities for correcting written errors. Reformulation involves a native-speaker rewriting the student's text in such a way as 'to preserve as many of the writer's ideas as possible, while expressing them in his/her own words so as to make the piece sound native-like' (Cohen, 1989: 4). This differs from the three main strategies as it involves reconstructing the *whole* of the student's text rather than focusing only on the erroneous parts. It lays the burden on the learner to identify and accept or reject the *specific* changes that have been made. Another possibility (see Shintani and Ellis, 2014) involves providing learners with a detailed metalinguistic explanation of a specific type of error (e.g. errors in the use of articles) without correcting the actual errors that occur in the learners' text. This differs from other forms of CF because the feedback is not individualized (i.e. all the students can receive the same metalinguistic explanation) and thus is less time-consuming and also because it requires the learners to locate the actual errors in their text.

As we have seen, these different types of oral and written corrective feedback are potentially effective in different ways depending on the theoretical perspective adopted. In the case of both oral and written CF, a key distinction is whether learners are given the correction or whether they are prompted to correct their own errors. Written CF is invariably explicit but oral CF can be implicit or explicit. Oral CF can occur online (immediate correction) or offline (delayed correction, as when a teacher postpones correction until the learners have completed a task); in contrast, written CF typically occurs only offline. We will now examine what the research has shown about the efficacy of CF and the relative effectiveness of the different strategies.

Corrective feedback research

Research on corrective feedback has proliferated in recent years. It has investigated a number of different issues. The key ones are as follows:

1 Does CF assist L2 acquisition?
2 Which type of CF is most effective in assisting L2 acquisition?
3 Does learner self-correction following CF (i.e. uptake or, in the case of written CF, text-revision) contribute to L2 acquisition?

These questions have been addressed in research conducted within both a cognitive–interactionist and a sociocultural framework. We will consider research based on both theoretical frameworks pointing out where the conclusions reached differ. We will also draw on research that has investigated both oral and written CF.

Does CF assist L2 acquisition?

Meta-analyses of studies that have investigated the effect of CF on acquisition (e.g. Russell and Spada, 2006; Mackey and Goo, 2007; Li, 2010; Lyster and Saito, 2010) show that CF is indeed effective in assisting acquisition. Li (2010), for example, meta-analysed a total of thirty-three oral CF studies involving 1,773 learners. He reported that 'corrective feedback had a medium effect on acquisition' (p. 335). This effect was evident in tests that immediately followed the treatment involving CF and over time. However, he also reported that the effect was much stronger in studies carried out in a laboratory than in a classroom. An obvious explanation for this is that learners are more likely to pay attention to the feedback they receive in the one-on-one interactions in a laboratory context than in the teacher–class interactions typical of the classroom studies. Li also found that the effect of CF was greater in foreign language than in second language settings and suggested that this might be because learners in the former are more predisposed to pay attention to the corrections they receive. Further evidence of the importance of the salience of the feedback as a factor influencing its effectiveness can be found in another variable Li investigated: CF proved more effective in treatments that involved discrete-item practice of grammatical structures (e.g. in drills), where the feedback is intensive and more likely to be noticed, than in communicative activities. A key issue in determining whether CF has any effect is the nature of the tests used to measure learning. Li also investigated this, reporting that the effects of CF were evident in both tests that measured controlled language use and free production. Two general conclusions can be drawn from Li's meta-analysis: (1) oral CF does assist L2 acquisition and (2) it is more likely to be effective in macro- and micro-contexts where it is salient to learners.

The studies that Li investigated were all experimental and conducted within a cognitive–interactionist framework. However, studies that draw on Sociocultural Theory also provide support for CF. Aljaafreh and Lantolf (1994), in the study referred to above, showed how the degree of scaffolding provided by the tutor for a particular learner diminished over time (i.e. whereas at one time the instructor needed to correct quite explicitly to enable a learner to self-correct, at a later time more implicit correction sufficed). In accordance with how learning is conceptualized in Sociocultural Theory, they argued that this demonstrated that learning was taking place. A later study (Erlam et al., 2013), however, failed to find evidence of any systematic reduction in the graduated assistance provided by a writing tutor over time, although it did result in gains in accuracy for articles and past tense in new pieces of writing, indicating that the CF had had an effect.

To date there has been no well-designed meta-analysis of written corrective feedback studies. However, a number of individual studies suggest that it too is effective in eliminating errors from learners' written work. Many of the early studies of written CF (e.g. Fathman and Whalley, 1990; Ferris and Roberts, 2001) showed that it was effective in helping learners correct their errors in a revised version of their initial text. However, as Truscott pointed out, this does not provide evidence that written CF assists acquisition. To show this it is necessary to demonstrate that the feedback leads to improved accuracy in new pieces of writing. Truscott and Hsu (2008) reported a study that suggested that written CF did not have such an effect. A limitation of this study, however, was that there was little room for improvement in accuracy as the learners were already using the target structure with a high level of accuracy at the beginning of the study. Also, this did not investigate whether corrections directed at specific grammatical features led to gains in accuracy in those features (i.e. it only investigated the effect on overall accuracy). Bitchener and Ferris (2011) undertook a narrative review of a range of studies. This provided clear evidence of the effectiveness of written CF when this is examined in terms of accuracy in new pieces of writing. They noted that the evidence is much stronger when the feedback is directed at a single feature that is rule-based than when it is directed at correcting multiple features. However, in one of the best studies carried out to date, Van Beuningen et al. (2012), reported that unfocused written CF had an effect on the general accuracy of a range of grammatical structures.

The answer to the question that informed this section is now quite clear. Both oral and written CF can assist L2 acquisition whether this is measured in terms of a reduction in graduated assistance or in tests that measure gains in accuracy. In other words, the results of the research do not support the claims of UG-based theorists but do lend support to those of cognitive–interactionist and sociocultural theories.

Which type of CF is most effective in assisting L2 acquisition?

The two theoretical frameworks that support a role for CF have taken very different positions regarding this issue. Research conducted within a cognitive–interactionist framework has investigated the two dimensions of CF shown in Table 10.2 (i.e. input-providing vs output-prompting and implicit vs explicit CF). The underlying assumption is that not all types of CF are equally effective and, therefore, the primary goal of CF research should be to establish which type works best. In contrast, research conducted within a sociocultural framework is based on the assumption that for CF to be effective it needs to be systematically tailored to the individual learner's developmental level, in order to jointly construct a zone of proximal development. From this perspective there is no one type of CF that will work best. We will consider a number of key studies conducted in both frameworks.

Lyster (2004) investigated 148 (grade 5) 10–11 year olds in a French immersion programme focusing on grammatical gender (i.e. choice of article with nouns). One experimental group received recasts and another prompts. There was also a control group that received no CF. All three groups also received explicit instruction in the target feature. A battery of oral and written tests was used to measure the effect of CF on acquisition, which was operationalized as gains in accuracy. The results favoured the group receiving prompts. Only this group outperformed the control in all the post-tests. However, the recasts group outperformed the control group in most of the tests. Also, there were no statistical differences between the recast and the prompt groups. One reason for this might be because both the experimental groups had received explicit instruction prior to CF. Lyster's study led to a number of other studies (e.g. Ammar and Spada, 2006; Yang and Lyster, 2010), comparing recasts and prompts which produced similar results. That is, both types of feedback benefited acquisition with prompts generally proving more effective than recasts (see also Lyster and Saito's (2010) meta-analysis of the classroom-based studies).

However, a number of caveats are in order. First, recasts constitute a single corrective strategy whereas prompts include four different strategies (i.e.

clarification requests, repetition of error, elicitation and metalinguistic clues). It is possible that the greater effect found for prompts is simply because many strategies are more effective than one strategy – a view compatible with Sociocultural Theory. Also, prompts include a mixture of implicit and explicit strategies, so it is possible that they are more effective not because they elicit self-correction but because they are more salient. Third, the effects of the two types of CF are likely to be mediated by a number of factors such as the instructional tenor of the classroom (i.e. whether it is primarily meaning or form-focused), the proficiency level of the learners, and the nature of the target feature (i.e. whether it is rule-based or item-based). For example, Lyster and Mori (2006) reported that recasts were more effective in an instructional context, where the learners were more inclined to pay attention to form and prompts more effective in a meaning-focused immersion context. Also, Yang and Lyster (2010) found that while prompts were more beneficial for regular past tense, both types of CF were equally effective for irregular past tense.

To investigate whether the advantage reported for prompts was because they included explicit types of CF, Mifka-Profozic (2012) carried out a study that compared the effects of recasts and just one implicit prompt (requests for clarification) on the acquisition of two French verb forms (*passé composé* and *imparfait*) by fifty high school students in New Zealand. She found that the learners who received recasts demonstrated significantly greater levels of post-treatment accuracy than the learners in a control group. Also, in some of the comparisons, the recasts group demonstrated significantly higher levels of acquisition than the prompts group. This study suggests that the reason for the apparent superiority of prompts in previous studies may lie in their explicitness rather than because they push learners to self-correct. Implicit prompts may be less effective than implicit recasts.

Studies that have investigated the relative effects of implicit and explicit CF have typically compared recasts (as an implicit strategy) with one or more types of explicit feedback (e.g. metalinguistic comments). A good example of such a study is Ellis et al. (2006). This investigated these two types of CF with thirty-four low-intermediate adult ESL students. The CF groups performed two 30-minute communicative tasks and received feedback on the errors they made in the use of regular past tense-*ed*. A feature of this study is that it attempted to measure acquisition in terms of both implicit knowledge (measured by means of an oral imitation test) and explicit knowledge (measured by means of an untimed grammaticality judgement test and a metalinguistic knowledge test). Ellis et al. first established that the frequency of the feedback provided to the learners in the two experimental groups was roughly equivalent. The results showed that the group receiving a repetition of an incorrect verb form followed by a metalinguistic comment outperformed both the control group and the recasts group in both the oral imitation test and the untimed grammaticality judgement test, although the differences only reached statistical significance in the delayed post-tests. Li's (2010) meta-analysis also found that explicit CF worked better than implicit CF. However, he also reported that implicit CF proved to be more effective in post-tests completed a long time after the instruction. This was because its effects increased over time whereas those of explicit CF did not change. Ellis et al.'s study did not investigate this possibility as their post-test was administered only two weeks after the treatment.

It should be noted, however, that recasts (the implicit CF strategy most commonly investigated) do not really constitute a single type of CF but vary considerably in how implicit or explicit they are and that the more explicit types of recasts have been shown more likely to promote learning (Loewen and Philp, 2006). Arguably, the recasts investigated by Mifka-Profozic (2012) were of the more explicit kind.

The debate about the relative efficacy of different types of CF is ongoing. Goo and Mackey (2013) critiqued the design of studies such as those by Lyster (2004) and Ellis et al. (2006) that have compared recasts and prompts and concluded that 'the case against recasts' is based on 'a shaky foundation'. They argued that recasts and prompts are 'apples' and 'oranges' and thus should not be compared. Lyster and Ranta (2013) responded to Goo and Mackey's article by pointing out that from a pedagogic perspective teachers do need to know 'when apples are a better choice than oranges'. They argued that CF research needs to be conducted with the needs of teachers (not just researchers) in mind and concluded that teachers' practice needs to be informed by empirical evidence from CF comparison studies. They also noted that in their own work with teachers they emphasize the need for the use of a variety of CF strategies rather than relying on recasts, which constitute the dominant type of CF strategy in most instructional contexts (Lyster and Ranta, 1997).

The case for applying multiple strategies to address errors has been made by sociocultural theorists, as in the study by Aljaafreh and Lantolf (1994) referred to above. From this perspective there is no one 'best' way of correcting errors. Aljaafreh and Lantolf proposed a number of general principles governing the effectiveness of feedback: (1) it must be graduated (i.e. no more help than is necessary is provided at any single time), (2) it must be contingent (i.e. it must reflect actual need and be removed when the learner demonstrates an ability to function independently) and (3) it is dialogic (i.e. it involves dynamic assessment of a learner's zone of proximal development). Clearly, conducting feedback in accordance with such principles requires considerable skill on the part of the teacher and, as Lantolf and Aljaafreh (1995) noted, the tutor they investigated was not always successful in fine-tuning his assistance to the learners' level of development.

A limitation of Aljaafreh and Lantolf's study is that it did not provide any evidence that the graduated assistance finally enabled learners to use those forms independently (i.e. that 'development' had taken place). However, Nassaji and Swain (2000) did attempt this. They investigated two Korean learners of English. One learner was provided with graduated assistance within her ZPD (i.e. the tutor systematically worked through Aljaafreh and Lantolf's scale to negotiate the feedback supplied) while the other learner was given only random help (i.e. the tutor was supplied with a random list of correcting strategies drawn from Aljaafreh and Lantolf's regulatory scale). Nassaji and Swain reported that providing feedback within the learner's ZPD was more effective in: (1) helping the learner to arrive at the correct form during the feedback session, (2) enabling the learner to arrive at the correct form with much less explicit assistance in subsequent sessions, and (3) enabling the learner to use the correct form unassisted in a post-test. This study provides some support for graduated CF although it should be noted that providing 'random feedback' is highly unnatural (as the tutor involved in this study observed) and thus is very unlikely to occur in actual teaching.

A comparison study that teachers might view as more pedagogically relevant is one that examines the relative effects of graduated assistance (which is quite time-consuming) and direct explicit feedback (which can be provided quickly and simply). Erlam et al. (2013) reported such a study. The results showed that the graduated feedback was much more successful in eliciting self-correction from the learners than the explicit correction. However, this study found no evidence of any systematic reduction in the explicitness of the teacher's strategies over time in the graduated feedback and in this respect differed from Aljaafreh and Lantolf's findings. Erlam et al. also investigated whether there was any difference in the effect of the two CF approaches on the learners' use of two target features (past tense and articles) in a new piece of writing. They reported no difference for past tense but found that graduated feedback was more effective than explicit feedback for learning articles. This study, then, suggests that the relative effectiveness of the two types of instruction might depend on the nature of structure being corrected (i.e. whether there is a clear rule of thumb or not).

We will turn now to consider briefly the research on written CF. Many of the early studies suffered from a variety of methodological flaws (e.g. they did not include control groups or pre-treatment measures of learners' ability to use the features targeted by the CF). Truscott (1996) reviewed these studies and concluded, with justification, that they failed to demonstrate that any type of written CF had any effect on learning. Later studies, however, remedied these defects by using the same kinds of design used in oral CF research. The studies examined two issues – the relative effect of direct as opposed to indirect CF and of unfocused as opposed to focused CF. Bitchener and Ferris (2011) concluded from their review of written CF studies that direct CF is more effective than indirect CF. For example, Van Beuningen et al. (2012) reported that whereas direct and indirect CF in conjunction with the opportunity to revise were equally effective for non-grammatical errors, only the direct CF resulted in significant gains in grammatical accuracy in new pieces of writing. This study investigated unfocused CF. Other studies (e.g. Bitchener and Knoch, 2009) have shown that focused CF is effective even if it involves only a single treatment, especially if it is directed at 'treatable' grammatical features (i.e. those that involve a clear rule of thumb). Few studies have compared unfocused and focused CF to date. However, Farrokhi and Sattarpour (2012) reported that focused CF was more effective than unfocused CF for both high- and low-proficiency adult Iranian EFL learners in improving accuracy in articles in narratives. As with oral CF, a variety of factors are likely to mediate the effects of these different types of written CF. One obvious variable is the extent to which learners attend to the feedback they have been given. As Guénette (2007) argued, students 'have to notice the feedback and be given ample opportunities to apply the corrections' (p. 52).

Does learner self-correction following CF (i.e. uptake) contribute to L2 acquisition?

Guénette's observation for written CF is equally applicable to oral CF. For either oral or written CF to be effective, learners need to pay attention to the corrections they have received. A number of studies have explored to what extent learners do notice oral corrections. Mackey (2006), for example, investigated the relationships between implicit corrective feedback (i.e. recasts and clarification requests), noticing and acquisition resulting from a task-based lesson. The target structures were questions, plurals and past-tense. Data on noticing were collected by means of learning journals filled out during class time, oral stimulated recall protocols, written responses in the learners' L1 to a focused question about the nature of the classroom activities, and written responses in English to a questionnaire. Measures of learners' use of the target structures were obtained from oral tasks administered as a pre-test and a post-test. The results indicated a higher level of noticing in a group that received CF than in a group that performed the task without CF. However, the level of noticing varied according to target structure, with higher levels evident for questions forms, much lower levels for past tense, and intermediate levels for plurals. Eighty-three per cent of the learners who reported noticing question forms also developed in their ability to form questions. However, the relationship between noticing and the other two target features was not established. This study showed that implicit corrective feedback is noticed by learners working on a task in a classroom context and that for some structures at least there is a relationship between noticing and acquisition. Arguably, however, learners are more likely to notice corrections when these are more explicit. This might be one reason why explicit CF has been found more effective than implicit CF for morphological features such as regular past tense, as in Ellis et al.'s study.

Mackey's study obtained evidence about noticing by eliciting self-reports from learners. Alternative evidence of noticing can be obtained by examining whether learners successfully self-correct an error following CF (i.e. whether 'uptake with repair' occurs). In Extract 1 on p. 260, the student does not respond to the recast by self-correcting, so it is impossible to tell whether noticing did or did not occur. In Extract 2, however, repair does occur in response to the clarification request, indicating that this learner did attend to the error. Some researchers have argued that successful uptake is important for acquisition. That is, they have suggested that when learners self-correct their errors, they are more likely to benefit from CF.

This is the position taken by Lyster. His research (e.g. Lyster and Ranta, 1997) showed that learner repair of lexical and grammatical errors was more likely after elicitations, requests for clarification, and metalinguistic clues (i.e. prompts) than other types of CF, in particular recasts. One reason why repair does not occur after recasts is because teachers often continue without giving students a chance to respond, as Oliver's (2000) study of recasts in an ESL classroom showed. However, there can also be marked differences in the level of uptake with repair in different classroom contexts. Lyster and Mori (2006) reported that the learners in a Japanese immersion programme in the US were more likely to repair their errors following recasts than learners in a French immersion programme in Canada and suggested that this was because there was a greater emphasis on accurate oral production and repetition in the former.

The importance of learners self-correcting their errors for acquisition, however, is a matter of controversy. Some researchers (e.g. Long, 2006) argued that recasts assist learning by inducing learners to notice the correction and that whether they subsequently uptake the correction is immaterial. Other researchers (e.g. Lyster, 2004) draw on skill-learning theory to argue that uptake of the correction is important for acquisition (see section above on cognitive–interactionist theories that have informed CF research). Lyster argued that the reason why prompts are more effective than recasts is precisely because they induce learners to self-correct. Sociocultural Theory also emphasizes the need for learner self-correction as the act of producing the correct form is viewed as evidence of learning. There is some evidence to show that uptake with repair assists learning. Loewen (2005) examined the relationship between corrective feedback episodes where uptake occurred in ESL lessons and their acquisition of those forms that had been corrected, in tailor-made tests administered one or two days after the lessons or two weeks later. He reported that successful uptake predicted the learners' test scores (i.e. learners who had corrected their errors during the lesson were more likely to demonstrate knowledge of the correct forms in the tests). A reasonable conclusion is that learners can benefit from oral CF even if they do not repair their errors but when they do, 'deeper processing' may occur and so also assist learning.

Immediate uptake is, of course, unlikely to occur in the case of written CF. However, there is an equivalent to uptake if learners are given the chance to revise an initial piece of writing following CF. In a carefully designed study, Chandler (2003) compared indirect CF plus the opportunity to revise with indirect CF where there was no opportunity to revise. Chandler reported that accuracy improved from the first to the fifth piece of writing significantly more in the group that was required to correct their errors, than in the group that just received indication of their errors. This study then suggests that asking learners to revise assists learning. In contrast, Van Beuningen et al.'s (2012) study found the indirect feedback plus revision did not result in improved accuracy in a new piece of writing although direct CF plus revision did. The crucial factor seems to be whether learners are able to use the feedback to correct their errors when revising and this is more likely to occur when the feedback is direct (i.e. they are provided with the corrections). A further factor may be the extent to which learners make use of the corrections they receive to develop metalinguistic understanding of the nature of the error and why it was corrected. Shintani and Ellis (2013) found that the low-intermediate level learners they investigated were not able to work out the rule for the use of indefinite articles (the feature corrected) when they revised.

Concluding comments

Ellis (2010a) proposed a framework for investigating CF. This involved considering:

1 The different types of CF.
2 The role played by individual learner factors in mediating the effects of CF.
3 The role played by contextual factors in mediating the effects of CF.
4 The extent to which learners engage with the CF (i.e. how they respond to it).
5 Learning outcomes (i.e. the effect CF has on learning).

By and large, the research has focused on the relationship between (1) and (5). It has shown that CF is effective in promoting learning. There is considerable controversy, however, regarding which type is most effective, with some researchers arguing that input-providing CF in the form of recasts (or in the case of writing, direct CF) is more effective than output-prompting CF, others claiming that what matters is how explicit the CF is, and still others drawing on Sociocultural Theory to claim that for CF to be effective it needs to be fine-tuned to the learner's level of development. We have seen that there is evidence to support all these positions. There has been much less attention to (2) and (3), although we have seen that individual factors such as the learners' level of proficiency do influence the effect that CF has on learning and that contextual factors such as whether the instruction is 'experiential' or 'analytic' (Stern, 1990) in nature also plays a role. In (4), investigation has been in terms of learners' uptake of corrections with the evidence suggesting that although it is not essential that learners repair their errors, it is helpful. A key issue regarding (5) is how the learning resulting from CF is measured. Here there is major difference between cognitive–interactionist research, which has used post-tests, and sociocultural research, which has sought for evidence of learning within corrective feedback episodes. In the case of the former, there is also the issue of whether the tests elicit constrained–constructed responses or free-constructed responses (Norris and Ortega, 2000). The results of the research suggest it benefits both.

Re-examining the role of corrective feedback in language pedagogy

A general concern of teachers, as reflected in the teacher guides, is that corrective feedback can have a negative effect on learners – for example, by increasing anxiety. We have seen that in SLA the affective aspect of CF has received little attention. The focus of the research we examined in the previous section was on the cognitive aspects of CF. The negative impact of CF on learners may have been overestimated in the pedagogic literature as learners typically state that they want to be corrected. This is not really surprising. Learners are in a classroom to learn a language and believe that having their errors corrected will help them to achieve this. However, teachers do need to monitor the extent to which their corrective feedback causes individual learners anxiety and adjust their feedback accordingly. Research has shown that teachers are often inconsistent in their practice of correcting learners – for example correcting some learners but not others. As Allwright (1975) pointed out, such inconsistency may reflect teachers' natural inclination to take account of individual differences in learners and to try to balance their cognitive and affective needs.

We saw that the teacher guides have addressed five key questions. We will now reconsider the answers that they gave to these questions in the light of the SLA research.

Should learners' errors be corrected?

The guides all acknowledge the need for teachers to correct learners' oral errors. This receives clear support from the SLA research, which has shown that both oral and written CF are effective in improving learners' accuracy. Ur (1996), while agreeing that correction is helpful, felt that it would be better for teachers to focus on avoiding errors rather than correcting them. From an SLA perspective this is doubtful. Learners are bound to make errors no matter what approach teachers adopt and certain types of error (i.e. those where positive evidence alone is not sufficient to ensure acquisition of the target form) may only be eliminated with the help of negative evidence. An approach that combines input providing positive evidence with corrective feedback is most likely to promote acquisition.

In one respect, there is a clear difference in the pedagogic position adopted in many of the guides and the research evidence. Some of the guides recommend making a clear distinction between accuracy-oriented and fluency-oriented instruction and claim that CF is desirable in the former but not in the latter as it leads to learners focusing on form rather than on meaning. Cognitive–interactionist theories, however, claim that CF is likely to be more effective if it occurs in response to learners' attempts to communicate as this is more likely to ensure transfer-appropriate learning. That is, the corrections are more likely to result in the implicit knowledge needed to engage in fluent natural language use. A number of studies (e.g. Lyster, 2004; Ellis et al., 2006) have shown that correcting learners while they are performing communicative tasks is effective. Nor is there any basis in the research for Scrivener's (2005) suggestion that teachers should only deploy 'unobtrusive immediate correction' in fluency work. For the feedback to work it has to be seen as corrective by the learners.

The guides also acknowledge the need for written CF. In this respect, they contradict Truscott's claims that written CF cannot contribute to learners' 'genuine knowledge of language' and thus will have no influence on accuracy in new pieces of writing. They are supported, however, by a number of recent studies that have shown that both focused and unfocused written CF can lead to significant improvements in accuracy in new pieces of writing. Thus, as with oral CF, there is a clear case for correcting learners' written errors.

When should learner errors be corrected?

There is much less consensus in language pedagogy about whether correction should be immediate or be delayed. Some teacher educators recommend delaying correction in fluency work until learners have completed an activity, while approving of immediate correction in accuracy work. But, as we have just seen, there is no basis for this in cognitive–interactionist theories. Sociocultural Theory also supports scaffolding learners' self-correction in communicative interactions.

However, there is to date no research that has compared the relative effects of the timing of CF. Just about all the studies to date have investigated online oral CF. Rolin-Ianziti (2010) reported a descriptive study of delayed oral CF carried out by teachers of L2 French following a role-play activity. The teachers took note of the learners' errors and then reviewed them later. This occurred in two ways. One teacher simply provided the corrections while another attempted to elicit correction from the students and only provided the correction if the students failed to self-correct. Rolin-Ianziti drew on Sociocultural Theory to argue that the second approach was likely to be more effective but offered no evidence to support this claim.

There are grounds for believing that delayed CF can assist learning, however. Written CF is invariably delayed and, as we have seen, it has been shown to contribute to improved accuracy in new pieces of writing. It is possible that immediate and delayed CF contribute to acquisition in different ways. Immediate CF may benefit the development of learners' procedural knowledge whereas delayed CF is perhaps more likely to foster metalinguistic understanding if learners reflect on the corrections they receive. Clearly, though, there is a need for more research investigating whether delayed CF is effective, what kind of knowledge it fosters, and, importantly, whether it is more effective than immediate CF.

Which errors should be corrected?

The various pedagogic proposals for deciding which errors to correct are hard to implement. It is unlikely that teachers will be able to distinguish between 'errors' and 'mistakes' in a consistent way, even in written CF. Burt's suggestion that teachers should focus on 'global' rather than 'local' errors receives some support from Long's Interaction Hypothesis (see Chapter 8). This views CF as arising in the negotiation of meaning when a genuine communicative problem arises. But there is plenty of evidence to suggest that CF is effective when it involves negotiation of form rather than meaning. In other words, correction assists acquisition even if there is no 'global' problem. The research has also shown that CF directed at 'local' errors can work. For example, both Ellis et al. (2006) and Lyster and Saito (2010) reported that CF resulted in learners acquiring past tense-*ed*. These studies do lend some support to Krashen's (1982) contention that CF should only be directed at grammatical features that are 'simple' and 'portable'. Past tense-*ed* is just such a feature. Many of the studies that reported an effect for written CF have also investigated what Ferris called 'treatable' features (e.g. the use of the definite and indefinite article for first and anaphoric reference). However, precisely what constitutes a 'simple' and 'portable' rule is far from clear. As we noted in Chapter 4, there is no widely accepted theory of grammatical complexity to help teachers or researchers decide which errors are treatable, and even if careful selection of errors were possible in written correction, it would be well nigh impossible in online oral correction.

There is, however, another way in which selection of errors for correction might be approached. Teachers could elect to adopt a 'focused approach' (i.e. predetermine the errors they will correct). In the case of a lesson that is directed at a specific linguistic feature, teachers could correct errors in that feature but ignore others (as Ur recommended). Alternatively, teachers could identify a specific feature that is clearly causing problems to learners and focus correction on that. Focused correction is practical and has been shown to be effective for addressing errors in both oral and written production. The research that has investigated oral CF has almost invariably investigated its effect on a specific, predetermined linguistic feature. Much of the recent written CF research has also been of the focused kind.

A possible objection to a focused approach is that it does not accord with normal pedagogic practice. Van Beuningen et al. (2012), for example, argued against it on the grounds that 'a teacher's purpose in correcting his/her pupils written work is to improve accuracy in general, not just the use of one grammatical feature' (p. 6). A similar argument could be made against focused oral CF. However, Van Beuningen et al.'s criticism can be addressed if teachers vary the focus in different lessons, thus achieving a wide coverage over time. One possibility might be 'tiered feedback' (i.e. feedback that begins by focusing on one grammatical feature and then adds an additional feature each time feedback is given). Andersen (2010) investigated this but found that the effectiveness of the feedback decreased as the number of corrected features increased. Overall, focused CF constitutes the most practical and useful basis for selecting which errors to correct.

How should errors be corrected?

One of the clear differences between the pedagogic treatment of error and the SLA research is that the strategies that can be used to correct errors are simply listed in the former but they are classified in the latter. In the guides, no theoretical justification is given for the choice of strategy. In SLA, the classification of strategies into two key dimensions (i.e. input-providing vs output-prompting and implicit vs explicit) is theoretically driven. Cognitive–interactionist theories differ in the importance they attach to input-providing CF (e.g. recasts) and output-prompting CF (e.g. elicitation or clarification requests). They also differ in the value they attach to implicit as opposed to explicit types of correction. The SLA research that has drawn on these theories has sought to identify which type of strategy is most likely to foster learning. Research based on Sociocultural Theory has also drawn on the implicit/explicit distinction to propose that feedback needs to be graduated to assure that the CF is tailored to the needs of individual learners.

The SLA research that has investigated oral CF has produced mixed results. It is clear that strategies relating to both of the two key dimensions can lead to acquisition when this is measured in terms of gains in accuracy. A general conclusion, therefore, might be that teachers should use a range of strategies – a view promulgated by the guides. However, it is also possible to identify a number of general principles that can guide the implementation of CF:

- Aim to provide intensive CF. A single correction directed at a linguistic feature cannot be expected to have much effect on learning. An advantage of focused CF is that it is intensive.
- For CF to be effective, learners need to recognize the corrective force of the CF. Explicitness is important.
- The extent to which learners are likely to identify CF as corrective varies according to context. In a fluency-oriented instructional context, learners may fail to recognize a recast as corrective as they are primarily focused on meaning. In an accuracy-oriented context, however, they are more likely to treat a teacher's recast as corrective. This suggests that teachers need to vary how they correct according to instructional context. In a communicative activity, brief explicit forms of correction may be needed. In a grammar exercise, recasts can be effective.
- Combine input-providing and output-prompting CF strategies. These two types of strategies cater to different senses of 'acquisition' (i.e. learning a 'new' form vs increasing control over an 'old' form). However, it is not practical to expect teachers to know whether the particular errors they are correcting involve a new or an old form and, in any case, what is 'old' for one student in the class may be 'new' for another. A possible solution to this problem might be to combine an output-prompting with an input-providing strategy. That is, first prompt learners to self-correct and then, if that fails, provide the correction. This can be achieved in various ways – for example, by means of 'corrective recasts'. Another way might be to begin with an elicitation and then move on to an explicit correction. This approach to combining strategies is *principled* and in this respect differs from the guides' recommendation that teachers should simply deploy a variety of strategies.
- Encourage uptake with repair. Learning can take place without uptake, providing learners notice the correction. But inducing learners to produce

the correct form may lead to deeper processing. In this respect, the SLA research lends support to the recommendation of the guides which emphasize the need to ensure learners successfully uptake the correction.

These principles are based on a cognitive–interactionist view of CF. Sociocultural Theory emphasizes the need for 'graduated assistance'. In the research based on this theory, this has been accomplished through one-on-one interactions between an expert (the teacher) and a novice (the learner). This may constitute a highly effective way of conducting CF in such a context – especially for those features such as articles that pose substantial learning problems for students – but it is not clear how 'graduated assistance' can be achieved in whole classes. In this respect, a more practical way is to combine strategies in the ways suggested above.

The guides demonstrate a clear preference for indirect written CF (see, e.g. Brumfit's 1977 model) in order to develop writers' autonomous ability to self-edit. The research, however, points to the advantage of direct CF where grammatical accuracy is concerned (e.g. Van Beuningen et al., 2012) and there would seem no reason why such a strategy cannot also help to foster learners' independent editing capacity over time. Combining CF with the opportunity for learners to revise their writing has also been found to promote learning. An important pedagogic issue is the laborious nature of written CF if the teacher corrects each student's writing. One way of addressing this problem might be to forego written CF in favour of explicit instruction directed at a specific type of error and conducted with the whole class as in Shintani and Ellis (2014).

Who should do the correcting?

Schegloff et al. (1977) distinguished different types of repair in conversations in terms of who initiates the repair (the speaker or the hearer) and who carries it out. The four basic types they found were: (1) self-initiated self-repair, (2) self-initiated other repair, (3) other-initiated self-repair and (4) other initiated-other repair. In the case of CF, as we have defined it in this chapter, repair is typically initiated by the teacher, so the choice lies between (3) and (4). The guides express a clear preference for (3) (i.e. eliciting a self-repair from the students). SLA researchers disagree about which type of repair is most effective. Prompts and indirect CF will result in type (3) repair work. However, recasts and direct CF involve type (4) repair work (i.e. the repair is both initiated and completed by the teacher). We have seen that research has shown both types of repair work to be effective, although in the case of writing, direct CF has been shown to be superior. The guides possibly overemphasize the merits of type (3) repair work. There is, perhaps, no need for teachers to be reluctant to 'other-correct'. However, as we noted, it is possible to conduct oral CF in a way that combines an opportunity for student self-correction with teacher-correction. Sociocultural Theory also proposes a combined approach by recommending that teachers first try to elicit student self-correction and only resort to providing the correct form if necessary.

Another way of accomplishing type (4) repair is by the teacher nominating another student to 'other-repair'. This is also favoured in many of the guides, especially in peer-correction of writing errors. However, this is not an option that SLA researchers have investigated. One reason for this is that it has been found to occur only rarely in classroom interaction (Seedhouse, 2004).

Conclusion

CF is clearly an aspect of instruction where the concerns of teachers and interests of SLA researchers coincide and, as such, constitutes an ideal construct for examining the contribution that SLA can make to language pedagogy. Reflecting this common concern, Ellis (2009) proposed a set of general guidelines for conducting CF, basing these on his review of the SLA research. We conclude this chapter with a revised version of these guidelines:

1   CF serves as one the major ways in which teachers can focus on form and thus accords with Principle 3 (Chapter 1) – 'Instruction needs to ensure that learners focus on form'. Research has shown that CF (both oral and written) works and so teachers should not be afraid to correct students' errors. The cognitive advantages of CF outweigh the possible affective disadvantages.
2   Both 'errors' and 'mistakes' need correcting if the purpose is to promote interlanguage development. Also, both 'global' and 'local' errors should be corrected.
3   The effectiveness of CF depends on the learners' readiness to acquire the feature. Thus, like explicit instruction (see Chapter 4), it will not always work. CF that is intensive, as in focused CF, is more likely to prove effective than extensive CF, as in unfocused CF.
4   CF is beneficial in both accuracy-based work based on a structure-of-the-day approach and in fluency work based on the performance of communicative tasks.
5   Both immediate and delayed CF may be beneficial. To date there is no clear evidence that one is superior to the other, so teachers need to experiment with the timing of oral CF. Given that written CF is delayed and has been shown to be effective, delaying feedback is a worthwhile option.
6   Teachers should not attempt to hide the corrective force of their CF moves from the learners. Learners need to know they are being corrected. However, while the corrective force needs to be explicit, it is not always necessary to use direct, explicit correction. Even recasts can be explicit.
7   There is no 'best' way of conducting oral CF. An approach that combines opportunities for learners to self-correct their errors followed if necessary by teacher correction (e.g. a combination of output-prompting and input-providing CF) accords with both the 'best practice' views of teacher educators and the findings of cognitive–interactionist and sociocultural SLA research.

8 In the case of written CF, the weight of the available evidence suggests that direct correction is more effective than indirect correction. However, if the learners have explicit knowledge of the feature, indirect CF may assist them to establish greater control over it.

9 Teachers need not be wary of other-initiated/other repair (i.e. CF initiated and completed by the teacher). However, leaving time for learner uptake of the correction (or in the case of writing for revision) can assist learning.

These guidelines are unlikely to satisfy all SLA researchers or teacher educators. Therefore, as Ellis (2009) argued, they are best viewed as a set of propositions that teacher educators and teachers can reflect on and debate. This is an approach to the use of SLA research that we will consider further in the final chapter of this book.

DISCUSSION QUESTIONS

1. The teacher guides emphasize the importance of 'positive feedback'. Do you agree? Can positive feedback aid acquisition? How?

2. Ur (1996) argued that it is better to try to prevent errors rather than correcting them. Do you agree? To what extent is it possible to prevent learners making errors? (You might like to refer back to the section on learner errors in Chapter 3.)

3. The teacher guides all propose that errors should be corrected in accuracy work but not in fluency work. What arguments support this position? Do you agree with them?

4. To what extent do you think teachers should correct learner errors in written work?

5. Various proposals have been made for deciding *which* errors to correct. Review these proposals. To what extent are they practical? Can you think of any other basis for selecting which errors to correct?

6. The teacher guides recommend that learners should be encouraged to correct their own errors rather than the teacher correcting them. Do you agree? Can you see any problems with this strategy?

7. Which of the three general strategies for correcting errors in writing (direct, indirect, metalinguistic) do you favour? Why?

8. There is a mismatch between the approach to error correction generally favoured by teachers and by learners. What is this mismatch? Do you think teachers should take more account of how learners already wish to be corrected?

9. Describe the approach to corrective feedback you would take if you were to base it on each of these theories of L2 acquisition:
    a. UG-based theory
    b. Cognitive–interactionist theories
    c. Sociocultural Theory.

10. Explain the difference between:
    a. Implicit and explicit corrective feedback
    b. Input-providing and output-prompting corrective feedback.

11. Use the results of the research referred to in this chapter to consider the potential for acquisition of each type of the four main types of corrective feedback.
12. How important for acquisition is it that learners 'uptake' the corrective feedback they receive?
13. In what ways are oral and written CF different?
14. In what ways do the findings of the corrective feedback research conflict with the recommendations found in the teacher guides?
15. Finally, formulate your own corrective feedback policy by addressing the five key questions initially posed by Hendrickson (1978).

Part IV

Learner differences

Any class of students is made up of individuals who differ in a variety of ways – for example, in the nature of their language aptitude, in the nature and strength of their motivation to learn, in how they cope affectively with the demands of performing in an L2 in a classroom setting, in their beliefs about how best to learn a language and in the learning strategies they employ. The importance of taking individual differences into account is reflected in Principle 9 of Instructed Language Learning (see Chapter 1) and is widely acknowledged in discussions of language pedagogy, as reflected in Harmer's (2007) comment:

> The moment we realise that a class is composed of individuals (rather than some kind of unified whole), we have to start thinking about how to respond to these students individually so that while we may frequently teach the group as a whole, we will also, in different ways, pay attention to the different identities we are faced with.
>
> (p. 85)

The challenge that teachers face is how they can effectively take account of student diversity. In the next section we will examine some of the ways of achieving this.

There is a long and rich tradition of research into individual learner differences in SLA. Learner factors such as motivation and language aptitude received attention some time before researchers began to investigate the process of L2 acquisition. However, as the previous chapters have shown, mainstream SLA focuses mainly on the universal aspects of L2 acquisition (i.e. the order and sequence of acquisition, the role of input and interaction and corrective feedback, and the effect of explicit instruction on learning). While research into individual learner factors has continued, it often figures as a separate strand of SLA, largely unrelated to the psycholinguistic or sociocultural theories of learning that inform research in SLA. It has typically probed the strength of the relationship between specific individual factors and learning outcomes (e.g. language proficiency) in order to identify which factors are important for successful learning. More recently, however, researchers have started to consider how individual learner factors impact on the social and cognitive processes involved in acquiring an L2. In other words, research into individual learner differences is now more clearly aligned with research focusing on the process of L2 learning.

11 Catering for learner differences through instruction

Individual difference factors

In this chapter we will make reference to a number of individual difference factors that have figured both in the language pedagogy literature and in SLA research. One of these is the learners' starting age. This mainly influences the rate of learning and ultimate attainment. Other factors are psychological in nature. Table 11.1 provides definitions and brief comments on each of the main psychological factors. They can be classified into those that represent more or less permanent and stable aspects of learners (e.g. intelligence, language aptitude, working memory and personality) and those that are mutable, dynamic and situated (e.g. motivation and anxiety). This distinction is potentially an important one for language pedagogy as it encapsulates two very different ways in which teachers can take account of individual differences. In the case of the permanent/stable factors, they will need to find ways of adjusting their teaching. Teachers cannot hope to change learners' aptitude or personality, at least in the short term, so they must accommodate their teaching to take account of how their learners differ. In the case of the mutable/dynamic factors, however, they can try to modify them in order to increase their impact on learning. For example, teachers can try to enhance learners' motivation or reduce the debilitating effect of language anxiety. There is a final category of factors consisting of learner beliefs and learning strategies. These function as mediating variables. That is, they influence the effect that other factors have on learning. Language aptitude or learning style, for example, can shape the beliefs learners hold about how to learn a language and the specific actions (strategies) that they employ to try to achieve their goals.

Individual learner differences in language pedagogy

A number of individual learner factors are recognized and discussed in the pedagogic literature. Nunan (1991) included a chapter entitled 'Focus on the Learner' in which he considered learning styles and strategies. He offered a lengthy discussion of the 'good language learner'. However, he provides only the briefest of comments about motivation in a list of 'things that helped learning the most'. Scarcella and Oxford (1992) included a chapter that discussed motivation and attitudes, anxiety, self-esteem, tolerance of ambiguity, and risk-taking,

Table 11.1 Psychological factors resulting in individual differences in language learning

Factor	Definition and commentary
Intelligence	Intelligence is 'a general sort of aptitude that is not limited to a specific performance area but is transferable to many sorts of performance' (Dörnyei, 2005: 32). According to this view, intelligence constitutes a single factor. However, an alternative theory posits multiple intelligences (e.g. mathematical intelligence, spatial intelligence and linguistic intelligence).
Language aptitude	Language aptitude is the special ability for learning an L2. It is considered to be separate from the general ability to master academic skills (i.e. *intelligence*). Language aptitude has been theorized as involving a number of distinct abilities – phonemic coding ability, grammatical sensitivity, inductive language-learning ability and rote-learning ability (Carroll, 1965).
Working memory	Working memory is a psychological term that refers to those mental functions responsible for storing and manipulating information temporarily. A popular model of working memory (Baddeley, 2003) distinguishes four subcomponents: (1) the central executive that controls attention, (2) the visuospatial sketchpad that stores and rehearses visual information, (3) the phonological loop that stores and rehearses oral information and (4) the episodic buffer that combines information from different sources. Working memory is now viewed as an important component of language aptitude.
Personality	Personality is generally conceived of as composed of a series of traits such as extraversion/introversion and neuroticism/stability. An array of different personality characteristics such as self-esteem, tolerance of ambiguity and risk-taking have been claimed to be significant in language learning (Long and Larsen-Freeman, 1991).
Learning style	Learning style refers to the characteristic ways in which individuals orientate to problem solving. It reflects 'the totality of psychological functioning' (Willing, 1987) involving affective as well as cognitive preferences. A variety of learning styles have been considered relevant to language learning (e.g. sensory preferences, inductive vs deductive, synthetic vs analytic).
Motivation	Motivation is a complex construct that involves the reasons or goals learners have for learning an L2, the effort they put into learning and the attributes they form as a result of their attempts to learn. Various theories of the role played by motivation in L2 learning have been proposed. In one theory of motivation, Gardner and Lambert (1972) distinguished 'instrumental' and 'integrative motivation'. Another key distinction is between extrinsic and intrinsic motivation. Recently Dörnyei (2005) has proposed a theory that relates motivation to the role that learners see the L2 playing in their personal identity.
Language anxiety	Different types of anxiety have been identified: (1) trait anxiety (a characteristic of a learner's personality), (2) state anxiety (apprehension that is experienced at a particular moment in response to a definite situation) and (3) situation-specific anxiety (the anxiety aroused by a particular type of situation). Language anxiety is seen as a specific type of situation-specific anxiety. It can be facilitating (i.e. have a positive effect on L2 acquisition) but is generally seen as debilitating (i.e. have a negative effect). A major cause of language anxiety is being required to communicate orally in front of the whole class.

Learner beliefs	Learners form 'mini theories' of L2 learning (Hosenfeld, 1978) consisting of the beliefs that they hold about language and language learning. Beliefs can be classified in terms of whether they reflect an experiential or analytic approach to learning. Learners also hold beliefs about their own self-efficacy as language learners.
Learning strategies	Learning strategies are techniques or procedures used consciously by learners to learn an L2. A distinction can be made between 'language-learning strategies' directed at acquiring or automatizing L2 knowledge and 'skill-learning strategies' directed at increasing efficiency in speaking, listening, reading and writing. Different kinds of learning strategies have been identified. For example, O'Malley and Chamot (1990) distinguished cognitive strategies (e.g. inferencing the meaning of a word), metacognitive strategies (e.g. deciding to pay selective attention to some specific aspect of the L2) and social/affective strategies (e.g. asking someone to repeat or paraphrase what they have said).
Willingness to communicate	Willingness to communicate is defined as 'the intention to initiate communication, given a choice' by MacIntyre et al. (2001: 369). It is viewed as a final-order variable, determined by other factors, and the immediate antecedent of communication behaviour.

learning styles and learning strategies. Ur (1996) provided a lengthy discussion of just two factors: motivation and age. She discussed motivation in terms of some of the key distinctions recognized in the SLA literature (e.g. integrative vs instrumental and extrinsic vs intrinsic). Ur acknowledged its 'sheer importance' for successful language learning. She also drew on the SLA literature in her discussion of age. She saw age as influencing language learning in terms of differences in learners' capacity for 'understanding and logical thought' and also in motivation (i.e. adult learners are more analytical than children and may have a stronger motivation to learn). Scrivener (2005) listed a whole host of ways in which learners differ but went on to consider only three – motivation, Multiple Intelligences (H. Gardner, 1983) and Sensory Preferences (an aspect of learning style). He then focused on whether teachers should 'teach the class or teach the individuals' but offered no concrete advice about how to address this. Hall (2011) distinguished 'attributes' (i.e. age, language aptitude, personality – in particular, extraversion vs introversion – and anxiety) and 'conceptualizations' (i.e. motivation, learner beliefs, learning styles and strategies). He provided a quite lengthy discussion of each, including a thoughtful look at the relevance of the 'good language learner' studies for language pedagogy.

Four points emerge from this analysis of the individual difference factors addressed in the pedagogic literature. First, there is a wide range of factors. Second, the authors of the books are quite selective in the specific factors they choose to focus on but do not attempt to justify their choice. Third, there is no mention at all of working memory although this is the factor that current SLA research sees as important for explaining differences in how learners process input for learning. Fourth, language aptitude – another factor SLA views as influential in learning – receives little attention.

The plethora of factors raises an obvious problem for language pedagogy. How can teaching take into account all these factors? One possibility might be to focus on a specific factor that is considered of special importance – a solution that we will discuss later in this chapter. But, as we have just seen, the teacher guides differ in the factors they view as important. Thus there is no consensus about which factor (or factors) to choose as a basis for individualizing instruction. In any case, the factors overlap in unclear ways (e.g. certain personality types are likely to favour certain learning styles). Tudor (2001) offered a more fundamental reason for not attempting to vary teaching in accordance with a single factor. He pointed out that learners cannot be really treated as 'discrete bundles of variables' (p. 14). They are individuals and how they differ will reflect their profile on an array of factors. Thus, there is 'little scope for neat, pre-packaged solutions to language teaching problems' (Tudor, 1996: x). According to Tudor, what is needed is to try to accommodate the individual learner in a more holistic manner.

One way in which this might be achieved is by identifying the characteristics of learners who have been highly successful in learning an L2. This is what motivated a series of studies of the 'good language learner'. This research, which began in the 1970s (see, e.g. Rubin (1975) and Naiman et al. (1978)), aimed to identify the approach to learning adopted by highly successful language learners. Researchers first identified learners with very high levels of proficiency and then interviewed them (or sometimes observed them) to find out how they achieved their success. R. Ellis (2008) summarized the results of a number of studies by suggesting that they revealed five major aspects of successful language learning: (1) a concern for language form, (2) a concern for communication (functional practice), (3) an active task approach, (4) an awareness of the learning process and (5) a capacity to use strategies flexibly in accordance with task requirements. These results led to proposals that teachers should assist students to adopt the learning strategies employed by these successful learners. There are, however, some obvious problems from such an approach. First, as R. Ellis (2008) pointed out, it is very easy to over-emphasize the commonalities among the good language learners and, second, as Hall (2011) noted, the characteristics seen as desirable reflect those of Western cultural norms and traditions of learning and ignore the strategies (e.g. rote-memorization) that learners from other cultures employ with success.

A common refrain in the pedagogic literature is that there is more than one way to learn an L2 and the way that works for one learner may not be so effective for another. This was one reason for the rejection of the 'method' construct (see Chapter 2) as a basis for language teaching. However, as we have seen, there are universal aspects of L2 learning and so, in some sense, all learners do learn in the same way. In order to cater for individual differences, then, it is necessary to consider how they impact on these universal processes. In addition it is necessary to examine how individual learner factors impact on the conscious behaviours that learners engage in to try to learn. In short, any discussion of individual differences needs to be based on a clear distinction between the universal processes involved in incidental learning and the variable strategy use that characterizes intentional learning.

Figure 11.1 shows the various options for addressing individual differences in language pedagogy. A basic distinction is between 'selecting learners', 'catering for differences' and 'promoting receptivity'.

Selecting learners

This option seeks to avoid the problem of how to accommodate individual differences in teaching by identifying learners who have the capacity to be successful and excluding those who have not from taking language courses. V. Cook (2008) lists this option as one way of addressing differences in language aptitude. This view of individual differences is premised on the assumption that learners are inherently 'good' or 'bad' at learning languages and was common up to the 1970s. In part it was what motivated the development of language aptitude tests as a means of predicting those learners who would benefit or be excused from taking a language course. Horwitz (2000), however, noted that from the 1970s onwards a marked change in thinking about individual differences occurred:

> The terms good and bad, intelligent and dull, motivated and unmotivated have given way to a myriad of new terms such as integratively and instrumentally motivated, anxious and comfortable, field independent and field sensitive, auditory and visual.

(p. 532)

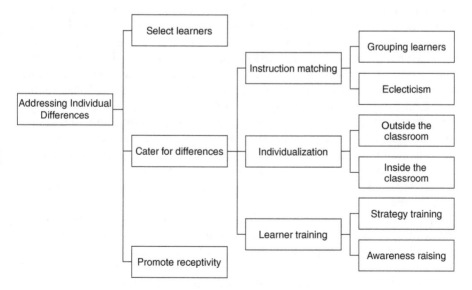

Figure 11.1 Addressing individual differences in language pedagogy

In other words, there has been a shift from viewing learners as either innately endowed with or lacking in language learning skills to seeing them as possessing different kinds of abilities and predispositions that influence learning in complex ways. However, the 'selection' option has not been entirely abandoned. For example, the Center for Advanced Study of Language of the University of Maryland developed a High-level Language Aptitude Battery (Hi-LAB), to identify individuals with the inherent capacity to reach very advanced levels of language proficiency (Mislevy et al., 2010). Such an option, then, might still be valuable when the aim of a language programme is to achieve very high levels of language proficiency. In most language teaching contexts, however, excluding learners on the basis of their language aptitude would not be considered appropriate.

Catering for differences

Figure 11.1 suggests that there are three major ways of catering for individual differences – instruction matching, individualization and learner training.

Instruction matching

V. Cook (2008) also proposed that instruction matching might be a way of coping with differences in learner aptitude (i.e. teachers should 'teach learners with different types of aptitude, for example, those with or without phonemic coding ability, in different ways and with different final examinations' (p. 146)). Examples of how instruction matching might be carried out can be found in aptitude–treatment–interaction (ATI) studies such as Wesche (1981) and Abraham (1985). In Abraham's study, learners were first distinguished in terms of whether their aptitude for learning suited them to inductive or deductive grammar teaching and then were taught accordingly. The results suggested that learners did learn better if the instruction matched their preferred way of learning.

However, it is one thing to conduct a carefully planned ATI study and entirely another to carry out instruction matching in a normal classroom. Learner-instruction matching requires teachers to first administer a language aptitude test, then group the students according to the result, and then devise and teach separate instructional packages for each group. As Ur (1996) pointed out, any attempt to vary the instruction to suit different learners will need to consider the 'degree of teacher work that needs to be invested' (p. 235). In the case of instruction matching, this is substantial. In addition to considerable lesson preparation, the teacher will also need to organize the teaching of two groups separately within the same classroom. A further problem, as we have already noted, is that learners differ in multiple ways, not just in terms of language aptitude, and thus grouping learners according to their aptitude (or any other single factor) is unlikely to achieve homogeneous groups. Thus for both theoretical and practical reasons, learner-instruction matching holds little promise for teachers.

The more practical way of carrying out learner-instruction matching is by including a mix of instructional activities for the whole class (i.e. providing something for everyone). However, addressing learner differences through a mix of activities calls for principled eclecticism not 'irresponsible adhocery' (Widdowson, 1979: 243). Eclecticism is widely recommended by teacher educators (e.g. Yalden, 1987; Scrivener, 2005) and favoured by teachers (Xiao-yun et al., 2007). It has generally been discussed in terms of a 'mixed method' approach involving the selection of activities from different methods. Mellow (2002), for example, proposed a set of principles for categorizing, selecting and sequencing activities in such a mixed method approach. There is, however, a lack of clear principles for defining and implementing eclecticism based on individual learner differences. Yorio (1987) advocated 'informed eclecticism' but offered no detailed advice about how teachers might go about this. Teachers, he argued, need to 'be well-informed, resourceful and open-minded' (p. 98) and able to 'compromise'. Scrivener (2005) also could see no 'easy answers' and suggested that achieving a satisfactory 'balancing act' involves 'a combination of gathering useful feedback from learners and using your intuition' (p. 66). It is hard not agree with Marton's (1988) assessment of eclecticism: 'practical eclecticism does not meet the criterion of efficiency, while theoretical eclecticism is suspicious on logical or theoretical grounds' (p. 86).

Individualization

Learner-instruction matching whether through ATI or through the eclectic provision of instructional activities relies on teacher-centred teaching – the teacher teaches either a group or the whole class. It is difficult for learners to express their individuality in such teaching. As Bowers (1980) noted 'formal, teacher-centred approaches may encourage suppression of the individual' because 'not only does teacher-talk dominate quantitatively but it dictates the communicative and cognitive patterns of classroom discourse' (p. 70). To cater for the learner-as-individual, individualized instruction is required – the next option in Figure 11.1. This is defined by Ur (1996) as 'a situation where learners are given a measure of freedom to choose how and what to learn' (p. 233). Ur pointed out that individualized instruction can be provided outside the classroom through self-access centres or inside the classroom by allowing learners to work on activities of their own choice. We will begin by considering individualization inside the classroom.

Individualized language teaching calls for activities that learners can work on independently. These activities can differ in a number of ways. Altman (1980) suggested that activities can be individualized according to:

- time allocated for learning;
- the curricular goal;
- the means for achieving the curricular goal (i.e. mode of learning);
- instructional expectations (i.e. the level of learning expected).

He then went on to suggest that these four dimensions can be permutated to yield eight different patterns of instruction. For example, in Pattern (1) all four dimensions are 'fixed' allowing no room for learner choice. This corresponds to the teacher-centred classroom. In Pattern (9) the rate and the curricular content are fixed but learners are left free to master the content in accordance with their preferred learning style and to do so with no expectation that they will all arrive at the same level of proficiency. Individualized instruction serves two purposes. In addition to catering to the wants and needs of individual learners, it also frees the teacher to work with individual or small groups of students.

It is clear that the task of implementing individualization in a classroom is a demanding one. First, the teacher needs to prepare a range of different learning activities. Cross (1980) recounted how he tackled this in a British high school. He described how he designed 'private study boxes' consisting of booklets on a wide range of topics and skills that the students could work on independently. In addition to teaching materials, the teacher will also need to develop evaluation instruments to assess students' progress on whatever aspect of the language they have chosen to work on. This will almost certainly require self-evaluation tools as teachers cannot be expected to develop separate instruments for each learner. Ur (1996) pointed out that it is necessary to acknowledge the amount of teacher preparation involved in individualizing instruction and emphasized the need to be practical. Logan (1971) concluded his own account of individualized instruction by advising teachers to 'proceed with caution' and advised setting one clear goal or objective to start with. Individualized instruction also places considerable classroom management demands on teachers as they need to organize the 'work stations' for individual students and also to monitor that each is functioning smoothly during the course of a lesson. Strevens (1980) argued that for individualized instruction to succeed, teachers need to become 'more sophisticated, better trained and more aware of what he or she is doing' (p. 28). Reflecting this, Niedzielski (1975) noted, 'there is only one thing that is wrong with truly and completely individualized instruction – it is too difficult to achieve and therefore discouraging' (p. 2).

According to Logan (1980), individualization began to appear in US classrooms in the 1960s and for a while attracted considerable attention. Disick published his often-cited book, *Individualizing Language Instruction: Strategies and Methods*, in 1975 and in 1980 Altman published an edited collection of papers on 'meeting individual needs'. More recent discussions of teaching (Ur and Scrivener, for example) include sections on individualization, acknowledging its importance for language teaching, but they offer no detailed guidance about how to implement it. An inspection of modern language teaching textbooks also suggests that individualized instruction has had little impact. Logan's comment that 'most standardized textbook and syllabuses are unsuitable for extensive periods of self-instruction' (1980: 104) remains as true today as when he made it. By and large, language pedagogy pays only lip service to the idea of individualized instruction in a classroom setting.

The picture is very different, however, when we leave the classroom and consider self-access centres. A self-access centre 'consists of a number of resources (in the form of materials, activities, and support) usually located in one place, and is designed to accommodate learners of different levels, styles, goals and interests. It aims at learner autonomy among its users' (Cotterall and Reinders, 2001: 24). Self-access centres are ideally suited to individualization both because they can provide learners with a wide range of learning materials to choose from and because they do not overburden the resources or management skills of the individual classroom teacher.

Our concern here, however, is how and to what extent self-access centres seek to cater for the kinds of individual difference factors that are the focus of this chapter. An inspection of the Language Resource Centre Handbook (LRC Project Partners 2003) suggests that these factors receive scant attention in the decision making involved in setting up a centre. That is, it is the 'levels' and the 'goals' of the learners that are prioritized rather than their 'styles' and 'interests'. Self-access centres, it would seem, cater to individual learners primarily by helping them identify their needs and providing them with learning materials appropriate for their proficiency level. Various lists of criteria for developing and evaluating materials for self-directed learning are available (see Reinders and Lewis (2006) for a review of these). However, these lists make scant reference to individual differences, although Sheerin (1989) did mention the importance of 'allowing learners to select their preferred learning style' (p. 24). Users of self-access centres, too, when asked about what they think are 'good materials', do not make any reference to the availability of materials that match their own preferred approach to learning. This failure to address individual differences[1] is in one respect surprising as the development of learner autonomy – one of the desired 'learning outcomes' of self-access centres – requires that learners are able to consider not just what to learn but also how to learn and this inevitably requires access to materials that cater to their own individual characteristics. Again, though, it is not so surprising because clearly it is no easy task creating resources that take account of how individual learners differ.

Self-access centres continue to be popular and play a major role in the provision for language learning in many universities around the world. Concerns about their effectiveness exist, however. Morrison (2005) documented how difficult it is for centres to show that they result in learning gains, especially if these are defined in terms of improved proficiency. It is virtually impossible to attribute any improvement directly to the use of a self-access centre given the complexity of a self-learning environment and the large number of variables involved. Reinders (2012) doubted whether what he considered the main goal of self-access centres – the development of learner autonomy – was actually achieved in many cases. He commented 'there is no clear focus on the individual' (p. 3) and argued that there was in fact less need for 'walled gardens' these days as learners are able to connect with multiple resources and communities via the World Wide Web in entirely individual ways.

Learner training

Educators acknowledge that for independent learning to be effective, learners may need some form of learner training to enable them to make the most of their learning opportunities. Instead of trying to match the instruction to the learner, learner training seeks to help the learner make the most of the instruction available. Crabbe (1993) proposed that learner training materials can provide a bridge between the 'public learning' of the classroom and the 'private learning' of a self-access centre. Figure 11.1 suggests that such materials can consist of either strategy-training or awareness-raising activities, the difference lying in whether the aim is to equip students with effective ways of learning or simply to make them aware of their own preferred ways of learning and of alternatives. It is, of course, possible to combine both and, in fact, this seems to be the preferred approach (see Cohen, 2003).

Strategy training involves both explicit instruction and practice (Cohen, 2003). In the explicit instruction phase of a lesson, the teacher explains how, when and why to use certain strategies and also models their use. In the practice stage, learners are given the opportunity to try out the strategies in a variety of tasks. Strategy training draws heavily on the learning strategies literature (e.g. O'Malley and Chamot, 1990; Oxford, 1990; Macaro, 2006). This claims that successful language learners have a range of strategies at their disposal and select strategies in accordance with both their long-term goals for learning the L2 and the particular task to hand. In particular, it emphasizes the importance of metacognitive strategies (i.e. the strategies involved in planning, monitoring and evaluating learning).

There are, however, problems with learner training. We have already taken note of one – the danger of assuming that there is a common set of strategies that characterize the 'good language learner'. Macaro (2006) pointed out another – the lack of standardization in the available intervention packages. He also noted that it was very difficult to reach any firm conclusions regarding the effectiveness of training learners to use specific strategies. In other words, it is not clear what strategies the training should focus on or whether training in the use of them actually improves learning. Nevertheless, learner training is frequently endorsed by teacher educators and many textbooks now include some form of strategy training. Also, teachers do not need to choose between strategy training and 'ordinary learning activities' as it is possible to systematically incorporate learning-how-to-learn tasks into normal teaching as some educators (e.g. Cohen, 2003) have proposed.

Awareness-raising activities consist of various kinds of tasks designed to both help learners make their own beliefs and preferred strategies explicit and also to expose them to alternatives (e.g. Ellis and Sinclair, 1989). As Scarcella and Oxford (1992) noted, learners tend to rely on those strategies that reflect their basic learning style but may be prepared to deploy alternative strategies when they are made aware of them. The aim is not to induce immediate change in strategic behaviour but to encourage learners to reflect on their beliefs and learning behaviours. The assumption is that such reflection will lead to experimentation with new strategies and, potentially, improve learning. As Nunan (1991) put it, awareness-raising tasks 'should encourage learners both to be more flexible in their approaches to learning and to experiment with a range of learning experiences' (p. 181). However, as with strategy training, there is only limited evidence that it is effective.

Promote receptivity

The final option involves creating a classroom climate which will maximize the learning of individual learners. This entails ensuring that learners are receptive to learning and preventing a defensive response to the instruction from developing. Allwright and Bailey (1991) define receptivity as 'a state of mind, whether permanent or temporary, that is open to the experience of becoming a speaker of another language' and defensiveness as 'the state of mind of feeling threatened by the experience and therefore needing to set up defences against it' (p. 157). They discuss a number of different ways in which a learner can be receptive or defensive – to the teacher as a person, to fellow learners, to the teacher's way of teaching, to course content, to the teaching materials and to the idea of communicating with others. Two affective individual factors play a major role in influencing the extent to which learners are receptive or defensive – motivation and language anxiety (see Table 11.1).

Most of the teacher guides we have examined have something to say about motivation. They offer brief accounts of the various types of motivation discussed in the research literature (e.g. instrumental vs integrative; extrinsic vs intrinsic) and then identify the factors that are likely to have an impact on student motivation. Harmer (1983), for example, focused on the distinction between extrinsic and intrinsic motivation. He noted that many students bring no extrinsic motivation to the classroom and that teachers can do little to promote it but suggested that demonstrating a positive attitude to the students' own culture will help. He examined intrinsic motivation at greater length and considered four factors that affect it – the physical conditions of the classroom, the choice of method, whether the students like the teacher, and ensuring the right level of challenge. Ur (1996) mentioned 'the sheer importance of motivation in successful language learning' (p. 275). She also focused on extrinsic and intrinsic motivation. In the case of extrinsic motivation, she noted that 'learners are often motivated by teacher pressure' (p. 279). In the case of intrinsic motivation, she emphasized the importance of selecting activities that have clear goals, varied topics, visual support, and both challenge and also entertain learners. Ur also pointed out that there are bound to be fluctuations in learners' level of interest. She noted that students attend better when the teacher addresses the whole class rather than individuals! Scrivener (2005) offered only a few cursory comments on motivation. He claimed that a common cause of difficulty in classes is the mismatch of motivation levels among the students but offered no suggestions for how this might be addressed. Hall (2011) concluded that the teacher is not wholly responsible but can play an important role by, for example, selecting 'motivating classroom activities'.

Motivation is a crucial factor determining receptivity; in contrast, language anxiety is likely to lead to defensiveness. Three major sources of anxiety have been identified – apprehensiveness about communicating in the L2 in front of the whole class, competitiveness (i.e. the negative self-evaluation that arises when learners consider themselves less successful learners than their classmates) and language tests (Horwitz et al., 1986). In general, the teacher guides have little to say about anxiety. Harmer, Ur and Scrivener, for example, have no entry for 'anxiety' in their indexes and offer no suggestions for how it might be addressed. This is surprising given that 'there are few, if any disciplines in the curriculum which lay themselves open to anxiety production more than foreign or second language learning' (Arnold and Brown, 1999: 9). However, there is one approach to language teaching, where the need to avoid anxiety holds a central place – humanistic language teaching. As Moskowitz (1999) put it, humanistic exercises aim at enhancing learners' self-esteem, developing 'closer and more satisfying relationships' and ensuring 'a positive outlook on life' (p. 178). She sees such exercises as 'promoting harmony, closeness and personal growth' (p. 192). In short, the main aim of activities such as 'I like you, you are different'[2] aim at personalizing language teaching and, in so doing, reducing defensiveness. Humanistic language teaching is premised on the assumption that anxiety is debilitating. However, this is not always the case. In some situations and within limits, anxiety can facilitate learning by inducing learners to make more effort.

Some concluding comments

The importance of individual learner differences is widely recognized in language pedagogy. In particular, learning style and motivation are acknowledged as key factors that need to be addressed. Learning strategies, too, receive considerable attention. However, the key issue – how teaching and learning can be organized to suit the individual learner – remains a problematic one. This is not surprising given the difficulty teachers face in addressing the multifarious ways in which learners can differ. We have examined a number of options – selecting learners, catering to differences through instruction matching, individualization and learner training, and promoting receptivity. Addressing individual differences is especially problematic when responsibility lies in the hands of the individual teacher. Addressing them through some form of independent-learning regime (as in a self-access centre), while potentially the best solution, is also not without its drawbacks. A limitation that runs through all the various possibilities we have considered is the failure to consider how learner differences impact on learning. Learner factors have been considered in isolation from the universal social and cognitive processes that characterize how an L2 is acquired.

Individual learner differences in SLA

Much of the early work investigating individual difference factors was correlational in nature. That is, it examined the extent to which measures of different factors were related to measures of L2 learning. Many of these studies investigated the relationship between learners' starting age and the rate and success of learning. Others investigated psychological factors, in particular language aptitude and motivation, which were found to account for a substantial portion of the variance in L2 proficiency. In other words, learners with higher aptitude and stronger motivation developed more rapidly and achieved higher levels of proficiency than those with lower aptitude and weaker motivation (Carroll, 1981; Skehan, 1989). In contrast, studies of other learner factors (e.g. learning style, personality, and anxiety) demonstrated much weaker relationships with L2 proficiency and, sometimes, none at all. Also research on learner beliefs and learning strategies has often failed to show clear and convincing relationships between specific beliefs (or types of beliefs) or strategies and learning outcomes. The differential impact of these learner factors, however, is not clearly reflected in the literature on language pedagogy, where, as we have seen, very little attention has been paid to age and aptitude and much more to learning style and learning strategies. In the examination of learner factors that follows, however, we will focus briefly on starting age and then on the two major psychological factors – language aptitude and motivation. We will also briefly examine the research that has investigated learning strategies.[3]

Starting age

SLA researchers were interested in the effect that learners' starting age has on learning because of what this could tell them about the nature of the language learning faculty. According to the Critical Period Hypothesis (CPH), attainment of full competence in an L2 was only possible if learners began to learn as children (i.e. before they reached puberty). Up to then they had access to the same language specialized faculty involved in L1 acquisition; after that, they would need to rely on general cognitive abilities. The key test of the hypothesis was whether learners who began to learn an L2 late were able to achieve native ability. Other researchers, motivated more by educational concerns, were interested in whether an early start resulted in more rapid learning and higher levels of ultimate attainment. A further issue, of considerable pedagogic interest, is whether the processes of acquisition differed in children and older learners.

We will not attempt to survey the voluminous research that has investigated the role of age in L2 acquisition. Readers should consult Singleton and Ryan (2004) for a comprehensive account of the research. Instead, we provide a summary of the main findings:

• Controversy exists as to whether there is a critical period for language acquisition. In the case of L2 acquisition, starting young is likely to result in higher levels of ultimate attainment, but there does not appear to be a distinct 'window of opportunity'. Rather, the ability to learn an L2 declines gradually with age, starting from a very young age.

- When learners acquire an L2 they do not develop a separate language system but meld the new language onto the old, achieving what V. Cook (1991) called 'multicompetence'. From such a perspective, it is inappropriate to take native-speaker competence as the yardstick of success.
- Learners who start learning in childhood achieve higher levels of proficiency in an L2 than those who start later, but this advantage of starting young only arises if learners have ample exposure to the target language.
- Older learners acquire an L2 more rapidly than younger learners in the initial stages except in the case of pronunciation. This may reflect the fact that older learners make fuller use of conscious learning strategies.
- Whether age has an effect on the process of L2 acquisition is uncertain. Some research shows that starting age has no effect on the order and sequence of acquisition but other research suggests that the analytical skills of older learners have an impact on how they acquire specific grammatical features.

A possible explanation for these findings is that younger learners are better equipped to engage in implicit learning and older learners rely more on explicit learning. As we have already seen, implicit learning is a slow process that requires massive exposure to the L2 so no immediate advantage is apparent for younger learners. In fact, explicit learning may lead to more immediate success. However, over time, implicit learning wins out because it is more likely to enable learners to develop high levels of L2 knowledge.

Language aptitude

Language aptitude is the special ability for learning an L2. It is a complex construct involving both general intelligence and a more specific ability for learning language (Sasaki, 1996). Also, language learning aptitude is componential rather than unitary. That is, it comprises a number of distinct abilities. This is important because it means that learners should not be classified as simply 'high' or 'low' in language aptitude but rather in terms of the different kinds of aptitude they possess.

The initial work on aptitude was conducted by John Carroll and associates in the 1950s. Building on Carroll's work, Skehan (2002) suggested a model of language aptitude that distinguished the abilities involved in the four macro stages of language acquisition: (1) noticing, (2) patterning, (3) controlling and (4) lexicalizing (see Table 11.2). His model draws on information processing theory to outline the processes by which a specific form is first attended to in the input, generalized in the form of a rule, restructured, integrated into the interlanguage system and then subsequently lexicalized, so that it is accessible both in the form of a ready-made chunk and as a rule for creative language use. The model, therefore, aims to relate work on the cognitive processes involved in L2 learning to language aptitude. Skehan accepted, however, that his model is programmatic and research is needed to both develop tests that can measure the different aptitude components and demonstrate the claims about their role played in the processes involved in L2 acquisition.

An implication of Skehan's model is that learners can be strong in some aptitude components and weak in others. For example, learners who are weak in auditory segmentation and phonemic coding are likely to experience problems in noticing, while other learners with less developed language analytical abilities may have difficulty in detecting patterns in the features they have noticed. This suggests that learners will differ in their ability to benefit from different types of instruction depending on the nature of their aptitude.

This possibility has been explored in two other models of language aptitude. Sternberg (2002) distinguished three types of aptitude: analytical intelligence (i.e. the ability to analyse, compare and evaluate), creative intelligence (i.e. the ability to produce novel solutions to problems) and practical intelligence (i.e. the capacity to adapt to, to shape and to select environments suited to one's abilities). Sternberg argued that tests have generally targeted analytic and, to a lesser extent, creative intelligence, largely because teaching methods have typically emphasized these. He proposed that instruction needs to be matched to the particular type of ability a learner is strong in. An equally tenable position, however, might be that learners need compensatory assistance for those aspects of acquisition that they experience difficulty with as a result of their particular aptitude profile.

Table 11.2 Skehan's (2002) model of language aptitude and L2 acquisition processes

Stage	Processes involved	Aptitude components
1. Noticing	Learner directs attention at some specific feature in the input.	Auditory segmentation; attention management; working memory; phonemic coding
2. Patterning	Learner constructs a hypothesis (implicitly or explicitly) about the feature, subsequently extends the domain of the hypothesis before recognizing its limitations and restructuring it and integrating the new representation into the interlanguage system.	Working memory; grammatical sensitivity; inductive language learning ability; restructuring capacity
3. Controlling	Learner is able to use the integrated feature with increasing ease and accuracy.	Automatization; proceduralization; retrieval processes
4. Lexicalizing	Learner is now able to produce the feature as a 'lexicalized element' (i.e. as a remembered whole rather than through applying a rule).	Memory; chunking; retrieval processes

The third model constitutes the most ambitious attempt to relate language aptitude to acquisition processes. Robinson (2002) proposed the Aptitude Complex Hypothesis, which distinguishes 'primary abilities' and 'second order abilities' (Figure 11.2). Primary abilities are those involved in the key processes involved in acquisition (e.g. pattern recognition, speed of processing in phonological working memory, and grammatical sensitivity). These underlie the second order abilities, which are directly related to the acquisition process (i.e. noticing-the-gap, memory for contingent speech, deep semantic processing, memory for contingent text, and metalinguistic rule rehearsal). Quoting Snow (1994), he proposed that these second order abilities combine into complexes that influence learning. Examples of such complexes are 'aptitude for focus on form' and 'aptitude for explicit rule learning'. In the case of the former, two primary abilities are involved – perceptual speed and pattern recognition. These contribute to the second order ability of noticing-the-gap. Learners who are 'high' in this ability may be better able to benefit from corrective feedback in the form of recasts than those who are 'low' in such abilities. In the case of the aptitude for explicit learning complex, the primary abilities involved are grammatical sensitivity and rote memory. These feed into the second order ability of metalinguistic rule rehearsal. Again, learners who are high in this ability will be better equipped to benefit from explicit explanation of linguistic features.

These models raise an important question. Is language aptitude only a factor in intentional/explicit L2 learning or is it also involved in incidental/implicit learning? Krashen (1981) argued that language aptitude is only relevant to what he called 'learning' (i.e. intentional/explicit learning). He suggested that high-aptitude learners were better equipped to engage in monitoring using their explicit knowledge and this was why they tended to show more rapid initial progress. He predicted that language aptitude would only show a strong relationship to L2 proficiency in test situations and when the instruction

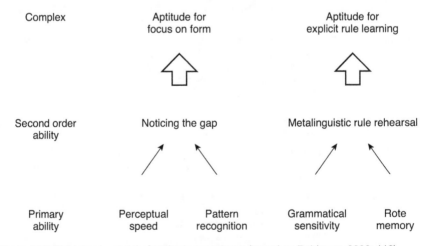

Figure 11.2 Robinson's model of aptitude complexes (based on Robinson, 2002: 119)

emphasized conscious learning. However, the three models we have just considered make it clear that language aptitude is important for both kinds of learning. This is clear once it is recognized that language aptitude is not an accumulated aggregation of abilities (as Krashen viewed it) but a number of quite distinct abilities involved in different types of learning. Thus, as Grigorenko et al. (2000) suggested, intelligence is a factor in explicit learning where linguistic–analytic ability is important, while phonemic-coding and memory abilities play a bigger role in incidental/implicit learning. Two points arise from such a position. The first is that there can be different types of learners who can achieve success in different ways. Skehan (1989) proposed a distinction between analytic and memory-orientated learners, arguing that both can achieve high levels of L2 proficiency. The second arises from the first: learners with different aptitude profiles will benefit from different types of instruction. For example, learners with the abilities required for focus-on-form will benefit from recasts, while those with the abilities involved in metalinguistic rule rehearsal will benefit from metalinguistic feedback.

The models also enable us to address a second issue that has proved contentious in the SLA literature – the relationship between language aptitude and age in L2 learning. DeKeyser (2000) claimed that language aptitude is only a factor in adult language learning. He proposed that differences in aptitude can explain differences in the ultimate attainment of learners who begin learning after the critical period but not before and reported a study that lent some support to this claim. However, DeKeyser only examined one aspect of aptitude – language analytical ability. It is reasonable to suppose that this will play a stronger role with adults, who are likely to rely on more conscious learning strategies. What would seem more likely is that different aspects of language aptitude become important at different ages. Younger learners may rely more on memory and phonemic discrimination abilities and less on language analytical ability, whereas the opposite may be true for some older learners, especially if they are receiving formal instruction. Harley and Hart's (1997) study of early and later immersion learners lends some support to this hypothesis. Age and type of instruction are likely to interact in determining which aspect of language aptitude is important for learning.

There is now a large body of research that has investigated language aptitude. We will not attempt to review this (see R. Ellis, 2008; Ortega, 2009). Instead, we will focus on some of the key studies that have examined how language aptitude mediates the effects of instruction on learning. In an early aptitude–treatment–interaction study, Wesche (1981) used aptitude tests to distinguish two types of learners – those who had a high overall score on the tests and those who manifested a high level of analytical ability but demonstrated problems with phonetic coding and listening. The two instructional treatments consisted of: (1) an audiovisual, inductive approach organized around the presentation of linguistic structures sequenced according to order of difficulty and (2) a more deductive, analytical approach, which taught oral and literacy skills together and provided explanations of grammatical points and of how to produce specific sounds. When students were matched to the type of instruction compatible with their aptitude profile, they gained higher scores and also reported greater interest in foreign language study, more initiative in practising French outside the classroom, and less anxiety in class.

A key issue is whether aptitude plays a role in communicative classrooms as well as more formal ones. There are two competing hypotheses here. One is that aptitude contributes most in formal classrooms that emphasize explicit learning – as proposed by Krashen. The other is that it will be more influential in communicative classrooms where students have to rely on their own abilities to extract structure from the input. White and Ranta (2002) reported that some students in an intensive, communicative ESL programme were able to acquire the grammatical rule for the use of 'his' and her' without any direct explicit instruction and that this could be explained by their higher levels of language analytical ability. Erlam (2005) examined the relationship between language analytic ability and three types of instruction (deductive instruction, inductive instruction and structured input instruction). She found that language analytic ability was not related to gains on a battery of tests in the deductive instructional group, but it was to gains made by the inductive and structured input groups. She concluded that language analytical ability becomes more significant when the instruction does not involve a structured presentation of the target features and, as a result, learners have to work out the grammatical rules for themselves. Both of these studies, then, lend support to the second of the two hypotheses. Other studies suggest that other aspects of language aptitude are involved in incidental learning. Robinson and Yamaguchi (1999), for example, found high significant correlations between measures of Japanese university students' phonetic sensitivity and rote memory and the learning that resulted from recasts provided during five weeks of task-based interaction.

Working memory has also been found to play a role in how learners respond to instruction. These studies have produced somewhat mixed results but there is some evidence to suggest that working memory contributes more when the instruction requires learners to process oral input, as suggested by Erlam's (2005) study than written input as found in Payne and Whitney's (2002) study. The explanation for this is that it is much more difficult for learners to hold and rehearse oral input in their working memories given its ephemeral nature.

While it is difficult to reach firm conclusions from these (and other) studies, one point seems clear. Different components of aptitude become significant for different types of instruction. This supports the predictions of Skehan's and Robinson's models. Language learning is a complex phenomenon, involving a range of cognitive processes. Language aptitude clearly plays a role in learners' ability to handle these processes but does so in different ways. As DeKeyser (2012) pointed out, investigating the interaction between instruction and aptitude 'can show *why* a treatment works best (or more precisely why sometimes it does and sometimes it doesn't)' (p. 192).

Finally, we can ask whether language aptitude is trainable. Carroll (1981) argued that aptitude is essentially innate and does not change as a result of experience. Sternberg (2002), however, claimed that what he termed 'practical intelligence' is trainable. One way in which this might be achieved is through strategy training, which we consider below. First, though, we turn to the other learner factor that research has shown is of major importance in language learning.

Motivation

Without motivation, an aptitude for learning an L2 is of little value. As Hatch (1978b) noted many years ago, learning a second language involves hard work. Therefore, no matter how able the learner is, if he/she is not prepared to put in the necessary hard work, little will be achieved.

Like language aptitude, motivation is a complex construct. It involves:

- The reasons a learner has for needing or wanting to learn an L2 (i.e. motivational orientation).
- The effort a learner is prepared to make to learn the L2 and the impact that the learner's immediate context has on this (i.e. behavioural motivation).
- The effect that the learner's evaluation of his/her progress has on subsequent learning behaviour (i.e. attributional motivation).

Theories of motivation have proliferated over the years. Dörnyei (2005) identified three phases in L2 motivation research. It began in the 1960s with the social psychological phase that emphasized the role of sociocultural factors such as language attitudes in shaping learners' motivational orientation. The key figure here was Gardner (1985), who distinguished two different motivational orientations – instrumental (learning a language for some functional purpose such as job enhancement) and integrative (learning a language because of the wish to engage with the culture of the L2). The second phase saw the development of cognitive-situated theories of L2 motivation. These theories sought to link motivation to the specific contexts in which learning took place, whether these are defined broadly (i.e. second vs foreign language settings) or more narrowly (i.e. in terms of the varying micro-contexts that arise within a classroom). Some of the key theories that emerged in this period are Self-determination Theory (Noels et al., 2000) and Attribution Theory (Williams and Burden, 1999). The former drew on the important distinction between intrinsic motivation (i.e. motivation that is self-initiated and sustained by a personal sense of enjoyment in learning an L2) and extrinsic motivation (i.e. motivation that derives from external causes such as the instrumental need to pass an exam). Attribution theory sought to explain how the subjective reasons that learners attribute to their success or failure in learning a language affect their future learning behaviours. Dörnyei labelled the third phase 'the process-oriented period'. Whereas earlier theories treated motivation as a trait phenomenon, the theories in this period viewed it as dynamic in nature, fluctuating not just over a period of time but from moment to moment in a single lesson. Dörnyei and Otto (1998) developed a process mode of L2 motivation that distinguished a pre-actional stage, an actional stage and a post-actional stage and suggested that each stage is associated with different motives (see below).

The most recent theory attracting attention from researchers is Dörnyei's L2 Motivational Self System (Dörnyei, 2005). This was based on a large-scale study of 8,593 Hungarian school learners of foreign languages (Csizer and Dörnyei, 2005). Dörnyei used the results of this study to argue that there are three main dimensions of L2 motivation:

1 Ideal L2 self (i.e. whether 'the ideal person we would like to become speaks an L2').
2 Ought-to self (i.e. whether the attributes a person feels they ought to possess in order to avoid negative outcomes includes speaking an L2).
3 L2 Learning Experience (i.e. 'the situation specific motives related to the immediate environment and experience' p. 106).

This theory reflects Ushioda's (2001) general observation that 'we can classify all the factors in each language learner's motivational configuration as either *causal* (deriving from the continuum of L2-learning and L2-related experience to date) or *teleological* (directed toward short-term or long-term goals and future perspectives)' (p. 107). Dörnyei claimed that the Ideal L2-self and the Ought-to Self involve teleological motivation whereas L2 Learning Experience relates to causal motivation. In short, the motivation to learn an L2 derives from positive experiences of learning an L2 and/or from the learner's visions for the future. Dörnyei argued that the L2 Motivational Self System incorporates constructs from previous theories and therefore provides an overall picture of L2 motivation and what shapes it.

The main context that we are concerned with in this chapter is the classroom. Therefore, in the following discussion of motivation we will focus on theoretical perspectives that are especially relevant to the classroom. We will also examine the rather sparse research that has investigated the interaction between motivation and the process of acquisition. Finally, we will take a look at the proposals for enhancing motivation that have emanated from research.

Dörnyei and Otto's (1998) process model of L2 acquisition

This model is of importance to language teaching because it allows us to see what aspects of motivation teaching is likely to impact on and which aspects it is less likely to influence. It also recognizes that L2 motivation is a dynamic phenomenon. The model consists of two dimensions: Action Sequence and Motivational Influences. The model is complex so we will provide only a brief sketch here.

The Action Sequence involves three phases, each involving a number of subprocesses. In the *pre-actional phase*, the learner decides what course of actions to implement. This involves goal setting and formulating a concrete intention to act. Thus the model distinguishes between the learner's long-term plans and the learner's commitment to engage in specific actions. The learner needs to develop a manageable 'action plan' for implementing the intention to act. However, whether the action plan is implemented will depend on situational opportunities. The *actional phase* begins when learners begin to implement their action plan. This involves a switch from 'choice motivation' to 'executive motivation'. Three basic processes come into play: (1) implementation of the subtasks in the action plan – this is a dynamic process because it will inevitably involve the generation of new subtasks and goals as action proceeds and as (2) appraisal takes place, and (3) action control involves the use of self-regulatory strategies such as motivational maintenance strategies, language learning strategies and goal-setting strategies. The *post-actional phase* takes place when the goal has been achieved or the action plan terminated. This is when the learner evaluates the outcome of the actions undertaken and forms causal attributions about the reasons for the success or failure of the action plan. During this phase, too, the learner will consider what changes need to be made to the choice of action-specific strategies to ensure more successful outcomes in the future.

Motivational Influences impact on: (1) goal setting, (2) actional processes and (3) post-actional evaluation. Included in (1) are the learner's subjective values and norms (e.g. whether the orientation is integrative and/or instrumental) and the extent to which the learner is self-determined and so can visualize the action to be undertaken. Included in (2) are all the influences that have impacted on the formation of the action plan together with others associated with the immediate context of learning, the perceived quality of the learning experience and the learner's perception of progress. Influences on post-actional evaluation include the attributional style of the learner – some learners tend to attribute an outcome to personal factors and ignore crucial situational factors.

Motivation as a dynamic phenomenon

Dörnyei and Otto's process model recognizes the dynamic nature of motivation. Change can originate in any of the three phases but is most likely to arise in the action phase (i.e. in the course of carrying out an action plan). In this respect, it is the learning experiences that arise when learners are performing instructional activities that will be crucial. If the learner's interest is aroused by the activities and if the learner is able to carry out the activity successfully, motivation will be sustained. Conversely, if the learner feels the activity is neither interesting nor relevant to his/her needs or if the learner is unable to carry out the activity successfully, motivation will atrophy. The maintenance of motivation will also depend on the attributions the learner performs. It will decline if the learner attributes failure to factors outside his/her control but it may increase if the learner feels able to address the causes of the failure.

However, the process model enshrines what is essentially a linear view of motivation – the very labels (pre-action, action, post-action) assume this. An alternative way of viewing motivation may be even more effective in accounting for its dynamic nature. Ushioda (2009) argued for an approach that she calls a 'person-in-context relational view of motivation' (p. 220). This rejects the dualism of 'context' and 'learner' (with the attendant assumption that contextual variables determine the learner's motivation) and instead views the learner as part of the context, not only influenced by it but also able to influence and shape it. From this perspective, motivation becomes 'an organic process that emerges through the complex system of interrelations'. Motivation, in other words, is inherently emergent. Ushioda suggested that the nature of this emergent motivation is best captured not through questionnaires (the instrument favoured in mainstream studies of motivation) but by examining the discourse that learners participate in. By way of example, she cited Richards (2006) study of how the identities of learners and teacher in a classroom shape their involvement in discourse. Richards showed how evoking what he called 'transportable identities' (the identities that the classroom participants possess as individuals and can bring into the classroom) has a powerful motivational impact on the nature of classroom talk. Ushioda concluded by suggesting that learners' current experiences and self-states dynamically shape their engagement with their future possible selves.

Motivation and acquisition processes

The discussion so far has focused on motivation in relation to learning outcomes. Thus, while motivation itself has been viewed as a process, learning has only been viewed as a 'product' achieved as a result of motivation. This constitutes an overly narrow view of 'learning' as it ignores mainstream work in cognitive–interactionist theories of L2 acquisition which treat acquisition as a process (see Chapters 7 and 8). Like language aptitude, if motivation has an effect on learning, it must do so by impacting on the interactional and cognitive processes that are responsible for interlanguage development.

Schmidt (2010) suggested two ways in which motivation can influence how learners learn. In accordance with Krashen's (1985) views, it can function as an affective filter preventing input from reaching the brain. Alternatively, it can lead to more attention being paid selectively to morphosyntactic information. Schmidt favoured the second view: motivation results in more noticing and also higher levels of awareness. Manolopoulo-Sergi (2004) proposed that the type of motivation is important in this respect: whereas extrinsically motivated learners are likely to attend only to the surface characteristics of the input, intrinsically motivated learners process input in a more elaborated, deeper manner.

There has been relatively little research that has investigated the relationship between motivation and learning processes. But there is evidence that motivation is a factor in 'focus on form'. Takahashi (2005) examined the relationship between Japanese EFL learners' motivation and their noticing of the pragmalinguistic features of complex request forms (e.g. 'Would it be possible for you to...?'). The results of her study supported Manolopoulo-Sergi's claim about the importance of intrinsic motivation. There was a positive correlation between a measure of this aspect of motivation and the learners' reported awareness of a number of pragmalinguistic features. Bassiri (2011) reported a study that examined the relationship between Iranian learners' motivation (measured by means of a questionnaire) and their noticing of L2 question forms in interactional feedback (measured by means of the learners' self-reports). He reported a strong correlation (r = .70).

The motivational basis of tasks

A potentially important area of enquiry is how students' motivation affects the way they perform tasks. Dörnyei (2002) reported a study that investigated this. He obtained measures of the motivation of Hungarian secondary school learners' of L2 English by means of a self-report questionnaire, that focused on a standard set of attitudinal and motivational variables (e.g. integrativeness and attitudes towards the English course) and also their attitudes to task-based teaching. He then asked them to perform an argumentative task in pairs and obtained measures of the number of words and turns produced by each student. He found surprisingly high correlations between the motivational measures and the performance measures but only in those learners who held positive opinions about performing tasks. He also reported evidence to show that the learners were strongly influenced by their partner's motivational disposition. He reached two main conclusions. The first was that task motivation involves both general motives and situation-specific motives. The second was that task motivation is co-constructed (i.e. one learner's motivation affects the other's). This study goes some way to showing that motivation is an important variable in task-based teaching as it affects the extent to which learning opportunities will occur.

Enhancing learners' motivation

Crookes and Schmidt (1991: 502) called for a model of motivation that is 'congruent with the concept of motivation that teachers are convinced are critical for L2 learners'. While we still have no such model, we do have a clearer idea of how teachers can promote students' motivation. In line with the preceding discussion, we can see that there are two ways of examining motivation enhancement. We can ask first 'What does the teacher have to do to promote motivation?' More importantly, perhaps, we can ask 'How is motivation constructed through classroom interaction?'

Dörnyei (2001), building on a study by Dörnyei and Csizér (1998), offered a comprehensive account of the motivational strategies teachers can deploy. Table 11.3 provides a selection of these in terms of the different phases of the process model. These strategies may seem rather abstract and general but Dörnyei offers very concrete suggestions for how they can be implemented.

Table 11.3 Selected teaching strategies for promoting motivation (from Dörnyei, 2001)

Phase	Motivational strategies
Pre-actional phase: generating initial motivation	Raise the learners' intrinsic interest in the L2 learning process.
	Increase the students' goal-orientedness by formulating explicit goals that are accepted by them.
	Make the curriculum and the teaching materials relevant to the students.
Actional phase: maintaining and protecting motivation	Make learning more stimulating and enjoyable by breaking the monotony of classroom events.
	Use contracting methods with your students to formalize their goal commitment.
	Provide learners with regular experiences of success.
	Increase student motivation by promoting cooperation among the learners.
	Increase the students' self-motivating capacity.
Post-actional phase: encouraging positive self-evaluation	Promote effort attributions in the students (i.e. by encouraging them to reject ability attributions).
	Offer rewards in a motivational manner (e.g. by making sure students are not preoccupied with rewards).

In an interesting study, Guilloteaux and Dörnyei (2008) investigated the relationship between teachers' motivating strategies and their students' motivation. They used a classroom observation scheme consisting of twenty-five strategy variables to measure the teachers' motivational practice in EFL lessons in Korea and then calculated the mean amount of time spent on each strategy. The students' situation-specific motivational dispositions were investigated by means of a Student Motivational State Questionnaire and also a Post-lesson Teacher Evaluation Scale. The results showed a significant positive correlation between the teacher's motivational practice and the learners' motivated behaviour, which Guilloteaux and Dörnyei interpreted as showing that it was the teachers' motivated practices that enhanced the students' motivation. However, it might also be possible to interpret this result as showing that the relationship between teachers' motivating practices and students' motivation is an interactive one (i.e. they feed off each other). Such an interpretation would be more compatible with Ushioda's view of motivation as emerging though interaction.

Very little is known about how motivation arises out of the interactions that learners participate in. The most complete attempt to examine motivation in terms of interaction can be found in Preston's (2009) study of French classes in a UK secondary school. Through the detailed analysis of classroom interactions she argued that interactional practices can be understood as social displays of L2 motivational states. She identified a number of 'participation concepts' that she claimed constituted such social displays. For example, she proposed that when a teacher confers 'next-turn speakership positions' on students after they have indicated a readiness to speak by hand-raising, they become 'rewarded bidders', which promotes the short-term motivation of learners and, potentially, contributes to the development of their longer-term motivation.

Learning strategies

We conclude this account of individual difference factors in SLA with a brief consideration of learning strategies (LSs). There is now an enormous literature on LSs and a substantial body of empirical research. This has been motivated to a considerable extent by the conviction that helping learners to make effective use of LSs is one way to improve language pedagogy.

Cohen (2011) gave this definition of learning strategies:

> Language learning strategies can be defined as thoughts and actions, consciously selected by learners to assist them in learning and using language in general, and in the completion of specific language tasks.
>
> (p. 682)

This definition raises some of the major problems involving learning strategies. Should LSs be restricted to those strategies directed at language learning or should they also include communication strategies and strategies involving specific skills such as reading and listening? Should learning strategies be viewed as general ways of learning or as specific actions for tackling particular tasks? Cohen, like other LS researchers, grappled with these questions but, as he admitted, there is no consensus on how to answer them. Not surprisingly then there is no well-established list of LSs nor is there any agreement about how they can best be classified. A further problem is that LSs are used in clusters but are listed as individual strategies in the available taxonomies. Dörnyei (2005) questioned the value of 'strategy' at a theoretical level, arguing that there is no clear distinction to be made between an ordinary learning activity (e.g. 'using a bilingual word list') and a learning strategy (e.g. 'colour coding words in a list to learn them'). Dörnyei argued that LSs should be replaced by the more theoretically sound concept of 'self-regulation' (i.e. 'the degree to which individuals are active participants in their own learning' p. 191). In this section, however, we will avoid theoretical disputations and focus instead on how LSs might be important for language pedagogy.

Assuming that it is possible to identify distinct LSs and assuming that at least some of the LSs that have been identified facilitate language learning, it becomes possible to think about training students to use them. Hassan et al. (2005) conducted a review of twenty-five strategy training studies. The main findings were as follows:

1 In general, strategy training is effective, at least in the short term. However, it was not possible to conclude whether the effects are long-lasting.
2 The effectiveness of the training varies according to the different language skills. Its effect is most robust in improving reading comprehension and

writing skills. Training directed at improving overall language ability produced mixed results.

3   It was not possible to determine the effect of awareness-raising training as opposed to behaviour strategy training or which particular training techniques were effective. Nor was it possible to determine whether training based on discrete strategies or packages of strategies worked best.

4   The studies investigated mainly non-school populations so little can be said about the effectiveness of strategy training with school-based learners.

5   The survey did not shed light on whether the learners' stage of development was a significant factor influencing the success of learner training.

In short, this review failed to find convincing evidence to support strategy training. Indeed, many of the individual studies that have investigated the effects of training specific strategies failed to show that it benefits learning.

However, there are grounds for optimism. Plonsky's (2011) meta-analysis of sixty-one studies that had investigated the effect of strategy instruction showed that the instruction was effective in the case of reading, speaking, vocabulary and pronunciation but not in the case of listening, grammar or general proficiency. There is also an interesting study that suggests which type of strategy instruction might be effective.

Holunga (1995) investigated the effects of metacognitive strategy training on the accurate use of verb forms by advanced learners of English. It involved three instructional conditions: (1) metacognitive strategy training plus communicative practice, (2) metacognitive strategy training plus a requirement to verbalize the strategies plus communicative practice, and (3) communicative practice only. During the instructional period, the learners performed a communicative task designed to elicit a specific linguistic feature (i.e. a focused task – see Chapter 6). Whereas groups (1) and (3) attended predominantly to message content, group (2) focused on both message content and the conditional verb form that the task required. This group demonstrated significantly greater gains in the ability to use complex verb forms accurately than the other groups. This study points to two ways in which strategy training can be effective. First, it needs to be directed at a specific language learning activity (e.g. the performance of a particular communicative task). Second, in accordance with one of the tenets of Sociocultural Theory, learners need to verbalize the strategy as they apply it. It is through the process of verbalization that they achieve self-regulation.

Learner training is popular. It has been endorsed by a number of researchers (e.g. Macaro, 2006). Many textbooks now include some form of strategy training and there are also whole books given over to strategy training activities. Our own view is that there is insufficient evidence overall to show that strategy training has a direct effect on learning. However, verbalizing strategy use may assist with the internalization of new language as Holunga's study showed. Also, strategy training has a potential role to play in sustaining learners' motivation. Dörnyei (2001) included this teaching strategy in his list of strategies for maintaining and protecting motivation: 'Build your learners' confidence in their learning abilities by teaching them various learning strategies' (p. 97).

Individual differences and language pedagogy

We return now to consider how individual learner differences can be accommodated in language pedagogy. We use the term 'accommodated' deliberately because it is clearly easier for a teacher to treat learners as homogeneous and devise instructional activities for the whole class. Clearly, though, learners do differ and teachers need to find ways of adjusting their teaching to take account of these. Thus, while the teacher guides are primarily concerned with how to teach the whole class, they all also acknowledge the need to consider the individual learner. The fact that they offer little hard advice about how this can be achieved is understandable, because the very nature of classrooms (where one person is responsible for the behaviour of many) makes simple recipes untenable. In short, adjusting teaching to accommodate learner differences constitutes one of the greatest challenges facing teachers. In what follows we suggest a number of general principles that can guide teachers in taking up this challenge.

Distinguish the roles of individual difference factors in incidental and intentional L2 acquisition

A conspicuous gap in both how language pedagogy and SLA has tackled individual learner differences is the failure to examine their roles in incidental and intentional language learning. By and large, individual differences are discussed with some general and vague notion of 'learning' in mind.

There is evidence to show that the three factors we have focused on in this chapter – starting age, language aptitude and motivation – are implicated in both types of learning. We have suggested that children differ from adults because they rely more on incidental/implicit learning. Once learners reach puberty they tend to engage in intentional/explicit learning. Although language aptitude is a factor both in communicative classrooms, which cater primarily to incidental learning, and in more formal classrooms, which cater to intentional learning, different components of language aptitude may be important for the two types of learning. For example, phonetic sensitivity and working memory have been shown to mediate learners' ability to process and rehearse material from input (an essentially incidental process), whereas language analytical ability contributes to their ability to formulate explicit rules (an intentional process) and appears to play a greater role with older learners (DeKeyser, 2012). Different aspects of motivation, too, may contribute in different ways to incidental and intentional learning. Pre-actional motivation, with its focus on forming 'action plans', implies a high level of intentionality on the learners' part. The executive motivation of the actional phase, however, would seem to relate to both types of learning. 'Appraisal', for example, can take place at a high level of consciousness but, as Ushioda and Preston have pointed out, it also arises in the contextualized interactions that learners participate in – a process that is surely more incidental than intentional.

Given the importance of the distinction between incidental and intentional learning in SLA, there is a clear need for more thought to be given to how individual difference factors affect both. Learners differ in terms of their capacity and their motivation to learn incidentally or intentionally but, with the exception of occasional references to differences between child and older learners, we could find no consideration of this in the teacher guides. The focus on learning strategies, for example, assumes the importance of intentional learning (i.e. the conscious application of explicitly taught strategies) and thus may be well suited to those learners who favour this type of learning but may not be so useful for learners who prefer incidental learning.

Focus on how individual difference factors influence the process of acquisition and not just on learning outcomes

This principle builds on the preceding one. We have seen that individual factors affect learning outcomes via the influence they have on the processes involved in acquisition. For example, different dimensions of language aptitude are involved in focus on form and explicit rule learning (see Figure 11.2). Robinson suggested that different instructional techniques (e.g. recasts and metalinguistic feedback) favour different dimensions of aptitude. Motivation, too, has been shown to play a role in some of the key L2 processes – for example, noticing – and that this can influence the learning opportunities that arise when learners perform an instructional activity (e.g. a task). Teachers need to be aware of *how* individual factors such as age, aptitude and motivation impact on the central processes involved in acquisition. Again, the guides we have inspected demonstrate little awareness of this.

Accommodate differences in language aptitude eclectically

One of the main ways of addressing individual learner differences is by instruction matching (see Figure 11.1). However, this approach is only really possible with those factors that are stable and therefore fixed. It makes no sense trying to match instruction to learners' motivation, for example. In the case of age, however, it is clearly possible to conceive of different approaches catering to incidental and intentional language learning. In the case of language aptitude, instruction matching is also feasible by distinguishing different types of language aptitude (e.g. one learner may be strong in auditory segmentation while another is strong in inductive language learning ability).

Figure 11.1 suggested two ways in which learner-instruction matching can be achieved within the same class – by grouping learners according to their abilities and then devising instruction that matched these or by offering an eclectic selection of activities, some of which will suit all the learners at least some of the time. We also saw the danger of such eclecticism, namely that it can result in 'irresponsible adhocery'. The logistic problems of organizing instruction matching through grouping preclude this option in most classroom contexts. It will overburden the teacher with the need to prepare different instructional materials for different groups and is also very demanding of a teacher's classroom management skills. Even though, as DeKeyser (2012) noted, 'various forms of technology are beginning to make true individualization possible' (p. 197), in most instructional contexts instruction matching will still need to be achieved eclectically rather than by design. The SLA research offers some suggestions for how this can be achieved by identifying the kinds of instructional strategies that correlate with different dimensions of language aptitude. For example, in the case of corrective feedback, recasts will suit learners who possess an aptitude for perceptual speed and pattern recognition, whereas metalinguistic feedback is suited to learners with an aptitude for grammatical sensitivity and rote memory. An eclectic approach to corrective feedback would involve the teacher using a mix of corrective feedback strategies so as to cater to the mixed types of aptitude in the class as a whole. This approach, it should be noted, runs contrary to the direction of much CF research in the cognitive–interactionist tradition, which has focused on trying to identify the particular type of CF that is most effective overall. But it accords with the approach to CF found in sociocultural research. (See Chapter 10 for a discussion of these different approaches.) Clearly, though, more research is required to explore how aptitude interacts with a whole range of instructional procedures.

Promote motivation through classroom interaction

Motivation is open to influence. Thus, the aim of instruction should be to ensure that learners are motivated and remain motivated. The importance of motivation is recognized in the teacher guides although there is a surprising lack of specific advice about what teachers need to do to promote learners' motivation. In contrast, motivation researchers such as Dörnyei (2001) have drawn on models of motivation and the research these have spawned to propose detailed sets of motivational strategies that teachers can use. Such lists are doubtlessly helpful but to be truly useful teachers need to know how to implement them. How, for example, does a teacher 'develop a personal relationship with the students'? We have examined studies which show that motivation is ultimately something that is constructed interactionally. So, ultimately, if teachers wish to promote their students' motivation, they need to understand how they can do this through what Preston (2009) has termed 'localised formations of L2 motivation experience' (p. ii). In the case of task-based teaching, this is achieved through the way in which learners (and the teacher) engage collaboratively when performing tasks. Egbert (2003), for example, explored what she called 'flow' (i.e. 'an experiential state characterized by intense focus and involvement that leads to improved performance on a task' (p. 499)) in group work. Flow occurred when there was: (1) a perceived balance of skills and challenges, (2) opportunities for intense concentration, (3) feedback on whether the learners were succeeding, (4) a lack of self-consciousness on the part of the learners and (5) the perception of time passing quickly. Such a list is helpful not because it provides concrete suggestions for how to achieve 'flow', but as a checklist that teachers can use to evaluate to what extent learners are motivated by a task. In whole-class interaction, learners' motivation depends on the extent to which learners feel involved in the discourse. Richards (2006), for example, showed how learners' interest in the interactions they were participating in depended to a considerable extent on the 'identities' they and the teacher enacted in the discourse of the classroom, with those interactions involving 'transportable identities' much more likely to arouse interest than those based on 'teacher–student identities'.

If motivation is situated, dynamic and relational, as current L2 motivation theory emphasizes (Dörnyei and Ushioda, 2009), then it has to be understood in terms of the contexts in which it is constructed – through interaction. If teachers wish to promote and maintain motivation, they need to ensure the learners are receptive to and engaged in the talk that goes on in a classroom.

Focus strategy training on helping learners achieve self-regulation

In our opinion, traditional strategy training holds out much less promise of assisting language learning than advocates such as Oxford (1990) or Cohen (2011) have claimed. By 'traditional' we refer to training that isolates specific strategies and teaches them explicitly through explanation, examples and practice. Awareness-raising activities hold out more promise as they are not designed to change learners 'actions' but to encourage them to subject their beliefs about language learning to critical scrutiny. However, they are better suited to older learners than to children. Also, we know of no research that clearly demonstrates that raising awareness about specific learning strategies impacts on either their actual use in instructional activities or on learning. In general, learner beliefs have been found to be only indirectly and weakly related to learning (R. Ellis, 2008).

However, an approach to strategy training based on the precepts of Sociocultural Theory holds out much more promise. This involves three requirements:

1 The strategy has to be explained 'scientifically'. It is not enough to tell learners to 'use context to infer the meaning of a word'; they need to be informed of the exact procedure they will need to follow to execute this strategy as in Nation's (1990) proposal for teaching this strategy.
2 The use of the strategy must be embedded in an authentic instructional task, not just in decontextualized exercises designed to practice the strategy.
3 Learners must be encouraged to verbalize their application of the strategy as they perform the instructional task.

The aim of such an approach is to help the learner achieve self-regulated use of the strategy. We have seen one example of this approach to training in Holunga's study. Another example can be found in the account of Concept-based Language Teaching in Chapter 4.

Conclusion

We have seen that learners differ in a multitude of ways and that accommodating these differences in language teaching is challenging. We have also noted that some commentators reject 'neat, pre-packaged solutions to language teaching problems' (Tudor, 1996: x), arguing instead for a holistic approach based on individuals rather than a differentiated approach based on specific, isolated learner factors. In one respect, this is sound advice. There are a large number of individual factors – Table 11.1 shows only a selection. In this chapter, we have only examined three key factors – age, language aptitude and motivation – and learning strategies. We have had nothing to say about a number of other factors (in particular, learning style and language anxiety) that have been the subject of attention from both researchers and teacher educators. Tudor is right, therefore – it is impossible for teachers to systematically take account of all these factors.

However, based on our understanding of the current SLA research, we feel that Tudor has somewhat overstated his position. Where age is concerned, there should be no difficulty in adopting pedagogic approaches suited to children and older learners. Also, it is very clear that both language aptitude and motivation are major factors accounting for a high proportion of the variance in the success of individual learners. Thus, there is a case, for considering how teaching can accommodate these two factors separately. This we have tried to do, although we recognize that there is still much work to be done to relate the research and theory to actual practice. We have also argued for strategy training, providing it is approached from an adequate theoretical base.

Perhaps, the major lesson for teachers that comes from the SLA research is to recognize that catering for individual differences is not just a matter of choosing instructional materials to suit different students and even less a matter of teaching learning strategies. Above all, it is a matter of engaging fully with learners through the interactions that take place for, as we saw in Chapter 8, teaching is interaction. We accommodate age and psychological differences in the people we meet in our daily lives in the way we interact with them and this is how teachers can best ensure that they treat learners as 'complex human beings who bring with them to the classroom their own individual personality' (Tudor, 2001: 14).

Notes

1 The only explicit treatment of individual difference factors in relation to independent learning we have been able to locate is Hurd (2002). Hurd examined a range of factors, reviews research on each, and offers a few suggestions about how they can affect independent learners. Hurd argued that 'knowledge of learner differences and the implications for learning and teaching is vital' but offers no concrete proposals for how this knowledge can be built into independent-learning materials.

2 In 'I like you, you are different', students are asked to write three things that make them feel good and that make them different from other students in

the class. The teacher reads out the cards and asks the class to guess the identity of the student who wrote it (Moskowitz, 1999: 190).

3 Readers may be surprised that we have decided not to address learning style. However, we feel this is justified by the fact that the research that has examined this factor has failed to provide convincing evidence of how or to what extent it affects learning and also because – given the multiplicity of learning styles dealt with in the literature – it is difficult to see how the research can be applied to language pedagogy.

DISCUSSION QUESTIONS

1. Read through the description of the psychological factors that affect L2 acquisition in Table 11.1. Which ones do you consider to be stable/permanent and which ones are mutable/dynamic?
2. Read through the section of the chapter that deals with how individual learner differences are addressed in language pedagogy and summarize what the teacher guides have to say about each of these factors:
   a. Age
   b. Motivation
   c. Language aptitude
   d. Language anxiety.
3. Tudor (2001) argued that learners cannot be really treated as 'discrete bundles of variables' (p. 14). They are individuals and how they differ will reflect their profile on an array of factors. Do you agree? If this is the case, how can teachers take account of the 'whole individual'?
4. Make a list of what you would consider to be the main characteristics of a 'good language learner'. One way to do this might be to think about a learner who is very successful and who you know well.
5. The chapter distinguishes three broad approaches for dealing with individual differences in learners:
   a. by selecting which learners to teach
   b. by trying to cater to individual differences by means of instruction matching, individualization or learner training
   c. by promoting receptivity.
   Which of these approaches do you find the most promising? Give your reasons.
6. What impact does age have on L2 acquisition? In what ways do you think instruction can take account of differences in the age of learners?
7. Explain how learners will differ in their ability to benefit from different types of instruction depending on the nature of their aptitude. Can you suggest how teachers might adjust their teaching to take account of this?
8. Why does language aptitude play a more important role in L2 learning with children than with adults?
9. In this chapter, we claim that motivation is a 'complex construct'. In what ways is it complex?
10. In what ways can Dörnyei and Otto's Process Model of Motivation serve as a basis for teacher intervention aimed at fostering motivation in learners?

11. The results of research that have investigated strategy training are very mixed. Why do you think that a number of studies have found it has no effect on learning or L2 use? Which type of strategy training do you think has the best chance of success?

12. Why is it important to distinguish the roles okayed by individual difference factors in incidental and intentional language learning?

13. Discuss some of the ways in which teachers can take account of how language aptitude and motivation affect the *process* of L2 learning.

14. Suggest some of the ways in which teachers can accommodate individual differences 'eclectically' while avoiding 'irresponsible adhocery'.

15. Motivation 'emerges through interaction'. In what sense does this happen? How can teachers influence learners' motivation through interaction?

Part V

Conclusion

The main goal of teaching a second language (L2) is to help learners learn the L2. There may be other goals (e.g. the development of cultural awareness or, from an educational perspective, the development of lifelong learning skills or the social skills needed to learn with others) but these are secondary. We teach an L2 so that learners can learn it. It is axiomatic, then, that teaching needs to be conducted in such a way that it accords with how learners learn an L2. This being so, any account of how to teach a language must also take into consideration about how learners learn a language.

In this final chapter, we examine two ways in which this can be achieved. The first is to examine what SLA has discovered about L2 acquisition and then apply it to language teaching. The second way is to submit pedagogical proposals to critical scrutiny through an examination of relevant SLA research. We have adopted the second approach in this book. We conclude by identifying some of the ways in which the discourse of language pedagogy might benefit from a closer inspection of SLA research.

12 Teaching for learning

Introduction

The purpose of this book was to explore how what is known about how people learn an L2 can inform language pedagogy so as to maximize its effectiveness. There are two ways of going about this. One way is to familiarize teachers with what researchers have found out about L2 learning and then apply the findings to language pedagogy:

SLA research → language pedagogy

There are now a number of comprehensive surveys of SLA theory and research (e.g. Gass and Selinker, 2002; Ellis, 2008; Ortega, 2009). These books, however, treat 'SLA' as an academic discipline and it is questionable whether such books have much direct relevance to language pedagogy. Other surveys (e.g. Lightbown and Spada, 2006), however, have been written with teachers in mind and, therefore, are client-centred. Nevertheless, even these do not directly address the 'questions that teachers ask' (Pica, 1994). Teachers' starting point, understandably, is not 'How do learners learn?' but rather 'How should I teach?' The second way, therefore, is to start with commonly held views about what constitutes sound language pedagogy and then consider these in the light of how learners learn:

Language pedagogy → SLA research

This is the approach we have adopted in this book. We have examined a variety of pedagogical proposals drawn from popular handbooks for teachers and asked to what extent these proposals are compatible with the findings of SLA. Such an approach, we would argue, accords more with how teachers and teacher educators view SLA. Hedge (2000), for example, speaking from the teacher educator's point of view, noted that it would be a mistake 'to assume that research in the contributing disciplines produces an agreed theory on language use or language learning that we can apply in immediate and direct ways'. Instead, 'it is more a question of having a foundation of knowledge against which we can evaluate our own ideas about teaching and learning, to which we can apply for insights in our attempts to solve pedagogic problems' (p. 2). This has been the perspective that has informed this book.

In this concluding chapter, we will explore a little more fully these two approaches to using SLA in language pedagogy. First, we will explore the possibilities of 'applying SLA' and, second, the advantages of 'exploring language pedagogy through SLA'.

Applying SLA

SLA researchers have not been slow to assert the importance of SLA for language pedagogy. Spolsky (1990), for example, commented 'we have a traditional concern to consider not just the explanatory power of a theory but also its relevance to second language pedagogy' (p. 610). Long (2006), with teachers and teacher educators in mind, viewed SLA as a 'field with considerable social consequences for millions of people all over the world' (p. 156). There is, however, no consensus among SLA researchers about how SLA should inform language pedagogy, reflecting Bardovi-Harlig's (1995) observation that the 'relationship of pedagogy to second language acquisition is a complex one that is not clearly agreed on by applied linguists' (p. 151). For some, SLA provides 'hard evidence' which should be used to advise teachers about what techniques and procedures work best (Long, 1990). In general, however, SLA researchers have been wary of prescribing or proscribing ways of teaching, preferring instead to suggest that the SLA findings can do no more than afford 'provisional specifications' (Stenhouse, 1975) about how to teach and that it is up to teachers to decide whether to act on these in their own classrooms (Ellis, 1997).

The customary way in which researchers seek to make the results of their research available to teachers is by means of an 'implications' section tacked on to the end of a research report. However, this does not meet with the agreement of all researchers as an interesting exchange in *TESOL Quarterly* 41(4) demonstrates. Han (2007) criticized the tendency of research articles to 'ostentatiously link the research to practice' (p. 31) but Chapelle (2007) responded by arguing that 'if an author can state no implications for teaching and learning, *TESOL Quarterly* is the wrong journal' (p. 405) and went on to point out that the author is in the best position to make the first attempt at pedagogical implications and so should do so. While Chapelle has a point, there is an obvious danger in trying to apply the results of an individual study; it does not follow that the implications drawn from a single study are of relevance to all teachers in all instructional contexts. It is also doubtful whether teachers (or many teacher educators) read research articles so the 'implications' – if drawn – have no impact on language pedagogy. It is striking that the teacher guides we examined in this book rarely cited any SLA research and only occasionally demonstrated any familiarity with it.

An approach that is perhaps more likely to gain some traction in pedagogical circles is to base advice on theories that have been tried and tested through research. Krashen (1983) argued for this approach, noting that initially he made the mistake of trying to apply the results of research to pedagogy before realizing that what was needed was a theory of L2 acquisition that could inform teaching. The problem, however, is that there are a lot of theories to choose from and, to date, there is no agreement in SLA about which theory provides the most robust explanation of L2 acquisition. Krashen had his own theory in mind – the Monitor Model (later relabelled as the Input Hypothesis). This did have a considerable impact on language pedagogy but it has come in for considerable criticism from other SLA researchers and clearly lacks explanatory adequacy in a number of respects. No other single theory has replaced it as a guide for pedagogy. We are now in a situation where there is a plethora of SLA theories, all of which have some merit, but which also in some respects offer fundamentally different accounts of L2 acquisition. In this book, for example, we have seen that cognitive–interactionist and sociocultural theories offer conflicting explanations about the role of interaction in L2 learning. Thus, while there might be merit in exploring the applications of specific theories to language pedagogy, it is doubtful whether a theory-based approach holds much promise. It would be asking a lot of the authors of the teacher guides to find their way through the varying applications of all the different theories.

There is, however, another way. Lightbown (1985b, 2000) attempted to summarize SLA research in terms of a set of generalizations which were 'consistent with the research to date' and which could serve as a 'source of information which could help teachers set appropriate expectations for themselves and their students' (2000: 431). Table 12.1 summarizes these generalizations and provides a commentary based on the research Lightbown referred to in support of them. It should be noted that she chose to cite only research carried out in classroom contexts on the grounds that such research was of more direct relevance to language pedagogy.

Lightbown is cautious in applying these generalizations to language pedagogy. She is critical of researchers such as Krashen and Truscott who are less cautious, as she feels their recommendations are not consistent with her own reading of the research. She argued that while SLA research is valuable in helping to question teachers' intuitions about how to teach, it is also important to guard against advocating pedagogical behaviours that are 'not compatible with their understanding of their role as teachers' (p. 453). She commented:

> when researchers make strong claims that are at odds with the views teachers have developed through their experience with learners, and when those claims are made on the basis of research which has been done in contexts which do not reflect reality as the teachers know it, they are likely to alienate teachers and lead them to dismiss researchers as ivory tower oddities.
>
> (p. 453)

This is why she views SLA research as a body of knowledge that can help to shape teachers' 'expectations' rather than as a source of specific recommendations. She called for researchers to 'enter into a dialogue with classroom teachers', listening to what they are saying as well as informing them about SLA.

Table 12.1 Lightbown's ten generalizations

Generalization	Commentary
1. Adults and adolescents can 'acquire' a second language.	While there is clear evidence that incidental acquisition can take place in a classroom, it is also clear that 'guided instruction' benefits learning.
2. The learner creates a systematic interlanguage which is often characterized by the same systematic errors as the child learning the same language as a first language, as well as others which appear to be based on the learner's own native language.	Exposure to formal instruction does not prevent 'systematic interlanguage patterns' emerging. These patterns, however, are not identical with those observed in L1 acquisition as the learner's L1 influences them in subtle ways.
3. There are predictable sequences in L2 acquisition such that certain structures have to be acquired before others can be integrated.	Progress in learning an L2 cannot be assessed purely in terms of whether learners can use the L2 in target-like ways; progress is also evident in movement along a developmental sequence.
4. Practice does not make perfect.	Practice directed at rote-learning is ineffective but it may assist the acquisition of formulaic chunks which learners may later break down for language acquisition.
5. Knowing a language rule does not mean one will be able to use it in communicative interaction.	While there are limits to what explicit instruction can achieve, there is growing evidence that the explicit teaching of grammatical rules is beneficial and, in some case, may be necessary to overcome the influence of the learners' L1.
6. Isolated explicit error correction is usually ineffective in changing language behaviour.	Error correction does not result in instant elimination of the error but it can be effective if sustained, focused on a feature the learner is capable of learning, and occurs in response to the learner's attempt to communicate.
7. For most adult learners, acquisition stops before the learner has achieved native-like mastery of the target language.	Even if there is a 'critical period' for language acquisition, it does not follow that 'younger is better'. Also the 'critical period' is of little relevance in a foreign language context.
8. One cannot achieve native-like (or near native-like) command of a second language in one day.	To be successful learners, irrespective of the age they start learning, needs both extensive and intensive exposure to the L2.
9. The learner's task is enormous because language is enormously complex.	Because of the complexity of a language, it is doubtful that learners can achieve mastery of morphosyntax or the sociolinguistic and pragmatic features of a language if they are dependent entirely on the classroom.
10. A learner's ability to understand language in a meaningful context exceeds his/her ability to comprehend decontextualized language and to produce language of comparable complexity and accuracy.	Receptive ability exceeds productive ability and acquisition can be promoted through manipulating the input to induce noticing of grammatical forms. Mastery of an L2 for use in everyday social interaction does not imply mastery of its use in complex/academic contexts.

However, there is one other way in which SLA might be applied more directly to language pedagogy – by engaging teachers in SLA research. Vasquez and Harvey (2010) provide a good example of how this might be accomplished. They asked a group of MA and doctoral students taking a course in SLA to replicate Lyster and Ranta's (1997) study of corrective feedback. To assist these novice researchers, they broke down the research process into a number of steps. First, they asked them to video record their own classes, then to prepare transcripts of the lessons, and then, after extensive discussion of Lyster and Ranta's categories, to code the data. They were also given the opportunity to share their results before finally writing a research report. Vasquez and Harvey were interested in what effect their research had on the teachers' own views about corrective feedback. They reported that the teachers were surprised to find how prevalent recasts were in their own teaching and that they became more aware of the importance of learner uptake. Interestingly, they were more inclined to acknowledge the cognitive rather than the affective dimension of corrective feedback as a result of their research – a change that we also suggested might be justified on the basis of our own evaluation of commonly held pedagogical views about corrective feedback (see Chapter 10). Replicating SLA studies in this manner seems an excellent way of encouraging teachers to examine their own intuitions about teaching. However, it is time-consuming and probably not something that most teachers would wish or were able to undertake.

Exploring language pedagogy through SLA

The alternative to applying SLA to language pedagogy is to take pedagogic issues as a starting point and then examine these in terms of findings from SLA. This is the approach we have adopted in this book. Our starting point was to identify a series of pedagogic topics. This was not easy as language pedagogy is now a rich and complex body of 'thinking about teaching in practice' (Levine and Phipps, 2011), informed not only by actual experience of learning and teaching but also by theories of language, language use and learning. It covers thinking about how both language-as-a-system and the four language skills can be taught. In its critical form, language pedagogy also addresses how teachers can assist learners to confront inequality and oppression (Crookes, 2010). Clearly it was necessary to make some kind of selection of the pedagogic issues we would examine.

We elected to define 'language pedagogy' quite narrowly in terms of how it addresses language-as-a-system (i.e. teaching directed at developing the linguistic knowledge learners need to communicate in an L2). Thus, we did not consider the four language skills or sociocritical issues. Nor have we dealt thoroughly with the taxing question of whether the goal of an instructional programme should be target-language norms or the functional lingua franca observed in communication between non-native speakers (Seidlhofer, 2011). We justify our choice in two ways. First, mainstream language pedagogy, as reflected in the popular pedagogic literature we inspected (e.g. teacher guides such as those by Harmer, Hedge, Nunan and Scrivener), is focused primarily on language-as-a-system and has still not taken on board critical perspectives or English-as-a-lingua franca. Second, SLA has been largely concerned with how learners acquire linguistic knowledge of an L2 and so it made sense to choose pedagogic issues that were readily examinable through SLA. We acknowledge the limitations of our choice but would also claim that the issues we have chosen are likely to be perceived as relevant to teacher educators and teachers in a wide range of instructional contexts.

The issues we identified were all 'interface issues' (i.e. issues that are of central importance in language pedagogy but are also issues that SLA clearly speaks to). We divided these issues into those that entail an 'external' and 'internal' perspective on language teaching. The former is evident in descriptions of what and how to teach. It constitutes 'technical knowledge' about teaching and is most clearly evident in the teacher guides. The latter treats teaching as an interactional event – the classroom talk that creates the contexts in which learning takes place. As we have seen, this receives much less attention in the teacher guides, understandably perhaps, given that it is much more difficult to provide advice about how teaching functions as a process than as a body of explicit techniques and procedures. However, arguably, it is the 'internal perspective' that SLA is best equipped to address and the relative absence of this perspective in the teacher guides is indicative of the failure of SLA to impact on mainstream accounts of language pedagogy.

To identify the issues that concern teachers we undertook an inspection of the pedagogic literature. This literature is voluminous so we focused on a number of popular guides for teachers, first identifying common topics relating to the teaching of language-as-a-system. These topics provided the content for the various chapters in this book. We then examined the positions taken by the authors of the guides on each topic, noting both commonalities and differences among them. In general, the commonalties far outweighed the differences. As Hedge (2000) noted in the introduction to her own teacher guide, it is possible 'to discern a number of persistent concerns in the professional practice of teachers' despite the 'vast heterogeneity of activity' that characterizes language teaching in classrooms (p. 1). She went on to list these concerns, starting with the issue that lies at the core of this book – 'What should the aims of language teaching be and what kinds of activities are needed to achieve them?'

The guides varied in the approach they adopted to each pedagogic topic. In some cases, they simply provided descriptions of the various approaches, techniques and procedures and avoided specific recommendations. In other cases, however, they were more forthright in proscribing and prescribing instructional practices. In still other cases (e.g. Ur, 1996), they invited teachers to explore their own thinking about particular aspects of teaching (e.g. how to conduct written corrective feedback) before giving their own opinions. In one respect, the guides were 'how-to' books designed to provide teachers with a comprehensive account about the practice of teaching. The authors often drew explicitly on their experience of teaching as teachers and thus were well placed to give practical advice. In addition, however – and in varying degrees – the authors demonstrated familiarity with educational theory and, on occasions, the findings of SLA research. This is reflected in the broader aim of the guides. They sought to identify underlying principles that could help teachers develop a theory of teaching and to offer teachers a range of options to select from in accordance with the needs of their own instructional context.

The guides provide excellent surveys of current thinking about language pedagogy and are important sources of knowledge for teachers. Our purpose in writing this book was not to critique them but rather to examine them to see to what extent they reflect what is known about how learners learn. We will turn now to some of the main findings of this examination.

None of the guides promotes a specific method for teaching language and, thus, in this respect they adopt a post-method approach (Kumaravadivelu, 2001). However, the guides do frequently refer to different methods and in one example (Klapper, 2006) an explicit case was made for familiarizing teachers with the theoretical premises and procedures of different methods. In Chapter 2, we noted that a case can still be made for including an examination of different methods in language pedagogy. Some of the earliest research in SLA was directed at evaluating the effectiveness of methods popular at that time. One way in which teachers can be made aware of the limitations of basing their teaching on a specific method is to examine why the comparative method studies were largely unsuccessful in demonstrating that one method was superior to another. We also argued that a case can still be made for 'local' (rather than 'global') method comparisons as there is still a need to establish whether the claims made on behalf of a method (or approach) are empirically justified.

Even though the guides were post-method in their orientation, it is possible to identify a commonality of 'approach'. All the guides address how to teach language-as-a-system assuming that this should be based on a structural syllabus. They devote considerable space to 'accuracy-work' through explicit instruction involving present–practice–produce. The guides take no account of the order and sequence of acquisition, assuming instead that a carefully crafted lesson can succeed in enabling learners to not just learn a new structure (in the sense of understanding it) but also to use it accurately in free communication. SLA does provide ample evidence that explicit instruction can assist learners to perform linguistic features more accurately (see Chapter 4) but it also questions whether a 'new' (as opposed to partially acquired) structure can be taught successfully if learners are not ready to do so – see Lightbown's second generalization in Table 12.1. If teachers are to have realistic expectations of what they can achieve through instruction, they need to be aware of the limitations of an approach based on a structural syllabus (see Chapter 3) and explicit instruction.

All the guides also recognize the importance of 'fluency-work'. However, by and large, 'accuracy-work' and 'fluency-work' are treated as distinct and separate ways of teaching. Accuracy activities are required to teach new language; fluency activities are needed to develop communicative abilities. The guides recognize the importance of 'tasks' but see these as contributing to fluency rather than accuracy and they figure most clearly in accounts of how to develop speaking skills. It is perhaps in this respect that the guides differ most clearly from the perspective afforded by SLA, which views accuracy and fluency as closely linked. In SLA, new linguistic knowledge is not seen as a prerequisite for communicative activity but as occurring within it when learners engage in interactions that, in one way or another, facilitate or create opportunities for learning. In Chapter 10, for example, we noted that the guides recommend that teachers should avoid correcting errors until students have completed a communicative task. Willis (1996) too considers that accuracy work is best left to the post-task stage of a task-based lesson. In contrast, SLA emphasizes the need to provide corrections while students are communicating as this helps learners with the form-function mapping that learning a language entails. From an SLA perspective, accuracy-work needs to be embedded in fluency-work. There is now a rich body of research that shows how this can be achieved.

It would be unfair to characterize mainstream accounts of language pedagogy as treating language entirely as an 'object' with the emphasis on a list of discrete items to be taught. Clearly, there is awareness that language is also a 'tool' for communicating. But, by and large, the emphasis in the teacher guides is on language-as-an-object and on intentional learning. This is understandable as it provides the easiest way of specifying the aims of teaching, which Hedge rightly saw as the main concern of teachers. But it ignores the importance of incidental learning in a classroom. Language is hugely complex and as SLA researchers have noted there are limits to what can be learned intentionally. Learners cannot be taught all the collocations a word can enter into nor can they be taught everything there is to know about the grammar of a language. While it is undoubtedly useful to divide language up into a series of bits and pieces which can be systematically taught, it is crucial that teachers recognize the limitations of such an approach. Consideration also needs to be given to how incidental learning can be fostered in the classroom.

The main way in which the pedagogic literature addresses this is through the advocacy of extensive reading (see Chapter 7). This is seen as not just helping to develop reading skills but also providing learners with exposure to vocabulary and grammar that they can learn incidentally. However, the pedagogic literature also includes recommendations that are not compatible with what is known about incidental learning. As we saw in Chapter 7, there is a strong commitment to the importance of authentic materials but this takes no account of how input works for acquisition. Incidental acquisition only becomes possible if learners are able to comprehend the input they are exposed to and an insistence on authentic materials – especially in the early stages of learning – is unlikely to ensure it. It is not authentic input that learners need but input that they are able to authenticate. Authentic input may have a place in language pedagogy for more advanced learners but from an SLA perspective it has been over-valued. There is also a neglect of the importance of teacher-talk as a source for incidental learning. The rather simplistic claims sometimes made in the guides about restricting the amount of teacher-talk in order to maximize opportunities for learner-talk in the classroom need re-evaluating.

The pedagogic approach that is most clearly directed at incidental learning is task-based teaching, where language is treated as a tool for making meaning and thereby creating opportunities for learners to acquire new language as well as develop fluency. In general, however, the teacher guides we inspected pay little attention to this. 'Tasks', when they do figure in the guides, are typically seen as devices for providing opportunities for free production in PPP. There is very little consideration of the possibility of defining the content of a syllabus (or of part of a syllabus) in terms of tasks in the teacher guides. In recent years – as we saw in Chapter 6 – interest in task-based teaching has been growing, in part as a result of SLA research which has investigated the design of tasks and how they can be implemented. SLA has shown how tasks can create the interactional conditions for incidental learning by fostering the negotiation of meaning and form and the types of mediation (e.g. 'languaging') that Sociocultural Theory claims are needed. It has shown how the design and implementation variables can be manipulated to influence the extent to which learners focus on fluency, complexity and accuracy. There are problems that still need to be worked out to make task-based teaching an effective pedagogic approach – not the least how to grade and sequence tasks in a task-based syllabus – but mainstream pedagogy surely cannot continue to ignore its potential for learning for much longer. It is noticeable that task-based teaching has attracted the criticism of advocates of traditional pedagogy (e.g. Swan, 2005) on the grounds that it is based on 'theory' and is untested empirically. Such criticism, however, ignores the very substantial amount of research in SLA that has shown that task-based teaching is effective and, in fact, more effective for some learners than traditional teaching (see, e.g. Shintani and Ellis, 2010). Our own position, however, is that this debate is unproductive. SLA research has shown that traditional teaching (i.e. explicit instruction) is also effective, especially with older learners. What is needed is an approach that balances instruction that treats language as an 'object' and as a 'tool' and thus caters to both intentional and incidental learning.

Teaching is best seen not as a set of techniques and procedures but as 'interaction'. Techniques and procedures are of value only if they give rise to the kinds of interactions in which and through which learning can take place. In general, teaching-as-interaction receives little attention in the guides, reflecting the emphasis placed on the 'external' as opposed to 'internal' aspects of teaching. Where 'interaction' is considered, it is discussed in terms of giving opportunities for student talk – viewed primarily in terms of quantity rather than quality. SLA theories – whether cognitive–interactionist or sociocultural – point to the need for the importance of the *quality* of learner talk rather than *quantity* (see Chapter 8). Learners need to be 'stretched' by being pushed to experiment with and extend their output. SLA research suggests ways in which this can be achieved. It also points to the need to reconsider the contribution that initiate–respond–follow-up (IRF) exchanges can make to learning. A number of the guides point out the dangers of this type of classroom discourse but none suggest how it might be adapted to foster learning. From an SLA perspective, perhaps, the central question that teachers need to consider is 'How can teaching ensure that the interactions that occur in a classroom create the conditions for successful learning?' This requires a fuller answer than we could find in the guides.

There were two topics that received careful attention in the guides – the role of the L1 and corrective feedback. The common view in language pedagogy is that teachers should strive for maximal use of the target language and also encourage students to avoid use of the L1. In Chapter 9, however, we saw that in fact teachers often do resort to the L1 and that SLA research on language transfer points to the positive way in which the L1 can contribute to L2 learning, as well as the possibilities of negative transfer. There needs to be a much more discriminating account of how the L1 can be used by both teachers and students to manage instructional activities and to facilitate interlanguage development. Translation, for example, can function as an effective pedagogic tool for both teachers and learners and can assist learning.

The guides all recommend that teachers should correct both oral errors (although not in fluency-work) and written errors. Correction is seen as both necessary – because students expect it – and helpful for learning. In two major respects, however, the views expressed in the guides and the findings of SLA research diverge. First, the guides emphasize the importance of the affective dimension of corrective feedback, pointing out the potential dangers in arousing a negative emotional response in learners. We saw that the teachers in Vasquez and Harvey's (2010) study started off with the same view. In contrast, SLA has focused on the cognitive dimension, exploring the effect of different types of correction on learning. Second, the guides simply list the different corrective strategies available to teachers with no consideration of their role in learning. SLA distinguishes strategies in terms of clearly defined general categories (i.e. input-providing vs output-prompting and implicit vs explicit). There is now a rich body of research that has investigated the effect of strategies belonging to these categories on the learning of new and partially acquired linguistic features. The findings of this research, summarized in Chapter 10, are now sufficiently robust to provide a much more detailed and nuanced account of corrective feedback than is currently available in the pedagogic guides.

The final topic we considered was 'individual differences' in learners. This, again, is very much an 'interface' topic: it receives attention in both pedagogic circles and in SLA. In some ways, however, this is the most intractable topic for both teachers and researchers. For a start, there are a large number of ways in which learners differ (see Table 11.1 in Chapter 11) and the approach adopted in the guides and in SLA has been to treat each separately. This runs the danger of losing sight of the learner as a whole person. From a research perspective, perhaps, it makes sense to investigate individual learner factors, although there is a growing recognition of the limitations of such an approach. From the teaching perspective, however, it is impossible to devise instructional materials that take all the different factors into account. It was for this reason that we elected to focus on the two factors that research has shown play the major role in language learning – language aptitude and motivation – and argued that there is a case for examining how teaching can accommodate these. We noted that whereas motivation is addressed in the guides, language aptitude is ignored. The guides pay more attention to learning strategies and the role of strategy training. We suggested, however, that this is a much less promising approach than some of its advocates have claimed, although we did see merit in encouraging students to verbalize the use of a specific strategy as they perform an instructional task. Individual learner differences are clearly important but how to take account of them in an effective pedagogy remains a challenge. With the exception of Dörnyei's (2001) work on 'motivational strategies', which deserves full consideration, we found it difficult to see how the research on individual difference factors in SLA can make an effective contribution to the pedagogic literature. Clearly, more work is needed to explore the interface between language pedagogy and SLA on this topic.

Concluding comments

In the Introduction to Part I, we pointed to the distinction between 'practical discourse' and 'theoretical discourse' and also noted the problems of trying to explain the former in terms of the latter. As Brumfit (1983) commented, 'learning to perform competently is never the same as learning to explain the process of performance' (p. 61). Practical discourse draws primarily on 'practical knowledge'; theoretical discourse deals with 'technical knowledge'. The question, then, is how the latter can inform the former.

There is no easy answer to this question (Ellis, 2010b) but one way of bridging the divide between the two discourses is to devise a theoretical discourse that is accessible to teachers. This is what the pedagogic literature – in particular, teacher guides – seeks to achieve by attempting to explain the 'process of performance' in terms that teachers can understand and relate to. In contrast, the theoretical discourse of SLA typically makes no attempt to be accessible to teachers. It is motivated by the concerns of researchers and cultivates a style that will be rewarded by publication in academic journals but is often incomprehensible. Busy teachers are likely to ignore SLA research. There are two ways of addressing this problem. One is to prepare a simplified account of SLA research aimed at teachers. As we have noted, there are books that have attempted this. The other way is more indirect. It involves an attempt to influence the theoretical discourse of language pedagogy itself. This involves an examination of the interface between two manifestations of 'technical discourse' – that of SLA and that of language pedagogy. This is what we have attempted to do in this book. Teachers do read teacher guides as they constitute the most obvious source of information about how to teach, so if SLA is to have an impact on the practical discourse of teaching, this might best be achieved as shown in Figure 12.1.

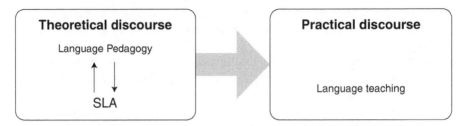

Figure 12.1 The interface of language pedagogy, SLA and teaching

There are two ways of achieving a nexus between the theoretical discourses of SLA and language pedagogy. One is to review SLA research and then derive a set of general instructional principles. This was the approach we followed in Chapter 1, which concluded the brief survey of SLA with the eleven general principles of instructed language learning. There are merits in such an approach as it provides a clear basis for conducting and evaluating teaching and can provide a useful resource for teacher educators (see, e.g. Erlam, 2008). However, it is still necessary to operationalize such principles in terms of concrete descriptions of language teaching. In other words, there is still a need for the discourse of language pedagogy. In the rest of this book, we took a different approach. We opted to examine language pedagogy through the lens of SLA, identifying proposals that could be supported and those that perhaps need modifying. In so doing, we hoped to have an impact on the pedagogic literature by helping to fine-tune the 'technical knowledge' it imparts to teachers. Perhaps, too, as suggested by the direction of the arrows in Figure 12.1, it is possible (and desirable) for the discourse of language pedagogy to have an influence on the discourse of SLA. How that might be achieved, however, would be the subject for another book.

DISCUSSION QUESTIONS

1. 'There are a lot of theories to choose from and, to date, there is no agreement in SLA about which theory provides the most robust explanation of L2 acquisition.' Which of the SLA theories that you have read about in this book do you find most helpful for thinking about language teaching?
2. Consider the relevance of each of Lightbown's ten generalizations in Table 12.1 to language teaching. How can each generalization inform what and how teachers teach?
3. If you were asked to select ONE study you have read about in this book, which one would you choose? Why?
4. How helpful have your found the distinction between the 'external' and 'internal' perspectives on language teaching which has informed the structure of this book?
5. The teacher guides make a clear distinction between 'accuracy' and 'fluency' work. To what extent is this distinction justified from the perspective of SLA?

6. The guides place the emphasis on 'intentional learning' through the teaching of specific linguistic items. How much consideration do you think needs to be given to 'incidental learning' in language teaching?
7. We claim that 'from an SLA perspective perhaps the central question that teachers need to consider is "How can teaching ensure that the interactions that occur in a classroom create the conditions for successful learning?"' (p. 330). Do you agree that this is the central question?
8. Which of the various pedagogic topics addressed in this book did you find of most value for your own teaching?

Glossary

accuracy
'The extent to which the language produced conforms to target language norms' (Skehan, 1996: 22). A typical measure of accuracy is percentage of error-free clauses.

affective filter
A psychological mechanism that governs the extent to which learners are able to process input for acquisition. Key factors governing whether the affective filter is 'high' or 'low' are motivation and anxiety. If learners are motivated and have little anxiety, they are able to make use of the input.

Audiolingual Method
A method of foreign or second language teaching based on behaviourist learning theory. It emphasizes the use of dialogues and drills and avoidance of the use of the L1 to develop correct L2 'habits'.

authenticity
A term applied to language teaching materials based on texts intended for native speakers or on natural interactions involving native speakers.

behaviourist learning theory
A general theory of learning (i.e. it applies to all kinds of learning) that views learning as the formation of habits. These are formed when the learner is confronted with specific stimuli which lead to responses, which are, in turn, reinforced by rewards, or are corrected.

built-in syllabus
A term used by Corder (1967) to refer to the natural order in which learners acquire the grammatical features of an L2. It assumes that learners are in control of the acquisition of grammar in much the same way as children in L1 acquisition.

code-switching
A kind of intra-speaker variation. It occurs when a speaker changes from one variety or language to another variety or language in accordance with situational or purely personal factors.

Cognition Hypothesis
A hypothesis proposed by Robinson (2001). It states that, in task-based teaching, pedagogic tasks should be sequenced on the basis of their cognitive complexity so that they increasingly approximate to the demands of real-world tasks.

Cognitive-Code Method
An approach to language teaching which emphasizes active analysis of a language on the part of the learner and not just mechanical habit-formation. It lends support to the explicit teaching of grammatical rules followed by practice activities.

cognitive theory of L2 learning
A theory developed by Skehan (1998). It claims that learners possess a dual system of language – an exemplar-based and a rule-based system – and draw on this system differently depending whether conditions lead to fluency or accuracy/complexity being prioritized.

communication strategies
Communication strategies such as circumlocution or requesting assistance are employed when learners are faced with the task of communicating meanings for which they lack the requisite linguistic knowledge (e.g. when they have to refer to some object without knowing the L2 word).

Communicative Language Teaching
An approach to teaching aimed at fostering communicative competence in a language. There is a both a weak form involving the teaching of the linguistic means for expressing 'notions' (e.g. possibility) or 'functions' (e.g. apologizing) and a strong form involving basing teaching entirely on tasks.

Community Language Learning
A language teaching method where the teacher functions as a 'counsellor' by translating the learners' L1 comments in the L2. The learners then repeat this to other members of the group. It emphasizes the importance of taking into account learners' personal feelings and their reactions to language learning.

complexity
An aspect of language production involving the elaborate use of a wide range of linguistic features. Skehan (1998) claims that complexity arises when learners are prepared to take risks rather than focusing on using language accurately.

comprehensible input
A term used by Krashen (1985) to refer to oral or written language that learners are able to understand. Input can be made comprehensible in various ways: through simplification, with the help of context, or by negotiating non-understanding and misunderstanding.

comprehensible output
A term used by Swain (1985) to refer to output that is made comprehensible. Swain proposed that when learners have to make efforts to ensure that their output is comprehensible (i.e. produce 'pushed output'), acquisition may be fostered.

comprehension-based instruction (CBI)
A type of instruction that emphasizes developing linguistic competence through listening or reading activities rather than through speaking or writing. It is based on the claim that productive language skills emerge naturally when learners have well-developed comprehension skills, which should therefore be the initial focus of a language course.

consciousness raising (CR)
A term used to refer to attempts to focus learners' attention on the formal properties of the language. Ellis (1991) used the term to refer to attempts to help learners understand a

grammatical structure and learn it as explicit knowledge. In this narrower sense it contrasts with 'practice'.

consciousness-raising tasks
Tasks that are designed to guide learners to discover how linguistic features function in a language. They provide learners with 'data' which learners are then helped to analyse so they understand an underlying rule.

Contrastive Analysis Hypothesis
A hypothesis that claims that L2 errors are the result of differences between the learner's L1 and the L2. The strong form of the hypothesis claims that these differences can be used to predict all errors that will occur. The weak form of the hypothesis claims that these differences can be used to identify only some out of the total errors that actually occur.

conversation analysis
A method for analysing social interactions in order to uncover their orderliness, structure and sequential patterns. It is used to investigate both casual conversation and institutional interactions (i.e. in the school, doctor's surgery, or law court). Key aspects of interaction studied in CA are turn-taking and repair.

corrective feedback
A type of feedback that provides learners with 'negative evidence' (i.e. indicates that they have made a linguistic or pragmatic error). Corrective feedback can be implicit or explicit; it can also be input-providing (in which case it also provides 'positive evidence') or output-prompting.

Critical Period Hypothesis
A hypothesis that claims that learners can only achieve full competence in an L2 if they start learning it as children.

deductive instruction
Instruction that provides learners with an explicit rule which they then practise in one way or another. It contrasts with *inductive instruction*.

Direct Method
A language teaching method which stipulates that only the target language is used in the classroom, the meaning of a sentence is demonstrated through actions and objects, speaking is prioritized, and grammar is taught only inductively.

Error Analysis
A method of analysing learner errors by identifying, describing and explaining them. Error Analysis for pedagogical purposes has a long history but its use as a tool for investigating how learners learn a language only began in the 1960s.

explicit form-focused instruction
Instruction that involves 'some sort of rule being thought about during the learning process' (DeKeyser, 1995). Learners are encouraged to develop metalinguistic awareness of the rule through *deductive* or *inductive instruction*.

explicit L2 knowledge
Knowledge of rules and items that exists in an analysed form so that learners are able to report what they know. Explicit L2 knowledge is *metalinguistic* in nature. It contrasts with *implicit knowledge*.

explicit L2 learning
Learning that takes place consciously and usually intentionally. It can be investigated by giving learners an explicit rule and asking them to apply it to data or by inviting them to try to discover an explicit rule from an array of data provided.

extensive reading
Reading large quantities of written material to gain a general understanding of what is read. Proponents of extensive reading claim that it develops good reading habits, builds up knowledge of vocabulary and structure, and promotes a liking for reading. It contrasts with intensive reading.

fluency
The 'capacity to produce language in real time without undue pausing or hesitation' (Skehan, 1998). It can be measured in different ways (e.g. by calculating the number of syllables produced per minute or counting the number of repetitions).

focus on form
A type of instruction that 'overtly draws students' attention to linguistic elements as they arise incidentally in lessons whose overriding focus is on meaning or communication (Long, 1991: 45–46). It contrasts with *focus on forms*.

focus on forms
A type of traditional language teaching that draws on a structural syllabus and involves teaching different language features one at a time. The underlying assumption is that language learning is an accumulative process involving mastering linguistic features one by one.

focused task
A task that is designed to elicit natural language use but also elicits the use of a predetermined linguistic feature.

foreigner talk
Talk that involves adjustments to the way a native speaker normally speaks to facilitate the interlocutor's understanding. Foreigner talk has been hypothesized to aid L2 acquisition in a number of ways (e.g. by making certain features more salient to the learner).

form-focused instruction
Instruction that involves some attempt to focus learners' attention on specific properties of the L2 so that they will learn them. Different types of form-focused instruction can be distinguished, including *explicit instruction* and *implicit instruction*.

formulaic sequence
'A sequence, continuous or discontinuous, of words or other meaning elements, which is, or appears to be, prefabricated; that is stored and retrieved whole from memory at the time of use, rather than being subject to generation or analysis by the language grammar' (Wray, 2000: 465).

fossilization
A term coined by Selinker (1972) in recognition of the fact that most L2 learners fail to reach target-language competence (i.e. they stop learning while their internalized rule system contains rules different from those of the target system). It can also be viewed as a cognitive process, whereby new learning is blocked by existing learning. It remains a controversial construct with some researchers arguing that learners never completely stop learning.

Frequency Hypothesis
A hypothesis that states the order of development in L2 acquisition is determined by the frequency with which different linguistic items occur in the input.

Grammar Translation Method
A traditional language teaching approach involving the presentation of grammatical rules, the study of lists of vocabulary, and translation exercises. It emphasizes reading rather than the ability to communicate in a language.

grammatical syllabus
One type of structural syllabus consisting of a graded list of grammatical structures to be taught.

implicit instruction
A type of instruction directed at enabling learners to infer rules without any awareness of what they are learning. It contrasts with *explicit instruction*.

implicit L2 knowledge
Knowledge of an L2 that is intuitive and tacit (i.e. it cannot be directly reported). The knowledge that most speakers have of their L1 is implicit. See also *explicit L2 knowledge.*

implicit L2 learning
Learning that takes place without either intentionality or awareness. It can be investigated by exposing learners to input data, which they are asked to process for meaning, and then investigating (without warning) whether they have acquired any L2 linguistic properties as a result of the exposure.

incidental L2 learning
Learning of some specific L2 feature that takes place without any conscious intention to learn it. It is investigated by giving learners a task that focuses their attention on one aspect of the L2 and, without pre-warning, testing them on some other feature.

individual differences in language learning
Individual learner differences occur in how learners learn an L2, how fast they learn and how successful they are. The factors responsible for individual differences are cognitive (e.g. language aptitude), affective (e.g. motivation), or social (i.e. relating to the learning environment) in nature.

inductive instruction
A form of explicit instruction that involves requiring learners to induce rules from examples given to them or simply from the opportunity to practise the rules. It contrasts with *deductive instruction*.

initiate–respond–feedback (IRF) exchange
A type of interaction that occurs in classrooms where the teacher initiates an exchange, the student responds, the teacher follows up by accepting or rejecting the student's response.

input-based task
A type of task used in task-based teaching that requires learners to comprehend input in order to achieve a communicative outcome.

Input Hypothesis
A hypothesis advanced by Krashen (1985) to explain how 'acquisition' takes place. It states that 'we acquire…only when we understand language that contains a structure that is a little beyond where we are now' (1982: 21). Elsewhere Krashen referred to the idea of input that is 'a little bit beyond' as 'i + 1'.

Input Processing Theory
A theory developed by VanPatten (1996), who proposed that because learners have a limited working memory capacity, they process input in accordance with a set of principles that allocate attention selectively to input. An example of such a principle is 'Learners process input for meaning before they process it for form'.

Interaction Hypothesis
A hypothesis proposed by Long (1983b). It initially claimed that the interactional modifications that arise during the negotiation of meaning provide learners with comprehensible input and thereby assist acquisition. In a later version, Long (1996) broadened the scope of the hypothesis by claiming that 'negotiation for meaning, and especially negotiation work that triggers interactional adjustments by the NS or more competent interlocutor, facilitates acquisition because it connects input, internal learner capacities, particularly selective attention, and output in productive ways' (pp. 241–42).

Interface Hypothesis
A hypothesis that emphasizes the distinctiveness of L2 implicit and explicit knowledge and maintains that explicit knowledge cannot transform directly into implicit knowledge.

Interlanguage
A term coined by Selinker (1972) to refer to the systematic knowledge of an L2 which is independent of both the learner's L1 and the target language. The term has come to be used with different but related meanings: (1) to refer to the series of interlocking systems which characterize L2 acquisition, (2) to refer to the system that is observed at a single stage of development ('an interlanguage') and (3) to refer to particular L1/L2 combinations (e.g. L1 French/L2 English vs L1 Japanese/L2 English).

interlingual error
An error which occurs as a result of transferring an L1 feature into the L2.

internalization
A term used in Sociocultural Theory to refer to the process by which a person moves from object/other-regulation to self-regulation. Ohta (2001) referred to this as 'the movement of language from environment to brain' (p. 11).

intralingual error
An error that arises as a result of mental processes such as *overgeneralization*. For example, L2 learners may say 'They explained her what to do' by overextending the use of the pattern in sentences such as 'They told her what to do'.

L1 transfer
The incorporation of L1 items and features into the learners' L2 system. It results in interlingual errors.

L2 motivational self-system
A theory of L2 motivation developed by Dörnyei (2005) that distinguishes three dimensions of motivation: (1) the learner's ideal L2 self (i.e. whether the person the learner would like to become is a speaker of the L2), (2) the learner's ought-to L2 self (i.e. whether the learner believes he or she has an obligation to learn the L2) and (3) L2 learning experience (i.e. the specific motives related to the learner's immediate learning environment).

language analytical ability
The ability to distinguish and understand the formal properties of a language, especially the grammatical properties. Language analytical ability is one of the components of *language aptitude*.

language anxiety
An affective factor that has been shown to influence L2 acquisition. Language anxiety can constitute a trait (i.e. it is a characteristic of a learner's personality) or a state (i.e. the apprehension that is experienced at a particular moment in response to a definite situation) or be situation-specific (i.e. the anxiety aroused by a particular type of situation). It can be both facilitating (i.e. it has a positive effect on L2 acquisition), or debilitating (i.e. it has a negative effect).

language aptitude
The special set of abilities required to be successful in learning an L2. These abilities include the ability to identify sound patterns in a new language, the ability to recognize the different grammatical functions of words in sentences and to infer language rules (i.e. language analytical ability) and rote-learning ability.

language-related episode
A term used by Swain and Lapkin (2001) to refer to an interactional sequence where the speakers focus on a specific linguistic feature and engage in talk about it.

language transfer
The transfer of linguistic features from one language to another. The most common form of language transfer is L1 transfer but it is also possible for transfer to occur from the L2 into the L1. Language transfer can manifest itself in errors, avoidance of overuse.

languaging
A term coined by Swain (2006) to refer to the role that language production (oral or written) plays in making meaning when learners are faced with some linguistic problem related to the use of the L2. It is claimed to facilitate language learning.

learner beliefs
The beliefs that language learners have about what is involved in learning a language, how to learn it and their own language-learning ability. Beliefs can be 'analytic', 'experiential' or 'affective' in nature. Learner beliefs influence how learners set about learning an L2.

learner training
Instruction directed not at teaching the L2 but at enabling learners to learn effectively. Learner training can focus on teaching effective learning strategies or on making learners aware of their own approach to learning and alternative approaches.

learning strategy
A specific device or procedure used by learners to learn. Learning strategies consist of both 'language-learning strategies' for mastering the linguistic properties of an L2 (e.g. inferencing the meaning of a word from context) and 'skill-learning strategies' for improving speaking, listening, reading and writing (e.g. using a heading to predict the content of a reading passage).

learning style
The characteristic ways in which individuals orientate to problem solving. For example, some learners are field-dependent (i.e. tend to see things as wholes) and others field-independent (i.e. distinguish the parts that make up a whole). Instruction is believed to be more effective if it matches a learner's learning style.

Levelt's Model of Speech Production
Levelt (1989) proposed that speech production could be accounted for in terms of four overlapping operations: (1) conceptualization, (2) formulation, (3) articulation and (4) monitoring. His model has been used in studies that have investigated the effects of planning on L2 performance.

lexical syllabus
A syllabus that is organized in terms of lexical units (i.e. words or formulaic chunks). It serves as a basis for the 'lexical approach' which aims to develop L2 competence – including grammatical competence – by teaching lexical phrases and helping learners to analyse them into their parts.

linguistic syllabus
A statement of what is to be taught that draws on linguistic descriptions of a language. A linguistic syllabus may specify the phonological, lexical or grammatical content of a course.

meaning-focused instruction
Instruction that is not intended to teach learners any specific linguistic features but aims to facilitate language learning through activities that have a primary focus on meaning.

mediation
A term used in *sociocultural SLA* to refer to various ways in which learning is assisted. Assistance can involve others through social interaction, the self through private speech, or artefacts (e.g. learning aids such as dictionary or grammar reference book).

metalanguage
The terminology available for analysing or describing a language. Metalanguage can be highly technical (e.g. 'hypothetical conditional') or everyday (e.g. 'verb').

metalinguistic explanation
An explanation of a linguistic feature that makes use of metalanguage. Descriptions of grammatical rules in the presentation stage of explicit instruction involve metalinguistic explanation.

method
A way of teaching a language which is based on systematic principles and procedures. Different methods of language teaching such as the Direct Method, the Audiolingual Method, the Grammar Translation Method result from different views of: 1) the nature of language, 2) the nature of language learning, 3) goals and objectives in teaching, 4) the type of syllabus to use, 5) the role of teachers, learners and instructional materials and 6) the techniques and procedures to use (Richards and Rodgers, 1986).

motivation
The effort that learners put into learning an L2 as a result of their need or desire to learn it. In one theory of motivation, Gardner and Lambert (1972) distinguished 'instrumental motivation', which occurs when a learner has a functional goal (such as to get a job or pass an examination), and 'integrative motivation', which occurs when a learner wishes to identify with the culture of the L2 group. Other types of motivation have also been identified. See in particular the *L2 motivational self-system*.

negotiation of form
An interactional sequence where attention to form occurs even though there is no communication difficulty (i.e. when the problem is entirely linguistic). Such sequences are uncommon in conversational interaction (although sometimes learners do request them) but have been shown to be very common in classroom contexts.

negotiation of meaning
An interactional sequence that arises when a problem in understanding occurs and there is a temporary communication breakdown leading to attempts to remedy it. It is characterized by interactional modifications such as comprehension checks and requests for clarification. It has been shown to assist learning when learners recognize the linguistic source of the communication problem and attend to the target language forms needed to resolve it.

Noticing Hypothesis
The strong version of the hypothesis claims that learners will only learn what they consciously attend to in the input. The weak version allows for representation and storage of unattended stimuli in memory but claims that 'people learn about the things they attend to and do not learn much about the things they do not attend to' (Schmidt, 2001).

noticing-the-gap
A term used by Schmidt and Frota (1986) to refer to the cognitive process involved when learners notice the linguistic differences between their own deviant output and the input they are exposed to. This process is claimed to facilitate L2 acquisition.

notional syllabus
A syllabus organized in terms of the meanings a learner needs to express. It lists 'notions' (i.e. semantic meanings such as 'possibility') and 'functions' (i.e. the actions that utterances perform, such as 'apologizing'). A notional syllabus also specifies the language needed to express the different notions and functions.

Oral-Situational Method
An approach to teaching that involves presenting and practising linguistic items (lexical and grammatical) in situations. Like the *Audiolingual Method*, it draws on behaviourist learning theory but differs from it by emphasizing the meanings of linguistic items.

order of acquisition
The order in which L2 learners achieve mastery of the grammatical features of a language. SLA research has shown that morphemes such as verb(ing) and verb(ed) are acquired in a fixed order irrespective of the learners' L1 or their age.

Output Hypothesis
A hypothesis proposed by Swain (1985). See *comprehensible output*.

Overgeneralization error
A type of *intralingual error*. Language learners in both L1 and L2 acquisition produce errors such as 'comed', which can be explained as extensions of a general rule to items not covered by this rule in the target language.

postmethod pedagogy
An approach to teaching a language that is not based on the concept of 'method'. It emphasizes the importance of teachers' autonomy in choosing what and how to teach and of their taking the specific instructional context and needs of their students into account.

present–practice–produce
An approach to teaching based on a linguistic syllabus. It involves presenting specific linguistic items, practising them in a controlled way (e.g. using drills) and then providing an opportunity for students to use them in free production.

private speech
The speech that a person uses when talking to him/herself. It often occurs when the person experiences some kind of problem and seeks to understand and resolve it. Some L2 learners who go through a *silent period* to engage in private conversations with themselves, thus, perhaps, preparing themselves for social speech later.

Processability Theory
A theory developed by Pienemann (1985). It seeks to explain acquisitional orders/sequences in terms of a set of hierarchical processing procedures. As Pienemann (2005) put it, 'once we can spell out the sequence in which language processing routines develop we can delineate those grammars that are processable at different points of development' (p. 2).

Processing Instruction
'A type of grammar instruction whose purpose is to affect the ways in which learners attend to input data. It is input-based rather than output-based' (VanPatten, 1996: 2). It is a form of *comprehension-based instruction* designed to assist learners to construct form-function mappings in line with the target language.

production-based instruction
A type of instruction that attempts to promote interlanguage development by requiring learners to produce the targeted L2 features in either oral or written form. The key difference between production-based instruction and *comprehension-based instruction* is that the former requires learners to produce the target feature whereas the latter does not.

recast
A type of corrective feedback. It takes the form of an utterance that 'rephrases the learner's utterance by changing one or more components (subject, verb, object) while still referring to its central meaning' (Long, 1996).

reformulation
A technique for teaching L2 writing. It involves taking a learner's text and rewriting it so that it keeps the same content but conforms to target language norms. The learner is then asked to use the reformulated text to revise his/her original text.

scaffolding
An interactional process where one speaker (an expert or a novice) assists another speaker (a novice) to perform a skill that the novice is unable to perform independently. It is a term used in *sociocultural SLA*.

semantic simplification
A process observed to occur in early L2 acquisition. Learners have been observed to frequently delete content words from their utterances and to rely on context to make their meanings clear (e.g. 'No today' = 'I am not coming today').

sequence of acquisition
This refers to the stages of acquisition through which a learner passes in acquiring specific grammatical structures such as interrogatives, negatives and relative clauses. These stages of acquisition involve 'transitional constructions' (i.e. constructions that differ from the target-language construction and that constitute a necessary step in acquisition). See also *order of acquisition.*

silent period
A period in early L2 acquisition where the learner refrains from speaking. However, acquisition can still take place as a result of exposure to L2 input.

Silent Way
A teaching method that emphasizes the importance of the teacher remaining silent to maximize opportunities for student talk. It makes use of gesture, mime, visual aids, wall charts and in particular Cuisinere rods (wooden sticks of different lengths and colours) to elicit utterances from students.

simplified input
Input that is simplified linguistically (e.g. by using high-frequency vocabulary and simple sentence structures) and/or interactionally (e.g. by means of repetition or by paraphrasing a word or expression). Simplifying the input helps to make it comprehensible to learners.

Skill Acquisition Theory
A theory that treats language learning, like other kinds of skill-learning. It claims that learning involves a progression from an initial declarative knowledge stage involving controlled processing, to a final procedural stage where knowledge is automatic. Skills are learnt as a result of 'practice'.

Social Identity Theory
A theory that claims learners' social identities affect how successful they will be in learning an L2. Norton (2000) demonstrated through a series of case studies of immigrant women in Canada how the social identity they accepted or insisted on impeded or facilitated their opportunities for learning English.

Sociocultural Theory
A theory that draws on the work of Vygotsky in viewing learning as the product of mediated activity. Higher order language functions are seen as developing both in and out of social interaction. Learners progress from object- and other-regulation to self-regulation through interacting with others. See also *zone of proximal development* and *scaffolding*.

stimulated recall
A technique for eliciting a retrospective report from learners. It seeks to investigate learners' thought processes at the time they performed an activity. Learners are presented with examples of what they said or wrote and then are asked to recall what they were thinking about at that time. It has been used to investigate to what extent learners 'notice' linguistic forms in the interactions they participated in.

structural simplification
A way of simplifying the structure of an utterance by omitting grammatical functors (e.g. articles and verb inflections). It occurs in some kinds of *foreigner talk* and also in learner utterances. Extreme structural simplification results in learner language that resembles a pidgin language.

structural syllabus
A syllabus that specifies the content of a language course as a list of linguistic items in the order in which they are to be taught.

task-based language teaching
An approach to the teaching of second/foreign languages based on a syllabus consisting of communicative tasks and utilizing a methodology that makes meaningful communication rather than linguistic accuracy primary, but which also requires a *focus on form*. Task-based language teaching caters to incidental rather than intentional language learning.

task-based syllabus
A syllabus is organized around tasks, rather than in terms of grammar or vocabulary. The syllabus consists of a variety of different kinds of task graded in terms of the different demands that they place on the language needed to carry them out.

teacher-talk
The way teachers talk when communicating with students in a classroom. Teachers make adjustments to both language form and language function in order to facilitate communication with language learners. See also *foreigner talk* and *simplified input*.

text-creation activities
Instructional activities that require students to use their own linguistic resources to create utterances. A good example of such an activity is a 'task'.

text-manipulation activities
Instructional activities that require students to operate on language that is given to them. Examples of text-manipulation activities are fill-in-the-blank or completion exercises.

Total Physical Response
A comprehension-based teaching method developed by James Asher (1969). It involves the teacher giving commands and the students responding by performing actions. It is based on a structural syllabus as the commands are designed to expose learners to different grammatical structures.

Trade-off Hypothesis
A hypothesis proposed by Skehan (1998) to account for the fact that learners will prioritize one aspect of production (e.g. accuracy) over another (e.g. complexity) when performing different kinds of tasks under different conditions.

transfer appropriate processing (TAP)
A principle that claims the conditions under which a language is learned will determine the conditions under which it can be used. For example, 'the learning environment that best promotes rapid, accurate retrieval of what has been learned is that in which the psychological demands placed on the learner resemble those that will be encountered later in natural settings' (Lightbown, 2005).

unfocused task
A task that is designed to elicit L2 processing of language in general rather than the use of a specific, predetermined linguistic feature. See also *focused task*.

willingness to communicate
The extent to which learners are prepared to initiate communication when they have a choice. It constitutes a factor believed to lead to individual differences in language learning.

working memory
A mental construct that accounts for how the key processes of perception, attention and rehearsal take place. It is believed to play a central role in L2 acquisition. There are different models of working memory including a capacity-limited model and a multiple-resources model.

zone of proximal development
'The distance between the actual developmental level as determined by independent problem solving and the level of potential development as determined through adult guidance or in collaboration with more capable peers' (Vygotsky 1978: 86). It is a term used in *Sociocultural Theory*.

References

Abbs, B., and Freebairn, I. (1982) *Starting Strategies*. Harlow: Longman.

Abbs, B., Ayton, J., and Freebairn, I. (1975) *Strategies*. London: Longman.

Abraham, R. (1985) Field independence-dependence and the teaching of grammar. *TESOL Quarterly* 20(4), 689–702.

Achiba, M. (2003) *Learning to Request in a Second Language*. Clevedon: Multilingual Matters.

Alderson, J. C. (1997) *Models of language? Whose? What for? What use?* Paper presented at the Evolving Models of Language: British Association for Applied Linguistics.

Alderson, J. C., and Urquhart, A. H. (1984) *Reading in a Foreign Language*. Harlow: Longman.

Aljaafreh, A. L. I., and Lantolf, J. P. (1994) Negative feedback as regulation and second language learning in the Zone of Proximal Development. *Modern Language Journal* 78(4), 465–83.

Al-Jabri, S. S. (2005) *The effects of semantic and thematic clustering on learning English vocabulary by Saudi students*. Unpublished doctoral dissertation, Indiana University of Pennsylvania, Indiana, PA.

Allan, R. (2009) Can a graded reader provide authentic input? *English Language Teaching Journal*, 63(1), 23–32.

Allen, J. P., Swain, M., Harley, B., and Cummins, J. (1990) Aspects of classroom treatment: toward a more comprehensive view of second language education. In B. Harley, J. P. Allen, J. Cummins, and M. Swain (eds.) *The Development of Second Language Proficiency*. Cambridge: Cambridge University Press.

Allen, L. Q. (2000) Form-meaning connections and the French causative. *Studies in Second Language Acquisition* 22(1), 69–84.

Allwright, D. (1984) Why don't learners learn what teachers teach – the Interaction Hypothesis. In D. Singleton and D. Little (eds.) *Language Learning in Formal and Informal Contexts*. Dublin: Irish Association of Applied Linguistics.

——(1988) *Observation in the Language Classroom*. London: Longman.

Allwright, D., and Bailey, K. (1991) *Focus on the Language Classroom: An Introduction to Classroom Research for Language Teachers*. Cambridge: Cambridge University Press.

Allwright, R. (1975) Problems in the study of the language teachers treatment of error. In M. K. Burt and H. D. Dulay (eds.) *On TESOL 75, New Directions in Second Language Learning, Teaching, and Bilingual Education* (pp. 96–109). Washington, DC: TESOL.

——(1980) Turns, topics and tasks: patterns of participation in language teaching and learning. In D. Larsen-Freeman (ed.) *Discourse Analysis in Second Language Research*. Rowley, MA: Newbury House.

——(1984) The importance of interaction in classroom language learning. *Applied Linguistics*, 5(2), 156–71.

Altman, H. (1980) Foreign language teaching: focus on the learner. In H. Altman and C. Vaughan James (eds.) *Foreign Language Teaching: Meeting Individual Needs*. Oxford: Pergamon.

Ammar, A., and Spada, N. (2006) One size fits all?: recasts, prompts, and L2 learning. *Studies in Second Language Acquisition* 28(4), 543–74.

Andersen, T. (2010) *The effect of tiered corrective feedback on second language academic writing*. Unpublished Master of Arts thesis, University of British Columbia, Vancouver.

Anderson, J. R. (1983) *The Architecture of Cognition*. Cambridge, MA: Harvard University Press.

——(1993) Production systems and the ACT-R theory. In J. R. Anderson and F. S. Bellezza (eds.) *Rules of the mind* (pp. 1–16). Hillsdale: Lawrence Erlbaum Associates.

Anderson, M. C. (2003) Rethinking interference theory: Executive control and the mechanisms of forgetting. *Journal of Memory and Language* 49(4), 415–45.

Anthony, M. (1963) Approach, method and technique. *English Language Teaching* 17(2), 63–67.

Antón, M. (1999) The discourse of a learner-centred classroom: sociocultural perspectives on teacher-learner interaction in the second-language classroom. *Modern Language Journal*, 83(3), 303–18.

Antón, M., and DiCamilla, F. J. (1998) Socio-cognitive functions of L1 collaborative interaction in the L2 classroom. *Canadian Modern Language Review* 54, 314–42.

Arnold, J., and Brown, H.D. (1999) A map of the terrain. In J. Arnold (ed.) *Affect in Language Learning*. Cambridge: Cambridge University Press.

Artigal, J. (1992) Some considerations on why a new language is acquired by being used. *International Journal of Applied Linguistics* 2(2), 221–40.

Asher, J. J. (1969) The Total Physical Response approach to second language learning. *Modern Language Journal* 53(1), 3–17.

——(1977) *Learning Another Language Through Actions*. Los Gatos, CA: Sky Oaks Productions.

Aubrey, S. (2011) Facilitating interaction in East Asian EFL Classroooms: Increasing students willingness to communicate. *Language Education in Asia* 2(2), 237–45.

Auerbach, E. (1993) Reexamining English only in the ESL classroom. *TESOL Quarterly* 27(1) 9–32.

Bachman, L. (1990) *Fundamental Considerations in Language Testing*. Oxford: Oxford University Press.

Baddeley, A. (1997) *Human memory: Theory and Practice*. Hove: Psychology Press.

——(2003) Working memory and language: An overview. *Journal of Communication Disorders* 36(3), 189–208.

——(2003) Working memory: Looking back and looking forward. *Nature Reviews: Neuroscience* 4(10), 829–39.

Bailey, N., Madden, C., and Krashen, S. (1974) Is there a natural sequence in adult second language learning? *Language Learning*, 24(2), 235–43.

Bardovi-Harlig, K. (1995) The interaction of pedagogy and natural sequences in the acquisition of tense and aspect. In F. Eckman, D. Highland, P. Lee, J. Milcham and J. Weber (eds.) *Second Language Acquisition and Pedagogy*. Mahwah, NJ: Erlbaum.

——(2000) *Tense and Aspect in Second Language Acquisition: Form, Meaning and Use*. Language Learning Monograph Series. Malden, MA: Blackwell.

Bardovi-Harlig, K., and Dörnyei, Z. (1998) Do language learners recognize pragmatic violations? Pragamatic vs. grammatical awareness in instructed L2 learning. *TESOL Quarterly* 32(2), 233–59.

Barnes, D. (1976) *From Communication to Curriculum*. London: Penguin.

Barraja-Rohan, A. (2011) Using conversational analysis in the second language classroom to teach interactional competence. *Language Teaching Research* 15(4), 479–505.

Bassiri, M. (2011) Interactional feedback and the impact of attitude and motivation on noticing L2 form. *First language and Literature Studies* 1(2), 61–73.

Bax, S. (2003) The end of CLT: A context-based approach to language teaching. *ELT Journal* 57(3), 278–87.

Bell, D. (2003) Method and postmethod: Are they really so incompatible? *TESOL Quarterly* 37(2), 325–36.

Benati, A. (2005) The effects of processing instruction, traditional instruction and meaning – output instruction on the acquisition of the English past simple tense. *Language Teaching Research* 9(1), 67–93.

Berry, M. (1981) Systemic linguistics and discourse analysis: a multi-layered approach to exchange structure. In M. Coulthard and M. Montgomery (eds.) *Studies in Discourse Analysis*. London: Routledge and Kegan Paul.

Bitchener, J., and Ferris, D. (2011) *Written Corrective Feedback in Second Language Acquisition and Writing*. Abingdon: Routledge.

Bitchener, J., and Knoch, U. (2009) The value of a focused approach to written corrective feedback. *ELT Journal*, 63(3), 204–11.

Block, D. (2001) An exploration of the art and science debate in language education. In M. Bax and J.-W. Zwart (eds.) *Reflections on Language and Language Learning: In Honour of Arthur van Essen* (pp. 63–74). Amsterdam: John Benjamins.

Borg, S. (1998) Teachers pedagogical systems and grammar teaching: A qualitative study. *TESOL Quarterly* 32(1), 9–38.

——(1999) Teachers theories in grammar teaching. *ELT Journal*, 53(3), 157–67.

Bower, J., and Kawaguchi, S. (2011) Negotiation of meaning and corrective feedback in Japanese/English eTandem. *Language Learning and Technology* 15(1), 41–71.

Bowers, R. 1980. The individual learner in the general class. In H. Altman and C. Vaughan James (eds.) *Foreign Language Teaching: Meeting Individual Needs* (pp. 66–80). Oxford: Pergamon.

Breen, M. (1987) Learner contribution to the task design. In C. N. Candlin and D. Murphy (eds.) *Language Learning Tasks* (vol. 7, pp. 23–46). London: Prentice-Hall International.

——(2001) *Learner Contributions to Language Learning*. London: Longman.

Bright, J. A., and McGregor, G. P. (1970) *Teaching English as a Second Language*. London: Longman.

Brindley, G. (1987) Factors affecting task difficulty. In D. Nunan (ed.) *Guidelines for the Development of Curriculum Resources* (pp. 45–56). Adelaide: Adelaide National Curriculum Resource Centre.

British Council/ BBC (2009) *Teaching English. Using L1 in the ESL classroom*. Online: http://www.teachingenglish.org.uk/forum-topic/using-l1-esl-classroom

Brock, C. A. (1986) The effects of referential questions on ESL classroom discourse. *TESOL Quarterly* 20(1), 47–59.

Broner, M. A. (2001) *Impact of Interlocutor and Task on First and Second Language Use in a Spanish Immersion Program*. Center for Advanced Research on Language Acquisition.

Brooks, F., and Donato, R. (1994) Vygotskyan approaches to understanding foreign language learner discourse during communicative tasks. *Hispania* 77(2), 262–74.

Brooks, N. (1960) *Language and Language Learning: Theory and Practice*. New York: Harcourt, Brace and World.

Brooks-Lewis, K. (2009) Adult learners perceptions of the incorporation of their L1 in foreign language teaching and learning. *Applied Linguistics* 30(2), 216–35.

Brown, R. (1973) *A First Language: the Early Stages.* Cambridge, MA: Harvard University Press.

Brumfit, C. (1977) Correcting written work. *Modern English Teacher* 5, 22–23.

——(1978) Communicative language teaching: an assessment. In P. Strevens (ed.) *In Honour of A. S. Hornby* (pp. 33–44). Oxford: Oxford University Press.

——(1983) The integration of theory and practice. In J. Alatis, H. Stern and P. Strevens (eds.) *Applied Linguistics and the Preparation of Second Language Teachers: Towards a Rationale.* Washington DC: Georgetown University Press.

——(1984) *Language and Languages; Communicative Competence; Study and Teaching.* Cambridge: Cambridge University Press.

——(1993) Simplification in pedagogy. In M. L. Tickoo (ed.) *Simplification: Theory and Application* (pp. 1–6). Singapore: SEAMEO Regional Language Centre.

——(1995) Teacher professionalism and research. In G. Cook and B. Seidlhofer (eds.) *Principle and Practice in Applied Linguistics* (pp 27–42). Oxford: Oxford University Press.

Brumfit, C., and Johnson, K. (1979) *The Communicative Approach to Language Teaching.* Oxford: Oxford University Press.

Bruton, A. (2002) From tasking purposes to purposing tasks. *ELT Journal* 56(3), 280–88.

Burt, M. (1975) Error analysis in the adult EFL classroom. *TESOL Quarterly* 9(1) 53–63.

Bygate, M., Skehan, P., and Swain, M. (eds.) (2001) *Researching Pedagogical Tasks: Second Language Learning, Teaching, and Assessment.* London: Pearson.

Byrne, D. (1986) *Teaching Oral English.* 2nd edition. Harlow: Longman.

Candlin, C. N. (1987) Towards task-based learning. *Lancaster Practical Papers in English Language Education* 7, 5–22.

Candlin, C. N., and Murphy, D. (1987) *Language Learning Tasks.* London: Prentice-Hall.

Carroll, J. (1965) The prediction of success in foreign language training. In R. Glaser (ed.) *Training, Research, and Education.* New York: Wiley.

——(1981) Twenty-five years in foreign language aptitude. In K. Diller (ed.) *Individual Differences and Universals in Language Learning Aptitude.* Rowley, MA: Newbury House.

Carroll, J., and Sapon, S. (1959) *Modern Language Aptitude Test—Form A.* New York: The Psychological Corporation.

Carroll, S. (2001) *Input and Evidence: The Raw Material of Second Language Acquisition.* Amsterdam: John Benjamins.

Carter, R. A., and McCarthy, M. (2003) What is a native speaker? *XXIII Annual IATEFL Conference Proceedings.*

Cathcart, R. L., and Olsen, J. E. W. B. (1976) Teachers and students preferences for correction of classroom conversation errors. In J. F. Fanselow and R. H. Crymes (eds.) *On TESOL 76* (pp. 41–53). Washington, DC: TESOL.

Celce-Murcia, M. (1991) *Teaching English as a Second or Foreign Language.* Boston, MA: Heinle and Heinle.

Celce-Murcia, M., and Larsen-Freeman, D. (1999) *The Grammar Book.* New York: Heinle and Heinle.

Chandler, J. (2003) The efficacy of various kinds of error feedback for improvement in the accuracy and fluency of L2 student writing. *Journal of Second Language Writing* 12(3), 267–96.

Chapelle, C. (2007) Pedagogical implications in TESOL Quarterly? Yes, please. *TESOL Quarterly* 41(2), 404–406.

Chaudron, C. (1977) A descriptive model of discourse in the corrective treatment of learners errors. *Language Learning* 27(1), 29–46.

——(1988) *Second Language Classroom: Research on Teaching and Learning.* Cambridge: Cambridge University Press.

Chomsky, N. (1959) Review of *Verbal Behavior* by B. F. Skinner. *Language* 35, 26–58.

Choudhury, S. (2005) Interaction in second language classrooms. *BRAC University Journal* 2(1), 77–82.

Clarke, M. (1994) The dysfunctions of the theory/practice discourse. *TESOL Quarterly* 28(1), 9–26.

Cohen, A. (1989) Reformulation: A technique for providing advanced feedback in writing. *Guidelines*, 11(2), 1–9.

——(2003) Strategy training for second language learners. *ERIC Digest August.* Washington, DC: Center for Applied Linguistics.

——(2011) Second language learner strategies. In E. Hinkel (ed.) *Handbook of Research in Second Language Teaching and Learning,* vol. II. New York: Routledge.

Cohen, A., and Brooks-Carson, A. (2001) Research on direct vs. translated writing: Students strategies and their results. *Modern Language Journal* 85(2), 169–88.

Cole, S. (1998) The use of the L1 in communicative English classrooms. *The Language Teacher.* Online: http://jalt-publications.org/old_tlt/files/98/dec/cole.html

Collentine, J. (1998) Processing instruction and the subjunctive. *Hispania* 81(3), 576–87.

Conrad, L. (1989) The effects of time-compressed speech on native and EFL listening comprehension. *Studies in Second Language Acquisition* 11(1), 1–16.

Consolo, A. (2000) Teachers action and student oral participation in classroom interaction. In J. Hall and L. Verplaetse (eds.) *Second and Foreign Language Learning Through Classroom Interaction.* Mahwah, NJ: Lawrence Erbaum.

Cook, G. (1994) Repetition and learning by heart: an aspect of intimate discourse, and its implications. *ELT Journal* 48(2), 133–41.

——(2010) *Translation in Language Teaching.* Oxford: Oxford University Press.

Cook, V. (1991) The poverty of stimulus argument and multicompetence. *Second Language Research* 7, 103–17.

——(2001) Using the first language in the classroom. *Canadian Modern Language Review* 57(3), 402–23.

——(2005) Basing teaching on the L2 user. In E. Llurda (ed.) *Non-native Language Teachers: Perceptions, Challenges and Contributions to the Profession* (pp. 47–61). New York: Springer.

——(2008) *Second Language Learning and Language Teaching.* 4th edition. London: Hodder Education.

Corder, S. P. (1967) The significance of learners errors. *IRAL – International Review of Applied Linguistics in Language Teaching* (5)4, 161–70.

Cotterall, S., and Reinders, H. (2001) Fortress or bridge? Learners perceptions and practice in self-access language learning. *TESOLANZ* 8, 23–38.

Coxhead, A. (2011) The academic word list ten years on: research and teaching implications. *TESOL Quarterly* 45(2), 355–62.

Crabbe, D. (1993) Fostering autonomy from within the classroom; the teachers responsibility. *System* 21(4), 443–52.

Crace, A., and Wileman, R. (2002) *Language to Go: Intermediate. Students Book.* Harlow: Longman.

Crookes, G. (2010) The practicality and relevance of second language critical pedagogy. *Language Teaching* 43(3), 333–48.

Crookes, G., and Gass, S. (eds.) (1993) *Tasks and Language Learning: Integrating Theory and Practice*. Philadelphia, PA: Multilingual Matters.

Crookes, G., and Schmidt, R. (1991) Language learning motivation: reopening the research agenda. *Language Learning* 41(3), 469–512.

Cross, D. (1980) Personalized language teaching. In H. Altman and C. Vaughan James (eds.) *Foreign Language Teaching: Meeting Individual Needs* (pp. 111–24). Oxford: Pergamon.

Csizer, K., and Dörnyei, Z. (2005) The internal structure of language learning motivation and its relationship with language choice and learning effort. *Modern Language Journal* 89(1), 19–36.

Cummins, J. (1981) *Bilingualism and Minority Children*. Ontario: Ontario Institute for Studies in Education.

——(2005) A proposal for action: strategies for recognizing heritage language competence as a learning resource within the mainstream classroom. *Modern Language Journal* 89(4), 585–92.

Czerwionka, L. (2009) Motivations and perceptions of participation in Spanish second language classrooms: the case of high achieving introverted students. *TPFLE* 13(1), 1–10.

Day, E., and Shapson, S. (1991) Integrating formal and functional approaches to language teaching in French immersion: an experimental study. *Language Learning* 41(1), 25–58.

Day, R., and Bamford, J. (1998) *Extensive Reading In The Second Language Classroom*. Cambridge: Cambridge University Press.

De Bot, K. (1996) The psycholinguistics of the Output Hypothesis. *Language Learning* 46(3), 529–55.

De Graaff, R., and Housen, A. (2009) Investigating the effects and effectiveness of L2 instruction. In M. H. Long and C. J. Doughty (eds.) *The Handbook of Language Teaching* (pp. 726–55). Oxford: Wiley-Blackwell.

De la Fuente, M. (2002) Negotiation and oral acquisition of L2 vocabulary: the roles of input and output in the receptive and productive acquisition of words. *Studies in Second Language Acquisition* 24(1), 81–112.

——(2006) Classroom L2 vocabulary acquisition: investigating the role of pedagogical tasks and form-focused instruction. *Language Teaching Research* 10(3), 263–95.

De Villiers, J., and de Villiers, P. (1973) A cross-sectional study of the development of grammatical morphemes in child speech. *Journal of Psycholinguistic Research* 1, 299–310.

DeKeyser, R. (1995) Learning second language grammar rules. *Studies in Second Language Acquisition* 17(3), 379–410.

——(1997) Beyond explicit rule learning: automatizing second language morphosyntax. *Studies in Second Language Acquisition* 19(2), 195–221.

——(1998) Beyond focus on form: cognitive perspectives on learning and practicing second language grammar. In C. Doughty and J. Williams (eds.) *Focus on Form in Classroom Second Language Acquisition*. Cambridge: Cambridge University Press.

——(2000) The robustness of critical period effects in second language acquisition. *Studies in Second Language Acquisition* 22(2), 499–533.

——(2007) *Practice in a Second Language: Perspectives From Applied Linguistics and Cognitive Psychology*. New York: Cambridge University Press.

——(2012) Interactions between individual differences, treatments, and structures in SLA. *Language Learning* 62(2), 189–200.

DeKeyser, R., and Sokalski, K. J. (1996) The differential role of comprehension and production practice. *Language Learning* 46(4), 613–42.

Diller, K. (1978) *The Language Teaching Controversy*. Rowley, MA: Newbury House.

Disick, R. (1975) *Individualizing Language Instruction: Strategies and Methods*. New York: Harcourt Brace Jovanovich.

Djigunovic, J. (2006) Language anxiety and language processing. In S. Foster-Cohen, M. Krajnovic, and J. Djigunović (eds.) (pp. 191–212). Amsterdam: John Benjamins.

Donato, R. (1994) Collective scaffolding in second language learning. In J. Lantolf and G. Appel (eds.) *Vygotskian Approaches to Second Language Research*. Norwood, NJ: Ablex.

——(2000) Sociocultural contributions to understanding the foreign and second language classroom. In J. Lantolf (ed.) *Sociocultural Theory and Second Language Learning*. Oxford: Oxford University Press.

Dörnyei, Z. (2001) *Motivational Strategies in the Language Classroom*. Cambridge: Cambridge University Press.

——(2002) The motivational basis of language learning tasks. In P. Robinson (ed.) *Individual Differences in L2 Learning* (pp. 137–58). Amsterdam: John Benjamins.

——(2005) *The Psychology of the Language Learner: Individual Differences in Second Language Acquisition*. Mahwah, NJ: Lawrence Erlbaum.

Dörnyei, Z., and Csizér, K. (1998) Ten commandments for motivating language learners: results of an empirical study. *Language Teaching Research* 2(3), 203–29.

Dörnyei, Z., and Otto, I. (1998) Motivation in action: a process model of L2 motivation. *Working Papers in Applied Linguistics* 47, 173–210. Thames Valley University.

Dörnyei, Z., and Ushioda, E. (2009) Motivation, language identities and the L2 self: future research directions. In Z. Dörnyei and E. Ushioda (eds.) *Motivation, Language Identity and the L2 Self* (pp. 350–56). Bristol: Multilingual Matters.

Doughty, C. (2001) Cognitive underpinnings of focus on form. In P. Robinson (ed.) *Cognition and Second Language Instruction*. Cambridge: Cambridge University Press.

Doughty, C., and Varela, E. (1998) Communicative focus on form. In C. Doughty and J. Williams (eds.) *Focus on Form in Classroom Second Language Acquisition* (pp. 114–38). Cambridge: Cambridge University Press.

Duff, P., and Polio, C. (1990) How much foreign language is there in the foreign language classroom? *Modern Language Journal* 74(2), 154–66.

Dulay, H., and Burt, M. K. (1973) Should we teach children syntax? *Language Learning* 23(2), 245–58.

——(1974a) Natural sequences in child second language acquisition. *Language Learning* 24(1), 37–53.

——(1974b) Errors and strategies in child second language acquisition. *TESOL Quarterly* 8(1), 129–36.

Dulay, H., Burt, M., and Krashen, S. (1982) *Language Two*. New York: Oxford University Press.

Dupuy, B., and Krashen, S. (1993) Incidental vocabulary acquisition in French as a foreign language. *Applied Language Learning* 4(1), 55–63.

East, M. (2012) *Task-based Language Teaching from the Teachers Perspective: Insights from New Zealand*. Amsterdam: John Benjamins.

Eckerth, J. (2008) Task-based learner interaction: investigating learning opportunities, learning processes, and learning outcomes. In J. Eckerth and S. Siekmann (eds.)

Task-based Language Learning and Teaching: Theoretical, Methodological, and Pedagogical Perspectives. Frankfurt: Peter Lang.

Eckerth, J., and Siekmann, S. (eds.) (2008) *Task-based Language Learning and Teaching: Theoretical, Methodological, and Pedagogical Perspectives*. Frankfurt: Lang.

Edge, J. (1989) *Mistakes and Correction*. London: Longman.

Edstrom, A. (2006) L1 use in the L2 classroom: one teachers self-evaluation. *Canadian Modern Language Review* 63(2), 275–92.

——(2009) Teacher reflection as a strategy for evaluating L1/L2 use in the classroom. *Babylonia* 1, 12–15.

Egbert, J. (2003) A study of flow theory in the foreign language classroom. *Modern Language Journal* 87(4), 499–518.

Ehrlich, S., Avery, P., and Yorio, C. (1989) Discourse structure and the negotiation of comprehensible input. *Studies in Second Language Acquisition* 11(4), 397–414.

Elder, C. (2009) Validating a test of metalinguistic knowledge. In R. Ellis, S. Loewen, C. Elder, R. Erlam, J. Philip and H. Reinders (eds.) *Implicit and Explicit Knowledge in Second Language Learning, Testing and teaching* (pp. 113–38). Bristol: Multilingual Matters.

Elder, C., and Manwaring, D. (2004) The relationship between metalinguistic knowledge and learning outcomes among undergraduate students of Chinese. *Language Awareness* 13(3), 145–62.

Elgort, I. (2011) Deliberate learning and vocabulary acquisition in a new language. *Language Learning* 61(2), 367–413.

Elgort, I., and Nation, P. (2011) Vocabulary learning in a second language. In P. Seedhouse, S. Walsh and C. Jenks (eds.) *Conceptualising 'Learning' in Applied Linguistics* (pp. 89–104). Basingstoke: Palgrave Macmillan.

Elley, W. B., and Mangubhai, F. (1981) *The impact of a book flood in Fiji primary schools*. Wellington: New Zealand Council for Educational Research.

Ellis, G., and Sinclair, B. (1989) *Learning to Learn English*. Cambridge: Cambridge University Press.

Ellis, N. (1996) Sequencing in SLA: phonological memory, chunking, and points of order. *Studies in Second Language Acquisition* 18(1), 91–126.

——(2002) Frequency effects in language processing: a review with implications for theories of implicit and explicit language acquisition. *Studies in Second Language Acquisition* 24(2), 143–88.

——(2005) At the interface: dynamic interactions of explicit and implicit knowledge. *Studies in Second Language Acquisition* 27(2), 305–52.

——(2007) The Associative-Cognitive CREED. In B. VanPatten and J. Williams (eds.) *Theories of Second Language Acquisition: An Introduction* (pp. 77–95). Mahwah, NJ: Lawrence Erlbaum.

Ellis, R. (2009) Corrective feedback and teacher development. *L2 Journal* 1(1). Online: http://repositories.cdlib.org/uccllt/l2/vol1/iss1/art2

——(1984a) Formulaic speech in early classroom second language development. In J. Handscombe, R. Orem and B. Taylor (eds.) *On TESOL 83, The Question of Control*. Washington, DC: TESOL.

——(1984b) *Classroom Second Language Development*. Oxford: Pergamon.

——(1988) The effects of linguistic environment on the second language acquisition of grammatical rules. *Applied Linguistics* 9(3), 257–74.

——(1989) Are classroom and naturalistic acquisition the same? A study of the classroom acquisition of German word order rules. *Studies in Second Language Acquisition* 11(3), 305–28.

——(1991) Grammar teaching—practice or consciousness-raising. In R. Ellis (ed.) *Second Language Acquisition and Second Language Pedagogy* (pp. 167–74). Clevedon: Multilingual Matters.

——(1992) Learning to communicate in the classroom. *Studies in Second Language Acquisition* 14(1), 1–23.

——(1993) Second language acquisition and the structural syllabus. *TESOL Quarterly* 27(1), 91–113.

——(1994) A theory of instructed second language acquisition. In N. Ellis (ed.) *Implicit and Explicit Learning of Languages* (pp. 79–114). San Diego, CA: Academic Press.

——(1995) Modified oral input and the acquisition of word meanings. *Applied Linguistics* 16(2), 409.

——(1997) *SLA Research and Language Teaching*. Oxford and New York: Oxford University Press.

——(1999) Input-based approaches to teaching grammar: a review of classroom-oriented research. *Annual Review of Applied Linguistics* 19(1), 64–80.

——(2002a) Does form-focused instruction affect the acquisition of implicit knowledge? *Studies in Second Language Acquisition* 24(2), 223–36.

——(2002b) Methodological options in grammar teaching materials. In E. Hinkel and S. Fotos (eds.) *New Perspectives on Grammar Teaching in Second Language Classrooms* (pp. 155–79). Mahwah, NJ: Lawrence Erlbaum.

——(2003a) Principles of instructed language learning. *System* 33(2), 209–24.

——(2003b) *Task-based Language Learning and Teaching*. Oxford: Oxford University Press.

——(2004) The definition and measurement of L2 explicit knowledge. *Language Learning* 54(2), 227–75.

——(2005) Measuring implicit and explicit knowledge of a second language: a psychometric study. *Studies in Second Language Acquisition* 27(2), 141–72.

——(2006) Modelling learning difficulty and second language proficiency: the differential contributions of implicit and explicit knowledge. *Applied Linguistics* 27(3), 431–63.

——(2008) *The Study of Second Language Acquisition*. 2nd Edition. Oxford: Oxford University Press.

——(2009) Task-based language teaching: sorting out the misunderstandings. *International Journal of Applied Linguistics* 19(3), 221–46.

——(2010a) Epilogue. *Studies in Second Language Acquisition* 32(s02), 335–49.

——(2010b) Second language acquisition, teacher education and language pedagogy. *Language Teaching* 43(2), 182–201.

——(2012) *Language Teaching Research and Language Pedagogy*. London: Wiley-Blackwell.

Ellis, R., and Gaies, S. (1999) *Impact Grammar: Grammar Through Listening*. Hong Kong: Addison Wesley Longman Asia ELT.

Ellis, R., and Heimbach, R. (1997) Bugs and birds: childrens acquisition of second language vocabulary through interaction. *System* 25(2), 247–59.

Ellis, R., and Tomlinson, B. (1980) *Teaching Secondary English*. Hong Kong: Longman Group Ltd.

Ellis, R., Basturkmen, H., and Loewen, S. (2001) Learner uptake in communicative ESL lessons. *Language Learning* 51(2), 281–318.

Ellis, R., Loewen, S., and Erlam, R. (2006) Implicit and explicit corrective feedback and the acquisition of L2 grammar. *Studies in Second Language Acquisition* 28(2), 339–68.

Ellis, R., Tanaka, Y., and Yamazaki, A. (1994) Classroom interaction, comprehension, and the acquisition of L2 word meanings. *Language Learning* 44(3), 449–91.

Erlam, R. (2005) Language aptitude and its relationship to instructional effectiveness in second language acquisition. *Language Teaching Research* 9(2), 147–72.

——(2008) What do you researchers know about language teaching? Bridging the gap between SLA research and language pedagogy. *Innovation in Language Learning and Teaching* 2, 253–67.

Erlam, R., Batstone, R., and Ellis, R. (in-press) The effects of graduated corrective feedback and direct explicit feedback on the acquisition of two grammatical structures: a comparison of corrective feedback in two theoretical paradigms. *Modern Language Journal*.

Erten, I. H., and Tekin, M. (2008) Effects on vocabulary acquisition of presenting new words in semantic sets versus semantically unrelated sets. *System* 36(3), 407–22.

Estaire, S., and Zanon, J. (1994) *Planning Class Work: A Task-based Approach*. Oxford: Heinemann.

Ewald, J. (2004) A classroom forum on small group work: learners see and change themselves. *Language Awareness* 12(3), 163–79.

Færch, C., and Kasper, G. (1980) Processes and strategies in foreign language learning and communication. *Interlanguage Studies Bulletin* 5(1), 47–118.

——(1986) The role of comprehension in second-language learning. *Applied Linguistics* 7(3), 257–74.

Farley, A. P. (2001) Processing instruction and meaning-based output instruction: a comparative study. *Spanish Applied Linguistics* 5(2), 57–94.

Farrokhi, F., and Sattarpour, S. (2012) The effects of direct written corrective feedback on improvement of grammatical accuracy of high-proficient L2 learners. *World Journal of Education* 2(2), 49–57.

Fathman, A., and Whalley, E. (1990) Teacher response to student writing: focus on form versus content. In B. Kroll (ed.) *Second Language Writing: Research Insights for the Classroom* (pp. 178–90). Cambridge: Cambridge University Press.

Felix, S. (1981) The effect of formal instruction on second language acquisition. *Language Learning* 31(1), 87–112.

Fernandez, C. (2008) Re-examining the role of explicit information in processing instruction. *Studies in Second Language Acquisition* 30(3), 277–305.

Ferrer, V. (2005) The use of the mother tongue in the classroom: cross-linguistic comparisons, noticing and explicit knowledge. Online: http://www.teachenglish worldwide.com/Articles.htm

Ferris, D. (1999) The case for grammar correction in L2 writing classes: a response to truscott (1996). *Journal of Second Language Writing* 8(1), 1–11.

——(2002) *Treatment of Error in Second Language Student Writing*. Ann Arbor, MI: University of Michigan Press.

——(2006) Does error feedback help student writers? New evidence on the short- and long-term effects of written error correction. In K. Hyland and F. Hyland (eds.) *Feedback in Second Language Writing: Contexts and Issues* (pp. 81–104). Cambridge: Cambridge University Press.

Ferris, D., and Hedgcock, J. S. (2005) *Teaching ESL Composition: Purpose, Process, and Practice*. Mahwah, NJ: Lawrence Erlbaum Associates.

Ferris, D., and Roberts, B. (2001) Error feedback in L2 writing classes: how explicit does it need to be? *Journal of Second Language Writing* 10(3), 161–84.

Firth, A., and Wagner, J. (2007) Second/foreign language learning as a social accomplishment: elaborations on a reconceptualized SLA. *Modern Language Journal* 91, 798–817.

Folse, K. S. (2004) *Vocabulary Myths*. Ann Arbor, MI: University of Michigan Press.

Fortune, A. (1998) Survey review: grammar practice books. *ELT Journal* 52(1), 67–80.

Foster, P. (1998) A classroom perspective on the negotiation of meaning. *Applied Linguistics* 19(1), 1–23.

Foster, P., and Ohta, A. (2005) Negotiation for meaning and peer assistance in second language classrooms. *Applied Linguistics* 26(3), 402–30.

Foster, P., and Skehan, P. (1996) The influence of planning and task type on second language performance. *Studies in Second Language Acquisition* 18(3), 299–323.

Fotos, S. (1993) Consciousness raising and noticing through focus on form: grammar task performance versus formal instruction. *Applied Linguistics* 14(4), 385–407.

——(1994) Integrating grammar instruction and communicative language use through grammar consciousness-raising tasks. *TESOL Quarterly* 28(2), 323–51.

Fotos, S., and Ellis, R. (1991) Communicating about grammar: a task-based approach. *TESOL Quarterly* 25(4), 605–28.

Fraser, C. A. (1999) Lexical processing, strategy use and vocabulary learning through reading. *Studies in Second language Acquisition* 21(3), 225–41.

Fries, C. (1948) As we see it. *Language Learning* 1(1), 12–16.

Galperin, P. I. (1989) Organization of mental activity and the effectiveness of learning. *Soviet Psychology* 27(3), 65–82.

——(1992) Stage-by-stage formation as a method of psychological investigation. *Journal of Russian and East European Psychology* 30(4), 60–81.

Gan, Z., Humphreys, G., and Hamp-Lyons, L. (2004) Understanding successful and unsuccessful EFL students in Chinese universities. *Modern Language Journal* 88(2), 229–44.

Gardner, H. (1983) *Frames of Mind: The Theory of Multiple Intelligences*. New York: Basic Books.

Gardner, R. (1985) *Social Psychology and Second Language Learning: The Role of Attitude and Motivation*. London: Edward Arnold.

Gardner, R., and Lambert, W. (1972) *Attitudes and Motivation in Second Language Learning*. Rowley, MA: Newbury House.

Gass, S. (1979) Language transfer and universal grammatical relations. *Language Learning* 29(2), 327–44.

——(1988) Integrating research areas: a framework for second language studies. *Applied Linguistics* 9(2), 198–217.

——(1997) *Input, interaction, and the second language learner*. Mahwah, NJ: Lawrence Erlbaum Associates.

Gass, S., and Mackey, A. (2002) Frequency effects and second language acquisition. *Studies in Second Language Acquisition* 24(2), 249–60.

——(2007) Input, interaction and output in second language acquisition. In B. VanPatten and J. Williams (eds.) *Theories in Second Language Acquisition* (pp. 175–200). Mahwah, NJ: Lawrence Erlbaum Associates.

Gass, S., and Selinker, L. (2001) *Second Language Acquisition: An Introductory Course*. 2nd edition. London: Lawrence Erlbaum Associates.

——(2002) *Second Language Acquisition: An Introductory Course*. 3rd edition. New York: Routledge.

Gass, S., Mackey, A., and Ross-Feldman, L. (2005) Task-based interactions in classroom and laboratory settings. *Language Learning* 55(4), 575–611.

Gatbonton, E., and Segalowitz, N. (2005) Rethinking communicative language teaching: a focus on access to fluency. *Canadian Modern Language Review* 61(3), 325–53.

Gattegno, C. (1972) *Teaching Foreign Languages in Schools*. New York: Educational Solutions.

Genesee, F. (1984) French immersion programs. In S. Shapson and V. Doyley (eds.) *Bilingual and Multicultural Education: Canadian Perspectives*. Clevedon: Multilingual Matters.

George, H. (1972) *Common Errors in Language Learning: Insights from English*. Rowley, MA: Newbury House.

Gilmore, A. (2007) Authentic materials and authenticity in foreign language learning. *Language Teaching* 42(2), 97–119.

Goldschneider, J., and DeKeyser, R. (2001) Explaining the 'natural order of L2 morpheme acquisition' in English: a meta-analysis of multiple determinants. *Language Learning* 51(1), 1–50.

Goo, J. M., and Mackey, A. (2013) The case against the case against recasts. *Studies in Second Language Acquisition* 35(1), 127–65.

Goodlad, J. (1982) Lets get on with reconstruction. *Phil Delta Kappa* 64, 19–20.

Gower, R., and Walters, S. (1983) *Teaching Practice Handbook: A Reference Book for EFL Teachers in Training*. London: Heinemann.

Granger, S. (1998) *Learner English on Computer*. London: Addison Wesley Longman.

Greenbaum, S. (1996) *The Oxford English Grammar*. Oxford: Oxford University Press.

Grellet, F. (1981) *Developing Reading Skills: A Practical Guide to Reading Comprehension Exercises*. Cambridge: Cambridge University Press.

Griffiths, R. (1990) Speech rate and NNS comprehension: a preliminary study in time-benefit analysis. *Language Learning* 40(3), 311–36.

Grigorenko, E., Sternberg, R., and Ehrman, M. (2000) A theory-based approach to the measurement of foreign language learning ability: the Canal-F theory and test. *Modern Language Journal* 84, 390–405.

Guénette, D. (2007) Is feedback pedagogically correct?: Research design issues in studies of feedback on writing. *Journal of Second Language Writing* 16(1), 40–53.

Guilloteaux, M., and Dörnyei, Z. (2008) Motivating language learners: a classroom-oriented investigation of the effects of motivational strategies on student motivation. *TESOL Quarterly* 42(1), 55–77.

Guk, I., and Kellogg, D. (2007) The ZPD and whole class teaching: teacher-led and student-led interactional mediation of tasks. *Language Teaching Research* 11(3), 281–99.

Hafiz, F. M., and Tudor, I. (1989) Extensive reading and the development of language skills. *ELT Journal* 43, 4–13.

——(1990) Graded readers as an input medium in L2 learning. *System* 18(1), 31–42.

Hakansson, G. (1987) *Teacher Talk*. Lund: Lund University Press.

Hakuta, K. (1974) A preliminary report on the development of grammatical morphemes in a Japanese girl learning English as a second language. *Working Papers on Bilingualism* 3(2), 18–43.

——(1976) A case study of a Japanese child learning English as a second language. *Language Learning* 26(2), 321–51.

Hall, G. (2011) *Exploring English Language Teaching: Language in Action*. London: Routledge.

Hall, G., and Cook, G. (2012) Own-language use in language teaching and learning. *Language Teaching*, 45(3), 271–308.

Halliday, M. (1973) *Explorations in the Functions of Language*. London: Edward Arnold.

Han, X. (2010) The empirical study of the effects of comprehensible input on incidental vocabulary recognition. *Chinese Journal of Applied Linguistics* 33(1), 91–108.

Han, Z. (2007) Pedagogical implications: genuine and pretentious. *TESOL Quarterly* 41(3), 387–93.

Harley, B. (1989) Functional grammar in French immersion: a classroom experiment. *Applied Linguistics* 19(3), 331–59.

Harley, B., and Hart, D. (1997) Language aptitude and second language proficiency in classroom learners of different starting ages. *Studies in Second Language Acquisition* 19(3), 379–400.

Harmer, J. (1983) *The Practice of English Language Teaching*. London and New York: Longman.

——(1998) *How to Teach English: An Introduction to the Practice of English Language Teaching*. Harlow: Longman.

——(2007) *The Practice of English Language Teaching*. 4th edition. London and New York: Longman.

Harwood, N. (2010) Issues in materials development and design. In N. Harwood (ed.) *English Language Teaching Materials: Theory and Practice* (pp. 3–30). Cambridge: Cambridge University Press.

Hassan, X., Macaro, E., Mason, D., Nye, G., Smith, P., and Vanderplank, R. (2005) *Strategy Training in Language Learning – A Systematic Review of Available Research*. In Research Evidence in Education Library. London: EPPI-Centre, Social Science Research Unit, Institute of Education, University of London.

Hatch, E. (1978a) Discourse analysis and second language acquisition. In E. Hatch (ed.) *Second Language Acquisition*. Rowley, MA: Newbury House.

——(1978b) *Second Language Acquisition*. Rowley, MA: Newbury House.

——(1983) *Psycholinguistics: A Second Language Perspective*. Rowley, MA: Newbury House.

Hatch, E., and Wagner-Gough, J. (1976) Explaining sequence and variation in second language acquisition. *Papers in Second Language Acquisition, Language Learning* (Special Issue, 4), 39–57.

Hawkins, B. (1985) Is an 'appropriate response' always so appropriate? In S. Gass and C. Madden (eds.) *Input in Second Language Acquisition* (pp. 162–80). Rowley, MA: Newbury House.

Hayn, G. A. (1967) After Colorado, what? *Hispania* 50(1), 104–107.

Hedgcock, J. S., and Ferris, D. R. (2009) *Teaching Readers of English: Students, Texts, and Contexts*. New York: Routledge.

Hedge, T. (2000) *Teaching and Learning in the Language Classroom*. Oxford: Oxford University Press.

Hendrickson, J. M. (1978) Error correction in foreign language teaching: recent theory, research, and practice. *Modern Language Journal* 62(8), 387–98.

Hill, D. R., and Thomas, H. R. (1988) Survey review: graded readers part 1. *ELT Journal* 42(1), 44–52.

Hirst, P. (1966) Educational theory. In J. Tibble (ed.) *The Study of Education* (pp. 29–58). London: Routledge.

Holunga, S. (1995) *The effect of metacognitive strategy training with verbalization on the oral accuracy of adult second language learners.* Unpublished doctoral dissertation, University of Toronto, Ontario Institute for Studies in Education.

Hornby, A. (1959) *The Teaching of Structural Words and Sentence Patterns.* Oxford: Oxford University Press.

Horwitz, E. (2000) Teachers and students, students and teachers: an ever-evolving partnership. *Modern Language Journal* 84(4), 523–35.

Horwitz, E., Horwitz, M., and Cope, J. (1986) Foreign language classroom anxiety. *Modern Language Journal* 70, 125–32.

Hosenfeld, C. (1978) Students mini-theories of second language learning. *Association Bulletin* 29(2), 2.

Howatt, A. (1974) The background to course design. In J. Allen and S. P. Corder (eds.) *The Edinburgh Course in Applied Linguistics,* vol. 3, *Techniques in Applied Linguistics* (pp. 1–23). Oxford: Oxford University Press.

——(1984) *A History of English Language Teaching.* Oxford: Oxford University Press.

Hu, G. (2010) A place for metalanguage in the L2 classroom. *ELT Journal* 65(2), 180–82.

Huckin, T., and Bloch, J. (1993) Strategies for inferring word meaning in context: a cognitive model. In T. Huckin, M. Haynes and J. Coady (eds.) *Second Language Reading and Vocabulary Learning* (pp. 153–76). Norwood, NJ: Ablex.

Huckin, T., and Coady, J. (1999) Incidental vocabulary acqusition in a second language: a review. *Studies in Second Language Acquisition* 21(2), 181–93.

Hughes, A. (1983) Second language learning and communicative language teaching. In K. Johnson and D. Porter (eds.) *Perspectives in Communicative Language Teaching.* New York: Academic Press.

Hulstijn, J. H. (1992) Retention of inferred and given word meanings: experiments in incidental vocabulary learning. In P. J. L. Arnaud and H. Bejoint (eds.) *Vocabulary and Applied Linguistics* (pp. 113–25). London: Macmillan.

——(2003) Incidental and intentional learning. In C. J. Doughty and M. H. Long (eds.) *Handbook of Second Language Acquisition* (pp. 349–81). Oxford: Blackwell.

Hulstijn, J. H., Hollander, M., and Greidanus, T. (1996) Incidental vocabulary learning by advanced foreign language students: the influence of marginal glosses, dictionary use, and reoccurrence of unknown words. *Modern Language Journal* 80(3), 327–39.

Hurd, S. (2002) Learner difference in independent language learning contexts. In *The Guide to Good Practice for Learning and Teaching in Languages, Linguistics and Area Studies.* LTSN Subject Centre for Languages, Linguistics and Area Studies, University of Southampton.

Hyltenstam, K. (1984) The use of typological markedness conditions as predictors in second language acquisition: the case of pronominal copies in relative clauses. In R. Andersen (ed.) *Second Language: A Crosslinguistic Perspective.* Rowley, MA: Newbury House.

Hymes, D. (1970) On communicative competence. In J. J. Gumperz and D. Hymes (eds.) *Directions in Sociolinguistics.* New York: Holt, Rinchart and Winston.

——(1971) Competence and performance in linguistic theory. In R. Huxley and B. Ingram (eds.) *Language Acquisition: Models and Methods* (pp. 3–28). London: Academic Press.

Izumi, K., Uchimoto, K., and Isahara, H. (2004) Standard Speaking Test (SST) speech corpus of Japanese learners' English and automatic detection of learners' errors. *ICAME Journal* 28, 31–48.

Izumi, S., Bigelow, M., Fujiwara, M., and Fearnow, S. (1999) Testing the output hypothesis: effects of output on noticing and second language acquisition. *Studies in Second Language Acquisition* 21(3), 421–52.

Jacobs, G. (1998) Cooperative learning or just grouping students: the difference makes a difference. In W. Renandya and G. Jacobs (eds.) *Learners and Language Learning* (pp. 145–71). Singapore: SEAMEO.

James, C. (1980) *Contrastive Analysis*. London: Longman.

Jenkins, J. (2000) *The Phonology of English as an International Language*. Oxford: Oxford University Press.

Jenkins, J., Matlock, B., and Slocum, T. (1989) Two approaches to vocabulary instruction: the teaching of individual word meanings and practice in deriving word meaning from context. *Reading Research Quarterly* 24(2), 215–35.

Jiang, N. (2002) Form-meaning mapping in vocabulary acquisition in a second language. *Studies in Second Language Acquisition* 24(4), 617–37.

Johns, A. M. (1990) L1 composition theories: implications for developing theories of L2 composition. In B. Kroll (ed.) *Second Language Writing: Research Insights for the Classroom* (pp. 24–36). Cambridge: Cambridge University Press.

Johnson, K. (1979) Communicative approaches and communicative processes. In C. Brumfit and K. Johnson (eds.) *The Communicative Approach to Language Teaching*. Oxford: Oxford University Press.

——(1982) *Communicative Syllabus Design and Methodology*. Oxford: Pergamon.

——(1995) *Understanding Communication in Second Language Classrooms*. Cambridge: Cambridge University Press.

Johnson, R., and Swain, M. (eds.) (1997) *Immersion Education: International Perspectives*. Cambridge: Cambridge University Press.

Just, M. A., and Carpenter, P. A. (1992) A capacity theory of comprehension. *Psychological Review* 99(1), 122–49.

Kalivoda, T. (1990) Teaching grammar in the target language. *Hispania* 73(1), 267–69.

Kaneko, T. (1991) *The role of the L1 in second language classrooms*. Unpublished EdD dissertation, Temple University Japan, Tokyo.

Kasper, G. (2001) Four perspectives on L2 pragmatic development. *Applied Linguistics* 22(4), 502–30.

——(2006) Beyond repair: conversation analysis as an approach to SLA, *AILA Review*, 19, 83–99.

Kasper, G., and Kellerman, E. (1997) Introduction: approaches to communication strategies. In G. Kasper and E. Kellerman (eds.) *Communication Strategies: Psycholinguistic and Sociolinguistic Perspectives*. London: Longman.

Kasper, G., and Rose, K. (2002) *Pragmatic Development in a Second Language*. Language Learning Monograph Series. Oxford: Blackwell.

Katayama, A. (2007) Students perceptions of oral error correction. *Japanese Language and Literature* 41(1), 61–92.

Kellerman, E. (1977) Towards a characterization of the strategies of transfer in second language learning. *Interlanguage Studies Bulletin* 2, 58–145.

——(1978) Giving learners a break: native language intuitions as a source of predictions about transferability. *Working Papers on Bilingualism* 15, 59–92.

——(1979) Transfer and non-transfer: where are we now? *Studies in Second Language Acquisition* 2(1), 37–57.

——(1983) Now you see it, now you don't. In S. Gass and L. Selinker (eds.) *Language Transfer in Language Learning*. Rowley, MA: Newbury House.

——(1986) An eye for an eye: crosslinguistic constraints on the development of the L2 lexicon. In E. Kellerman and M. S. Smith (eds.) *Cross-linguistic Influence in Second Language Acquisition*. Oxford: Pergamon.

——(1995) Crosslinguistic influence: transfer to nowhere? *Annual Review of Applied Linguistics* 15, 125–50.

Kim, S., and Elder, C. (2005) Language choices and pedagogic functions in the foreign language classroom: a cross-linguistic functional analysis of teacher talk. *Language Teaching Research* 9(3), 335–80.

Kim, Y. (2006) Effects of input elaboration on vocabulary acquisition through reading by Korean learners of English as a foreign language. *TESOL Quarterly* 40(2), 341–73.

——(2009) The effects of task complexity on learner-learner interaction. *System* 37(2), 254–68.

Kinginger, C. (2002) Defining the zone of proximal development in US foreign language education. *Applied Linguistics* 23(2), 240–61.

Klapper, J. (2006) *Understanding and Developing Good Practice: Language Teaching in Higher Education*. London: CILT National Centre for Languages.

Krahnke, K. (1987) *Approaches to Syllabus Design for Foreign Language Teaching*. Englewood, NJ: Prentice-Hall, Inc.

Kramsch, C. (1993) *Context and Culture in Language Teaching*. Oxford: Oxford University Press.

——(2009) *The Multilingual Subject*. Oxford: Oxford University Press.

Krashen, S. (1981) *Second Language Acquisition and Second Language Learning*. Oxford: Pergamon.

——(1982) *Principles and Practice in Second Language Acquisition*. Oxford: Pergamon.

——(1983) Second language acquisition theory and the preparation of teachers. In J. Alatis, H. Stern and P. Strevens (eds.) *Applied Linguistics and the Preparation of Teachers: Toward a Rationale*. Washington DC: Georgetown University Press.

——(1985) *The Input Hypothesis: Issues and Implications*. London and New York: Longman.

——(1989) We acquire vocabulary and spelling by reading: additional evidence for the Input Hypothesis. *Modern Language Journal* 73(4), 440–64.

——(1998) Comprehensible output? *System* 26(2), 175–82.

——(2004) The case for narrow reading. *Language Magazine* 3(5), 17–19.

Krashen, S., and Scarcella, R. (1978) On routines and patterns in second language acquisition and performance. *Language Learning* 28(2), 283–300.

Krashen, S., and Terrell, T. (1983) *The Natural Approach: Language Acquisition in the Classroom*. Oxford: Pergamon.

Kumaravadivelu, B. (1993) The name of the task and the task of naming: methodological aspects of task-based pedagogy. In G. Crookes and S. Gass (eds.) *Tasks in a Pedagogical Context* (pp. 69–96). Cleveland, UK: Multilingual Matters.

——(1994) The postmethod condition: (e)merging strategies for second/foreign language teaching. *TESOL Quarterly* 28(1), 27–48.

——(2001) Toward a postmethod pedagogy. *TESOL Quarterly* 35(4), 537–60.

——(2006) *Understanding Language Teaching: From Method to Postmethod*. Mahwah, NJ: Erlbaum.

Labov, W. (1970) The study of language in its social context. *Studium Generale* 23(1), 30–87.

Lado, R. (1957) *Linguistics Across Cultures: Applied Linguistics for Language Teachers*. Ann Arbor, MI: University of Michigan.

——(1964) *Language Teaching: A Scientific Approach*. New York: McGraw Hill.

Lalande, J. F., II. (1982) Reducing composition errors: an experiment. *Modern Language Journal* 66(2), 140–49.

Lally, C. (2000) First language influences in second language composition: the effect of pre-writing. *Foreign Language Annals* 33, 428–32.

LRC Project Partners (2003) *Language Resource Centre Handbook*. Athens: Kastaniotis Editions.

Lantolf, J. (2000a) Introducing sociocultural theory. In J. Lantolf (ed.) *Sociocultural Theory and Second Language Learning*. Oxford: Oxford University Press.

——(2000b) Second language learning as a mediated process. *Language Teaching* 33(2), 79–96.

——(2005) Sociocultural and second language learning research: an exegesis. In E. Hinkel (ed.) *Handbook of Research on Second Language Teaching and Learning*. Mahwah, NJ: Lawrence Erlbaum.

——(2006) Sociocultural theory and L2. *Studies in Second Language Acquisition* 28(1), 67–109.

Lantolf, J., and Aljaafreh, A. L. I. (1995) Second language learning in the Zone of Proximal Development: a revolutionary experience. *International Journal of Educational Research* 23, 619–32.

Lantolf, J., and Thorne, S. (2006) *Sociocultural Theory and the Genesis of Second Language Development*. Oxford: Oxford University Press.

Larsen-Freeman, D. (1976) An explanation for the morpheme acquisition order of second language learners. *Language Learning* 26(1), 125–34.

——(1995) On the teaching and learning of grammar. In F. R. Eckman, D. Highland, P. W. Lee, J. Mileham and R. R. Weber (eds.) *Second Language Acquisition Theory and Pedagogy* (pp. 131–48). Mahwah, NJ: Lawrence Erlbaum Associates.

——(2003) *Teaching Language: From Grammar to Grammaring*. Boston, MA: Thomson Heinle.

Larsen-Freeman, D., and Cameron, L. (2006) *Complex Systems and Applied Linguistics*. Oxford: Oxford University Press.

Larsen-Freeman, D., and Long, M. (1991) *An Introduction to Second Language Acquisition Research*. London: Longman.

Laufer, B. (2005) Focus on form in second language vocabulary learning. *EUROSLA Yearbook* 5, 223–50.

Laufer, B., and Girsai, N. (2008) Form-focused instruction in second language vocabulary learning: a case for contrastive analysis and translation. *Applied Linguistics*, 29(4), 694–716.

Laufer, B., and Hulstijn, J. (2001) Incidental vocabulary acquisition in a second language: the construct of task-induced involvement. *Applied Linguistics* 22(1), 1–26.

Laufer, B., and Nation, P. (1995) Vocabulary size and use: Lexical richness in L2 written production. *Applied Linguistics* 16(3), 307–22.

Laufer, R., and Eliasson, S. (1993) What causes avoidance in L2 learning: L1–L2 difference, L1–L2 similarity, or L2 complexity? *Studies in Second Language Acquisition* 15(1), 35–48.

Lee, J. (2000) *Tasks and Communicating in Language Classrooms*. Boston, MA: McGraw-Hill.

Lee, Y. A. (2006) Respecifying display questions: Interactional resources for language teaching. *TESOL Quarterly* 40(4), 691–713.

Leki, I. (1991) The preferences of ESL students for error correction in college-level writing classes. *Foreign Language Annals* 24(3), 203–18.

Lenneberg, E. (1967) *Biological Foundations of Language.* New York: John Wiley and Son.

Leow, R. P. (1993) To simplify or not to simplify. *Studies in Second Language Acquisition* 15(3), 333–55.

——(1997) Attention, awareness, and foreign language behavior. *Language Learning* 47(3), 467–505.

Levelt, W. (1989) *Speaking: From Intention to Articulation.* Cambridge, MA: MIT Press.

Levin, L. (1972) *Comparative studies in foreign-language teaching. Godteborg Studies in Educational Sciences* 9. Gothenberg, Sweden: Gothenburg School of Education.

Levine, G., and Phipps, A. (eds.) (2011) *Critical and Intercultural Theory and Language Pedagody.* Boston, MA: Heinle.

Lewis, M. (1993) *The Lexical Approach.* Hove: Language Teaching Publications.

——(1997) *Implementing the Lexical Approach.* Hove: Language Teaching Publications.

Li, S. (2010) The effectiveness of corrective feedback in SLA: a meta-analysis. *Language Learning* 60(2), 309–65.

Lightbown, P. (1983) Exploring relationships between developmental and instructional sequences in L2 acquisition. In H. Seliger and M. Long (eds.) *Classroom-Oriented Research in Second Language Acquisition.* Rowley, MA: Newbury House.

——(1985a) Can language acquisition be altered by instruction? In K. Hyltenstam and M. Pienemann (eds.) *Modelling and Assessing Second Language Acquisition.* Clevedon: Multilingual Matters.

——(1985b) Great expectations: second language acquisition research and classroom teaching. *Applied Linguistics* 6(2), 173–89.

——(2000) Anniversary article. Classroom SLA research and second language teaching. *Applied Linguistics* 21(4), 431–62.

——(2005) Perfecting practice. Plenary talk given at the IRAAL/BAAL Conference, Cork, Ireland.

——(2008) Transfer appropriate processing as a model for classroom second language acquisition. In Z. Han (ed.) *Understanding Second Language Process* (pp. 27–44). Clevedon: Multilingual Matters.

Lightbown, P., and Spada, N. (2006) *How Languages are Learned.* 3rd edition. Oxford: Oxford University Press.

Littlewood, W. (2007) Communicative and task-based language teaching in East Asian classrooms. *Language Teaching* 40(03), 243–49.

Loewen, S. (2005) Incidental focus on form and second language learning. *Studies in Second Language Acquisition* 27(3), 361–86.

Loewen, S., and Philp, J. (2006) Recasts in adults English L2 classrooms: characteristics, explicitness, and effectiveness. *Modern Language Journal* 90(4), 536–56.

Logan, G. E. (1971) Problems in testing, grading, and issuing credits in an individualized foreign language program. In H. B. Altman and R. L. Politzer (eds.) *Individualizing Foreign Language Instruction: The Proceedings of the Stanford Conference* (pp. 225–37). Rowley, MA: Newbury House.

——(1980) Individualized foreign language instruction: American patterns for accommodating learner differences in the classroom. In H. B. Altman and C. V. James (eds.) *Foreign Language Teaching: Meeting Individual Needs* (pp. 94–110). Oxford: Pergamon Press.

Long, M. (1981) Input, interaction and second language acquisition. In H. Winitz (ed.) *Native Language and Foreign Language Acquisition* (pp. 259–78). Annals of the New York Academy of Sciences 379.

——(1983a) Does second language instruction make a difference? A review of the research. *TESOL Quarterly* 17(3), 359–82.

——(1983b) Native speaker/non-native speaker conversation and the negotiation of comprehensible input. *Applied Linguistics,* 4(2), 126–41.

——(1988) Instructed interlanguage development. In L. Beebe (ed.) *Issues in Second Language Acquisition: Multiple Perspectives.* New York: Newbury House.

——(1990) Second language classroom research and teacher education. In C. Brumfit and R. Mitchell (eds.) *Research in the Language Classroom* (pp. 161–70). ELT Documents 133. London: Modern English Publications.

——(1991) Focus on form: a design feature in language teaching methodology. In K. D. Bot, R. Ginsberg and C. Kramsch (eds.) *Foreign Language Research in Cross-Cultural Perspective* (pp. 39–52). Amsterdam: John Benjamins.

——(1996) The role of the linguistic environment in second language acquisition. In W. Ritchie and T. Bhatia (eds.) *Handbook of Second Language Acquisition.* San Diego, CA: Academic Press.

——(2005) *TBLT: building the road as we travel.* Paper presented at the International Conference on Task-Based Language Teaching.

——(2006) *Problems in SLA.* Mahwah, NJ: Lawrence Erlbaum Associates.

——(2008) Methodological principles for language teaching. In M. Long and C. Doughty (eds.) *The Handbook of Language Teaching.* Malden, MA: Wiley-Blackwell.

Long, M., and Crookes, G. (1987) Intervention points in second language classroom processes. In B. Das (ed.) *Patterns of Classroom Interaction.* Singapore: SEAMEO Regional Language Centre.

Long, M., and Larsen-Freeman, D. (1991) *An Introduction to Second Language Acquisition Research.* Harlow: Longman.

Long, M., and Porter, P. (1985) Group work, interlanguage talk, and second language acquisition. *TESOL Quarterly* 19(2), 207–28.

Long, M., and Ross, S. (1993) Modifications that preserve language and content. In M. L. Tickoo (ed.) *Simplification: Theory and Application* (pp. 29–52). Singapore: SEAMEO.

Long, M., and Sato, C. J. (1984) Methodological issues in interlanguage studies: an interactionist perspective. In A. Davies, C. Criper and A. P. R. Howatt (eds.) *Interlanguage* (pp. 253–80). Edinburgh: Edinburgh University Press.

Loschky, L. (1994) Comprehensible input and second language acquisition: what is the relationship? *Studies in Second Language Acquisition* 16(3), 303–23.

Loschky, L., and Bley-Vroman, R. (1993) Grammar and task-based methodology. In G. Crookes and S. Gass (eds.) *Tasks and Language Learning: Integrating Theory and Practice* (pp. 123–67). Clevedon: Multilingual Matters.

Lynch, T. (1996) *Communication in the Language Classroom.* Oxford: Oxford University Press.

Lyster, R. (1994) The effect of functional-analytic teaching on aspects of French immersion students sociolinguistic competence. *Applied Linguistics* 15(3), 263–87.

——(2001) Negotiation of form, recasts, and explicit correction in relation to error types and learner repair in immersion classrooms. *Language Learning* 51(s1), 265–301.

——(2004) Differential effects of prompts and recasts in form-focused instruction. *Studies in Second Language Acquisition* 26(3), 399–432.

——(2007) *Learning and Teaching Languages through Content: A Counterbalanced Approach*. Amsterdam and Philadelphia, PA: John Benjamins.

Lyster, R., and Mori, H. (2006) Interactional feedback and instructional counterbalance. *Studies in Second Language Acquisition* 28(2), 269–300.

Lyster, R., and Ranta, L. (1997) Corrective feedback and learner uptake. *Studies in Second Language Acquisition* 19(1), 37–66.

——(2013) The case for variety in corrective feedback research. *Studies in Second Language Acquisition* 34(1), 167–84.

Lyster, R., and Saito, K. (2010) Oral feedback in classroom SLA. *Studies in Second Language Acquisition* 32(s2), 265–302.

Macaro, E. (2001) *Learning Strategies in Foreign and Second Language Classrooms*. London: Continuum.

——(2005) Codeswitching in the L2 classroom: a communication and learning strategy. In E. Llurda (ed.) *Non-Native Language Teachers: Perceptions, Challenges and Contributions to the Profession* (pp. 63–84). New York: Springer.

——(2006) Strategies for language learning and for language use: revising the theoretical framework. *Modern Language Journal* 90(3), 320–37.

——(2011) *The teachers codeswitching and the learners strategic response: towards a research agenda and implications for teacher education*. Plenary address at JACET Annual Conference, Fukuoka, Japan.

MacIntyre, P., and Gardner, R. (1991) Methods and results in the study of foreign language anxiety: a review of the literature. *Language Learning* 41(1), 25–57.

MacIntyre, P., Baker, S., Clement, R., and Conrad, S. (2001) Willingness to communicate, social support, and language learning orientations of immersion students. *Studies in Second Language Acquisition* 23(3), 369–88.

Mackey, A. (1999) Input, interaction and second language development: an empirical study of question formation in ESL. *Studies in Second Language Acquisition* 21(4), 557–87.

——(2006) Feedback, noticing and instructed second language learning. *Applied Linguistics* 27(3), 405–30.

Mackey, A., and Goo, J. M. (2007) Interaction research in SLA: a meta-analysis and research synthesis. In A. Mackey (ed.) *Input, Interaction and Corrective Feedback in L2 Learning* (pp. 379–452). Oxford: Oxford University Press.

Mackey, W. (1965) *Language Teaching Analysis*. London: Longman.

Manolopoulo-Sergi, E. (2004) Motivation within the information processing model of foreign language learning. *System* 32(3), 427–42.

Markee, N. (2008) Toward a learning behavior tracking methodology for CA-for-SLA, *Applied Linguistics* 29(3), 404–27.

Marsden, E. (2006) Exploring input processing in the classroom: an experimental comparison of processing instruction and enriched input. *Language Learning* 56(3), 507–66.

Marton, W. (1988) *Methods in English Language Teaching: Frameworks and Options*. Cambridge: Prentice Hall International.

Mayo, M. (ed.) (2007) *Investigating Tasks in Formal Language Learning* (pp. 7–26). New York: Multilingual Matters.

McCarten, J. (2007) *Teaching Vocabulary: Lessons from the Corpus, Lessons for the Classroom*. New York: Cambridge University Press.

McCarthy, M. (1991) *Discourse Analysis for Language Teachers*. Cambridge: Cambridge University Press.

McCarthy, M., and O'Dell, F. (2010) *English Vocabulary in Use Elementary.* Cambridge: Cambridge University Press.

McRae, J. (1996) Representational language learning: from language awareness to text awareness. In R. A. Carter and J. McRae (eds.) *Language, Literature and the Learner: Creative Classroom Practice* (pp. 16–40). London: Longman.

Meara, P., Lightbown, P. M., and Halter, R. (1997) Classrooms as lexical environments. *Language Teaching Research* 1(1), 28–47.

Mellow, J. (2002) Towards principled eclecticism in language teaching: the two-dimensional model and the centring principle. TESL-EJ 5 (4) A-1. Online: http://tesl-ej.org/ej20/a1.html (retrieved 3 August 2012).

Meyer, H. (2008) *The pedagogical implications of the use of the L1 in the L2 classroom.* Online: http://www.kyoai.ac.jp/college/ronshuu/no-08/meyer1.pdf.

Mifka-Profozic, N. (2012) *Corrective feedback, individual differences and the L2 acquisition of French preterite and imperfect tenses.* Unpublished PhD thesis, University of Auckland, Auckland.

Mishra, C. (2005) *Error Correction in English: A Training Course for Teachers.* New Delhi: Sarup and Sons.

Mislevy, R. J., Behrens, J. T., Bennett, R. E., Demark, S. F., Frezzo, D. C., Levy, R., Robinson, D. H., Rutstein, D. W., Shute, V. J., Stanley, K., and Winters, F. I. (2010) On the roles of external knowledge representations in assessment design. *Journal of Technology,Learning, and Assessment* 8(2). Online: http://escholarship.bc.edu/jtla/vol8/2

Mohamed, N. (2001) *Teaching grammar through consciousness-raising tasks.* Unpublished MA thesis, University of Auckland, Auckland.

Mohammed, A. M. (1996) Informal pedagogical grammar. *IRAL: International Review of Applied Linguistics in Language Teaching* 34(4), 283.

Mohr, K.J., and Mohr, E.S. (2007) Extending English-language learners classroom interactions using the response protocol. *The Reading Teacher* 60(5), 440–50.

Montgomery, C., and Eisenstein, M. (1985) Real reality revisited: an experimental communicative course in ESL. *TESOL Quarterly* 19(2), 317–33.

Morrison, B. (2005) Evaluating learning gain in a self-access language learning centre. *Language Teaching Research* 9(3), 267–93.

Morrow, K. (1979) Communicative language testing: revolution or evolution. In C. Brumfit and K. Johnson (eds.) *The Communicative Approach to Language Teaching.* Oxford: Oxford University Press.

Moskowitz, G. (1999) Enhancing personal development: Humanistic activities at work. In. J. Arnold (ed.) *Affect in Language Learning* (pp. 177–93). Cambridge: Cambridge University Press.

Myles, F. (2004) From data to theory: the over-representation of linguistic knowledge in SLA. *Transactions of the Philological Society* 102(2), 139–68.

Myles, F., Hooper, J., and Mitchell, R. (1998) Rote or rule? Exploring the role of formulaic language in classroom foreign language learning. *Language Learning* 48(3), 323–63.

Naiman, N., Fröhlich, M., Stern, H., and Todesco, A. (1978) *The Good Language Learner.* Research in Education Series No 7. Toronto: The Ontario Institute for Studies in Education. Reprinted in 1996 by Multilingual Matters.

Nakahama, Y., Tyler, A., and Van Lier, L. (2001) Negotiation of meaning in conversational and information gap activities: a comparative discourse analysis. *TESOL Quarterly* 35(3), 377–405.

Nassaji, H., and Swain, M. (2000) A Vygotskian perspective on corrective feedback in L2: the effect of random versus negotiated help on the learning of English articles. *Language Awareness* 9(1), 34–51.

Nassaji, H., and Wells, G. (2000) What's the use of "triadic dialogue"?: an investigation of teacher-student interaction. *Applied Linguistics* 21(3), 376–406.

Nation, I. S. P. (1990) *Teaching and Learning Vocabulary.* Boston, MA: Heinle and Heinle.

——(2000) Learning vocabulary in lexical sets: dangers and guidelines. *TESOL Journal* 9(2), 6–10.

——(2001) *Learning Vocabulary in Another Language.* Cambridge: Cambridge University Press.

——(2003) The role of the first language in foreign language learning. Online: http://www.asian-efl-journal.com/june–2003–PN.html (retrieve 31 January 2005).

——(2006) How large a vocabulary is needed for reading and listening? *Canadian Modern Language Review* 63(1), 59–82.

——(2009) *Teaching ESL/EFL Reading and Writing.* New York: Routledge.

Negueruela, E. (2003) *Systemic-theoretical instruction and L2 development: a sociocultural approach to teaching-learning and researching L2 learning.* Unpublished doctoral dissertation, the Pennyslvania State University, University Park.

Newell, A., and Rosenbloom, P. S. (1981) Mechanisms of skill acquisition and the law of practice. In J. R. Anderson (ed.) *Cognitive Skills and their Acquisition* (pp. 1–55). Hillsdale, NJ: Erlbaum.

Newman, F., and Holzman, L. (1997) *The End of Knowing: A New Developmental Way of Learning.* London: Routledge.

Newmark, L. (1966) How not to interfere with language learning. *Language Learning* 40(1), 77–83.

——(1981) Participatory observation: how to succeed in language learning. In H. Winitz (ed.) *The Comprehension Approach to Foreign Language Instruction.* Rowley, MA: Newbury House.

Niedzielski, H. (1975) *Rationalizing Individualized Instruction.* ERIC Document FL 006 925.

Nitta, R., and Gardner, S. (2005) Consciousness-raising and practice in ELT coursebooks. *ELT Journal* 59(1), 3–13.

Nobuyoshi, J., and Ellis, R. (1993) Focused communication tasks. *ELT Journal* 47(3), 203–10.

Noels, K., Pelletier, L., Clement, R., and Vallerand, R. (2000) Why are you learning a second language? Motivational orientations and self-determination theory. *Language Learning* 50(1), 57–85.

Norris, J. M. (2007) *Educational context, epistemological competition, and the future of task-based research: a program evaluation perspective.* Paper presented at the Social and Cognitive Perspectives on Language Learning and Teaching Conference.

Norris, J. M., and Ortega, L. (2000) Effectiveness of L2 instruction: a research synthesis and quantitative meta-analysis. *Language Learning* 50(3), 417–528.

Norton, B. (2000) *Identity and Language Learning: Gender, Ethnicity and Educational Change.* Harlow: Longman.

Nunan, D. (1988) *The Learner-Centred Curriculum.* Cambridge: Cambridge University Press.

——(1989) *Designing Tasks for the Communicative Classroom.* Cambridge: Cambridge University Press.

——(1991) *Language Teaching Methodology: A Textbook for Teachers*. New York: Prentice Hall International.

——(1999) *Second Language Teaching and Learning*. Boston: Heinle and Heinle.

——(2004) *Task-Based Language Teaching*. Cambridge: Cambridge University Press.

Nuttall, C. (1996) *Teaching Reading Skills in a Foreign Language*. Oxford: Heinemann.

Odlin, T. (1989) *Language Transfer*. Cambridge: Cambridge University Press.

——(1990) Word-order transfer, metalinguistic awareness and constraints on foreign language learning. In B. VanPatten and J. Lee (eds.) *Second Language Acquisition–Foreign Language Learning*. Clevedon: Multilingual Matters.

Oh, S.-Y. (2001) Two types of input modification and EFL reading comprehension: simplification versus elaboration. *TESOL Quarterly* 35(1), 69–96.

Ohta, A. (2001) *Second Language Acquisition Processes in the Classroom: Learning Japanese*. Mahwah, NJ: Lawrence Erlbaum.

Oliver, R. (2000) Age differences in negotiation and feedback in classroom and pairwork. *Language Learning* 50(1), 119–51.

Omaggio, A. C. (1986) *Teaching Language in Context: Proficiency-Oriented Instruction*. Boston: Heinle and Heinle.

O'Malley, J., and Chamot, A. (1990) *Learning Strategies in Second Language Acquisition*. Cambridge: Cambridge University Press.

O'Neill, R. (1994) *The myth of the silent teacher*. Paper presented at the Annual IATEFL Conference. Online: http://www.tedpower.co.uk/esl0420.html

Ortega, L. (2009) *Understanding Second Language Acquisition*. London: Hodder Education.

——(2011) Sequences and processes in language learning. In M. Long and C. Doughty (eds.) *The Handbook of Language Teaching* (pp. 81–105). Malden, MA: Wiley-Blackwell.

Owen, C. (1996) Do concordances need to be consulted? *ELT Journal* 50(3), 219–24.

Oxford, R. (1990) *Language Learning Strategies: What Every Teacher Should Know*. Rowley, MA: Newbury House.

——(2011) *Teaching and Researching: Language Learning Strategies*. London: Pearson Longman.

Palmer, A. (1979) Compartmentalized and integrated control: an assessment of some evidence for two kinds of competence and implications for the classroom. *Language Learning* 29(1), 169–80.

Palmer, H. E. (1917) *Extensive Reading: The Scientific Study and Teaching of Languages*. London: Harrap. Reprinted 1968 by Oxford University Press.

Papathanasiou, E. (2009) An investigation of two ways of presenting vocabulary. *ELT Journal* 63(4), 313–22.

Paradis, M. (1994) Neurolinguistic aspects of implicit and explicit memory: implications for bilingualism. In N. Ellis (ed.) *Implicit and Explicit Learning of Second Languages* (pp. 393–419). London: Academic Press.

——(2009) *Declarative and Procedural Determinants of Second Languages*. Amsterdam: John Benjamins.

Parker, K., and Chaudron, C. (1987) *The effects of linguistic simplification and elaborative modifications on L2 comprehension*. Paper presented at the 21st Annual TESOL Convention.

Paulston, C. B. (1970) Structural pattern drills: a classification. *Foreign Language Annals* 4(2), 187–93.

——(1972) The sequencing of structural pattern drills. *TESOL Quarterly* 6, 197–208.

Pavlenko, A., and Jarvis, S. (2002) Bidirectional transfer. *Applied Linguistics* 23(2), 190–214.

Pawley, A., and Syder, F. (1983) Two puzzles for linguistic theory: nativelike selection and nativelike fluency. In J. Richards and R. Schmidt (eds.) *Language and Communication*. London: Longman.

Payne, J., and Whitney, P. (2002) Developing L2 oral proficiency synchronous CMC: output, working memory, and interlanguage development. *CALICO Journal* 20(1), 7–32.

Peacock, M. (1997) The effect of authentic materials on the motivation of EFL learners. *ELT Journal* 51(2), 144–56.

Pennycook, A. (1989)The concept of method, interested knowledge, and the politics of language teaching. *TESOL Quarterly* 23(3), 589–618.

Peppard, J. (2010) *Towards a functional-lexicogrammatical syllabus*. Unpublished MA thesis, University of Birmingham.

Perez-Pereira, M. (1989) The acquisition of morphemes: some evidence from Spanish. *Journal of Psycholinguistic Research* 18(3), 289–312.

Pesce, S. (2008) Focused tasks in L2 Spanish grammar learning and teaching. In J. Eckerth (ed.) *Task-based Language Learning and Teaching: Theoretical, Methodological, and Pedagogical Perspectives* (pp. 67–88). Frankfurt: Peter Lang.

Phipps, S., and Borg, S. (2009) Exploring tensions between teachers' grammar teaching beliefs and practices. *System* 37(3), 380–390.

Pica, T. (1983) Adult acquisition of English as a second language under different conditions of exposure. *Language Learning* 33(4), 465–97.

——(1988) Interlanguage adjustments as an outcome of NS–NNS negotiated interaction. *Language Learning* 38(1), 45–73.

——(1991) Classroom interaction, negotiation, and comprehension: redefining relationships. *System* 19(4), 437–52.

——(1992) The textual outcomes of native speaker–non-native speaker negotiation: what do they reveal about second language learning. In C. Kramsch and S. McConnell-Ginet (eds.) *Text and Context: Cross-Disciplinary Perspectives on Language Study*. Lexington, MA: D.C. Heath and Company.

——(1994) Questions from the language classroom: research perspectives. *TESOL Quarterly* 28(1), 49–79.

——(1996) The essential role of negotiation in the communicative classroom. *JALT Journal* 78(1), 241–68.

——(1998) Second language teaching and research relationships: a North American view. *Language Teaching Research* 1(1), 48–72.

Pica, T., and Doughty, C. (1985) The role of group work in classroom second language acquisition. *Studies in Second Language Acquisition* 7(2), 233–48.

Pica, T., and Long, M. (1986) The linguistic and conversational performance of experienced and inexperienced teachers. In R. Day (ed.) *Talking to Learn: Conversation in Second Language Acquisition*. Rowley, MA: Newbury House.

Pica, T., Young, R., and Doughty, C. (1987) The impact of interaction on comprehension. *TESOL Quarterly* 21(4), 737–58.

Pica, T., Holliday, L., Lewis, N., and Morgenthaler, L. (1989) Comprehensible output as an outcome of linguistic demands on the learner. *Studies in Second Language Acquisition* 11(1), 63–90.

Pienemann, M. (1984) Psychological constraints on the teachability of languages. *Studies in Second Language Acquisition* 6(2), 186–214.

——(1985) Learnability and syllabus construction. In K. Hyltenstam and M. Pienemann (eds.) *Modelling and Assessing Second Language Acquisition*. Clevedon: Multilingual Matters.

——(1989) Is language teachable? Psycholinguistic experiments and hypotheses. *Applied Linguistics* 10(1), 52–79.

——(1998) *Language Processing and Second Language Development: Processability Theory*. Amsterdam: John Benjamins.

——(2005) An introduction to processability theory. In M. Pienemann (ed.) *Cross-Linguistic Aspects of Processability Theory*. Amsterdam: John Benjamins.

Pienemann, M., Johnston, M., and Brindley, G. (1988) An acquisition-based procedure for second language assessment. *Studies in Second Language Acquisition* 10(2), 217–43.

Plonsky, L. (2011) The effectiveness of second language strategy instruction: a meta-analysis. *Language Learning* 61(4), 993–1038.

Podromou, L. (2002) The great ELT textbook debate. *MET* 11(4), 25–33.

Polio, C., and Duff, P. (1994) Teachers language use in university foreign language classrooms: a qualitative analysis of English and target language alternation. *Modern Language Journal* 78(3), 313–26.

Porter, D., and Roberts, J. (1981) Authentic listening activities. *ELT Journal* 36(1), 37–47.

Poulisse, N. (1990) *The Use of Compensatory Strategies by Dutch Learners of English*. Enschede: Sneldruk.

Powell, S. (2005) Extensive reading and its role in Japanese high schools. *The Reading Matrix* 5(2), 28–42.

Prabhu, N. S. (1987) *Second Language Pedagogy*. Oxford: Oxford University Press.

Preston, A. (2009) *The contribution of interaction to learner motivation in the modern foreign language classroom*. Unpublished PhD thesis, University of Southampton.

Redman, S. (2003) *English Vocabulary in use Pre-Intermediate and Intermediate*. Cambridge: Cambridge University Press.

Reid, L. (1987) The learning style preferences of ESL students. *TESOL Quarterly* 21(1), 87–111.

Reinders, H. (2012) The end of self-access?: From walled garden to public park. *ELT World Online* 4, 1–5.

Reinders, H., and Lewis, M. (2006) An evaluative checklist for self-access materials. *ELT Journal* 60 (3), 272–78.

Reiss, M. (1985) The good language learner: another look. *Canadian Modern Language Review* 41, 511–23.

Richards, J. (1971) A non-contrastive approach to error analysis. *ELT Journal* 25, 204–19.

——(1996) Teachers maxims in language teaching. *TESOL Quarterly* 30(2), 281–96.

Richards, J., and Rodgers, T. (1986) *Approaches and Methods in Language Teaching*. Cambridge: Cambridge University Press.

——(2001) *Approaches and Methods in Language Teaching*. 2nd edition. Cambridge: Cambridge University Press.

Richards, J., Platt, J., and Platt, H. (eds.) (1992) *Longman Dictionary of Language Teaching and Applied Linguistics*. London: Longman.

Richards, K. (2006) Being a teacher: identity and classroom conversation. *Applied Linguistics* 27(1), 51–77.

Ringbom, H. (1992) On L1 transfer in L2 comprehension and L2 production. *Language Learning* 42(1), 85–112.

——(2007) *The Importance of Cross-Linguistic Similarity in Foreign Language Learning: Comprehension, Learning and Production.* Clevedon: Multilingual Matters.

Rivers, W. M., and Temperley, M. S. (1978) *A Practical Guide to the Teaching of English.* Oxford: Oxford University Press.

Robinson, P. (1995) Attention, memory, and the 'noticing' hypothesis. *Language Learning,* 45(2), 283–331.

——(2001) Task complexity, task difficulty, and task production: exploring interactions in a componential framework. *Applied Linguistics* 22(1), 27–57.

——(2002) Learning conditions, aptitude complexes and SLA: a framework for research and pedagogy. In P. Robinson (ed.) *Individual Differences and Instructed Language Learning* (pp. 113–33). Amsterdam: John Benjamins.

——(2003) Attention and memory during SLA. In C. J. Doughty and M. H. Long (eds.), *Handbook of Second Language Acquisition* (pp. 630–78). Oxford: Blackwell.

——(2005) Cognitive abilities, chunk-strength, and frequency effects in implicit artificial grammar and incidental L2 learning: replications of Reber, Walkenfeld, and Hernstadt (1991) and Knowlton and Squire (1996) and their relevance for SLA. *Studies in Second Language Acquisition* 27(2), 235–68.

——(2007) Criteria for classifying and sequencing pedagogic tasks. In M. D. P. G. Mayo (ed.), *Investigating Tasks in Formal Language Learning* (pp. 7–26). New York: Multilingual Matters.

——(2011a) Syllabus design. In M. Long and C. Doughty (eds.) *The Handbook of Language Teaching* (pp. 294–310). Malden, MA: Wiley-Blackwell.

——(2011b) Task-based language learning: a review of issues. *Language Learning,* 61(1), 1–36.

Robinson, P. (ed.) (2011c) *Second Language Task Complexity: Researching the Cognition Hypothesis of Language Learning and Performance.* Philadelphia and Amsterdam: John Benjamins.

Robinson, P., and Yamaguchi, Y. (1999) *Aptitude, task feedback and generalizability of focus on form: a classroom study.* Paper presented at the 12th AILA World Congress, Waseda University, Tokyo.

Rodrigo, V., Krashen, S., and Gribbons, B. (2004) The effectiveness of two comprehensible-input approaches to foreign language instruction at the intermediate level. *System* 32(1), 53–60.

Roehr, K. (2008) Metalinguistic knowledge and language ability in university-level L2 learners. *Applied Linguistics* 29(2), 173–99.

Rolin-Ianziti, J. (2010) The organization of delayed second language correction. *Language Teaching Research* 14(2), 183–206.

Rosansky, E. (1976) Methods and morphemes in second language acquisition. *Language Learning* 26(2), 409–25.

Rubin, J. (1975) What the 'good language learner' can teach us. *TESOL Quarterly* 9(1), 41–51.

Russell, J., and Spada, N. (2006) The effectiveness of corrective feedback for the acquisition of L2 grammar. In J. M. Norris and L. Ortega (eds.) *Synthesizing Research on Language Learning and Teaching* (pp. 133–64). Amsterdam: John Benjamins.

Rutherford, W. (1988) *Second Language Grammar: Learning and Teaching.* London: Longman.

Salaberry, M. R. (1997) The role of input and output practice in second language acquisition. *The Canadian Modern Language Review* 53(2), 422–51.

Sampson, G. (1984) Exporting language teaching materials from Canada to China. *TESOL Canada Journal* 1(1), 19–31.

Samuda, V. (2001) Guiding relationships betweem form and meaning during task performance: the role of the teacher. In M. Bygate, P. Skehan and M. Swain (eds.), *Researching Pedagogic Tasks: Second Language Learning, Teaching, and Testing.* London: Longman.

Samuda, V., and Bygate, M. (2008) *Tasks in Second Language Learning.* Basingstoke: Palgrave Macmillan.

Sasaki, M. (1996) *Second Language Proficiency, Foreign Language Aptitude, and Intelligence.* New York: Lang.

Sato, C. (1986) Conversation and interlanguage development: rethinking the connection. In R. Day (ed.) *Talking to Learn: Conversation in Second Language Acquisition* (pp. 23–45). Rowley, MA: Newbury House.

Savignon, S. (1972) *Communicative Competence: An Experiment in Foreign Language Teaching.* Philadelphia, PA: Center for Curriculum Development.

Savignon, S. J. (1997) *Communicative Competence: Theory and Classroom Practice.* 2nd edition. New York: McGraw-Hill.

Saville-Troike, M. (1988). 'Private speech: evidence for second language learning strategies during the 'silent period'. *Journal of Child Language* 15(3), 567–90.

Scarcella, R. (1990) *Teaching Language Minority Students in the Multicultural Classroom.* Englewood Cliffs, NJ: Prentice Hall Regents.

Scarcella, R., and Oxford, R. (1992) *The Tapestry of Language Learning.* Boston, MA: Heinle and Heinle.

Schegloff, E., Jefferson, G., and Sacks, H. (1977) The preference for self-correction in the organization of repair in conversation. *Language* 53(2), 361–82.

Scherer, A., and Wertheimer, M. (1964) *A Psycholinguistic Experiment in Foreign Language Teaching.* New York: McGraw Hill.

Schmidt, R. (1983) Interaction, acculturation and the acquisition of communication competence. In M. Wolfson and E. Judd (eds.) *Sociolinguistics and Second Language Acquisition.* Rowley, MA: Newbury House.

——(1990) The role of consciousness in second language learning. *Applied Linguistics* 11(2), 129–58.

——(1993) Awareness and second language acquisition. *Annual Review of Applied Linguistics* 13, 206–26.

——(1994) Deconstructing consciousness in search of useful definitions for applied linguistics. *AILA Review* 11, 11–26.

——(1995) Consciousness and foreign language learning: a tutorial on the role of attention and awareness in learning. In R. Schmidt (ed.) *Attention and Awareness in Foreign Language Learning* (pp. 1–65). Honolulu, HI: University of Hawaii Press.

——(2001) Attention. In P. Robinson (ed.) *Cognition and Second Language Instruction* (pp. 3–32). Cambridge: Cambridge University Press.

——(2010) Attention, awareness, and individual differences in language learning. In W. M. Chan et al. (eds.) *Proceedings of CLaSIC 2010, Singapore, December 2–4* (pp. 721–37). Singapore: National University of Singapore, Centre for Language Studies.

Schmidt, R., and Frota, S. (1986) Developing basic conversation ability in a second language: A case-study of an adult learner. In R. Day (ed.) *Talking to Learn: Conversation in Second Language Acquisition.* Rowley, MA: Newbury House.

Schmitt, N. (2008) Review article: instructed second language vocabulary learning. *Language Teaching Research* 12(3), 329–63.

Schumann, J. (1978) The acculturation model for second language acquisition. In R. Gingras (ed.) *Second Language Acquisition and Foreign Language Teaching*. Arlington, VA: Center for Applied Linguistics.

Schwartz, B. (1986) The epistemological status of second language acquisition. *Second Language Research* 2(2), 120–59.

Schweers, C. W. (1999) Using L1 in the L2 Classroom. Online: http://exchanges.state.gov/forum/vols/vol37/no2/p6.htm

Sciarone, A., and Meijer, P. (1995) Does practice make perfect? On the effect of exercises on second/foreign language acquisition. *International Review of Applied Linguistics* 35(7), 107–108.

Scollon, R. (1976) *Conversations with a One-Year Old*. Honolulu, HI: University of Hawaii Press.

Scott, V., and de la Fuente, M. (2008) What's the problem? L2 learners' use of the L1 during consciousness-raising, form-focused tasks. *Modern Language Journal* 92(1), 100–113.

Scovel, T. (2001) *Learning New Languages: A Guide to Second Language Acquisition*. Boston, MA: Heinle and Heinle.

Scrivener, J. (2005) *Learning Teaching: A Guidebook for English Language Teachers*. Oxford: MacMillan Education.

Seedhouse, P. (1999) Task-based interaction. *ELT Journal* 53(3), 149–56.

——(2004) *The Interactional Architecture of the Language Classroom: A Conversation Analysis Perspective*. Malden, MA: Blackwell.

——(2005) 'Task' as research construct. *Language Learning* 55(3), 533–70.

Seidlhofer, B. (2005) English as a lingua franca. *ELT Journal* 59(4), 339–41.

——(2011) *Understanding English as Lingua-Franca*. Oxford: Oxford University Press.

Selinker, L. (1972) Interlanguage. *International Review of Applied Linguistics* 10(3), 209–31.

Sfard, A. (1998) On two metaphors for learning and the dangers of choosing just one. *Educational Researcher* 27(2), 4–13.

Sharwood-Smith, M. (1993) Input enhancement in instructed SLA. *Studies in Second Language Acquisition* 15(2), 165–79.

Sheen, R. (2003) Focus on form – a myth in the making? *ELT Journal* 57(3), 225–33.

——(2006) Focus on forms as a means of improving accurate oral production. In A. Housen and M. Pierrard (eds.), *Investigations in Instructed Second Language Acquisition* (pp. 271–310). Berlin: New York: Mouton de Gruyter.

Sheerin, S. (1989) *Self-access*. Oxford: Oxford University Press.

Shehadeh, A. (2002) Comprehensible output, from occurrence to acquisition: an agenda for acquisitional research. *Language Learning* 52(3), 597–647.

Shimizu, M. (2006) Monolingual or Bilingual policy in the classroom: pedagogical implications of L1 use in the Japanese EFL classroom. *Maebashi Kyoai Gakuen College Ronsyu* 6, 75–89.

Shin, S., and Milroy, L. (1999) Bilingual language acquisition by Korean schoolchildren in New York City. *Bilingualism: Language and Cognition* 2(2), 147–67.

Shintani, N. (2011) A comparative study of the effects of input-based and production-based instruction on vocabulary acquisition by young EFL learners. *Language Teaching Research* 15(2), 137–58.

——(2012) Input-based tasks and the acquisition of vocabulary and grammar: a process-product study. *Language Teaching Research* 16(2), 253–79.

——(2013) The effect of focus on form and focus on forms instruction on the acquisition of productive knowledge of L2 vocabulary by young beginning-level learners. *TESOL Quarterly* 47(1), 36–62.

——(forthcoming) Using tasks with young beginner learners: the role of the teacher. In V. Samuda (ed.) *Teaching to the Task: How Teachers Interpret and Apply Task-based Principles in the Classroom.* Amsterdam: John Benjamins.

Shintani, N., and Ellis, R. (2010) The incidental acquisition of English plural-s by Japanese children in comprehension-based and production-based lessons. *Studies in Second Language Acquisition* 32(4), 607–37.

——(2014) The comparative effect of metalinguistic explanation and direct written corrective feedback on learners explicit and implicit knowledge of the English indefinite article. *Journal of Second Language Writing* 23(2).

Shintani, N., Li, S., and Ellis, R. (2013) Comprehension-based versus production-based instruction: a meta-analysis of comparative studies. *Language Learning* doi: 10.1111/lang.12001.

Shook, D. J. (1994) FU/L2 reading, grammatical information and the input-to-intake phenomenon. *Applied Language Learning* 5(2), 57–93.

Shulman, L. S., and Keislar, E. R. (eds.) (1966) *Learning by Discovery: A Critical Appraisal.* Chicago, IL: Rand McNally and Company.

Sinclair, J. (1991) *Corpus, Concordance, Collocation.* Oxford: Oxford University Press.

Sinclair, J. M., and Coulthard, M. (1975) *Towards an Analysis of Discourse: The English used by Teachers and Pupils.* Oxford: Oxford University Press.

Sinclair, J. M., and Renouf, A. (1988) A lexical syllabus for language learning. In R. Carter and M. McCarthy (eds.) *Vocabulary and Language Teaching* (pp. 140–58). Harlow: Longman.

Singleton, D., and Ryan, L. (2004) *Language Acquisition: The Age Factor.* 2nd edition. Clevedon: Multilingual Matters.

Sjöholm, K. (1976) A comparison of the test results in grammar and vocabulary between Finnish- and Swedish-speaking applicants for English. In H. Ringbom and R. Palmberg (eds.) *Errors Made by Finns and Swedish-speaking Finns in the Learning of English.* ERIC Report ED 122628. Abo, Finland: Department of English, Åbo Akademi.

Skehan, P. (1989) *Individual Differences in Second-Language Learning.* London: Edward Arnold.

——(1996) A framework for the implementation of task-based instruction. *Applied Linguistics* 17(1), 38–62.

——(1998) *A Cognitive Approach to Language Learning.* Oxford: Oxford University Press.

——(2002) Theorising and updating aptitude. In P. Robinson (ed.) *Individual Differences and Instructed Language Learning.* Amsterdam: John Benjamins.

——(2011) *Researching Tasks: Performance, Assessment and Pedagogy.* Shanghai: Shanghai Foreign Language Education Press.

Slimani-Rolls, A. (2005) Rethinking task-based language learning: what we can learn from the learners. *Language Teaching Research* 9(2), 195–218.

Smith, P. (1970) *A Comparison of the Audiolingual and Cognitive Approaches to Foreign Language Instruction: The Pennsylvania Foreign Language Project.* Philadelphia, PA: Center for Curriculum Development.

Snow, R. (1994) Abilities in academic tasks. In R. Sternberg and R. Wagner (eds.) *Mind in Context: Interactionist Perspectives on Human Intelligence* (pp. 3–37). New York: Cambridge University Press.

Song, Y., and Andrews, S. (2009) *The L1 in L2 Learning: Teachers Beliefs and Practices*. Munich: Lincom Europa.

Spada, N. M. (1986) The interaction between type of contact and type of instruction: some effects on the L2 proficiency of adult learners. *Studies in Second Language Acquisition* 8(2), 181–99.

Spada, N., and Lightbown, P. (1999) First language influence and developmental readiness in second language acquisition. *The Modern Language Journal* 83(1), 1–21.

Spada, N., and Tomita, Y. (2010) Interactions between type of instruction and type of language feature: a meta-analysis. *Language Learning* 60(2), 263–308.

Spada, N., Lightbown, P. M., and White, J. (2006) The importance of form/meaning mappings in explicit form-focused instruction. In A. Housen and M. Pierrard (eds.) *Investigations in Instructed Second Language Acquisition* (pp. 199–234). Berlin: Mouton de Gruyter.

Sparks, R. L., Ganschow, L., and Javorsky, J. (2000) Déjà vu all over again: a response to Saito, Horwitz, and Garza. *Modern Language Journal* 84(2), 251–59.

Speelman, C. P., and Kirsner, K. (2005) *Beyond the Learning Curve: The Construction of Mind*, vol. 1. New York: Oxford University Press.

Spolsky, B. (1990) Introduction to a colloquium: the scope and form of a theory of second language learning. *TESOL Quarterly* 24(4), 609–16.

Stapa, S., and Majid, A. (2009) The use of first language in limited English proficiency classes: Good, bad or ugly? *Journal e-Bangi* 1(1), 1–12.

Stenhouse, L. (1975) *An Introduction to Curriculum Research and Development*. London: Heinemann.

Stenson, B. (1974) Induced errors. In J. Schumann and N. Stenson (eds.) *New Frontiers in Second Language Learning*. Rowley, MA: Newbury House.

Stern, H. H. (1990) Analysis and experience as variable in second language pedagogy. In B. Harley, P. Allen, J. Cummins and M. Swain (eds.) *The Development of Second Language Proficiency* (pp. 93–109). Cambridge: Cambridge University Press.

Sternberg, R. (2002) The theory of successful intelligence and its implication for language aptitude-testing. In P. Robinson (ed.) *Individual Differences and Instructed Language Learning*. Amsterdam: John Benjamins.

Stockwell, R., Bowen, J., and Martin, J. (1965) *The Grammatical Structures of English and Spanish*. Chicago: Chicago University Press.

Storch, N. (2001) Comparing ESL learners attention to grammar on three different classroom tasks. *RELC Journal* 32(2), 104–24.

——(2002) Patterns of interaction in ESL pair work. *Language Learning* 52(1), 119–58.

Storch, N., and Aldosari, A. (2010) Learners use of first language (Arabic) in pair work in an EFL class. *Language Teaching Research* 14(4), 355–75.

Storch, N., and Wigglesworth, G. (2003) Is there a role for the use of the L1 in an L2 setting? *TESOL Quarterly* 37(4), 760–70.

Strevens, P. (1980) The paradox of individualized instruction: it takes better teachers to focus the learner. In H. Altman and C. Vaughan James (eds.) *Foreign Language Teaching: Meeting Individual Needs* (pp. 17–29). Oxford: Pergamon.

Svartvik, J. (1973) Introduction. In Svartvik, J. (ed.) *Errata: Papers in Error Analysis*. Lund, Sweden: CWK Gleerup.

Swain, M. (1985) Communicative competence: some roles of comprehensible input and comprehensible output in its development. In S. Gass and C. Madden (eds.) *Input in Second Language Acquisition* (pp. 235–56). Rowley, MA: Newbury House.

——(1995) Three functions of output in second language learning. In G. Cook and B. Seidhofer (eds.) *Principles and Practice in the Study of Language: Studies in Honour of H. G. Widdowson.* Oxford: Oxford University Press.

——(1998) Focus on form through conscious reflection. In C. Doughty and J. Williams (eds.) *Focus-on-Form in Classroom Second Language Acquisition.* Cambridge: Cambridge University Press.

——(2000) The output hypothesis and beyond: mediating acquisition through collaborative dialogue. In J. Lantolf (ed.) *Sociocultural Theory and Second Language Learning.* Oxford: Oxford University Press.

——(2006) Languaging, agency and collaboration in advanced second language learning. In H. Byrnes (ed.) *Advanced Language Learning: The Contributions of Halliday and Vygotsky.* London: Continuum.

Swain, M., and Lapkin, S. (1982) *Evaluating Bilingual Education: A Canadian Case Study.* Clevedon: Multilingual Matters.

——(1998) Interaction and second language learning: two adolescent French immersion students working together. *Modern Language Journal* 82(3), 320–37.

——(2000) Task based language learning: the use of the first language. *Teaching Research* 4(3), 251–74.

——(2001) Focus on form through collaborative dialogue: exploring task effects. In M. Bygate, P. Skehan and M. Swain (eds.) *Researching Pedagogic Tasks: Second Language Learning, Teaching and Testing* (pp. 99–118). New York: Longman.

——(2002) Talking it through: two French immersion learners response to reformulation. *International Journal of Educational Research* 37(3/4), 285–304.

——(2007) The distributed nature of second language learning: a case study. In S. Fotos and H. Nassaji (eds.) *Focus on Form and Teacher Education: Studies in Honour of Rod Ellis.* Oxford: Oxford University Press.

Swain, M., Kinnear, P., and Steinman, L. (2011) *Sociocultural Theory in Second Language Education: An Introduction through Narratives.* Bristol: Multilingual Matters.

Swan, M. (1994) Design criteria for pedagogic language rules. In M. Bygate, A. Tonkyn and E. Williams (eds.) *Grammar and the Language Teacher* (pp. 45–55). New York: Prentice Hall.

——(2005) Legislation by hypothesis: the case of task-based instruction. *Applied Linguistics* 26(3), 376–401.

Swan, M., and Walter, C. (1984) *The Cambridge English Course.* Cambridge: Cambridge University Press.

Swanborn, M. S. L., and de Glopper, K. (2002) Impact of reading purpose on incidental word learning from context. *Language Learning* 52(1), 95–117.

Takahashi, S. (2005) Pragmalinguistic awareness: is it related to motivation and proficiency. *Applied Linguistics* 26(1), 90–120.

Tarone, E. (1977) *Conscious communication strategies in interlanguage: a progress report.* Paper presented at the On TESOL 77, Washington DC.

——(1982) Systematicity and attention in interlanguage. *Language Learning* 32(1), 69–82.

Tarone, E., and Swain, M. (1995) A sociolinguistic perspective on second-language use in immersion classrooms. *Modern Language Journal* 79, 166–78.

Taylor, L. (1991) Review: Collins COBUILD English Course. *ELT Journal* 45(1), 74–77.

Thornbury, S. (1996) Teachers research teacher talk. *ELT Journal* 50(4), 279–89.

——(1998) The lexical approach: a journey without maps. *Modern English Teacher* 7(4), 7–13.

——(1999) *How to Teach Grammar*. London: Longman.

Tian, L., and Macaro, E. (2012) Comparing the effect of teacher codeswitching with English-only explanations on the vocabulary acquisition of Chinese university students: a lexical focus-on-form study. *Language Teaching Research* 16(3), 367–91.

Tinkham, T. (1997) The effects of semantic and thematic clustering on the learning of second language vocabulary. *Second Language Research* 13(2), 138–63.

Tomasello, M., and Herron, C. (1988) Down the garden path: inducing and correcting overgeneralization errors in the foreign language classroom. *Applied Psycholinguistics* 9(3), 237–46.

——(1989) Feedback for language transfer errors: the garden path technique. *Studies in Second Language Acquisition* 11(4), 385–95.

Tomlin, R. S., and Villa, V. (1994) Attention in cognitive science and second language acquisition. *Studies in Second Language Acquisition* 16(2), 183–203.

Tomlinson, B. (2010) Principles of effective materials development. In N. Harwood (ed.) *English Language Teaching Materials: Theory and Practice* (pp. 81–108). Cambridge: Cambridge University Press.

——(2011) *Materials Development in Language Teaching*. 2nd edition. Cambridge: Cambridge University Press.

Trim, J. (1973) *Systems Development in Adult Language Learning*. Strasbourg: Council of Europe.

Truscott, J. (1996) The case against grammar correction in L2 writing classes. *Language Learning* 46(2), 327–69.

——(1998) Noticing in second language acquisition: a critical review. *Second Language Research* 14(2), 103–35.

——(1999) The case for ' the case for grammar correction in L2 writing classes': A response to Ferris. *Journal of Second Language Writing* 8(2), 111–22.

——(2004) Evidence and conjecture on the effects of correction: a response to Chandler. *Journal of Second Language Writing* 13(4), 337–43.

——(2007) The effect of error correction on learners ability to write accurately. *Journal of Second Language Writing* 16(4), 255–72.

——(2010) Some thoughts on Anthony Brutons critique of the correction debate. *System* 38(2), 329–35.

Truscott, J., and Hsu, A. Y-P. (2008) Error correction, revision, and learning. *Journal of Second Language Writing* 17(4), 292–305.

Truscott, J., and Sharwood-Smith, M. (2011) Input, intake, and consciousness. *Studies in Second Language Acquisition* 33(4), 497–528.

Tsui, A. (1996) Reticence and anxiety in second language learning. In K. Bailey and D. Nunan (eds.) *Voices from the Language Classroom* (pp. 145–67). Cambridge: Cambridge University Press.

Tudor, I. (1996) *Learner-Centredness as Language Education*. Cambridge: Cambridge University Press.

——(2001) *The Dynamics of the Language Classroom*. Cambridge: Cambridge University Press.

Turnbull, M., and Arnett, K. (2002) Teachers uses of the target and first languages in second and foreign language classrooms. *Annual Review of Applied Linguistics* 22, 204–18.

Underhill, A. (1985) Working with the monolingual learners' dictionary. In R. Ilson (ed.) *Dictionaries, Lexicography and Language Learning* (pp. 103–114). Oxford: Pergamon.

Ur, P. (1996) *A Course in Language Teaching: Practice and Theory.* Cambridge: Cambridge University Press.

——(2011) Grammar teaching research, theory, and practice. In E. Hinkel (ed.) *Handbook of Research in Second Language Teaching and Learning Volume II* (pp. 507–22). New York: Routledge.

Ushakova, T. (1994) Inner speech and second language acquisition: an experimental-theoretical approach. In J. Lantolf and G. Appel (eds.) *Vygotskian Approaches to Second Language Research.* Hillsdale, NJ: Ablex.

Ushioda, E. (2001) Language learning at university. Exploring the role of motivational thinking. In Z. Dornyei and R. Schmidt (eds.) *Motivation and Second Language Acquisition* (pp. 93–125). Honolulu, HI: University of Hawaii Press.

——(2009) A person-on-context relational view of mergent motivation, self and identity. In Z. Dornyei and E. Ushioda (eds.) *Motivation, Language Identity and the L2 Self* (pp. 215–28). Bristol: Multilingual Matters.

Van Beuningen, C. G., De Jong, N., and Kuiken, F. (2012) Evidence on the effectiveness of comprehensive error correction in second language writing. *Language Learning* 62(1), 1–41.

Van den Branden, K. (1997) Effects of negotiation on language learners output. *Language Learning* 47(4), 589–636.

Van den Branden, K., Bygate, M., and Norris, J. (2009) Task-based language teaching: Introducing the reader. In K. Branden, M. Bygate and J. Norris (eds.) *Task-Based Language Teaching: A Reader.* Amsterdam: John Benjamins.

Van Lier, L. (1996) *Interaction in the Language Curriculum: Awareness, Autonomy and Authenticity.* London: Longman.

Vann, R. J., Meyer, D. E., and Lorenz, F. O. (1984) Error gravity: a study of faculty opinion of ESL errors. *TESOL Quarterly* 18(3), 427–40.

VanPatten, B. (1990) Attending to form and content in the input. *Studies in Second Language Acquisition* 12(3), 287–301.

——(1996) *Input Processing and Grammar Instruction: Theory and Research.* Norwood, NJ: Ablex.

——(2004) Input processing in second language acquisition. In B. VanPatten (ed.) *Processing Instruction: Theory, Research, and Commentary* (pp. 5–32). Mahwah, NJ: Laurence Erlbaum Associates.

——(2007) Input processing in adult second language acquisition. In B. VanPatten and J. Williams (eds.) *Theories in Second Language Acquisition* (pp. 115–35). Mahwah, NJ: Lawrence Erlbaum.

VanPatten, B., and Cadierno, T. (1993) Explicit instruction and input processing. *Studies in Second Language Acquisition* 15(2), 225–43.

VanPatten, B., and Oikkenon, S. (1996) Explanation versus structured input in processing instruction. *Studies in Second Language Acquisition* 18(4), 495–510.

VanPatten, B., and Sanz, C. (1995) From input to output: processing instruction and communicative tasks. In F. Eckman, D. Highland, P. W. Lee, J. Mileham and R. R. Weber (eds.) *Second Language Acquisition Theory and Pedagogy* (pp. 169–85). Mahwah, NJ: Lawrence Erlbaum Associates.

Vasquez, C., and Harvey, J. (2010) Raising teachers awareness about corrective feedback through research replication. *Language Teaching Research* 14(4), 421–43.

Vigil, N. A., and Oller, J. W. (1976) Rule fossilization: a tentative model. *Language Learning* 26(2), 281–95.

Von Stutterheim, C. (1991) Narrative and description: temporal reference in second language acquisition. In T. Huebner and C. Ferguson (eds.) *Crosscurrents in Second Language Acquisition and Linguistic Theories* (pp. 358–403). Amsterdam: Benjamins.

Vygotsky, L. (1978) *Mind in Society.* Cambridge, MA: MIT Press.

——(1986) *Thought and Language.* Newly revised and edited by A. Kozulin. Cambridge, MA: MIT Press.

——(1987) *The Collected Works of L. S. Vygotsky,* Vol. 1: *Thinking and Speaking.* New York: Plenum Press.

Walsh, S. (2006) *Investigating Classroom Discourse.* New York: Routledge.

Warren-Price, T. (2003) *Action research investigating the amount of teacher talk in my classroom.* Unpublished MA paper. University of Birmingham.

Weaver, R. R., and Qi, J. (2005) Classroom organization and participation: College students' perceptions. *The Journal of Higher Education,* 76 (5), 570–601.

Weinert, R. (1987) Processes in classroom second language development: the acquisition of negation in German. In R. Ellis (ed.) *Second Language Acquisition in Context.* London: Prentice Hall International.

Wells, G. (1985) *Language Development in the Pre-School Years.* Cambridge: Cambridge University Press.

Wesche, M. (1981) Language aptitude measures in streaming, matching students with methods, and diagnosis of learning problems. In K. Diller (ed.) *Individual Differences and Universals in Language Learning Aptitude.* Rowley, MA: Newbury House.

West, M. (1953) *The General Service List of English Words.* London: Longman.

White, J. (1998) Getting the learners attention: a typographical input enhancement study. In C. Doughty and J. Williams (eds.) *Focus on Form in Classroom Second Language Acquisition* (pp. 85–113). Cambridge: Cambridge University Press.

White, J., and Lightbown, P. (1984) Asking and answering in ESL classes. *Canadian Modern Language Review* 40(2), 288–344.

White, J., and Ranta, L. (2002) Examining the interface between metalinguistic task performance and oral production in a second language. *Language Awareness* 11(4), 259–90.

White, L. (1991) Adverb placement in second language acquisition: some effects of positive and negative evidence in the classroom. *Second Language Research* 7(2), 133–61.

——(2003) *Second Language Acquisition and Universal Grammar.* Cambridge: Cambridge University Press.

White, L., Spada, N., Lightbown, P. M., and Ranta, L. (1991) Input enhancement and question formation. *Applied Linguistics* 12(4), 416–32.

White, R. (1988) *The ELT Curriculum, Design, Innovation and Management.* Oxford: Basil Blackwell.

——(1998) *The ELT Curriculum.* Oxford: Blackwell.

Widdowson, H. G. (1978) *Teaching Language as Communication.* Oxford: Oxford University Press.

——(1979) *Explorations in Applied Linguistics.* Oxford: Oxford University Press.

——(1990a) *Aspects of Language Teaching.* Oxford: Oxford University Press.

——(1990b) Grammar, Nonsense, and Learning. In H. Widdowson (ed.) *Aspects of Language Teaching.* Oxford: Oxford University Press.

——(2003) *Defining Issues in English Language Teaching.* Oxford: Oxford University Press.

Wilkins, D. (1976) *Notional Syllabuses.* Oxford: Oxford University Press.

Williams, E. (1983) Communicative reading. In K. Johnson and D. Porter (eds.) *Perspectives in Communicative Language Teaching* (pp. 171–88). London: Academic Press.

Williams, M. (1988) Language taught for meetings and language used in meetings: is there anything in common? *Applied Linguistics* 9(1), 45–58.

Williams, M., and Burden, R. (1999) Students developing conceptions of themselves as language learners. *Modern Language Journal* 83(2), 193–201.

Willing, K. (1987) *Learning Styles and Adult Migrant Education*. Adelaide: National Curriculum Resource Centre.

Willis, D. (1990) *The Lexical Syllabus: A New Approach To Language Learning*. London: Collins ELT.

Willis, D., and Willis, J. (1996) Consciousness-raising activities in the language classroom. In J. Willis and D. Willis (eds.) *Challenge and Change in Language Teaching* (pp. 63–76). Oxford: Heinemann.

——(2007) *Doing Task-Based Teaching*. Oxford: Oxford University Press.

Willis, J. (1996) *A Framework for Task-based Learning*. Harlow: Longman.

Willis, J., and Willis, D. (1988) *Collins COBUILD English Course*. London: Harper Collins.

Winitz, H. (1981) *The Comprehension Approach to Foreign Language Instruction*. New York: Newbury House.

Wode, H. (1983) *Papers on Language Acquisition, Language Learning and Language Teaching*. Heidelberg: Julius Groos.

Wong Fillmore, L. (1976) *The second time around: cognitive and social strategies in second language acquisition*. Unpublished PhD dissertation, Stanford University.

——(1985) When does teacher talk work as input? In S. Gass and C. Madden (eds.) *Input in Second Language Acquisition* (pp. 17–50). Cambridge, MA: Newbury House.

Wong, W. (2001) Modality and attention to meaning and form in the input. *Studies in Second Language Acquisition* 23(3), 345–68.

Wood, D., Bruner, J., and Ross, G (1976) The role of tutoring in problem-solving. *Journal of Child Psychology and Psychiatry* 17(2), 89–100.

Wray, A. (2000) Formulaic sequences in second language teaching: principle and practice. *Applied Linguistics* 21(4), 463–89.

Wright, T. (2005) *Classroom Management in Language Education*. Basingstoke: Palgrave MacMillan.

Wu, K. Y. (1993) Classroom interaction and teacher questions revisited. *RELC Journal* 24(2), 49–68.

Xiao-yun, Y., Zh-yang, Z., and Peixing, D. (2007) *Asian EFL Journal* 17 (Article 1). Online http://www.asian-efl-journal.com/pta—Jan—07—yuy.pdf (retrieved 3 August 2012).

Yalden, J. (1983) *The Communicative Syllabus: Evolution, Design and Implementation*. Oxford: Pergamon.

——(1987) *Principles of Course Design for Language Teaching*. Cambridge: Cambridge University Press.

Yang, Y., and Lyster, R. (2010) Effects of form-focused practice and feedback on chinese EFL learners? Acquisition or regular and irregular past tense forms. *Studies in Second Language Acquisition* 32(2), 235–63.

Yates, J. (2006) *Practice Makes Perfect: English Vocabulary for Beginning ESL Learners*. New York: McGraw-Hill.

Yorio, C. (1987) Building multiple bridges: eclecticism in language teaching. *TESL Canada Journal* 5(1), 91–100.

Yuan, F., and Ellis, R. (2003) The effects of pre-task planning and on-line planning on fluency, complexity and accuracy in L2 monologic oral production. *Applied Linguistics* 24(1), 1–27.

Zhao, Y. (1997) The effects of listeners control of speech rate on second language comprehension. *Applied Linguistics* 18(1), 49–68.

Zobl, H. (1983) Markedness and the projection problem. *Language Learning* 33(3), 293–313.

——(1985) Grammars in search of input and intake. In S. M. Glass and C. Madden (eds.) *Input in Second Language Acquisition* (pp. 329–44). Rowley, MA: Newbury House.

Index